Matrix of Redemption

Contemporary Multi-Ethnic English
Literature from Northeast India

Matrix of Redemption

Contemporary Multi-Ethnic English Literature from Northeast India

Edited by
NIGAMANANDA DAS

ADHYAYAN

Adhyayan Publishers & Distributors
New Delhi-110002

Published by
ADHYAYAN PUBLISHERS & DISTRIBUTORS
4378/4 B, 105, J.M.D. House, Murari Lal Street
Ansari Road, Darya Ganj, New Delhi-110002
Ph. : 011-23263018, 011-23277156, Fax : 011-23280028
E-mail : adhyayanpublishers@yahoo.com

Matrix of Redemption : Contemporary Multi-Ethnic English Literature from Northeast India

Edition : 2011
ISBN : 978-81-8435-255-9

Printed in India

Published by Harish Chandra Yadav for Adhyayan Publishers & Distributors, Laser Typesetting at Net Graphics and Printed at Tarun Offset Printers, Delhi.

Acknowledgements

The editor owes the debt of gratitude to all the contributors of this anthology for their contributions on various aspects of the contemporary writing in English from Northeast India. He is thankful to all his well-wishers and colleagues . He also likes to record the constant support of his daughter Ankita and wife Geetanjali. His thanks are due to Mr. H.C. Yadav, M/s. Adhyayan Publishers, New Delhi, for his support in nicely bringing out the book.

—**Nigamananda Das**

Preface

The Northeast India comprising of eight provinces of Arunachal Pradesh, Assam, Manipur, Meghalaya, Mizoram, Nagaland, Sikkim and Tripura is an ecological paradise and anthropological museum. Known as Assam the provinces excluding Sikkim, are popularly called seven sisters. The vernacular literature of Assamese has a long history and tradition. It is as old as any vernacular literature of India.The literatures of the other provinces of Northeast were basically oral literature for many years until the roman script was adopted as script for the Tribal literatures.Tripura has a tradition of Bengali literature as the province has been dominated by Bengalis and their culture and literature.The writing in English which developed during the colonial period in other provinces of India beyond its Northeast, could not develop in Northeast. The first Indian Writing in English from this region to introduce the region to the outside world is Hem Barua's *The Red River and the Blue Hill*(1954). The writing in English from this part of the country has a distinct trend, a set of distinct concepts and techniques.

Though writing in English has been produced slowly, the tempo of writing has gathered momentum after 1990s. Established writers like Bhupati Das, Temsula Ao, Robin S. Ngangom, Kynpham Sing Nongkynrih, Lakshahira Das,Dayananda Pathak, Mamang Dai, R.K. Madhubir, Mitra Phukan, Easterine Iralu, Homen Borgohain, Nirupama Borgohain,Dhruba Hazarika, Siddhartha Deb, Arup Kumar Dutta, Sanjoy Hazarika, Umakanta Sarma,Esther Syiem, Indira Goswami, Birendra Kumar Bhattacharya, Ratan Thiyam, Arun Sarma,Yeshe Dorjee Thongchi, Nilakshi Borgohain, Rajendra Bhandari and Bhaskar Roy Barman have been assessed by various contributors in this anthology. The work is supposed to pave the ground for further critical harvest in this field.

Some writers have been discussed in this anthology and have not been explicated sufficiently. As such I beg pardon of the readers and concerned writers also. I have a plan to edit another anthology as the second volume of the present work.The response of the readers, researchers and all concerned will decide it.The present work came out after more than four years. I began collecting essays in 2006. After a long process of selection and rejection, I decided upon the present shape. The Northeast India has a very talented band of writers.Some writers of other provinces domiciled in Northeastern states have also produced a good quantum of writing in English which have not been discussed in the present volume. I consider the band of writers discussed in the present volume as the first generation of writers in English from Northeast India.The second generation who have studied this first generation of writers and have been inspired by them have arrived in the literary map of the Northeast. But it will take time to collect and assess their works and also some time is required to distinguish them as the second generation with proper voice of their own.The present volume is the first ever representative volume assessing Indian writing in English from the Northeastern part of the country. I thought of writing a long introduction to this literature distinguishing it from the mainstream Indian Writing in English. But I gave up the idea allowing the essays to speak of their own merits.Earlier I worked on poetry in English from this region.But that other forms writing in English are available, that is represented in this volume.There are volumes/ monographs on biography of the prominent personalities of the region. Autobiography, travel writing,plays and non-fictional prose works are available in good number. As in mainstream Indian Writing in English, in the writing in English from Northeast also novel and poetry have been written profusely. Some works from vernacular literatures translated into English have also been discussed in this anthology.

The Northeastern Indian Writing in English has been prescribed in different Indian Universities in both the UG and PG syllabuses.Several M.Phil. and Ph.D. dissertations have also been written on this trend of writing.The students, research scholars, teachers and general readers will find this work a good companion volume.The editor and contributors of chapters will find their labour rewarded if the readers appreciate the work.

Nigamananda Das

Contents

(1)

Mapping Contemporary NEIWE: The Road Not Taken

Bijay K. Danta

Opportunists prosper, goes an old saying, when specializations proliferate. This may appear true when we plead for NEIWE(North Eastern Indian Writing in English). For, NEIWE in essence means yet another addition to the already baggy discipline of English studies, stretched as it is by shifting intellectual foci and changing perspectives in global and local power structures. In fact, there are already discomforting signs that we may have done too much too soon. It is natural therefore to take a close hard look at what we call or propose to call NEIWE. I wish to address these very issues. What needs to be done, in my opinion, is greater problematization and theoretical exploration of the very concept of NEIWE. Once we accept that any topographical definition is provisional, and therefore alterable, it is not surprising to see the North East paradoxically available as different exclusive sites to different groups: a colonial construct, a national imaginary, and a homeland. Each fact and figure has its own history and politics, and not to address them would be fraught with dangers, both disciplinary and interdisciplinary.

1

Tony Howard, a travel writer once wrote something that captures one's imagination, and yet shocks one to recognizing the incongruity of figures: "If India was the Jewel in the Crown of the British Empire, the remote North East of that country is its Hidden

Jewel". Given that the North East is available both as fact and figure, and given the implications of such a position, the very idea of a separate course comprising North East Indian Writing in English appears a little tremulous. There is also the feeling that the corpus of NEIWE is a little too slight for any long-term evaluation. What is more important is the fear that NEIWE may not be reflective of or responsive to what could be called a northeast spirit or worldview.

Thus, the ungainly phrase, north-east, which owes its origin to the centre-periphery model of state-formation and location, carries on the colonial legacy meant to describe what is territorially contained and culturally "contained" within the Indian nation-state. Culturally, a significant part of the territory is seen as an extension of Aryan otherness available in puranic subtexts and also as a Hindu outpost, especially in *Mâhâbhârata, Yoginitantra* and *Kalikâpurâna.* Geographically, the place begins by adverting for its between-ness, caught as it is between the flimsy Siliguri (chicken) neck and the international borders of Bhutan, China/Tibet, Myanmar and Bangladesh, each compelling a certain categorical recognition. In India's political imaginary the term serves to describe a region that is both fascinating and yet dangerous. In other words, the term seems to homogenize a location where homogeneity is neither automatic nor autochthonous.

Given that there was literature in the North East before there was the North East itself, we must ground our assumptions on inherited beliefs and specific realities. We should begin by re-reading some of the fascinating figures associated with writing in English in the North East. Verrier Elwin has produced fascinating accounts of the place and the people and pleaded for a particular kind of North East, but needs to be critically analyzed.

There is first of all a feeling that poets are not as successful as novelists. For, poetry in the north-east once meant, and in many ways still means, poets based in Shillong: Robin S. Ngangom, Desmond L. Kharmawphlang, Kynpham S. Nongkynrih. There are new names but the odds still favour the older poets. The issues that I address here would be mostly along expected lines, and they are: who writes poetry here and of what kind? Do we have enough of what could be called good poetry, and, in that case, is the poetry worth serious reading? How Indian is this poetry? I believe that readers would read these poets not only with an eye to what is here and now, but also with a sense of tradition. Could we say that we have here poetry with a different focus, but the difference is rewarding and in a way rooted? It may therefore make sense to move beyond the immediate questions and look at the region's contested histories, contesting cultures, dramatically varying topography, and remarkable identity politics. I think the major strength of the poetry of this region lies in two features: its rootedness and its political consciousness. Having said that, the rootedness is neither unidimensional nor uniform or unilinear. The rootedness that we speak of is a kind of rootedness that we see in the poetry of Jayanta Mahapatra. His Orissa is not just a setting, it is the soul of his poems. It may not be out of place here to say that in many ways Mahapatra is an Oriya poet who writes in English, unlike somebody like Nissim Ezekiel whose preferred idiom is Indian English, different, but unmistakably Indian English.

The English poets of the North East are contestatory and dialectical sites where the private and the public coalesce. So in every private lyric utterance we see a complex web of social consequences. If we miss these resonances, we miss the poetry. The speaking 'I' of the lyrics of the region is not the reflective artist, who can withdraw from his material, and produce an impersonal modernist poem. On the contrary, we have romantics and rebels melting into each other where the lover of a young girl is also lover of the hills and the rivers. But it is not swooning over spring flowers and winter suns. Nature is not just an object to be de/refamiliarized as an art object, but a crowded melting pot of history, politics, and local and global mythologies.

This for instance is Desmond's poem on the city man U Di's visit to the village to know more about his past:

> The stories burn our memories like
> a distant meteor searing
> the unnamed gloom; by their light I examine
> the great hurt I carry in my soul
> for having denied my own.
>
> ("Letter from Pahambir")

Or,

> I remain silent all the while
> as I did yesterday, when he
> took me to deep jungles and
> taught me the meaning of
> an upturned leaf, the furtiveness

of birds, the age of animal droppings
("Letter from Paham Ri-oh Village")

A woman's anger is heard in the poetry of Indari Syiem Warjri (b. 1962). "The God of Revenge" is bold in its theme and her utterance sincere. Published in the *New Welsh Review* this poem shows how poetry can address inhuman brutality that follows militant nationalism. The scene is that of a violent day of ethnic conflict.

I do not call you "brother"
Who wage war on children and watch as they
Choke in silent anguish
The word brother has an ironical ring about it in that it is as much about the alienation caused by insurgents fighting for local rights as about Christianity.

Monalisa Changkija (1960-) writes of the uncorrupted land, Naga myths and legends and mourns the destruction of its old glory:

Yes, I have seen our rice fields
Turn into factories and hills
Reduced to barren brown
Our rivers have dried
And our once sparkling fish
Lie dead on sandy banks.

Mamang Dai (1957-), from Arunachal Pradesh, seems to have avoided political concerns, but her poetry is rooted in her soil. There is a concern for a rapidly disappearing past:

I know
From faces that I meet
In these lives
That have crumbled
That the past lives
In these eyes
That the jungle shows

But as I said earlier, the poet who has made all the difference to the poetry in the North East is Robin S. Ngangom. In a poem titled "Poetry" he says:

And I saw my self-selected pain,
the entire history,
unveiled by memory and thirst
And the last reflection I saw,
was my naked shame, my empty hands,
a lifetime of silence.
Again, the primary motif in his early poetry is silence:
When you write you are silent
silent with your thoughts,
alone without your friends,
silent without love,
alone without joy or pain.
("When You Write You Are Silent")

But not all by Ngangom are personal responses to the condition of Manipur. This is for instance his self-deprecatory tribute to his "Mother Apopki":

Forgive me, for all your dreams
of peace and rest during your remnant days
I only turned out to be a small man,
with small dreams and leading a small life.
("A Poem For Mother")

The poetry is therefore private yet public, combining the reflective power of the lyric poet with public muse, not unfamiliar to the singers and balladeers of the region. One has to explore the reasons behind this kind of poetic voice that separates the English poets of the North East from those of the rest of India. I would like to suggest that the poetry of this region has its roots in the indigenous bardic traditions but draws its new energy from the public voice of revolutionary poets. This later tradition is something with which students of English and American poetry may not be very familiar. For a perspective of this kind, one has to look more at somebody like Pablo Neruda or the Caribbean Walcott than T.S. Eliot. Then we must look at the role of translation, though there would be no consensus on what is and is not NE writing. For, there would always be texts that seem rooted in a specific state of the region and may not automatically form part of the kind of collective-critical imaginary that NEIWE entails. But these challenges would help us refine our skills and enlarge vision.

2

What interests me however is the new fiction of the region. As new novelists like Vikram Seth, Amitav Ghosh, Upamanyu Chatterjee, Arundhati Roy, Boman Desai, and Vikram Chandra did in the 1990s to Indian Writing in English, so two new novelists have forced us to notice the fiction of the North East. Though there are many writers who are worthy of serious attention I shall be talking about two recent books. Interestingly, both are based in Shillong, though the themes and techniques vary. The names may be familiar to most of you but I feel privileged that I have a forum to speak on the writings of Siddhartha Deb and Dhruba Hazarika. I use an old yardstick to judge the novels, which some of you may find a little dated, but I believe my readings will justify my decision. A good novel should organize, explore, objectify and evaluate the material it uses. For the novelist to do that what is essential is a technique to separate one's life from one's art, to let the medium do the talking. To my mind, technique in fiction is the difference between the lived experience of life and the felt experience of art. This would cover even autobiographical writing. But that's not our subject today.

I would begin by mentioning a novel by Mitra Phukan titled *The Collector's Wife*. The protagonist Rukmini is married to a District Collector and teaches English Literature to wide-eyed students at a local college. She is a suitable Indian wife. Her life is interwoven with the political situation in Assam. Being a teacher, especially of English Literature, as well as the collector's wife, she has a view from both sides: the administration led by her husband and the students who have begun a somewhat idealistic anti-migrant movement. Rukmini's personal life is in a mess. Taunted by others for her incapacity to bear a child she enters into an affair with a young man but finds that her husband too is not far behind.

As the political turmoil escalates, Rukmini's story too spirals into horror and tragedy. Her story becomes Assam's story, as everything else falls apart. There is kidnapping, extortion, killing and fight for an independent homeland. As a novel from or even of the North-East, *The Collector's Wife* has the right ingredients. Interestingly the narrative confirms the depiction of the region as a formula. The novel is ruined, as Mark Schorer once said of HG Wells' *Tono Bungay* by its material, as it fails to explore and evaluate it.

Dhruba Hazarika's *A Bowstring Winter* is a tightly organized novel on life in Shillong in the 1970s. First of all it is a novel on

Shillong. In a way Shillong is its primary theme and main character. The novel records the elements of Shillong as a lover would at once be feeling and guarding. It is in essence a story of friendship, or rather a code of friendship; "Like a bowstring: tight. Like an arrow: straight." Set in the three months of "U Naiwieng" (November), "U Nohprah" (December) and "U Kyllalyngkot" (January), the coldest and the most romantic period in Shillong, the novel deals with teer-gambling, love, and revenge.

The characters are drawn from diverse backgrounds but the setting is unmistakably Khasi Shillong. A college teacher unwittingly saves a bookie's life while having a meal at the latter's restaurant. He is drawn into a circle of violence that strengthens his friendship with a loyal group comprising a Chinese cook, a Bengali manager, a Bihari cab driver, and a motley committee of Khasis. He steals his friend's girl, a passionate young woman who loves both, but fears the man who discovered her. The story is a replay of an earlier story: the bookie had stolen the girl of an ugly man in the past. The conscience-keeper in the group is an ace archer who also is friend, philosopher, and forgiving father. The story ends in violence with the death of the man who had saved many families from ruin, but must die for the lovers to go forward. But we are also told that he had killed the woman he had stolen from the bad man because she returned to him one afternoon. The novel has a clearly visible Hemingway touch, both in language and tone.

To some one interested in tracking the origin of the novel, I would suggest the everpopular story of *Dosti* handed down to generations of young men and women. In lighter vein, one could even say that the novel is the fictional version of the Hindi movie with a Khasi cast and a Shillong setting. The narrative is urgent, gripping, and riveting. I would propose one more look at the theme of friendship and love, though. Interestingly, the ambience dominated by momo, roasted pork, rice, and rum. Much of the charm in the novel comes through drunkenness and fantasies of innocence. The novel more or less celebrates the kind of violent initiation rites one associates with the Nick Adams stories of Hemingway. What the novel lacks, however, is a sense of history. For, the novel offers a sanitized version of Shillong that is part of a middleclass dream: love, food, romance, winter, and an inviolable code of friendship and inner truth. We have the code heroes of Hemingway, operating in the wintry recesses of a hilly paradise.

The Shillong of Hazarika's novel is also the Shillong of anti-Bengali and anti-foreigner riots. Hazarika's novel has a code of friendship and truth that applies exclusively to the tribal inhabitants of the hills. Again as in the *Deerslayer* stories of James Fenimore Cooper the innocence of the zone must be protected. So when the old man in the book speaks about the inviolable of the hillmen over his hills, we only ask for considered opinion. It is a fine love story but a story that withholds the ugliness of Shillong, the opinion. It is a fine love story but a story that withholds the ugliness of Shillong, the Shillong that drives out the enemy and the friend, as it had only one word to define the foreigner: *dkhar*, foreigner, unwanted. It is a novel limited by its order of exploration and evaluation. It fails to capture the multivalent tapestry that Shillong already is.

In contrast to the Shillong of Dhruba Hazarika's *A Bowstring Winter,* Shiddhartha Deb's engagement with Shillong, and, by implication with the Northeast, in *Point of Return* (2002), and *Surface* (2005), is resonant, and in a way sobering. As I propose to show, the clinically sanitized and youthful world Hazarika's Shillong is now replaced by a politically sensitive world where the outsider is not a creation of his own youth or idealism. Instead, we have the Bangladeshi refugee, a commonplace but compelling by-product of war and geopolitical transformations of the subcontinent, repeating and replicating in a strange act of mimicry and defiance of colonialism and nationalism.

The partition emerges as a powerful trope, this time with echoes from and in East Bengal, Assam, and other areas of the region including Meghalaya. Interestingly, the tragedy of the Bangladeshi finds little sympathy because of the overwhelming presence-absence of the figure who is at once the condition and consequence of this tragedy. The transformation of the Bangladeshi from a persecuted figure, shorn of home, work, dignity, to one of a menacing presence, is already a complex and multilayered web of politics, deception, and inevitability. The signature of religion and electoral politics is everywhere. It is necessary to see the social consequences obtaining in the North-east where the Bangladeshi is a figure either of scorn or fun, depending on his re-location. While the state of the Bangladeshi Muslim migrants and refugees is explained away either in religious or political terms, the Bangladeshi Hindu remains a paradoxically an insider-outsider. Due to rising concerns with ethnicity and identity, the receiving community in the North-east is either skeptical of the Hindu refugees from East Bengal or remains adamant that the

Bengalis have not done enough to integrate themselves with the local culture. Deb's comment on this issue is interesting:

> We [Bengalis] were not perfect, we are not perfect now and never will be. We were insular and narrow-minded, with a false sense of superiority when we first came here [to Assam]. We saw the honesty of the tribal people as stupidity, and through that we taught them our own deviousness. That is the irony...that we should have learned to be more human only when they became less so.

In the novel, Babu, son of Dr. Dam, a veterinary surgeon in Meghalaya, actually a government official whose address and identity kept altering with the carving out of new hill states such as Meghalaya and Mizoram from what remained of Assam after the dissolution of the NEFA, reminisces about his father's life, trying to understand him—at least to the extent that sons can ever understand their fathers. Acutely aware that men of every generation are molded by the events and experiences which occur during their own lifetimes, Babu recognizes that though he and his father have shared many events, their views of these events are vastly different, in each case conditioned by their separate, though sometimes interesting, pasts. Part of a cultural minority which was threatened by religious and social upheavals in East Pakistan, Babu's family escapes to the then undivided Assam and settles down in Silchar.

In a narrative that is reminiscent of Naipaul's *A House for Mr Biswas,* Dr. Dam finds that he cannot build a house for himself anywhere in Assam except Silchar, neither in Guwahati, where he buys a plot of land to assert his independence from his parents and his past in another country, nor in Shillong, a place where he works with great sincerity and even greater insecurity. His Guwahati plot is eaten up by the highway expansion project, and all he can do is watch in anger and disbelief. In what is clearly an ironic acceptance of ethnic cleansing, Dr. Dam allows the bulldozer man to borrow his broomstick to clear the rubble from what was once his "belonging" and symbol of belonging. Assam already in turmoil because of the numerous demands on its territory and status, and the impending bowdlerizations of the state to accommodate tribal sentiments, cannot accept his type. The ethnic population, which was denied its rightful political space by the colonial government and their historical allies, the babus of Bengal, now regard the Dams, and all Bengalis as interlopers.

As Babu tries to understand his father, he does so as someone who was born in India, someone who has never known the places which were home to his father and grandparents and which shaped their lives and still live in their hearts. His own experiences in Shillong point at a "lost" world, but he also realizes that the loss is not unique or exclusive to him or his father or the Bengalis from East Bengal or the Assamese or the Biharis. He dislikes but recognizes a point of view that is unpalatable to the non-tribals: the point of view of the indigenous tribal, who, in turn, points to a loss that antedates the loss of the refugee or the foreigner.

There are multiple narratives involving the creation and destruction of Shillong, which emerges, in each case, as a paradise gone wrong, a paradise in ruins that must be either mourned or reclaimed. Each strand tells a different tale with its own built-in structural arrangements for heroes and villains. There is narrative that hints at the colonial origin of the place, essentially suggesting that the Shillong that the tribals claim as their own has a complex colonial past that cannot be ignored, implying that this Shillong perhaps belongs as much to the local and ethnic as to the colonial detritus called the *dkhar*, the alien, the unwanted foreigner. Then there is the Shillong that the men from the plains built or inherited from the free nation, the capital of Assam in independent India. This is where men like Dr. Dam worked with passion, honesty, and fearlessness, believing that they were contributing to the cause of the nation and, more importantly, to the welfare of the locals. This Shillong is different from the tourism paradise that is part of middleclass holiday fantasies. In addition, there is the Shillong of the missionaries that simultaneously spreads education and Christianity in the region. Shillong was till the early 1980s the destination for children looking for decent English-medium education. It is not just a coincidence that the entire region had for a long time Cotton College at Guwahati and St. Edmund's College at Shillong, two centres of learning that provided a window to the world outside the North-East. With the formation of the state of Meghalaya, Shillong has been forced to live a double life, with a colonial past that is now irrelevant but doubly resonant, and a present must perhaps disregard the past to move on its desired or destined path.

Each has a story to tell in Deb's Shillong. Even Shillong has a story: its air, its smell, its winter and summer rains have recorded stories of friendship and betrayal. The novel mirrors the more mundane realities of life in this mountainous province. Deb also concentrates on universal values and the father-son search for understanding, with the result that the novel is less exotic, despite its unusual setting, than some other Indian novels, but more accessible to readers from other cultures and more potent in its observations about life. In an ironic twist, the narrator and Babu switch roles to provide Dr. Dam's personal history in a chronology which, though linear, moves backwards in time, telling of events which begin in 1987 and end in 1979. Babu, at 17 in 1987, recalls what he knows of his father and the events and people which shape their combined destinies.

As the novel moves backwards, we see through Babu's eyes the level of graft and corruption under which Dr. Dam has managed to maintain his integrity as a public servant. Adding particular poignancy to this turn of events is Dr. Dam's family history as the oldest son, supporting his brothers and sisters for years after their expulsion from them. Dr. Dam's stroke has profound effects on the family, and Babu, in particular, and the second half of the novel takes the reader from 1987 to the present, as Dr. Dam struggles to walk again, and Babu learns the necessity of subordinating his personal goals and dreams for the good of his family. When their town in Meghalaya gets dangerous, the family moves to Silchar, to a house which was supposed to be retirement dream of his father, but which turns out to be closer to a nightmare in terms of its construction, space, and level of privation. On the eve of his departure for Silchar, Babu reflects, "People think that those who have gone away have relinquished their rights to the place left behind, [and] are gone forever...Me? I return every day, sometimes under the cover of sleep, at other times stepping in full daylight across the chicken's-neck strip that divides where I am from where I was, when a certain smell or song or face emerges from the city's contested grounds". In confronting the dangers and leaving the "home" where he grew up, Babu experiences the same uprooting and sense of loss as his father did a generation before, bringing him closer to his father and making the old man's life a bit more understandable to Babu.

In the conclusion of the novel, years after the death of his parents, an older Babu pays a return visit to the town where he grew up:

> I came back to find an end to the story other than Dr. Dam's death, and to find something that would recover the voice of the boy who had left with dreams of...another future where he would be free and successful and unafraid of his alienness...In the streets that had once been so familiar, [I expected] there would be two ghosts, one that of my father, the other of the child that was me. I thought it would be a way of seeing the two of them closer together than they had ever been actual life, without the wall of fear rising between them, without each trapped in self doubt.

Deb's point of view mirrors on the one hand the real-life experiences many of us have as we seek to understand our parents. It is in fact tempting to see in the reverse chronology an allegorical history created by children for parents. It should be much too easy to see in Babu's re-covery of family history as a humanistic effort seeking to combine one's present experiences with whatever knowledge one has of the past of one's lives. This may also look like a universal attempt to find common ground in multiple histories where each tries to understand who he or she is, and who the others are, who they really are, or were. In a sense, our own changing experiences ultimately affect what we think is relevant about their lives and influence our understanding of our loved ones. It would be in a sense convenient to look at the novel as the story of a man coming to terms with his father's life, and on the yearning for home, even after it is gone, after models provided by VS Naipaul (*The Mystic Masseur*), Amitav Ghosh (*The Shadow Lines*) in the wake of Rushdie and Garcia Marquez. But the novel provides observations which compel us to look at the North East, as a cartographic logic and a cartographic baggage. The novel accommodates and challenges the notion of art as universal and local. Viewed as a universal tale of a man growing up to understand his father, as his father had perhaps done before him, Babu's story is allegorically bound, the history of his family's peregrinations a confirmation of an overarching humanist credo. On the other hand, the story stabs us like a bitter drink, tells us it is local, relevant in its historicity and specificity, relevant as a document of the many tragedies of the North East, to be recognized as such.

We are back where we had begun. We have to do the tracks again.

I want to end my paper with a quote from Robin S. Ngangom's

"The Strange Affair of Robin S. Ngangom":

Patriotism is the need of the hour.
Patriotism is preaching secession
And mourning our merger with a nation,
Patriotism is honouring martyrs
Who died in confusion,
Patriotism is declaring we should
Preserve native customs, traditions,
Our literature and performing arts,
And inflicting them on hapless peoples,
Patriotism is admiring
The youth who fondles grenades,
Patriotism is proclaiming all men as brothers
And secretly depriving my brother,
Patriotism is playing the music of guns
To the child in the womb.

And a few lines from a poem by the noted Assamese poet Hiren Bhattacharjya "Of the Country and Others":

1

Name my country and I need no commands.
In my teeming blood gallop
A thousand and one fighting horses.

2

Let there be a procession of my words,
Let them guard the cruel, crooked night
Let the sharp sword of anger shine
in the enthused flow of blood of lively words.

Works Cited

Dai, Mamang. *River Poems*. Calcutta: Writers Workshop, 2004.

Deb, Siddhartha. *The Point of Return*. London: Picador, 2002.

Hazarika, Dhruba. *A Bowstring Winter*. New Delhi: Penguin, 2006.

Kharmawphlang, Desmond. *Touchstone/U Mawshamok*. Shillong, 1988.

Nongkynrih, KS and Robin S Ngangom, Eds. *Anthology of Contemporary Poetry From Northeast*.Shillong: NEHU 2003.

Ngangom, Robin S. *Words and the Silence*. Calcutta: Writers Workshop, 1988.

—. *Time's Crossroads*. Hyderabad: Orient Longman, 1994.

(2)

Contemporary Poetry in English from the North-East: A Quick Glance

Jaydeep Chakrabarty

Have you no language of our own
no way of doing things
did you spend all those holidays
at England's apron strings?
E.K. Brathwaite, 'The Emigrants'
(Cited in *Postcolonial Poetry in English* by Rajeev S. Patke)

As early as 1970, V. K. Gokak in what remains till date the most comprehensive anthology on the field, claimed that "INDO-ANGLIAN POETRY is now nearly a hundred and fifty years old" (Gokak 19). However, the comprehensiveness of the laudable work of Gokak is sufficiently undermined by the conspicuous absence of writers of English poetry from the North Eastern Part of India. Though creative writing in English has been there in the North-East for some period of time, it has not received the attention of the mainstream audience and critics in India and abroad. With all its beauty and serenity, it is like Wordsworth's Lucy-'A violet by a mossy stone/ Half hidden from the sky'. This is part of the general trend of dis/ mis-recognition of the periphery on the part of the centre. This could also be related with some 'real' or attributed inherent 'lack' of originality and variety in the literature in English from region. The purpose of the above quotation from Brathwaite is to generate a critical safeguard against possible unproblematic celebration of poetry in English from the North East as some excellent achievement while I do not hint at not awarding them the merits they deserve. The basic problem with these writings is that what is common to all postcolonial culture-the imperative and predicament of expressing indigenous reality and experience in an "alien" tongue. Raja Rao phrased it best: "One has to convey in a language that is not one's own the spirit that is one's own" (Cited in Iyenger 391) selves and worlds in a language which is not our own. One has there to look at how the poets from the North East make the best (or the worst) of a bad bargain. However before going to some of the poems/poets of the region, it is important here to point out that the category "North East" is highly contentious, even more than "Indian"- as there are extremely divergent realities present in the states clubbed under the term. Even in colonial times the status or reality of a state like the present Assam was very different from that of the present states of Tripura or Mizoram. Let us have a speedy glance at the composition of the geo-political area in/after the British period: 'Out of the most North eastern seven states of present-day administration, after the independence of India, Arunachal Pradesh was known as NEFA, Manipur and Tripura were princely states and all other provinces were known as one province, that is Assam' (Das). It quite naturally follows that such a disparate compendium of languages, cultures, ethnicities and literary traditions cannot be adequately addressed to by the identity 'Northeast'; which should best be treated as a category of convenience or a nominal take-off point. And countering the previous thesis of the alien nature of English, the language should also be seen as the common minimal unifying factor among the states.

Assam, if not the largest, is at least the most ancient and richest among these states in written literary heritage and also in oral traditions. It has produced literature in Sanskrit in the Eleventh century (especially *Kalikapurana and Yogini Tantram*) and has continued ever since with glaring instances of literary excellence difficult to find in its counterparts. No discussion of poetry in English from Assam can afford to ignore the native tradition. In fact the first foray of Assamese poetry into English was through the publication of Dr. Hem Barua's *Modern Assamese Poetry* in 1960 'which enshrines the English translations of the poems of twenty six Assamese poets out of which nine poets translated their own poetry into English' (Das 7). This is also chronicled in K.R.S. Iyenger's *Indian Writing in English*—the source book of Indian English literature criticism

(Iyenger 642). He terms them as "The 'New' Poets" (Iyenger 641). From the seventies to the nineties, the poets who came up with commanding voices were Maheswar Neog, Amaresh Datta, Dayananda Pathak, Lakshahira Das, Umakanta Sharma and Bhupati Das. The pioneering work on the field, Nigamananda Das's *Mosaic of Redemption* offers precise and contextual critiques of their English poems.

An introductory paper like this can only be indicative but never exhaustive or conclusive. For the sake of convenience, let us commence with a very brief engagement with Amaresh Datta's poetry. The veteran octogenarian from Assam, Amaresh Datta (recently conferred honorary D. Litt. by Assam University) has been a brilliant teacher and eloquent analyzer of English Literature and his poems bear testimony to his erudition and imagination. The reinterpretation of the Biblical myth of Origin in an ironical tone brings him close to the spirit of a modernist:

In the beginning was the dream
He said: let there be light
And pressed the button
And light was there
In his walled globe.
And water too
For his lackey brought it cool from the bar.

(Cited in Das 8)

Datta's poems are romantic lyrics of introspection, but often woven with contemporary issues and ethics. His poems about nature and earth evokes the age old relationship between God and creation:

You have given me
The freedom
To traverse my sky
To gain my nest's paradise
Or lose it. (ibid.)

Nature and its representation is also the major concern of Bhupati Das's poems who has shown adequate skill and imagination to be labeled as the finest poet from Assam writing in English (*Mosaic* 13). His ecological concerns, however, do not overshadow the romantic mystic in him:

The lonely road
I walk it
alone
counting the dead leaves
falling
vibrations
of my thoughts
ripple through them
and make the dead leaves
alive.
Are you my love
counting your steps
on some other path
some other time
thinking
about
you and me (Cited in *Mosaic* 14)

Two significant poetic voices to come out of the dense forests of Arunachal Pradesh are Mamang Dai and Yumlam Tana. Quite naturally, the Arunachalian topography and geography are major issues in their creation. Lament, implicit and explicit, for past ways of life is also a recurrent theme, expecially in the poems of Dai. At times she chronicles the changes in Arunachal tribal societies almost with an Achebean acuteness: "I know/from the faces that I meet/in these lives/that have crumbled/that the past lives/in these eyes/ that the jungle shows" ("The Balm of Time":3)

Legends, myths, rites, rituals and customs of the Nyishi tribe find reflection in the poems of Yumlam Tana in sync with postcolonial self assertion. He is vocal about the problematic of English as a creative medium, which reminds one of Raja Rao, Kamala Das, Chinua Achebe or Ngugi wa Thiong'o: "I write in English/ which is not my language/You see I am a Nyshi/ A tribal claiming to be a man" (*The Man and the Tiger* 2000).

Robin S. Ngangom from Manipur has been an able maker of verse and can be said to be the representative poetic voice of Manipur with little disagreement. Published by the Writer's Workshop in 1988, his first volume of poetry, *Words and Silence,* engages with multifarious themes of World War II, tribal life, Manipuri legends, love and sensuality etc. Bitter realities of contemporary Manipur, not withstanding its legendery past, makes Robin deeply pessimistic:

Our necks and hands shake with perverse lust
We respect with avarice only the richest new
And a pot-belly and a manipulating wife
Are our status symbols (Ngangom 20)

R.K. Madhubir is also from Manipur and is chiefly concerned with initiating witty dialogues between mainstream Indian and Christian myths and legends, re-assessing their validity for contemporary life. For instance, he uses the Ravan-Sita motif in his attempt to protest the chase and haunting of innocent wild animals. Myths have not only related the ancient epics, modern legendary figures are no less mythical in their complete ideological failure or incompatibility with changing times. Madhubir's satire on these Gods that failed is scathing, to say the least:

What Karl Marx said for economic freedom?
What Lenin did for socialism?
And what Gandhi fought for liberty?
Ought we to adore them?
Who cares for the Das Kapital?
Who cares for the Utopia?
And who cares for the Truth? (Madhubir 69)

Meghalaya, which literally means 'the abode of clouds' has a strong presence of Christian-European culture in its socio-religious world, and English for all purposes is often almost the mother tongue or 'L_1'. It is more so in the capital Shillong and there is quite a few Shillong based poets who address their worldviews in English. The Manipuri poet Robin Ngangom (discussed above) is also seen as part of this Shillong group due to his enthusiasm about and representations of the folk life and culture of Meghalaya. Desmond L. Kharmawaphlang is a bilingual poet and moves frequently between Khasi and English writing in both and translating to and fro. 'Contemporary socio-cultural concerns of Meghalaya, the cultural past and environmental changes are main subjects of his poetry' (*Mosaic* 45). The barbaric communal riots of Nellie (1983), cyclones of Andhra Pradesh, floods in Bangladesh-such are the chosen themes of Ananya S. Guha's poems, whose two chief books are *In this My Land* (1986) and *What Else is Alive?* (1988). A strong female and feminist voice is discernible in the upcoming poet Anjum Hasan, presently residing at Bangalore. But the autobiographical quasi-mystic note is also present in her, as in many of her peers:

> Life is a woman
> Night, a stolen sobbing chamber
> Of unnamed girls
> I see centuries of slavery
> In the shadows
> Within one dark room (cited in Das 48)

Meghalaya has a lot more to offer, but I leave it for other papers and request you to peep at the poetic trend of Mizoram. Landscape is a prominent concern in the poems of both the famous Mizo poets in English-H. Ramdinthari and Mona Zote. In her poems, Ramdinthari shows a sincere celebration of nature and humanity. When at her best, she can offer some superb poetic lines like "The sky is back and blue tonight/until stars hang up their lights/from the treetops/lit by stray lights/(...) soon voices leave the back cobalt street,/whispers of empty rivers/and bird cries in crescendo;/the hill slope is dark, galvanic and barren." (Nongkynrih et al. 2003:195). Mona Zote is able to offer a correlation among myth, nature, humanity, divinity and psychology in the same dimension of reality. As Nigamananda Das observes: "The landscape of Mizoram haunts both the poets constantly. In the quest of the poetic realities, they have invested novel images chosen from the ecology and culture of the land" (*Mosaic* 58).

Celebration of nature and liberal feminist ideology in sync with humanism is the hallmark of the major poetic voice from Nagaland-Temsula Ao. Being born in Assam and serving in Meghalaya as a University teacher in English, she has definitely more than one cultural tradition at her back. Her earliest collection of poetry *Songs That Tell* (1988) is primarily concerned with identity, existence, subjectivity and a search for the 'roots'-all common features of Indian English literature. What marks her out however is her distinctly individual response to the issues and in her search for the mechanics/origin of her writing, she approximates a Wordsworthian mysticism:

> These are songs which
> Sometimes come
> On lonely nights

And make bright
And fading lights
Songs
Which sometimes
Imitate
Greater bards to indicate
Similar response
To corresponding chords. (Ao 10)

Ecstasy, agony, memory, fantasy-these perennial human emotions and realities are always addressed to in Temsula Ao's poetry. She has also been called a nature poet par excellence whose poetic vision is often haunted by 'the cultural and physical ecology of Nagaland' (Das 58).

Significant poetic creations are yet to emerge from Sikkim and Tripura-Rajendra Bhandari and Bhaskar Roy Barman being, respectively, the lone voices of some prominence from these states. The cursory glance I wanted to give you must end here to give way to papers with deeper and specific engagements with poets and poems from the North East.

Works Cited

Ao, Temsula. *Songs That Tell.* Calcutta: Writers workshop, 1988.

Chandra, N.D.R. and Nigamananda Das. *Ecology, Myth and Mystery: Contemporary Poetry in English from Northeast India.* New Delhi: Sarup and Sons, 2007.

Dai, Mamang. "The Balm of Time": *Chandrabhaga,* Vol.-I, Cuttack, 2000, pp.3-4.

Das, Nigamananda. *Mosaic of Redemption: Poetry in English from the North East.* Cuttack: M.G. Publications, 2004.

Gokak, Vinayak Krishna. *The Golden Treasury of Indo-Anglian Poetry.* 1970. New Delhi: Sahitya Akademi, 2006.

Iyenger, K.R.S. *Indian Writing in English.* 1962. New Delhi: Sterling Publishers, 2001.

Madhubir, R. K. *The Time bomb and other Poems.* Imphal: Vagya Publication, 1987.

Ngangom, Robin S. *Words and the Silence.* Calcutta: Writers Workshop, 1988.

Patke, Rajeev S. *Postcolonial Poetry in English.* New Delhi: Oxford UP, 2006.

(3)

Contemporary Poetry in English from Assam

Nigamananda Das

In 1960 Hem Barua published English translations of Assamese poems entitled *Modern Assamese Poetry*. In this collection, out of the twenty six Assamese poets, nine poets translated their own poems into English. This shows that in 1960 in Assam there were poets who could have written in English. Assamese poetry which has yet to renounce romanticism, is quite different from the poetry of the other provinces of India in its emotional effects and aspects. Even, at present, except a few, Assamese poets writing in Assamese are seldom obscure. The publications of Assamese poets writing in English do not reflect the essence of the Assamese culture significantly. In this regard it is different from the English poetry written in other Indian provinces.

The poetry in English from Assam abounds in a good quantum of translations from folk and religious vernacular literatures and ethnic literatures. The *Bhagavat, Kirtan, Namghosha, Bhaona* and other forms of Vaishnavite or ethnic literatures have been translated into English, which have enriched the reservoir of poetry in English. Discussion of a few samples will provide us some information about the works in this field. Pradip Acharya, Ajit Barua and some other English teachers of Assam have published commendable works in this field. Mahapurush Sankardeva (1449-1569) who propagated *Ekasarannamdharma,* the neo-vaishnavite faith of surrendering to the single Lord by chanting His holy name etched a good number of songs that dilate the glory of the Almighty. Some of these verses bear mark of literary excellence of universal appeal:

> Numbered are the years that measure your life;
> Half the life slips away in the hours of sleep;
> A score of years fly in the winds of boyish pranks;
> Ten years go in counting coins on the finger-tip.
> Think of the twenty years at the other end of it
> When life shall grow too heavy to drag on;
> Each hour in the sand-glass shall be an eternity of aches,
> Each sunrise bringing dullness and disease unknown.
> And shall melt away the dreams of your eyes and starry hues;
> Confined in a cabin it shall pile up a welter of woes.
> (*Prahlad Caritra*)(Barua 27)

The English rendering of Sankardeva's works by various scholars is mostly prosaic as it is very difficult to bring the felicity of poetry in translation:

> Madhava, Rama Hari,
> O Jadava! Rama Hari.
> Being Vyasa, son of Satyabati, you saw the people becoming very foolish.
> Then you spread the teachings of the four Vedas and wrote the epic of 'Mahabharat'...
> You fought with the demons for gods and Indra won the battle at your blessings....
> Shri Shankardeva, the disciple of Krishna says such, "All say Hari Hari in order to destroy your vices."
> (Tr. Punya Hazarika, 5-6)

Sankardeva propagated the various modes of bhakti and equity of human beings,and keenly desired for caste and creedless society and upliftment of the downtrodden. In his *Kirtan ghosha,* he declares from the mouth of Lord Krishna:

> If women and sudras cultivate bhakti for me
> Impart to them this knowledge, great minded one.
> (Dev Goswami 20)

He propounded the doctrine of self-surrender to the Almighty Lord and advised his disciples:

Throw thy body, soul and all at the feet of that vast one
With single minded devotion and thou wilt enjoy the
Bliss of human life. (ibidem 22)

Madhavadeva, the prominent disciple of Sankardeva in his works propagated the bhakti dharma to uplift the downtrodden and to cleanse the society from all sorts of evils:

My obeisance to that devotee
Who is indifferent even to salvation.
Verily, I crave for ecstatic devotion.
My adoration to that Lord Yadupati
Who, being the crown-gem of all,
Remains enslaved to His worshipper. (Dutta 1)

He also wrote many lyrical songs about many aspects of the worldly life like the sense of apathy or indifference to worldly pursuits:

O Hari, how can I be saved, sinful as I am
Unless you shower your mercy on me?
The sinful mind does not forsake worldly desires:
I am deeply plunged in the dreadful world.
(Sarma 1985:55)

A Sufi saint named Ajan Fakir who migrated to Assam from Baghdad in the later part of 16th century is credited with the composition of 200 jikir songs for muslims of Assam. In his jikirs he has spread the bhakti principles both for the Hindu and Muslim communities of Assam. He says:

The *Quran* and purans preach the same
If you are a wise man, you will understand

Ajan Fakir has emphasized on the control of mind and sense to overcome the worldly illusions. He said to his disciples:

Keep your wild senses under control
You will be victorious. (Malik 31)

These poet-saints, who were pillars of society once upon a

time, have been so even now and their works in English translations have been enriching the reservoir of new literatures of the postcolonial times.

Besides translations from the works of the saints, there have been ample translations from Assamese poetry. Famous poet, Hiren Bhattacharya's poems have been rendered into English in an anthology entitled *Ancient Gongs*(1985) where the profound thoughts of the stalwart have found deft expression in the other tongue. The following poem speaks of Bhattacharya's vital concerns:

> My pen is the hammer in the blacksmith's hands.
> I hammer words into shape sharp as the
> Farmer's plough-share, the golden Sita on
> The furrows, ragged like the carpenter's saw,
> I extract from the grains of hard timber,
> Words stained by the blood of experience,
> Like sure arrows from the Santhal male's bow,
> Words become ardent in my blood, flesh and desire,
> Some of them stand high as mountains,
> Some lie low like rivers,....
>
> I am a poet of the vast continent
> Studded with rivers and mountains,
> the earth is my poem.(70)

A collection of songs of Bhupen Hazarika in English translation entitled *Where Seas Meet* (1993) speaks of the great singer's concerns and patriotism:

> No room, in my new land
> For traders of religion
> Or champions of parochialism
> I'll destroy with my own hands
> The spectre of untouchability
> And build a new Assam
> I'll make love flow
> Through all races and communities
> I'll break all barriers of discrimination
> And build a heaven
> Of equality. (3)

Nagen Saikia's new form of short expressions called *Mita Bhash* translated into English as *Aching Void* (2005) speak of mystical expressions about life and living being's explorations of realities in life:

> Drops of melody hung upon the rattle of flower has become dry
> Now only the agony of the petals are floating
> A little bird is bathing there
> It is his last bath (113)

A collection of poems by Megan Kachari (Mithinga Daimary, the Publicity Secretary of ULFA) entitled *Melodies and Guns*(2006) translated into English by Pradip Acharya and Manjeet Baruah and introduced by Indira Goswami exposes the ideology of the revolutionary:

> The quiet sandy beaches, golden in the sun,
> The cascading waves of the river, across that bank,
> Our games in the past, from the water to the earth.
> The pungent smell of the corpse, afloat now
> And stuck to the mud
> And this smell of death,... from the river to the bank...
> But your breasts?....
> Naked to my skin
> I stood watching the new temples, of sand
> Along the golden bank, to enter
> The New World of our pledge.(35)

A collection of poems by Kathita Hatibaruah on mother Earth entitled *Earth Song* (1999), translated by Pradip Acharya reveals the poet's love for Nature and her festivities:

> Such a sweet name,life-giving
> Fertile, loaded with
> The rich sweetness of creation
> Rich, abundant, the golden field
> The primordial mother
> Of thirst and hunger
> The panacea....
> Fertility is the field

The field is fertility
The banner of victory
At the threshold of the twenty-first century. (29)

The translations have proved to be a good harvest of English poems.

Though love for nature is intense in the poets of Assam who are writing in English, yet profuse descriptive passages about ecological awareness are rare in their poetry. Maheswar Neog (1918-1995) in his *Under One Sky (1970)* writes about the people and landscape of the East European countries which he visited under the Indo-Foreign Cultural Exchange Programme. The Indian landscape finds casual references in his poems. In "Pranams to the Danube", he writes:

Here is no Gangã, no Yamunã, no Sarasvati, No Godavari, no Kaveri, or no Brahmaputra.
Yet here am I touching the water of the Danube in my pilgrimage.
Here are no Mughal Gardens;
Yet here do I look at every strange face, every beautiful face,
And it blossoms forth into kindness and grace. (1970:1)

Amaresh Datta (1920–), is a fine romantic poet. His momentary impressions abound references to nature, though a serious attempt to expose ecological disaster in India and an awareness concerning ecology is untraceable in his stanzas. In his poem "My God", his romantic use of some ecological terms can be seen:

You have given me
The freedom
To traverse my sky
To gain my nest's paradise
Or lose it. (1992: 34)

In another poem "In the beginning", such uses continue to appear:

In the beginning was the dream
He said: let there be light

And pressed the button
And the light was there
In his walled globe.
And water too
For his lackey brought it cool from the bar.
(ibidem 35)

In the poem "Wonder" he exposes the mystery of the universe, which is still murky to every imagination:

I would not ask a creator-God
Why a strange ball of fire
Yielded finally to the clamours of inchoate life
Raring to be born of a random blend Or how a tiny globe
Among thousands of gigantic orbs
Turned slowly into a universe of dappled dreams (2005:1)

Amaresh Datta is a gifted poet. He has control over the use of words and images. Besides the use of ecological terms, the poems sound his sad and sensuous strains of the soul:

When nothing happens to the soul
I do not know what really to do:
To brood on the nothingness of life
Or contemplate the mystery of the will of God, (1971:9)

Amaresh Datta's collection of poems, *Captive Moments* (an anthology of thirty lyrics) was published by Writers Workshop, Calcutta in 1971. He is at a stretch a poet, critic and playwright. His other works are *Time's Harvest* (a collection of poems), (Seagull Books Pvt. Ltd., Calcutta, 1996) and *Lotus and the Cross* (a poetic trilogy) (National Publishing House, New Delhi, 1997). *Shakespeare's Tragic Vision and Art* (Kitab Mahal, Allahabad, 1964) is a work of criticism. *Lotus and the Cross,* a verse play, is designed as a modern morality play dealing with the problems of our times like violence, greed, pollution and mad rush for individual success. Its meaning therefore relates to various levels of consciousness and the frontier between the realistic and the symbolic is not clearly marked though the characters have been conceived realistically with the usual dramatic foils and juxtapositions. *Time's Harvest* is a part of the colourful tradition set by the *Ramayan* and the *Mahabharat.* The human psyche and emotion have been pierced and revealed in *Time's Harvest* with a modern individual interpretation.

Lakshahira Das's *Between Births* (1990) contains sixty nine poems out of which ten poems are originally written by her in English. Other poems have been translated into English by Pradip Acharya and others. In her original English poems, Lakshahira has very beautifully exposed her sentiments. But because of the lack of her consciousness as to the growth of poetry in English, which she felt late, she could not compose profusely in English, though she has a fine lyric genius. Writing on various themes, she plays on a whole gamut of feelings and sensations– love, anxiety, sense of death, passions, love-hate relations, hopes, frustrations and anger' (Sarma 1996: 97).

In her later poetry she extended her theme of love beyond the personal level to cover the whole of earth and the human race. The crisis, violence, sorrows and anxieties which ravage the land have been depicted vividly. In her flight of poetic passions, in this period she has been the home-bound pilgrim and thus has buried her emotions in the soil of her birth. In her original English poems by acclimatizing the indigenous tradition to the English language she has produced Indian English poetry. With innate lyrical and emotional fervour, her poetry seems to be a lark's singing of the poetry of the earth at heaven's gate, Her poems heighten the glory of the soulscape. Thus Lakshahira, the *Sangeet Deepika of Assam*, may be called the *Skylark of North Eastern India*. (Das, N. 1998:29)

After her visit to Neli in 1983, she writes about the hellish scenes of the place and her compassion expresses her concern over the cruelty and ethnic violence which have pervaded her land of peace. Addressing the dead children in Neli (the site of communal violence and massacre), Lakshahira, the *Sangeet Deepika* of Assam, sings:

> Sleep my son
> sleep in silence
> No weapon of man can pierce you now
> Nor any fire burn
> only the blood stains
> bear testimony to
> Man's immense senselessness and cruelty (1990:30)

Her finer lyric sensibility has been exposed telling us about her concept of 'time' in the poem entitled 'The Eternal':

> I have taken in my hands
> A broken piece of time glittering like glass
> Wherein is woven the threads of all dreams
> I am prepared this time for enormous nights.
> (ibidem 31)

Against the decency of traditional social life, the deception of modern life spreads a network of illusion. So Lakshahira writes,

> That circle, that path
> The well-rounded globe:
> Broken water-pictures in whirlpool
> Deeds, Life Insurance, Babyfood, household wars.
> Huts and moors
> Hospitality in ancient homes;
> We ever gather from them new wealth
> And a laugh in a circle. (ibidem 34)

Her concept of life in the modern world has been depicted as:

> Life is here but a cry of disgust
> of a bird, in bondage. (ibidem 37)

Her Indianness and lyric sensibility have been depicted very lucidly in a poem entitled "The lingering light":

> From some hidden source
> the note of the magic flute fills the air
> leaving the petals of poesy
> amidst crushed Rajanigandhas (ibidem 28)

Though the poetess contributes only one collection to Indian English poetry, yet her romantic mooring has been made clear in her poems and her later poetry exposes her consciousness of contemporary reality in her surroundings.

In 1993, a collection of English verse entitled *The Protest* by one Hareswar Deka has been published. This collection is a translation of Assamese poems into English by the poet himself. The sixty one poems of this anthology are simple and most of them deal with simple themes. In some of these poems simple Indian myths from epics like *The Ramayan* and *The Mahabharat* have been used. Many of the poems are immature, without any depth of thought and also have grammatical errors. Perhaps the poet has ceased writing now-a-days and this single collection though not a serious attempt at poetry, yet is a landmark in the Indian English verse from Assam. Hunger, grief, illusion, slavery, truth, happiness, self-realization are some of the themes of the poems of this collection. In the first poem of the collection Deka voices his protest and this is perhaps the best one in the collection. Entitled as *The Protest* the text of the poem exposes his dilemma as follows:

> I have no time
> to relax
> pondering about stories
> of the past,
> that led to my coronation;
> sleeping on the lap of power,
> I have also not thought
> of dreaming about
> the noises of the ghosts. (ibidem)

Dayananda Pathak's *Coral Island (1998)* has been introduced by Prof. Amaresh Datta. About his craft, Datta writes in 1980: "Shri Pathak is a serious and sensitive youngman, fully alive to the world about him. What he has seen has made him, more often than not, sad and shaken to the core and like many conscientious youngmen of his generation he seems to have been disillusioned by the spectacle presented by the modern city life in its various ramifications. But he is in search of something beyond the noise and glitter of this phenomenal world." (Foreword). C. Paul Verghese introducing the poetry of Pathak speaks of the flexibility and richness of the English language and its historicity making it an integral part of the cultural and linguistic life of the people of India mainly as a medium of creative expression. Pathak's poetry exposes his emotions and experiences and his themes concern the world, life, love, loneliness and pain of living. His style and art of versification show his originality of expression and imagery (introduction, iii).

As a poet of Assam writing in English, Pathak has not tried to picturise the ethos and contemporary situations of Assam which should have made his poetry expose the authenticity of Assamese contribution to Indian English poetry. As an Assamese poet, his poems also contribute to the Indian writing in English in a novel way and in the context of post-modern Indian writing, this presents a new mode. Like the family poems of Ramanujan and Kamala Das, Pathak also lingers on his nostalgia. About his art and themes he writes:

> My grand-father bought me a sword
> and a pen to play with
> Besides, I have my own words,
> the weapon to fight with
> and to redesign the rickety globe
> my father bought me
> in my birth day
> years past. (ibidem 14)

His attitude to and concept of the modern world in which he is living has been made clear in his lines:

> We are born flowers,
> pure and holy,
> life makes us stones,
> rugged and rude ("Diamond") (ibidem 27)

The same feeling of agony has been voiced in a poem entitled 'feed':

> Plateful of injustice
> my daily feed,
> I munch
> and digest.
> There is none better
> in the market complex
> around me
> for a fresh relish
> cupful of ignominy
> my daily drink
> I live on them and thrive. (ibidem 33)

Pathak uses simple vocabulary and his images are also comprehensive and thought-provoking.

Umakanta Sarma's *Thawing out (1998)* contains ten poems. Sarma is an old man aged above eighty. A prolific writer in Assamese he has been awarded the Assam Valley Literary Award by the Magor Foundation Trust in 1997. A poet of old school, his verses contain the passions of his youth and his use of language seems to be Aurobindo-like. He is mystic, passionate and grave in exposition. The prologue of the book expresses his depth and themes:

> With an agonising turbulence
> deep inside
> I had a fantasy
> as though I glimpsed a universe
> in its splendour, pillage and wrath. (ibidem 9)

He also uses Indian myths and concerns his life with the worldly struggles:

> Long long ago
> how long
> none can tell,
> a silk-cotton tree died.
> Uprooted by the storm!
> Poisoned by cruelty!
> Perished on its own!
> A Rama
> scanning the sea
> A Vasco De Gama
> on turbulent waves
> A hermit
> At Gangotry
> bathing in cosmic ray. ("A life floats") (ibidem 17)

Sarma's contribution to Indian English poetry from Assam is important. Even his single collection sufficiently reflects his poetic sensibilities.

Bhupati Das is the finest among the poets of Assam writing in English. His first collection *May I* (1998) is a unique contribution to Indian English poetry. Writing his introduction to the book in verse, he exposes his romantic and mystic concept of existence as follows:

> May I/ intrude into the/ privacy of your heart and soul with a few thoughts and feelings/ of mine wrapped affectionately/ in words/ that you may or may not like/

> but the emotions are honest and frank/ may be some would resonate/ with your inner thoughts/ quietly tuckled away/ somewhere in the inner recesses while getting on with life and living/ how about/ revisiting/ those feelings/ here.

A fine romantic poet of the North Eastern India, Bhupati Das is very tough in his exploration of worldly reality. His romantic mooring is very evocative and mystic. The following lines show the serene thoughts of the poet.

> the sky was an honest blue
> the stars were bright and the sea was a dancing dream
> with the waves echoing
> the joys of an expectant night
> a poignant moment
> in a cascading embrace
> with the love waves........ (Op.cit., unpaginated)

A deep sense of frustration pervades his poetry. The despair of his heart after the demise of the beloved has been depicted in his lines. His shortest poem "my prison" exposes his deep mystic sense.

> She died
> with it
> my world
> died
> and
> it stopped living. (op.cit.)

Life and its companion and the journey in the path of life are very decently exposed in his words.

> the lonely road
> I walk it
> alone
> counting the dead leaves
> falling
> vibrations
> of my thought
> ripple thro' them
> and

make the dead leaves
alive.
Are you my love
counting your steps
on some other path
some other time
thinking about
you and me.

The poet who "always introduces the conscious intervention of an artistic imagination without straying from the context of life" (2004: blurb), is a lyrical wordsmith. His telefilm 'Call of the Valley' based on his poems was selected for participation as India's entry in 23rd Japan festival for shortfilms in 1996. In *Life and beyond life* (2004), Bhupati furthers his quest for lyrical mellifluity. The eternal revolution in the human, celestial and spiritual world has been voiced with lucid words of the poet:

at the lost horizon
the moon was dying
in the arms of the elusive god
the blood-red sun
came out afresh
ambushing the night
and the pregnant dream
undelivered
She cried out
god
why are you silent (unpaginated)

Amidst his mystery-filled surreal melody, he has been consciously troubled at September 11, 2001, the event of world-terror. He is much above the narrow communal restrictions and as such is mourning of the great tragedy:

no matter/whether you're/a moslem, a hindu or a christian/...../cry/cry my conscience/for the death of sanity/for the remaining world of zombies/life itself is taken for ransom. (ibidem).

Bhupati Das's contribution to Indian English writing is highly praiseworthy and it is hoped that he will publish more of his poems.

Rupanjali Baruah's *All Things Passing & other poems* (2005) is her maiden attempt at writing poetry in English. Many momentary impressions find place in this collection.Her definitive poem "The beginning of poetry" explains how there is no season or exact time for writing poetry. On the other hand "poetry has its beginnings/ in some other surrounding/ when emotions are scattered/here and there/ like leaves on a dry autumn field"(24). She says:

> Poetry begins
> When words are weighed
> On palate of upper lip
> Travel through a psychedelic osmosis
> When thoughts creep in between
> Moments of sleep and waking.(ibid.)

About her craft of writing she says again:

> I cry with diligence
> That is one thing I do with passion best
> And the rest is a passable waste(25)

Rupanjali is a new voice and has a bright future to grow and compose many mellifluous forms of verses.

Though a few collections of English verse by Assamese writers have come out, yet a consciousness has already arisen among the writers and it is hoped that in future a large number of writings in English will be published from Assam.

Works Cited

Barua, B.K.1964. *History of Assamese Literature.* New Delhi: Sahitya Akademi.(1978 edn.).

Baruah, Rupanjali. 2005. *All Things Passing.* Calcutta: Writers Workshop.

Bhattacharya, Hiren.1985. *Ancient Gongs.*Tr. Pradip Acharya. Guwahati:Beaver Books.

Das, Bhupati. 1998. *May I.* Guwahati: Sabinay.

.... 2004. *Life and Beyond Life.* Guwahati: Katha Publications.

Das, Nigamananda. 1998. "Indian English Poetry from North East India": *Proceedings of North East India Forum for English Studies* (NEIFES). Vol.3. Tezu Conference (21-31).

....2004. *Mosaic of Redemption.* Cuttack: M.G. Publication.

....2007.*Ecology, Myth and Mystery: Contemporary Poetry in English from Northeast India*. New Delhi: Sarup and Sons. (with NDR Chandra).

....2009. "The Idea of Ecotopia and Ecocracy in Precolonial Indian Litereature: A Study of Literatures from Southeastern to Northeastern India"- paper presented at Indian Institute of Advanced Study, Shimla.(1-30).

Datta, Amaresh. 1971. *Captive Moments*. Calcutta: Writers Workshop.

....1992. "Three Poems": *Indian Literature*: 152(Nov–Dec). ed. K. Satchidanandan. New Delhi: Sahitya Akademi (34-36).

....2005. "Wonder":MS, Dibrugarh.

Deka, Hareswar. 1993. *The Protest*. published by the poet from Jorhat.

Dev Goswami, Keshabananda.1982. *Life and Teachings of Mahapurush Sankardeva*. Patiala: Punjab University.

Hatibaruah, Kathita.1999. *Earth Song*. Guwahati: Sabinay.

Hazarika, Bhupen.1993. *Where Seas Meet*. Guwahati: Lawyers Book Stall.

Hazarika, Punya.2006. *The Kirtan*. Guwahati: Beenapani Das

Iyengar, K.R.S. 1987. *Indian Writing in English*. New Delhi: Sterling.(rpt.)

Kachari, Megan.2006. *Melodies and Guns*.Tr. Pradip Acharya and Manjeet Baruah. Ed. Indira Goswami. New Delhi:UBSPD.

Madhavadeva, Sri Sri. 1997.*The Divine Verses* (*Naam Ghosha*). Tr.Soroj Kumar Dutta. Tinsukia: Vision Publications.

Malik, Syed Abdul.1990. *Ajan Fakir*. New Delhi: Sahitya Akademi.

Neog, Maheswar. 1970. *Under One Sky*. Gauhati: New Book Stall.

Pathak, Dayananda. 1998. *Coral Island*. Guwahati: Sabinay.

....2007.*The Golden Deer*. Kolkata: Jatiya Sahitya Prakashan.

Saikia, Nagen.2005. *Aching Void* (Mita Bhash). Tr. Gitali Saikia.Dibrugarh:Kaustubh Prakashan.

Sarma, Satyendranath.1985.*Madhavadeva*. New Delhi: Sahitya Akademi.

Sarma, Umakanta. 1998. *Thawing Out*. Guwahati: Sabinay.

Sarma, Upendranath. 1996. Review of Lakshahira Das's *Between Births: Kabita*. Vol.I ed. Shoneet Bijoy Das. Guwahati: Sabinay (96-99).

(4)

Feminist Voices in the Poetry from Nagaland

A.J. Sebastian sdb

'Feminism' is centred on the inequality in the relationships of sexes, leading to various forms, championing the identity of women and their rights. It also studies sexism, gender privilege, and the critical theories formulated by the male dominated literary field. Thus it aims at establishing a feminine critical tradition. Femininity as a cultural construct inscribes the society's views about women through conventions and inhibit woman's individuality. The statement 'one is not born a woman, but one becomes one' (Beauvoir 1997:295) calls attention to the issue under consideration. The term 'feminine' stands for woman herself and everything concerning her womanhood. It is body, passion and nature that define a woman's feminine traits, focussing on her mental and physical nature of mothering and nurturing life. A proper understanding of the issue presented by feminists is essential for a better debate as '...They argue that feminism should work to liberate women from a system of male-centred values and beliefs, and should empower them to discover their own uniquely female identity' (Tolan 2006:323).

In this paper it is my endeavour to present the feminine voice as reflected in the selected poems from the women poets of Nagaland. They voice their feminine concerns in a society that has defined their roles as per societal norms.

Introducing her first book of verse entitled *Weapons of Words on Pages of Pain,* **Monalisa Changkija** writes: " 'To whom it may concern' reflects some of my thoughts on battered and abused women, on domestic violence and on women's ability to rise above the 'second class citizenry.' Yes, I am empathizing with and also crying out at the same time along with women who have suffered and continue to suffer in a discriminate society" (WWPP : i). Domestic violence against woman haunts our society and has turned 'political' besides being 'personal'(Ibidem i). Monalisa with her pithy verse is very emphatic throughout the collection calling attention to societal concerns.

> If God made man
> In His own Image,
> Where shall the
> Battered seek Justice? (Ibidem 1).

She terms oppression of women as a sign of weakness on the part of men as it reveals male 'inadequacies and insecurities.' 'Female bonding' (Furman 1978:182) through language of violence continues unabated in her male dominated society.

> Masculine hands
> Raining blows
> On bodies
> Soft and feminine
> To me
> are battles lost
> but not
> wars won (*WWPP* 2).

Ironically the poet refers to bride burning of 'Dowry-less brides / Penniless Wives.../Son-less Mothers' (Ibidem 3). Feminine strength continues to daunt man with the 'unbroken spirits' of women who continue to nurture life as 'Mother' and 'Wives' despite being 'battered, bruised and bent.' (Ibidem 5). Social evils such as dowry deaths, female feticide, infanticide, rape, wife beating and desertion need eradication.

Monalisa draws attention to the patriarchal society where man conceals his inferiority in 'masculinity' (Ibidem 8). She challenges man to come to his senses and to let her be 'what I am' (Ibidem 11). The poet becomes very articulate as she recounts the untold stories of grieving women as 'weapons of words/ on ...Pages of Pain' (Ibidem 19).

Ayangla Longkumer's "I am woman" affirms her strength of character exemplified through the power of endurance. She is unafraid of physical and mental torture as she has to live with it by her very nature. She defines her role as creator of life, giving birth 'through pain.' As Gayatri Chakravorty Spivak opines, '...in the womb, a tangible place of production, there is the possibility that pain exists *within* the concepts of normality and productivity .' (Spivak 2003: 480). Seasoned thus in the furnace of experience, she has a wisdom innate in her very nature as mother.

> My silence is not weakness
> ...
> My cries do not stem from weakness
> ...
> My eyes
> Reflect the light of wisdom
> Gained through experience (*PFN* 33).

Patient endurance is her proven strength through submission and sacrifice. A woman's creative power makes her survive despite all obstacles of life.

> That in my core
> I have the power to create
> My instinct is to nurture
> ...
> I will endure
> I will survive (Ibidem 33-4).

Ayangla's thoughts are similar to Kamala Das who in her "Introduction" defines herself despite the various roles she has to play as a woman.

> ...it is I who lie dying
> With a rattle in my throat. I am sinner,
> I am saint. I am the beloved and the
> Betrayed...
> I too call myself I (*TGT* 273).

Rosemary Dzüvichü in "Womanhood" focuses on gender inequality in her society. The poet is very pointed in her queries with its didactic purpose. Her social criticism through a series of questions put into the mouth of a young girl are thought provoking. The poem aims to bring about a change in the mind-set of people.

> Why
> my brothers don't carry water
> from the distant pond
> ...
> Why
> men sit and drink
> from morn till dusk
> as their women sweat
> silently
> ...
> Why
> women only cry (*PFN* 111-12).

The child is puzzled by her mother's stoic and enduring spirit that makes her suppress her sorrow. With a final question the little girl wants to enter into the mystery of her mother's hidden grief. The intricate answer the child gets from her mother is that it is part of 'motherhood.' Rosemary vividly brings gender politics in her society that lives in a make-believe world of gender equality.

> Why
> mother I have never
> seen you cry
> ...
> Where
> did you hide
> all your hurt
> and your pain
> ...
> and yet you tell me
> this is Womanhood (Ibidem 112).

From a young girl's queries on gender politics in the previous poem in "Tell Me Mother" **Easterine Iralu** probes into questions of being a woman. Having her mother as a role-model '... a girl's core gender identity is positive and built upon sameness, continuity, and identification with the mother' (Showalter 2003:320). The girl as she matures to adolescence and adulthood, is embarrassed by her sudden physical growth. She finds herself very different from the boys of her age making her afraid and ashamed of her womanhood.

> Tell me mother,
> What is like to be a woman?
> Unafraid
> Unashamed
> ...
> Awkward with my limbs
> Ashamed of my menstruation
> Afraid of my womanhood? (*KA* 32).

Easterine's feminine concerns articulated through the question raised by the young girl can be contrasted with Eunice De Souza's character in the poem "de Souza Prabhu," defining her role in a male dominated society.

> I belong with the lame ducks.
> I heard it said
> My parents wanted a boy.
> I've done my best to qualify.
> I hid the bloodstains
> On my clothes
> And let my breasts sag.
> Words weapon
> To crucify (*TMIP* 119).

Anungla Imdong Phong's "Here I am" is a poem affirming her feminine identity in a world that ignores her inner self and its brokenness. She compares herself to time's 'broken vase' which in its beauteous form was admired by searching eyes. Now as she withers with age she is turned like 'a dry flower arrangement.' The poet ruminates on the brevity of life and beauty like Shakespeare in "Time and Love": 'When I have seen by Time's fell hand defaced/ ...But weep to have that which it fears to lose.' Anungla speaks of her protagonist's lonely existence with her unfulfilled dreams.

It is often found that though the experience of motherhood is a unique experience of woman, yet the 'institution of motherhood is controlled by man and this physical quality conditions her entire life' (Rich 1976:35).

> Here I stand
> as mute witness
> widowed, alone and lonely
> ...
> Here I run
> along with time
> running and looking back –
> ...
> and my unfulfilled spectrum
> forever (*PFN* 18).

The agony of a beleagured old mother is the focal point of **Anungla Longchari's** "An Old Mother's Lament." She has lived her life for her child's sake and has reached the end of her sojourn on earth. She groans in pain:

> I trudge along the last steps of my life,
> Weary and tired of being alive;
> No one to make joyous my last days on earth –
> Not even you to whom I gave birth (Ibidem 20).

She slaved, toiled and bled to get her child to reach the height of glory. Now the old lady is left in the lurch and has become a burden to her daughter. Recollecting nostalgic memories of the bygone days, the mother laments her pathetic situation and forewarns the daughter of similar abandonment in old age.

> Tell me, is it too big a crime
> To ask of you, my child, for me some time?
> ...
> Now when I ask you for a shoulder
> To rest my weary head,
> ...
> Or soon, as am I,
> You will be in the very same state
> When you, like me, become
> As old and mellow! (Ibidem 20).

Josephine Changkija's "Eve" is a fusion of myth and reality articulating her feminine voice. Reflecting on man's original sin, she recalls the Biblical account of the first fall: "So when the woman saw that the tree was good for food, and that it was a delight to the eyes... she took of its fruit and ate; and she also gave some to her husband, and he ate. Then the eyes of both were opened" (Genesis 3:6-7). The poet plays on words rendering the poem a modern metaphor of betrayals. Is the woman alone to be blamed for her beauty left at the feet of the man she loved? But at the end it is the woman who stands accused of the proto sin.

> With her beauty
> Standing out among
> The unbelievable orchard
> ...
> Where the only man she loved
> Left her at Eden one day
> And let her lust roam
> Till it found
> The slithering evil
> And
> Salivated
> The curse (*PFN* 56).

In "Man and Whore," **Nini Lungalang** examines the basic distorted gender positions in a male-female dialogue. The title itself reflects the woman in the darker side as the whore. He on the contrary remains the unsullied man. Is he not a whore too? For a dialogue to be successful, both the parties have to be on an equal pedestal. But the case in hand is of the man who begins with a male dominated position of looking down upon his female counterpart as a whore. He is excellent in his dissembling and looks down upon her only as a plaything of his lust.

> **He:** Woman,
> ...
> What you offer, is more
> Coarse relief
> Cheaper than the garland
> Of pink pearls
> Slung around your neck
> By a past lover (*TMY* 40).

The poem projects the woman as a subaltern in her victim position. Her utterances are very mellowed. She addresses him as 'brother' with great respect, though he is the villain who exploits her femininity. Her speech is one of subordination as she is nothing more than a whore to him. She becomes a mere cog in the machine of his lust.

> **She:** Brother, I'll meet you there
> Anonymous and furtive
> The hot dark passage
> Our common ground;
> ...
> Brother, I'll leave you there,
> And leave behind
> A spark of my essence
> With yours (Ibidem 40).

In "Mirror" **Nini** sees herself identical to her mother. She longs to determine her personal identity without any mirror image of the other. She presents her 'Matrophobia' which is the fear of becoming one's mother. Though she hates to be her mother's replica there is an underlying mysterious pull towards the mother (Rich 1976:62).

> They say I look a lot like mother:
> ...
> She's put much of herself into my making.
> After my birth, as well as before;
> ...
> Sometimes I'd see that phantom child
> And it would anger me to unreasoning hatred,
> I'd see it in the things she'd say
> ...
> And I would weep in wild frustration,
> ...
> Yes, I look a lot like my mother
> And my daughter looks
> A lot like me (*PFN* 86-7).

In "The Tale of a Woman" **Thejangü-ü Zümvü** projects the agony of a girl as she passes through the various stages of growth to womanhood and to motherhood. She makes her resolve to break with an androcentric society. The story begins with the father longing to have a male issue to head his clan.

> And...
> When my mother bore me,
> His poor heart fell,
> His head dropped heavy in disappointment
> ...
> I grew up then,
> Envying my brothers
> who grudgingly trotted off to school
> While I laboured with mother
> ...
> Till a man proposed
> to tie a nuptial knot (Ibidem 149-50).

Marriage being the destiny traditionally offered to women by society, she is married to a stranger at the tender age of fifteen. From then on her sufferings begin as she recounts:

> ...
> He battered me,
> Destroying my young body and health.
> I knew no love
> From my husband,
> who savagely ravished me every night
> In drunken frenzy (Ibidem 152).

Trotting back on memory lane, she recollects how her own mother suffered in silence in the hands of her father. And as she now beholds her first born daughter in her arms she is resolved to protect her from gender abuse. Disregarding all barriers and threats she is determined to educate her daughter to be free from the shackles of gender oppression.

> And I heard my own voice
> Calling out, to rise up;
> To break free
> From the laws of man,
> From the shackles of tradition (Ibidem 153).

As a fitting conclusion to the analysis of feminine concerns in this discourse, let me probe into **Temsula Ao's** fable "Bat Cloud " with allegorical significance.

> Once upon a time
> There lived two bats
> A mother and her
> Albino daughter.
> Even among the outcasts
> They were a class apart
> Living in a dark cave... (*SHT* 8).

Their peaceful life in the cave was disturbed by some creatures with gun on their shoulders. The little daughter 'crouched and shivered' while the bat-mother comforted her. As the mother prayed for protection from cave-goddess she was told:

> But only one of you
> And are you willing to pay the price?
> The bat-mother responded
> Any price mother, any price,
> Please save my daughter (Ibidem 9).

As the bat-mother consented to the sacrifice, a gun shot was heard that hit the mother and opened the cave-roof. As she lay dying the mother prompted her daughter to take her flight to freedom.

> Fly my little girl, fly
> Fly to the sky
> ...
> The little one then began to fly
> With her mother's whisper
> Ringing in her ear (Ibidem 10-11).

The women poets from Nagaland have very thought provokingly presented their feminine voices articulating their personal experiences in a society that ignores their right to be themselves. It is relevant to reflect on the statement of Luce Irigari: "It is also necessary for us to discover and assert that we are always mothers once we are women. We bring something other than children into the world, we engender...love, desire, language, art, the social, the political, the religious...and we must reappropriate the maternal dimension that belongs to us as women" (Irigary 2003:420-1).

Women suffer betrayals and are often victims of patriarchy in manifold ways. However they do not 'constitute *a muted group*, the boundaries of whose culture and reality overlap, but are not wholly contained by, the *dominant (male) group*' (Showalter 2003::322) since they have come forward asserting their role in society, seeking equal opportunities.

References

Beauvoir, Simone De.1997. *The Second Sex.* trans.H.M.Parshley. London: Vintage.

Furman, Nelly. 1978. *The Study of Women and Language*: Comment Vol.3, No.3 Signs 4.Autumn.

Irigaray, Luce. 2003. "The Bodily Encounter with the Mother." *Modern Criticism and Theory*. David Lodge, Nigel Wood. 2nd ed. Delhi: Pearson Education.

Pearce, Lynne. 1997. *Feminism and Politics of Reading*. London: Arnold.

Rich, Adrienne. 1976. *Of Woman Born: Motherhood as Experience and Institution*. New York: W.W. Norton.

Showalter, Elaine. 2003. "Feminist criticism in the wilderness." *Modern Criticism and Theory*. David Lodge, Nigel Wood. 2nd ed. Delhi: Pearson Education.

Spivak, Gayatri Chakravorty. 2003. "Feminism and Critical Theory." *Modern Criticism and Theory*. David Lodge, Nigel Wood. 2nd ed. Delhi: Pearson Education.

Tolan, Fiona. 2006. "Feminism." *Literary Theory and Criticism*. Ed. Patricia Waugh. New Delhi: Oxford University Press.

Works Cited:

Ao, Temsula. 2003. *Songs from Here and There*. Shillong: NEHU Publications. Abbreviated *SHT*.

Changkija, Monalisa. 1993. *Weaspons of Words on Pages of Pain*.Dimapur: Write-on Publication.Abbreviated: *WWPP*.

Department of English. Ed. 2005. *Poetry from Nagaland*. New Delhi: Savio Publications. Abbreviated *PFN*.

Gokak, Vinayak Krishna. 1992. *The Golden Treasure of Indo-Anglian Poetry*. New Delhi: Sahitya Academy. Abbreviated : *TGT*.

Kire, Easterine. 1982. *Kelhoukevira*. Calcutta: J.B.Lama. Abbreviated : *KA*.

Melhrotra, Arvind Krishna. 2003. *The Oxford India Anthology of Twelve Modern Indian Poets.* New Delhi: Oxford University Press. Abbreviated: TMIP.

Nini. 1994. *The Morning Years.* Dimapur: Write-on Publication. Abbreviated : *TMY.*

The Holy Bible, Revised Standard Version. London: Catholic Trust Society. 1966. (All references are taken from this edition)

(5)

Petrified Relics: Ecofeminism in Poetry from Meghalaya and Mizoram

Dikshita Bhuyan

Meghalaya possesses incredible natural beauty and is praised as the Scotland of East. This beautiful province has produced a band of poets who write regularly in English. Among them, Esther Syiem and Indari Syiem Warjri are two renowned women poets who have exposed their ecological aesthetics. Myth and tribal folklore are among the core subject matters of these two poets. Born in Shillong in 1958, Esther Syiem teaches English at North Eastern Hill University. The poems of Esther Syiem, discussed in this chapter are taken from her collection of poems entitled *Oral Scriptings* (2005).

Esther Syiem is continuously reminded of the Khasi myths and legends. As a poet she realizes that in every myth is embedded the wisdom of her race and that every legend speaks in symbolic overtones. Her quest, as such, is for this wisdom so that:

> Like a child who absorbs his strength and energy from the mother and who takes care of her in return; we too, should first sink our roots into our own past. (quoted in Nongkynrih 43)

In her poetic etches Esther Syiem reflects sorrowful fates of the innocent who have fallen prey of the destiny. In the poem entitled "Just One More Field My Child", the poet describes the story of a farmer woman's ill luck when her child kept upon a giant boulder is slowly swallowed up by it:

> *Mei* don't keep me on hold any longer
> Don't you know that my feet are clamped in its jaws?
> Don't ask me to wait as you plough your field
> My knees feel grazed as they're sucked deeper in
> ....
> don't turn a deaf ear my *mei*, yes I know
> your burden is your commitment to feed me at dusk
> ....
> my eyes, only my eyes left to embrace you
> even now you can still draw me out *mei*
> you plough your field as if bewitched by a labour that
> turns you away. I in terrifying death am enclosed.
> (2005: 43)

In Khasi '*mei*' means mother. The helpless child cries out of fear when the hard labouring mother is busy ploughing the paddy field. Bound by duty the mother consoles her child by saying "just one more field, my child"(ibidem). Although she well knows that her icon is indeed dying slowly, but life is too hard to compromise with the cries of her infant baby. No doubt, she lives in between desire and luck, but the urgency of survival compels the caring mother to be a careless one who ignores the difficulty of her child. The poet feels that the mother may lose the child to the giant boulder but issues like hunger, food and shelter are more important to her and so the child complains "you've abandoned me so cruelly to what you believed was a shelter" (ibidem). This complaint of the child and realization of the tragic reality of the mother enhance the tragic intensity of the legend.

In another poem "The Hill of Woman's Death", the poet depicts the tragedy of a legendary beautiful girl whose befitting suitor dies prematurely. The hill mentioned in the poem is found in Ri Bhoi area of the Khasi Hills near the Umiam reservoir. According to a legend which forms the basis of the poem, the father of a beautiful girl organized a race for all her suitors. The winner who could run the fastest up the hill would marry her. Tragically, even though, the one favoured by her won the race, he could not claim her for the sudden exertion caused his lungs to burst at the moment of victory. She chose to remain on the hill to mourn for him:

Father I know you decreed this for me.
My destiny you wrote
on these grassy steeps.
To choose with a *kwai shi kynitien* (betel nut)
Was my privilege denied.
You've stalled me forever
And the future is yours for the taking.
My vigil I'll keep.
And on this hill I'll wait... (ibidem 59)

The poetry of Esther Syiem exhibits a wonderful blending of myth and mystery related to the ecology. Among such "All about U Pyrthat" is a poem in which the poet speaks after a legend about fruitless labour of a lynx to get his sword back. The Khasi word *U Pyrthat* used in the title means the thunder. The narrative begins with a description of dance arranged by the earth. When the earth was young and the forest tender the earth hosted a mega dance that had never been before. All creatures who gathered were anxious to display their talents. In "this unfurlment of talent" (ibidem 12) the earth imagined as a fair maiden, danced with her womanly grace:

with womanly grace
slow step by slow step
The earth she scratched
as demure as a belle
at her first dance
The revelry was fired with
laughter and merriment
and the field rat's face
was fused with the moment. (ibidem)

The lynx, one of the participants in this merrymaking, had a sword which he brandished about and which the thunder envied. He asked to borrow it but then took it away with him to his abode in the heaven. Even since then, whenever there is lightning it is believed that the thunder is brandishing his sword. The tribal people also believe that the lynx vainly tries to get his sword back by depositing his dung in the same spot as a ladder to reach the thunder.

On that significant morn
when all else paused
for a ringside view

of creatures in dance,
U Pyrthat who had come,
to take stock of the others
took note of *U Kui* (Lynx)
who brandished a sword
He desired what he saw,
to piruotte agilely,
to flash it around
in a masquerade of power.
....
So to the dung that he makes
he must add another mass
to enable him to use
as stepladder to the heavens
to reach for his sword
before the pyramid starts crumbling
A tragically vain effort
to obtain a possession. (ibidem 14)

In the poem "Pinnus Khasia—some thoughts", Esther Syiem addresses the pine trees which are in fact the pride of Shillong. The thought that the human population is rising heaps and bounds and that at the same time man is exploiting natural resources much faster than these can regenerate and replenish themselves puts her in an awkward predicament. A large number of pine trees have thus disappeared from the geographical boundaries of Meghalaya and have become fragile. The rows of pine trees are seen as anachronism in present day bleak scenario. The persona is worried about the future at the loss of the glory of natural surrounding:

submerged in the
dampness of a grey mist
that veils your present
with motley configuration
you have become
an anachronism.
the scribes
passed you by,
and left you, to
the maiming indifference
of time. (ibidem 32)

In the next stanza the poet is seen more perturbed at the loss of the fertility of these pine trees which not only add beauty but bring bliss and joy and provide fresh air:

> your fibres
> have not wasted away
> but your seeds
> withhold their fertility,
> unable to reclaim
> the earth
> with the once luxuriant cover
> that was rejected
> by us, when we displaced
> by our woodness
> *ka jinkieng ksiar*
> as we are goaded
> by the desire,
> to be more than what we were.
> ....
> But you are the
> petrified relics
> of our land, as we are
> of ourselves. (ibidem 32-33)

According to the traditional belief of Khasi, *Ka Jingkieng Ksiar* is a bridge, in the form of a tree that connects heaven with the earth. Thus in a pensive mood the poet shows how the earth becomes bare and naked without the luxuriant green cover of pine trees. As Meghalaya is a beautiful hilly province the pine trees are a great asset of its ecology and their maintenance and germination are of paramount importance. Instead the grim reality is that these trees are not safe because of shifting cultivation, destruction of the hills and deforestation. Trees have been there before human beings have appeared on the earth and while trees can exist without human beings, the existence of humans without trees is not possible. The poet feels that her ancestors were conscious of the importance of the forests. Regrettably, there is lack of such consciousness in the mind of modern man. In the haphazard pace of development, urbanization and modernization, it is rarely realized how vast is our dependence on forests especially on trees. There is a sense of bitter dissatisfaction in her utterance when she says, "we are goaded by the desire to be more than what we are" (ibidem). Motivated by a strong urge to gather and gain more and more than actually they require, men in her land wipe out the pine trees without giving a second thought and thus have resulted into a serious ecological crisis. The image of the pine trees as "petrified relics" shows that these trees are now in danger of becoming extinct. The relations of the individual self to her environment, to the forest and trees, to the earth, to the legend and ancient relics, to the men and women who comprise her society are existing relations which make the poet a homebound pilgrim. This kind of attachment also reveals one of her preoccupations-search for an identity for herself and her land. Under the sway of western capitalism, the powerful forces it releases, she finds it quite difficult to preserve the culture and identity of her pristine homeland. She feels this mode of identity crisis at the core of her heart and admits "you are the petrified relics of our land as we are of ourselves" (ibidem). "Ka Tiew Lalyngngi Pepshad" (The flower that Missed the Dance) is a poem exultant in the self recognition of the poet. It is found in the oral literature of Meghalaya that this particular flower *Ka Tiew Lalyngngi Penshad* which grows beside rivers and streams failed to attend the dance organized by all the creatures of the earth. Any person who is known for his procrastination is a *Ka Tiew LalyngngiPepshad*. The poet finds similarity between herself and the flower as she moulds herself a *Tiew Lalyngngi Pepshad*:

I was
the one who never attended.
Ka tiew Lalyngngi pepshad they called me
a ; they labeled me
with words that sealed my fate
till I became the emblem
of a people's instinct for delay.
....
I was the flower that never went
I was she who smoothed her roughened heels
with a pumice from the river bed
and luxuriated in the bull of gentle waters.
The one who combed her tresses thick
and plaited them and piled them high
Till time stood still for me
And all else paled away. (ibidem 16)

The condition of the poet described here perhaps rose as much out of necessity-not being able to find the society she desired. So she defends herself:

> But if followed to have my say
> I'd rearrange the words
> and tell them all,
> the reasons for my procrastination
> from the point of view of one
> who wanted most of all
> to be the crowning beauty of a dance
> which eventually I missed. (ibidem 16-17)

The poet's ecological consciousness is seen here as she is creating a sense of belongingness to the flower.

Another poem "My child" highlights the close connections between woman and nature. The poem is primarily concerned with the themes of suffering, struggle, pain and agony of a hard-labouring mother:

> I've been crushed by pain
> bowed with the uncertainty of being;
> but as I have borne you
> so must I care for you
> with hands that have
> tilled and ploughed,
> and split the earth.

I bind you close with my *jainit* (a linen band to bind a child to one's back)

> And cover you with my *tapmoh.* (shawl)
> And as I carry you on my back
> I climb the stony uphill
> in the dampness of a lingering dawn
> to earn for our keep
> My soul's winter has left it withered and dry
> stretched with the fear that wrings it at all times.
> (ibidem 44)

A sentiment of this kind can be attributed to all women and may emerge from the philosophy of ecofeminism. The language used in the first stanza is symbolic one which shows the connections between sexist and naturist language, i.e. the language that inferiorizes women and non-human nature by naturalizing women and feminizing nature. It becomes apparent from the lines like, "I have borne you", "so must I care for you with hands that have tilled and ploughed / and split the earth" that the mother and the earth are both reproductive and productive. Thus they are closely connected. It is the speaker who shoulders the burden of her family and is always worried about their next day's bread. She suffers from a feeling of insecurity, uncertainty and barrenness in the financial crisis as "my soul's winter has left it withered and dry/ stretched with the fear that wrings it at all times". This is a state from which she might have tried to escape but does not succeed. This mental paralysis, anticipated with fear rather than hope is suggestive of the vulnerability of the speaker. The mood of despair, the burden and the feeling of disappointment go deeper in the last stanza. Her heart becomes as hard as stone and she admits her pathetic condition:

> My ears heard your cries
> but my heart was a numbed stranger
> that kept me from you
> My child. (ibidem 45)

These lines sum up the sorrow and tragedy of the poet. She is unable to hold her child and sings a lullaby to make it sleep "for the socket wrenching labour" (ibidem). The poet studies the different attributes of the subordination of a mother-bearing injustice, shouldering the burden of responsibility, serving without complaints and is aware that she is making a sacrifice. The circumstances under which these lines are written should not be ignored. Esther Syiem records her love and adoration for her home town Shillong in the poem "Shyllong: of a cold Evening":

> I am awed
> by the power
> of your love.
> ....
> in the dusk
> of a cold evening
> you strew my path

> with scrolls of dead leaves
> that are whipped by the wind
> which gathers itself
> strong again me. (ibidem 47)

There is an intense feeling and ardent enthusiasm in the first three lines. The poet seemed to be deeply involved in love with Shillong. She is spellbound and 'hushed' by enjoying the beauty of a cold wintry evening when "the silhouette of trees/ form a dark line/against the graying sky" (ibidem). As soon as evening falls, the crimson light of the setting sun spreads over the trees. She is overwhelmed to view the panoramic beauty of the nature. Thus she shows her keen observation in the shifting phenomena of nature like scrolling of dead leaves sunset and swaying of wintry wind. But the last stanza takes a different turn. Contrast to the calm and serene mood of the previous stanza, there is a kind of discontent, anguish and bitterness. The fact which discourages the poet from sharing the happy moments with her fellow beings is that the city dwellers around her show little interest in such changes in nature:

> But the flash touches no one,
> for my city
> has enclosed herself
> once more
> within the verbiage
> of her noise. (ibidem)

The people who live in the din and bustle of city, not only lack interest in nature but their materialistic attitude also keep them in a distant confinement far from the reach of the blessings of nature. Thus a strong sense of satire of artificial modes of modern life is undercurrent in this poem.

The ever increasing menace of environmental pollution at a very rapid pace can be attributed primarily to man's contemptuous attitude towards nature. The environment is being indiscriminately disturbed in utter disregard of the fact that the nature is one that the man cannot replace. It is this callous and systematic destruction of nature that now threatens man's very survival. Addressing a monolith, the poet appreciates its enduring capability to withstand a rough and unfavourable time when the world is submerged in heaps of plastic and other non-biodegradable materials which are a direct threat to ecological balance:

You appear
to have withstood
time's duress
as you watch
over a world
of plastic clutter.
Your sense of time
is forbidding
but you keep intact
our self respect
You have shut yours
in an aura
that is yours alone. (ibidem 57)

The monolith is standing motionless for ages. The poet asserts that it is the stability and silent repose of the monolith that enables it to guard and protect its identity. Thus with the change of time the monolith remains immutable, majestic and stands still there:

Your changelessness
in flux
is the only surety
against the inquisition
that assails you. (ibidem)

In this poem the monolith is depicted as a symbol of antiquity. The poet regards the monolith as "the keeper of our past, vertical guardian" (ibidem). The poem is a revelation of the contrast between naturalness and artificiality, modern age and primitive age, change and changelessness. The poet expresses her gratitude to the monolith in the last stanza:

Your commodity
is your soul
held still, in the
imbroglio of time,
as you provide
shelter and rest
for wayfarers,

drawn by your etchings
in their souls. (ibidem 58)

By extending this kind of rewardless help, the monolith perhaps tries to convey the message to the mankind that nature and natural object need cooperation, that nature is a great friend, not foe of human beings. Here lies the greatness of the monolith. The mental and emotional attitude of the poet is exquisitely reflected in the clear-cut, yet suggestive phraseology of the poem. "Cherries", a short poem of Esther Syiem, is a flowery description of beautiful cherry flowers. The poet is completely dumbfounded by the blossoms of cherry flowers nestle in bright red colour:

blossom of cherries
nestle in colour
as they touch the heavens
and cast me in wonder. (ibidem 48)

A passionate lover of nature, the poet is not alienated from nature but wholly merged in nature. She shares her joy with nature, the blooming of thousands of cherries in the bosom of nature which remains, through all the changes, fresh and beautiful. These flowers become an inexhaustible source of her inner peace and joy.

In the poem "Hybridity", Syiem remembers her past joyful days spending amidst natural surrounding. She reflects how happy they were while enjoying the hide and seek of the sun to shine through in a rainy afternoon. They leapt, laughed and danced in the green field. The images of nature's more remote and skiey phenomena are quite inseparable from her soul:

The rain was like a sieve
for the sun to shine through.
droplets of fun in the afternoon
tickled us with gaiety.
we danced in the shimmering confetti
for the fox had married the quail.
a moment of rejoicing
in the golden rain
trapping sun,
and sun, artful dodger,
bouncing back to us. (ibidem 72)

But such pleasure is short-lived. Now everything has been changed in her surrounding. There is the indiscriminate felling of trees and the jungle has been stripped off. This kind of deforestation and denudation has taken a dangerous proportion leading to extinction of various species of plants from the dark deep forest. So she says:

> Now that the jungle
> has been stripped
> the *tiew dieng* that they sell (orchid)
> is a hybrid,
> produced from the flower
> gone to seed. (ibidem)

The poet expresses her deep concern over the loss of the original beauty of wild orchid. She puts the onus of this problem on the ecologically harmful practices on the part of men. The magnificent tall trees are the only abode of the orchids. But deforestation and shifting cultivation of her land have turned the forest, once wrapped with tall trees into an almost barren land. Since the trees are chopped off so thoughtlessly, the question of the dark future of these orchids haunts the poet. As a result, such ruthlessness hastens the process of fast vanishing of the variety of orchids and other plants and wild flowers and thus hybrid replaces the original.

Indari Syiem Warjri (1967-) explores the nostalgic royal traditions and rich culture of Meghalaya in her poems. The way the tribal people of her land invokes the gods amidst the offerings., decorations of the king among his somber ministers, the head priest and others sitting cross legged, grasping a gourd of libation evoke an air of the glorious tribal ritual. A virgin princess sketches patterns on earth's face in adoration of the god. In this way the ceremony ends successfully:

> Rich gold, silken black tresses,
> Falling below your curved waist
> Interwoven with braided gold
> eyes downcast, head under a spell
> ....
> a royal sword will deflect lightning from the sky
> as sacrificial blood stain the white fleece

a pitiful bleat blessing the monarch.
The gods are satisfied. (188)

Nature's mysteries and mysterious folk tales enrich her composition. The contribution of myth and legend can't be underestimated as they enrich the folk literature and tradition of Meghalaya. According to Khasi legend *Pahsyntiew* is the mother of the kings in the Khasi hills. It is believed that she is a woman of divine origin. The poet pays her tribute to *Pahsyntiew* in this manner.

I heard of your beauty
blushing daughter of the deities
sheltered in your cave of chastity
no man dares explore. (ibidem 189)

The description of the dim and rain wet Khasi hills ruled by Syiems (kings, rulers) is quite attractive and beautiful:

the sons became men, royal in stature
having wisdom gifted by the gods
they came to rule the misty hills;
to dwell in pinewood mansions
where carpets of clouds
and cloaks of rain
conserve the forest of the Khasi hills. (ibidem 190)

The imagery used in the poem 'misty hill', 'pinewood mansion', 'Carpet of clouds', 'clouds of rain' are mostly drawn from nature.

Both Esther Syiem and Indari are poets of nostalgic eloquence. They have explored the ecology, myth and mystery of Meghalaya in their poetry and have thereby revealed their reminiscences of the glorious past of the land.

So far as the poets of Mizoram are concerned Mona Zote and H. Ramdinthari are two remarkable women poets. They are very nostalgic of the Mizo landscape. Mona Zote is a gifted poet. Her poems have favourable climate of myth and ecology mingled with mystery which exposes "how the hybrids shall inherit the land". (204). Her impressions on an environment, blossomed with lilyum in the poem entitled "Lylyum" reveal her mystery-mixed inclinations:

Thin-skinned October
with its cold religious air
Eyes of coal
Veins of ice
And the dark-enfolded insects
go to sleep insects
Go to sleep
O Allah she thinks of Jesu
When out of the honeycomb of night
Church drums busily advertise
the high percentage of faith. (ibidem)

In the month of November, the hybrid flower lilyum assumes new dimensions. The poet calls it "Gods own graffiti". (ibidem 205)

November obsessive punctual
Let's loose on the hemming hills
these yellow dead-men's flowers. (ibidem)

She brings out a symbolic and mythic significance of the flower and dissects its dimension for an intended meaning:

Lilyum, named for traitors,
Replace the burning tree and set
An alphabet that comprehends the need
for self-translation. Thank god I see
No synthesis
In your pained
Schizophrenic
sepals. (ibidem)

The poem is a unique expression of the poet's concept of myth and ecology. In the poem "Mary Winchester", Mona Zote shows her love of nature in her serene, sincere and nostalgic expressions:

The knew that snake berries
are shy and will often hide
under a mess
of larger leaves. They look
Life drops of blood
from a deer's flank. And so weet. (ibidem 199)

A blend of romantic imagination and sense of reality is observed in the poem of H. Ramdinthari. She portrays hills, valleys, sky, trees, rivers and extremely enticing nature vividly:

> the sky is black and blue tonight
> until stars hang up their lights
> from the treetops
> Lit by stray lights
> ....
> Soon voices leave the black cobalt street,
> whispers of empty rivers
> and bird cries in crescendo,
> the hill slope is dark, galvanic and barren.
> (ibidem 195)

Her nostalgia revolves round the landscape of Mizoram. Human habitations as well as the green surroundings are made charmful in her colourful imagination:

> For us the fogged light of tree leaves
> and the thick lamp-past of crushed boulders
> are antipodes where we build our huts. (ibidem 197)

Works Cited

Nongkynrih, K.S. "Hard-edged Modernism: Contemporary Poetry in Northeast India". *IIC Quarterly* 32, 2 & 3 (2005)

Ramdinthari, H. Poems: *Anthology of Contemporary Poetry from the Northeast.* ed. K. S. Nongkynrih & Robin S. Ngangom. Shillong: NEHU, 2003, pp.195-197.

Syiem, Esther. *Oral Scriptings.* Calcutta: Writers workshop, 2005.

Warjri, Indari Syiem. "Poems": *Anthology of Contemporary Poetry from the Northeast.* ed. K.S. Nongkynrih & Robin S. Ngangom. Shillong: NEHU, 2003, pp. 188-192.

Zote, Mona. "Poems": *Anthology of Contemporary Poetry from the Northeast.* ed. K.S. Nongkynrih & Robin S. Ngangom. Shillong: NEHU, 2003, pp.199-205.

(6)

Ecology, Myth and Mystery in Contemporary Poetry in English from Arunachal Pradesh, Manipur, Sikkim and Tripura

Nigamananda Das

More than two dozens of poets from various provinces of the north-eastern part of India have published their poems and poetry collections in English, both in India and abroad. These poets have been called "ethnic poets" (Guha 119). They may be called multi-ethnic poets because they hail from multifarious ethnic groups which are troubled by various ethnic crises. Hills, valleys, men, myths, legends, communal violence, tribal rites, mystic and profoundly aesthetic sensibilities, ecology, self-alienation, autobiographical exegeses of self, being some of the themes of their poetry, the poets are proved to be consistently home-bound pilgrims.

Mamang Dai (1957–), a famous Indian English poet of Arunachal Pradesh, (born in Pasighat, East Siang District), left the Indian Civil Service for maintaining a career in journalism and uplifting the social and eco-cultural standards of her people. A poet from the Adi community, she founded the Arunachal Heritage Society in 1992 and has been its president since then. An accreditted journalist to the Government of Arunachal Pradesh, she has been tirelessly devoted to social welfare through the NGO. She has published poems in various Indian journals and has brought out a collection of poetry, entitled *River Poems* (2004) from Writers Workshop, Calcutta. Dai is a home-bound pilgrim in her quest for identity. In her poetry, life in Arunachal Pradesh, peoples' faiths and her own, agriculture, mountains, streams, rivers and stones, myths, and nature's magic, reveal the myriad world of Arunachal's ecology and mysterious and glorious heritage. She reflects the Arunachalee culture and traditions and recent or modern transitions in the mosaic of living conditions. A keen explorer of heritage, she seems to be a sentinel of traditional tribal values. Environment/ ecology, profound serenity in nature, and an innocent voice about the things in the surroundings have been her important concerns. She voices her emotions and feelings through the images and metaphors chosen mostly from nature. Her search for identity has exposed her to be a nature-loving-humanist. She reveals her beliefs in tribal pantheon of Gods and mystery of environing ecology:

> Yes, I believe in gods,
> in the forest faith
> of good and evil,
> spirits of the river
> and the dream world
> of the dawn.
>
> ["The Balm of Time" 2000(a):3]

She also ponders over the contemporary systems of living in Arunachal and contrasts them with the ancient ways of life and agriculture. She has been an observer of the changes in the tribal society over the time:

> I know/from faces that I meet/in these lives/that have crumbled/that the past lives/in these eyes/that the jungle shows/sometimes........., the mountain knows/how we pressed our hearts/against its earth/we placed the shadows/where they are/in the leisure of dreams/the sky wind knows,/how we grew flowers/in fields of stone. (ibidem)

She has been a close observer of the wide socio-cultural changes in her land. The men, mountains, rivers, trees and harvest have been her important subjects. In her poem entitled "Sky Song", she says,–

> We left the tall trees standing.
> We left the children playing.

We left the women talking,
and the men are predicting
Good harvests, or bad
that winged summer
we left, racing with
the leopards of morning. (ibidem 5)

"Indian English poets are 'river poets'. Poems on rivers abound." (Sarang 1995:13). Living near the rivers amidst the natural surroundings, and varied feelings, experiences, and emotions, make the poetess remember the transactions of life and plights of the components of nature. The past of her ancient land, the red robed men, the tribal rituals, tribes living in caves and the favourite, mysterious ecology lurk in her mind. Such remembrances make her a mythmaker, a designer of living realities and the contemporary myths, or the ancient and present life in Arunachal Pradesh:

> I remember then/the great river/that turned, turning/ with the fire/of the first sun/away from the old land/ red robed men,/and the poisonous ritual,"/....Remember the flying dust/and the wind, /like a long echo/ snapping the flight/of the river beetle, /venomous in the caves/where men and women/dwelt, facing the night, guarding the hooded poison. ["The Missing Link": 2000(b):64]

The rivers, eastern mountains, the flash of summer, intricate nature, divinity in trees, starry skies, the great river: Brahmaputra, landscape full of memories, which the poetess calls "myth and mystery" (Dai 2001:154), crowd her lines in poetry. Hers is the poetry of landscape:

Without speech
We practised a craft
leaving imprints
on sky walls,
Linking the seasons,
coding the trailing mist
in silent messages
across the vast landscape. [Dai 2000(b): 66]

Mamang's *River Poems* (2004) containing fifty one poems, legitimatizes her voice of home-bound ballads. This single collection makes her presence felt when the poetess exposes her concerns for both the local and global events. She feels the palpitations of the rivers' hearts and recurrently says, "The river has a soul..... the river knows/the immortality of water" (2004:29). The Arunachalee *Tapu* dance and folk-faith associated with it that issueless women by joining the dance putting on male attire can conceive a son (ibidem 42-43), the funeral rites of the Adi tribes (46-47), the *ponung* dance of Adis during the festival of *solung* (ibidem 19-20), the man and tiger brotherhood (ibidem 50-51) are among several local concepts of Arunachal that have prompted the powerful feelings of the poet. Her Korea poems which express her emotional concern for the accident of a mid air explosion that killed many of the nation's top leaders reveal the mourning of her profoundly responsible soul. The words that narrate her mourning spring out of the ecology of her favourite nature:

> locked in our tears blind storm
> on this clearest of mornings
> we feel again the draining of strength
> when the hills are waiting
> acrid, sad
> smoky with autumn and her wild fires
> in the courtyards the old men sit
> like stone, remembering (ibidem 66-67)

The tragic images of Korea reflect the Arunachalee countryside in Mamang's description. Her poetic explorations concentrate on the rites of living in Arunachal Pradesh and are thus a conscious attempt for the quest for identity.

Yumlam Tana (1976–), born at Koloriang, Subansiri District of Arunachal Pradesh, teaches English literature at the Government School, Karsingsa in Papumpare District. He has published a collection of poetry in English entitled *The Man and the Tiger* (2000). In his poetry we see his constant clinging to the mores of quest for identity, a major concern of postcolonial Indian English literature. He belongs to the *Nyishi* tribe of Arunachal Pradesh and his poems allude to the *Nyishi* myths of brotherhood of the man and the tiger, *Nyishi* legends, superstitions, rites and rituals, customs, and costumes, etc. He writes about his identity by humanizing his status universally:

I write in English
which is not my language
You see, I am a Nyishi
A tribal claiming to be a man.
I am all humanity,
With no geographical boundary,
No social restrictions, no biological limitations.
...Nothing to divide me from my fellowmen.
(Tana: 2003:13)

He speaks of his brotherhood with the tiger, the *jhum* fields in his surroundings, his sojourn in the Dibang Valley and the life in the bosom of nature:

My brother, my mother nestled so fondly on her bosom
Singing lullabies in the night and
when away to the jhum fields in the mountains
We played various games around the house
He was my playmate. He was my nurse.
....
The Tsangpo flowing through the Dibang Valley
And the plains of India
And Bangladesh
....
So the tiger must stalk in the forest
To kill and spill blood for blind appetite
And the man, a social animal,
Search an Ideology to suit his Intellect.
(ibidem 14-15)

He dilates on tribal animist rituals to propitiate the spirits and the primordial sentiments and exposes a constant pre-occupation with tribal anthropomorphism:

In spite of all those talks about rationales
And scientific temper
A primordial sentiment lurks
Somewhere in us begotten in the days of chaos.
The *Nyibu* had read the entrails of

The chickens
And presaged that six dead monkeys
Shall lie beside a stranger in the house
And as required six horns of Mithuns to be slaughtered,
Besides the fat pigs from grandpa's sty
To appease the hungry spirits from the
World of the dead
Amidst chantings of prayers in four
Sleepless weeks. (ibidem 16)

Nyibus's (the traditional priests of the Nyishi people) power of divination and healing, the traditional attire of Nyishis, "*Pomo* and *Jupung*", the Nyishi and tiger brotherhood and Nyishis' similarity with the physical features of the tiger, the ecology of the land of Nyishis, their mysterious faiths and ideology, are the prime concerns in Tana's poetry.

Mamang Dai and Yumlam Tana have brought glory to Arunachal for their contribution to Indian Writing in English. They are trying to legitimatize their voices in giving expression to tribal cults, myth, mystery, history and ecology of Arunachal and contemporary transitions. Their future poetry will mirror their quest more in quality and quantum.

R.K. Madhubir(1942–) of Manipur uses common Indian and Christian myths in his poetry. His is very often a comic vision of the situations and surroundings of the modern life. He is recurrently worried for Manipur. But myths, legends, history and folk faith of the land have not been reflected enough in his works. Specific episodes from mythologies have not been applied in his poetry with contextual reference. Juxtaposition/admixture of Christian and Indian myths with reference to loss of ecological serenity reveals an agnostic view of life and a deep sense of responsibility:

Look in the dark
You'll see Christ daringly running
Like a fugitive from enemy's camp
To save himself from crucifixion
And Krishna you'll find lying dead
As pauper on railway platform
covered with numerous flies
Yes, you'll see
If you're an agnost. (1987:1)

Excessive materialism of modern times has shattered the delicate serenity and grace of nature, where the holiness of the gods and religious faith and feats has been devastated. As a result in his vision lies an endless horizon of a shattered world where the glorious trend of soul-searching has suffered a gross setback:

I look in the dark
And see
A ruined big city
Not a single soul at all
Thousand plastered pieces of walls I see
Falling down from the sky scrappers
which reached the blue yesterday
I see them falling down dusty. (ibidem 2)

His dreams are filled with comic vision of upturning myths and history. He sees fulfilment of unfulfilled desires in his dreams: where he sees Jesus coming out of his grave and killing Herod with an arrow when everybody praised him; Kalidas killed Dusyanta and brought Shakuntala to his old hut when Kanva danced with joy and laughter; Siddhartha suddenly woke up from meditation and scurried breathlessly towards Kapilabastu while Krishna came to the kingdom of Kamsa and Kamsa embraced him in his warm bosom; Shahjahan broke down the Tajmahal and cursed Mumtaj, Alexander came to Delhi as an ambassador, Hitler served Jews for their welfare and Madona sitting at the foot of an elm tree, keeping her child on her lap, anxiously waiting for the shepherd burst tears throughout the night (ibidem 3-4).

The poet remembers heroes and events of World History and that of the great wars which caused havoc to world civilizations. Ruminating the past, he envisions a rebirth or incarnation of a new civilization wherein we will have some new experience and a new 'time'. He welcomes wars and heroes like Hitler and Napoleon and reveals his contentment in the devastations in the sense that, that will bring an epoch-making change in the mindset and habit of the mankind. As such he says:

At the great cities of our desires
And torpedoes strike the ships of our selfish cargoes
And we are burnt
To be reborn (ibidem 13)

In every religion, the Almighty God is the saviour. At the time of the obliteration of the world (*Pralaya*), the deluge, it is the Saviour who saves the people He likes to save the world from the deluge. Finding ecological devastation in his surroundings, the poet is so much obsessed that at a time he prays the saviours of various religions and faiths to save him from the deluge. He finds his existence useless in the context of the ecological disaster and the pervasive perversion at all spheres:

> In my blood there is water
> in my breath there is air
> and in my diet there is protein
> but everything now useless
> will no one save me now
> either Krishna or Jesus or Allah
> or Shidaba, any one of you
> be kind and save me from the deluge
> save me kindly from the deluge. (ibidem 14)

He numbers the contemporary myths that aggravate his obsessions and thus exposes his sympathy and love for the serenity and pomp of nature and the traditional culture of the land and race:

> Everybody's heart tugging by nuclear holocaust
> everybody's hair raising by starwar
> everything now doing by computers
> moving the roads now instead of engines
> in this age you're picking sparrow-dung as coins
> encroaching like Pahom for a few more steps.
> (ibidem 15)

He uses the myths of Ravan, Sita and the like, in the context of abusing the pitiless hunter who kills birds and animals in the forests in a large scale. He advises him to kill the tiger that kills the innocent animals, but not to kill all deer in the forest like the Nazis' killing of innocent men:

> If
> dogs, hens, ducks and pigeons
> from yours the tiger had fetched
> if you think him to catch
> if you want him to punish

Come as transformed Ravana into golden deer
Come in the heart of the forest
take him away as Sita from Panchabati
to the palace of Lanka
take him away I do not worry. (ibidem 18)

To give a picture of the transactions of life in the modern times, he presents the mythic concept of time and life's transactions by certain reversals of characters and actions. He calls the modern times *balliyuga*, i.e., the age of exploitation and mischief, where there is no difference between male and female in their appearances, outlook, customs, behaviours, etc. The human behaviour of past ages has been traced by him by a deliberate displacement of time and character to evoke a sense of satire and fun. As a moralist he is critical of the human behaviour at various points of time:

Rama was born in Satyayuga
faithful were the people that time
Bharata was born in tretayuga
disciplinary ideals were there properly
Krishna was born in dwaparyuga
since then the universe had started flattering
Bhima was born in Kaliyuga
the yuga of might is right
and today
it is balliyuga
fathers and sons, brothers and sisters
relatives and friends
no one knows no one cares. (ibidem 22-23)

In these lines there are certain deliberate changes in the mythic time, such as, whereas both Rama and Bharat belonged to *tretayuga*, and Krishna and Bhima belonged to *dwaparyuga*, he has shown the difference as Rama and Bhima belonging to *Satya* and *Kaliyuga* respectively. The poet has made these changes to characterize the time in accordance with the human behaviours. He also depicts the contemporary scene in Indian politics where deceitful political rogues are exploiting the innocent men of the land:

amidst
chanting of the names of Mahatma and Panditji

by numerous political rogues
Chanting and looting many innocent people.
(ibidem 23)

He is reminded of the glories of his *Meitei* race in Manipur and feels pain to dilate the changes in the land due to various reasons:

but how ridiculous is my Meitrabak
everything everywhere is funny
looking towards the natural phenomena
no Meitei fruits growing in Meitrabak
the sound of oothum couldn't be heard again
the lovely folksongs of Meiteichanu
how is it I like to hear
I've never heard in life
when asked to aged ones. (ibidem 25)

Madhubir's vision is recurrently obsessed by inversion of myths. It is his typical method of exploring realities in poetry. He sees in Man, an old vulture for whose nature, there will be inversions in the course of nature's transactions and the behaviour of gods:

The eastern breeze will stop now
The western sea will sink to bottom
And Nataraj will stop now dancing
The angels will not come to you now
From Heaven to give message from God.
(ibidem 43)

The contemporary desertion of sweet and healthy ecology and glorious natural surrounding is reflected in his poem *A Deserted Temple* where he finds dead idols of many Gods or incarnations like Ratnakar (Valmiki), Radha, Krishna, Nityananda, and Jagannath which are lying smeared with mud on the dirty and dusty floor of the temple (ibidem 54-55).

In the era of biodiversity depletion, human relationships have also been shattered and all the human beings have become the mythic *Pandavas* and *Kauravas* on the bosom of nature (1998:2). The poet addresses the Almighty God as Saviour and compares him with the Polestar. Drawing an instance from the history of the defeat of King Ashok in the Kalinga War, he addresses his saviour, "but my dear maker, by whom you've been defeated?" (ibidem 33). He is disheartened about Lord God's behaviour like a misanthropist as He lives somewhere away from the human society and from all the human beings (ibidem). He employs some Greek myths in his imaginary sojourn of that glorious world as he is oblivious of the aim of his journey in the path of life. He does not know where to end the journey of his life. As such in his imagination, he is blithe of the bounties of the Greek mythic world as he sings:

> Floating so long on such a wide ocean
> I've gone to Greece and met Phidias
> visited Parthenon, visited Olympian Zeus
> offered flowers to Anthena and Zeus
> fell in love with sweet Aphrodite
> talked of valour with Antheno the matchless
> drank fine wine with Dionysus
> And today here I'm floating
> on the beautiful transparent breast of Pescidon
> floating so long on such a wide ocean. (ibidem 43)

A strong sense of satire of various modes of modern life is undercurrent in Madhubir's poetry. He always makes direct reference to the mythic characters to provide a generalized notion of the particular mythic characters. The ideals of Karl Marx, Lenin and Gandhi have been myths for the poet. Once upon a time, their ideals brought out revolutionary changes in the society. But in the postmodern period their ideals have become outdated and have lost their significance. Now we have turned gypsies crying for a sweet home. So the poet questions the *locus standi* of the Marxism, Socialism and Gandhism (Ahimsa) and says:

> What Karl Marx said for economic freedom?
> What Lenin did for socialism?
> And what Gandhi fought for liberty?
> Ought we to adore them?
> Who cares for the Das Kapital?
> Who cares for the Utopia?
> And who cares for the Truth (ibidem 69)

He sees turmoil everywhere in the inner and outer worlds. The myths have been upset in the world's turmoil. Madhubir envisions devastative upheavals in the world everywhere:

> Krsna, the Director of Mahabharata
> wounded and paralysed and died
> by the blows of one of his actors.
> Now the devils are playing cricket
> Sita sits on Ravana's throne
> heavier and heavier is the globe now (ibidem 71)

Lord Buddha appearing in the poet's dream and destroying the Lumbini garden, breaking down the monasteries, Jesus sitting among the rogues and Krsna scurrying with the smugglers (ibidem 77) are the prophetic visions of the poet as to present day trouble-torn society where the denizens of this world are engaged in destroying their own habitats and resorting to the ways of life moulded of perversions like smuggling, insurgency, robbing, killing, etc. In his haikus he has used some myths with new interpretations to create fun. His sense of satire is remarkable here:

> (17)
> Rama married Sita
> Ravana attacked Rama
> Smiled Sati Sita (ibidem 85)
> (37)
> Buddha's my Lord
> worshipped him always but
> He never knows me (ibidem 88).

Madhubir has not delved deep into his racial myth, memory and history. He is frivolous in manipulating myths to pierce into the inner recesses of life and culture and explore the existential possibilities of his times. The contemporary burning problems of his motherland have not been expounded by the use of Manipuri myths.

Lone poet from Sikkim who writes in English and Nepali and translates from Nepali, Rajendra Bhandari (1954–), makes landscape his haven for poetry. Stars, streams, flowers, trees and creatures of the surroundings are the means of explorations of his emotions and feelings:

> The naked sky is the witness.
> Sultry sun is the witness.

These words,
I haven't coughed out
from nowhere.
....
I haven't materialised these lines
by the sleight of my hand.
Reclaiming them from sliding land
I've lifted them from
the forests, the lowlands,
the grainfields, the cliffs (2000: 19/ 2003: 72)

He is sympathetic to the poor and downtrodden. Depicting the poverty of a girl and her parents, he consoles himself with the step taken up by the girl.

In the dark corner of the street,
the girl has opened a shop
going hungry for many days
At last she has learnt a trade,
Trembling from the death-bed
her father spat at the sky once
Shedding many a tear
the mother hid her face
in her two palms (1992: 23)

The poet reacts to loneliness during the rains and hailstorm, when the nature turns violent isolating the man in shivering and solitude:

Hostile is this loneliness to me.
The past and present have grabbed me.
History has assaulted me brutally, my dear!
Wounded all through the body, I'm here (2000: 21)

The poet, who finds, "In the midst of chaos, chaos itself sits quiet" (2003: 71), dissects the reality in his surroundings to trace the mystery in our existence:

What could be more explosive:
The city's lonely man
Or
the bomber's lonely briefcase abandoned at some

junction?
Memory's tree, lush branches
laden with fruits
where are the roots? (ibidem 75)

Momentary impressions of Rajendra Bhandari provide powerful stances for exploring the surreal. In 'An Unpoetic Afternoon' which narrates the persona's mood during the afternoon, when sorrow, monotony and laziness overpower our body and mind, we find the existence of a powerful poetry,

> Hurriedly I peep inside the mirror and find that,/
> my prehistoric face still nourishes my primeval dreams,/
> I feel elated/that my face still carries some archaeological value./
> I scream–/O come, excavate here, inside the wrinkles of my face/And you will find/that statue of a poem/ditched thousands of years ago. (2003:70)

The extraordinary enshrined in the matters we consider ordinary, has been a mysterious area of concern of the humankind from time immemorial. The poet in his quest for that extraordinary enumerates the 'ordinary' in worlds personal and impersonal:

> Suddenly as he walked/he remembered his own face/
> Ordinary eyes. Ordinary build/Ordinary face. That face vanished again/into an ordinary crowd./ ....
> Ordinary river made of ordinary streams
> Ordinary sea made of ordinary rivers.
> Ordinary wave of an
> Ordinary sea that could wash a village away.
> An ordinary sea?
> Ordinary wave? (ibidem 69)

Rajendra Bhandari is growing in concepts and techniques. His poems reveal his bond with the place and race he belongs to. Significant dimensional improvement in his art is expected in his future poetry.

The tribal ethos of Tripura are best exposed in the poetry of Bhaskar Roy Barman (1950–), where he has been reflecting the cultish designs of Tripura [Das 2000: 2/ 2009:246]. Recurrence of river, stream, mountain, tree, temple, priest, crow, stone and other forms of ecology is found in many of his poems. Through the image of river, the poet symbolically exposes the hard life of the tribes and their happy singing life in the midst of all hardships:

> The river knows not how
> it has come to be called a river,
> Know though it does where it was born,
> Since its birth on the mountain top
> It has been cascading down the mountain
> Through groups of stones
> Spread out down the path
> While treading its way it sings forth
> into existence (Roy Barman 1)

The sorrow-stricken rural life, the life of the tribes who have been driven away from the plains of Tripura by the Bengali refugees of Bangladesh, the tribal rites and practices, the harvest activities and the surrounding environment find recurrent exposition in his poetry:

> I resumed wending my way towards the village,
> On my ears impinged the sounds
> That emanate from beating of tomtoms
> Which generally accompanies a folkdance
> Danced round heaps of crop gathered on a courtyard.
> I remembered it was time farmers brought crops home.
> (ibidem 35)

Bhaskar Roy Barman in his simple poems finds the death of his friend and a theft in a temple mysterious. Once a friend hinting at a scurrying hare-like animal told the poet that the animal might have been killed by somebody who would have eaten its flesh. But mysteriously the next day the friend died in a road accident (Roy Barman 4). In a poem "The Temple Forlorn" the gorgeously ornamented deity was stolen away by "the thieves from city" (ibidem 9). The temple priest went mad out of his misery after the theft. Then in his mysterious faith, he has reset a mud-lump in the shrine and has been leading a poor life:

> He deified the mud-lump through his devotion
> He ate breadcrumbs the crow carried down on its beak

and threw down to the priest,
The crow was friends with the priest and the stream.
(ibidem)

This exposes the sorrow-stricken life of the tribes of Tripura who have been driven away from the plains by the terrorist activities of the Bangladeshi refugees and have turned terrorist to re-establish their right over the soil of Tripura. In this poem also the image of stream occurs. The temple after being stolen of its deity stands forlorn and dilapidated on the bend of a flowing stream.

The poet has not only tried to expose the various aspects of tribal ethos in his poetry; but also his metaphorical expositions of various momentary impressions in the lines of verse, have obliquely emanated the tribal ways or practices of life. All the situations commented upon in his poetry relate the practices or traditions of Tripura where the non-tribal refugees of Bangladesh dominate tribes. Life in Tripura has now been affected by terrorism, thieving, instability and all sorts of antisocial activities. The poet as a passive-observer is much concerned about it. In some poems even the persona (the narrator-poet) exposes the tribal practices: the activities of the tribes which bring hope and aspiration to their minds.

The world is crowded and shrouded by mysteries. The bards of Northeast have culled these mysteries from various sources and spun several webs. In these webs of mystery lies the identity of North-east's worlds of esoteric and exoteric mysticism. Roy Barman is growing in his themes and techniques. His poetry is rich in imagery and a vision of despair pervades it. His legitimate voice is yet to be clear. In his future poetry, his voice is expected to be more profound, visionary, and refined. The bards of North-east are expected to explore the myths of the region more profoundly in future.

Works Cited

Bhandari, Rajendra. 1992. "Two Poems". *Indian Literature* 152 (Nov-Dec). ed. K. Satchidanandan. New Delhi: Sahitya Akademi. (23-24).

.... 2000. "Four Poems". *I.L.* 197 (May-June). ed. H.S. Shiva Prakash. New Delhi: Sahitya Akademi. (19-22).

....2003. Seven Poems. *Chandrabhaga 8.* ed. Jayanta Mahapatra. Cuttack (69-75).

Dai, Mamang. 2000(a). "Two Poems" : *Chandrabhaga.* 1/2000 (3-6).

ed. Jayanta Mahapatra. Cuttack: Chandrabhaga Society.

.... 2000(b). "Four Poems" : *Indian Literature* : 197. May-June (62-66),New Delhi: Sahitya Akademi.

.... 2001. "With the Confidence of Things Impermanent" (154-156), *Dialogue*-VI.ed. Srutimala Duara, Guwahati : NEIFES.

.... 2004. *River Poems.* Calcutta: Writers Workshop.

Das, Nigamananda. 2000. "Tribal Ethos in the Poetry of North-Eastern India: Poetry from Tripura". *Proceedings of Seminar.* A.S.C. Banaras Hindu University. (MS. 01-14).

.....2009. Multi-ethnic Poetry in English from North Eastern India: Thematic Trends and Concepts. *Multicultural Literature in India: Critical Perceptions.* Ed. NDR Chandra. New Delhi: Sarup Book Publishers,(211-51).

Guha, A.S. 2000. "Poetry & the English Writing Scene": *Trends in Social Sciences and Humanities in North East India,* Shillong. (117-125).

Madhubir, R.K. (1987). *The Timebomb and other Poems.* Imphal: Vagya Publication.

.... (1998). *The Shadow of Darkness.* Imphal: Vagya Publication.

Sarang, Vilas. 1995. *Indian English Poetry since 1950.* Bombay: Disha Books.

Tana, Yumlam. 2003. "Three Poems". Chosen from *The Man & the Tiger* (2000), Ranchi : Writers Forum : *Anthology of Contemporary Poetry from the North East.* eds. K.S. Nongkynrih & Robin S. Ngangom. Shillong : NEHU. (13–16).

(7)

Temsula Ao's Poetry: A Thematic Study

AJ Sebastian sdb

A recipient of Padmashri in 2007 for Literature and Education, Temsula Ao (b.1945) holds a Ph.D in English Literature and is a Professor of English at North-Eastern Hill University, Shillong. She was Director of North East Zone Cultural Centre, Dimapur (1992-97), and was a Fulbright Scholar to the University of Minnesota (1985-86). Her publications include four collections of poetry *Songs that Tell* (1988), *Songs That Try to Say* (1992), *Songs of Many Moods* (1995), *Songs from Here and There* (2003) and *Songs from the Other Life* (2007). Her other works include *Henry James and the Quest for an Ideal Heroine, The Ao Naga Oral Tradition* and *These Hills Called Home.* Some of her poems that have appeared in *Anthology of Contemporary Poetry from the Northeast* published by NEHU, are taught in the MA English course of Nagaland University.

In this study I have tried to classify Temsula's selected poems thematically into various categories viz. on Women issues, poems on Death, on Love and Compassion, on Biblical themes, on Ecological concerns, on Ageing, on Folklore, Myth and Fable, and Poems of Reflections. Her poetry is marked by its basic 'quest for roots' (Das 2004: 63) and socio-ecological concerns.

Her first verse collection *Songs That Tell* (1988) begins like the "Introduction" of William

Blake's *Songs of Innocence.*
'Piper, sit thee down and write

In a book that all may read .'
....
And I wrote my happy songs
Every child may joy to hear.

Similarly Temsula begins her poetic career with her "Give Me a Book of Songs."

So I sat down
And collected
My stray thoughts
The hazy lines
To compose a bouquet
Of these songs (STT:9).

For Temsula her songs come to her on 'lonely nights' as songs of 'ecstasy' and in imitation of the 'great bards.' Yet, though the songs remain 'inarticulate,' they 'vibrate' for a 'kindred heart' who 'heard and understood.' Her final argument is:

And so I sing these songs
For him who said
'Give me a book of your songs' (STT: 10).

On Women issues

Temsula's reflections on women issues draw attention to what Irigary would opine: '...we must not once more kill the mother who was sacrificed to the origins of our culture. We must give her new life, new life to that mother, to our mother within us and between us. We must refuse to let her desire be annihilated by the law of the father. We must give her the right to pleasure, to *jouissance*, to passion, restore her right to speech, and sometimes to cries and anger' (Irigary 2003:421).

In "Woman" the poet examines a woman's role in life. She had been fashioned by nature to nurture life disregarding her own needs. But she has been a victim of social customs and roles assigned to her. She has become a prey of male domination despite protests.

Man beguiled her
Into submission
Thus establishing
Timeless dominion (STT:22).

In the process of her being subjugated she has been rendered 'a mother, lover/ And beast of burden.' But at times she rebelled to break free from such male oppression and subjugation in history in various heroines such as Clytemnestra, Cleopatra, Medea, etc. Temsula articulates women's role in society and longs 'to reclaim their female heritage and to celebrate woman's potent connection with nature and the body.' (Tolan 2006:324).

In "Man to Woman" a man courts a girl promising to build a new house after the harvest season as per Ao Naga tribal custom and to propose marriage to her. He woos her admiring her smile, gait, dancing and zest for work.

> When the time is right
> My maternal uncle will bring my offer in the night
> ...
> That I want you with a yearning
> Stronger than the jhum burning?
> And let me walk to next year's jhum by your side
> (SFTOL:58-9).

The romantic courting of the girl is easily forgotten once the marriage is celebrated. Thus issues concerning women are given due attention by Temsula.

In "Village Morning I, II & III" Temsula takes note of the role of a woman in a traditional village setting. Her responsibilities begin as the day dawns with 'myriad chores.' She has no choice despite her 'aching limbs' but to rise at daybreak while her husband sleeps on. Her diverse chores go on - feeding her family, pigs and chickens, breast-feeding her wailing child, and allotting daily chores to her children before she leaves for the fields. The man, her husband 'feels a stranger/In his own hearth' and gets out with his shawl and dao to join the other men, as if he is out to conquer the whole world. Though the real battle is won by the woman by managing her home, she is never acknowledged.

> The darkness of the pre-dawn
>
> Is still un-relieved
> Like the misery and loneliness
> Or her orphan-self now turned

Into a beast of burden
Showered with constant abuse
And given little sustenance (SFHAT:19).

Oppression of women takes various forms in contemporary Indian society. In "Requiem?" the poet narrates a case of bride burning for dowry. 'Who will mourn?' her fate 'roasted on the pyre / Of avarice.' The man goes scot-free labelling it an accidental death. The poet continues to ponder over questions that continues to haunt her.

Who will mourn?
Mothers and fathers
Millstoned with daughters?
Or daughters who are simply born? (STT.44).

Though women suffer betrayals and are often victims of patriarchy, they do not constitute *a muted group* (Showalter 2003:322) as they need to come forward asserting their role in society.

Poems on Death

"In Death Comes Calling" Temsula makes her reflection on death like Emily Dickinson in "We Pray – To Heaven." She renders the poem in the form of several questions raised with humour and irony.

When death comes calling nowadays
Does he wear a mask
Or does he display an identity card
...
Does he ride in his jet (STT:26).

The reflection is set in modern times and the poet notes the untraditional ways in which Death may be expected to come – perhaps riding in his jet or flying down. She wonders if he would come ringing the bell and with the book of life. Could there be some bargaining as in ancient times when gods used to offer extension of time? And the poem ends on a humorous note:

Now
If there is such an interim
For the modern victim

Would he ask for a moratorium
And would he know
Which gods to apply to
And how? (STT:27).

In "Dying" the poet reflects on how the act of dying itself is a moment of experiencing what it is to be 'Vacant.' She is able to look at dying from a different perspective like the metaphysical poets finding that it has 'an odour,' 'a texture,' 'a look' and yet it is 'as vacant/ As a pair of eyes/ From where/ The soul has/ Already fled (STTTS:28).

Her reflection in "Death" calls our attention to inevitability of death which is 'always with us/ The invisible companion to life' (STTTS:29). "What are you death?" is a challenge to death asking him to speak out if he is 'Friend, foe, deliverer?/... Benefactor, creditor, destinator?' (STTTS:30). The poet wants an answer to the puzzle.. Temsula tries to come to terms with life's ups and downs in "Disloyalty." In the midst of 'crippling death' the poet didn't wish to recover, yet 'life persisted' to give her a new lease of life.

Swiftly,
Life took precedence
And the dead
Seemed redundant.
...
In living
That I seem to neglect
My dead (SOMM:20).

As life keeps going taking precedence over 'the dead,' she has no choice and says:

In living
That I seem to neglect
My dead (SOMM:20).

In "Farewell" Temsula has yet another poem in which she reflects on life and death. The poet bids farewell to her beloved who has gone to his eternal reward.

So I concede
And say 'Farewell'

Only to affirm
That in your passing away
You have re-affirmed
Your permanence in my life (SOMM:23).

Temsula refers to the irony of death that brings people together in "The Empty Coffin." Some are genuinely grief-stricken while others await the execution of the will of the deceased to be shared. It is only avarice that lets the dead enter 'the minds of the living' (SOMM:26).

In keeping with the traditional tribal belief, in "Last Farewell" the poet bids adieu to a dear departed whose soul she believes has flown away to the heavens, carried away by the winds. She believes that the soul has 'become the breath/ Of the universe' and has become a star and hopes it to 'return in showers.'

And when I feel the rain
I will know
That you touch
The earth in me
Once again (SOMM:66).

On Love and Compassion

Temsula celebrates love in "A Lover's Prayer." The poem centres on the 'spark of love' that exists at all times in true lovers. She prays that such love continues to be.

Burn for me
Exclusively
Through eternity (STT:9).

But such love in youth can recede like the stars and the dream can be shattered ' in small hours.'

The poet's reflection on the various attributes of Mother Teresa ends in prayer as she utters – 'Amen' meaning 'so be it be.' Mother's love and compassion for the 'living dead' and 'the living skeletons' with her 'beatific smile' makes her an 'angel of mercy.' Her unconditional love has left its mark on her 'etched' face, 'gnarled hands,' and 'bent' back. What sustains mother is her love of God and man.

The energy is unfailing
The faith unyielding
In this "angel of mercy"
Bringing new light to humanity (STT:33).

On Biblical themes

Temsula has written several poems on biblical themes applicable to modern living with humour and irony. In "Lazarus" the poet juxtapositions the story of the poor man Lazarus as narrated in the Gospel of Luke chapter 16 and the story of Lazarus of Bethany in the Gospel of John chapter 11. The poet muses on the misery of the poor man Lazarus who desired to be fed by the crumbs that fell from the rich man's table. After death their roles are reversed "The poor man died and was carried by the angels to Abraham's bosom. The rich man also died ... and in Hades being in torment... and saw Abraham far off and Lazarus in his bosom. And he called out, 'Father Abraham, have mercy upon me, and send Lazarus to dip the end of his finger in water and cool my tongue; for I am in anguish in this flame" (Luke 16:23-24). The second Lazarus of Bethany died and was buried. When Jesus came after four days he told Lazarus' sister Martha ,"Your brother will rise again" (John 11:23). "...he cried with a loud voice, "Lazarus, come out." The dead man came out..." John 11:43-44).

The juxtaposition brings to focus the meaning of the resurrection from the dead. Lazarus who was denied food by the rich man gets the reward of resurrection, while the rich man was denied the same. The second Lazarus of Bethany gets it through a new lease of life as Jesus raised him from the dead. The poet pauses to reflect on the idea of death and after life:

Did this Lazarus then
Born again
From the womb of death
Live to witness
The other Resurrection
That transformed Life
Here
And hereafter? (STT:36).

"The Judgement" is a poem based on the gospel story of the woman caught in adultery narrated by St. John. The Pharisees brought a woman caught in adultery to be condemned to death by Jesus as per the Jewish custom. Jesus 'Saw only a forsaken woman' but the accusers 'saw only the fire and malice.' Perceiving their wickedness, pride and vanity, the Lord saw only the 'frailty' of the woman to make the declaration that the sinless among them cast the first stone. "...he stood up and said to them, 'Let him who is without sin among you be the firs to throw a stone at her.'... But when they heard it, they went away, one by one, beginning with the eldest, and Jesus was left alone with the woman standing before him" (John 8: 7-9).

As the accusers left in utter confusion Jesus had only one admonition for her, 'Woman, go home / And sin no more.' The final comment of the poet is central to the parable:

> The judgement of one
> Who knew
> What it meant
> To be human (STT:42).

"Serpent and I" is based on the biblical story of the first fall as recorder in the Book of Genesis. The Lord God had commanded Adam and Eve not to eat of the tree in the midst of the garden. But Eve was tempted by the serpent. "So when the woman saw that the tree was good for food, and it was a delight to the eyes...she took of its fruit and ate; and she also gave some to her husband, and he ate. Then the eyes of both were opened, and they knew that they were naked" (Genesis 3:6-7).

The dialogue between the serpent and Eve is made very dramatic with the tempter persisting and Eve getting restlessly trapped.

> "Eat"
> He said
> "Be like god"
> "Eat"
> He said to me
> "And be the goddess."
> I hesitated.

But he persisted.
...
I looked
And grew restless (STT:53-54).

The consequence is that it revealed her 'nakedness' which predicted her death. Her only hope is in the promise of redemption in Christ.

A new earth
To be born
Of the breached one
A new god
Of the fallen ones (STT:55).

In "Jezebel" Temsula tells the story of King Ahab's ruin and his wicked queen Jezebel's cursed end as described in 1 Kings 21. King Ahab in his greed got Naboth killed being counselled by his wife Jezebel to get possession of his vineyard. God sent prophet Elijah to prophesy doom for Ahab and his queen. "...you have sold yourself to do what is evil in the sight of the Lord.. Behold, I will bring evil upon you; I will utterly sweep you away, and will cut off from Ahab every male...because you have made Israel to sin. And of Jezebel the Lord also said, 'The dogs shall eat Jezebel within the bounds of Jezreel. Any one belonging to Ahab who died in the city the dogs shall eat..." (1 Kings 21:20-24).

The poet observes that there is only a dung-heap where the dogs ate the flesh of the wicked queen who prompted her husband with the wicked scheme to possess the field of Jezreel.

There is a dung-heap at Jezreel
Where beetles chirp and chant
'Jezebel, O Jezebel'
...
If you ask the dogs what royal remnants
'Formed the dung upon the face
Of the field of Jezreel'
They join the chorus
Of the beetles and howl
'O Jezebel' (SFHAT:52-53).

In "Salome" Temsula draws the attention of her readers to the Biblical narration of the beheading of John the Baptist. Herod was condemned by John the Baptist for keeping his brother's wife Herodias. She wanted to get rid of John to live her incestuous life. During a banquet on Herod's birthday, Herodias' daughter Salome pleased Herod with her dance and the king vowed her anything she wished including half his kingdom. The dancing girl was prompted by her mother to ask for the head of John. "I want you to give me at once the head of John the Baptist on a platter" (Mark 6:25). Thus John was beheaded by Herod to keep his promise to a dancing girl.

The poet gives the poem a new twist as it concludes with the hope of resurrection for the Baptist. In fact, when Herod heard about the fame of Jesus, he was curious to meet him supposing him to be John the Baptist risen to life.

> Ah... Salome,
> Thus reduced
> Will you execute
> Once more
> Your murderous dance,
> If the severed head
> Rise again
> And disdains
> Your proferred kiss? (STTS:52).

The grim realities of life on earth does not preclude "Blessings" as recounted by the poet like the beatitudes of Jesus wishing happiness to the poor and the humble: "Blessed are the poor in spirit, for theirs is the kingdom of heaven. Blessed are those who mourn, for they shall be comforted. Blessed are the meek, for they shall inherit the earth. Blessed are those who hunger and thirst for righteousness, for they shall be satisfied. Blessed are the merciful, for they shall obtain mercy...." (Matthew 5:3-7).

The poet renders a modern day interpretation of the teachings of Christ with ironical overtones, coupled with social criticism.

> Blessed are the poor,
> In rags,
> ...
> Blessed are the blind
> For they see not...

...
Blessed are the deaf
And the dumb
For they hear not
And cannot
Utter lies.
Blessed are the lame
For they are out of the game
...
Blessed are the unborn
For they cannot mourn
The loss
Of what
Never had (STT:20-21).

The final irony is that the blessings uttered remain purely illusory.

Blessed are these all
For theirs is the kingdom
That never was (STT:21).

On Ecological concerns

Like an eco-feminist, Temsula exposes the ever increasing deforestation and destruction of nature by man in "lament for Earth." The poet is Keatsian in her description of the 'verdant, virgin' forest that was the 'majestic splendour' of the earth made 'Silent / Stunned and stamped' in course of time. She continues to describe in eco-feminist terms and grieves for the rape of mother earth. She asserts like some feminists 'that women are closer to nature, to the environment, to a matriarchal principle at once biological and ecological' (Showalter 2003:324). On her breasts where once elephants roamed about is replaced by the rumble of lorries carrying logs. The river that flowed through her verdant green is muddied and bleached. The forest is made barren as:

No life stirs in her belly now
The bomb
And the bleaching powder
Have left her with no tomorrow.
...

Alas for this earth
Thus ravaged
Stripped of her lushness (STT:46-47).

Temsula laments the fading beauty of the forest that has thus been ravished and left 'old and decrepit.' Her symbolic expressions and personification of nature makes her also an ecocritic in expression as 'society would be so involved in taking care of 'it' (environment) that it would no longer be a case of some 'thing' that surrounds us, that environs us, and differs from us.' (Morton 2007: 706). The poet is deeply affected by the sorry sight of mountains and rocks, furrowed by constant logging. The sight of one of such giant rocks in her village makes the poet lament the sorry sight of "The Bald Giant." Like true ecocritics, Temsula finds 'a renewed version of Romantic joy in the contemplation of nature may offer the best chance of the sexiness and hedonism that environmentalism needs' (Kerridge 2006:541). The poem reminisces her childhood days when the giant rock looked very majestic, shining in the greenery of summer. In autumn the rock had its distinguishing beauty with golden patches on it. The winter appearance of the rock enveloped in the mist gave it a mystical look. Now the poet laments the sorry sight of the giant rock made bald by deforestation and awaiting its final disintegration and doom.

Once I thought him friendly
But now he looks menacing
And I resent his presence
In my horizon
Because I dread
That when the earth shakes
He will surely disintegrate
And carry me to our common doom (SFHAT:2).

"Prayer of a Monolith" is yet another pathetic poem on the way rocks are broken to suit man's ambition. The monolith speaks out how people cracked her out of the rock. The monolith's plea was ignored by all and she was 'chipped and chiselled.' They pulled her and planted in the village to stand there in mockery 'For someone else's fame.' She implores the elements of nature:

you elements,
When you pass by the forest

And my beloved queries
Just tell her
I have gone to my glory
But please, please, never
Tell her the story
Of my ignominy (SFHAT:5).

In "The Garden" the poet sings in praise of the gardener of all gardens who is the source of all life. The reflection pin points how 'a slice of the earth' put in a pot with a seed or sapling in it sprouts and grows with hormonal changes brought about by fertilizers. The miracle of life makes the poet bow in adoration as:

The slice of earth
Thus nurtured
Brings forth
Beauties
In praise
Of the GARDENER
Of all gardens (STTTS:16).

On Ageing

Ageing makes the poet reflect on human frailty and the end of life. In "Coming-of-Age" the poet realises suddenly that she has reached her forties with streaks of gray and wrinkled face. Her musing brings flashback of yester-years when she was twenty-one. Her youth declined by her maturing in years.

And that coming –of-age
So remote
And so removed
From this vintage (STT:14).

"I Fear" is also evocative of "Coming of age" in which the poet expresses her fear of ageing.

I fear
The dreaded fate
Of being rendered
Redundant
Before my formal death (SOMM:68).

As years go by, the poet is disturbed by the fear of physical changes leading to furrowing face, degeneration of muscles and mental retardation.

Ageing is always painful and yet the poet has to reckon with the reality of "the symphony of life/ Beyond forty,' and reminisces the bygone days of 'twenty one.'

Folklore, Myth and Fable

With regard to folk narratives, narrators and singers often attribute their tales and songs to the collective tradition of the community (Ben-Amos 2006: 11). Temsula has been very proud of the story-telling legacy of her forebears and longs to preserve the folklore tradition. Anthropologically these stories present the fantasises of people who present their popular themes with the purpose of entertaining and instructing their people (Ibid. 265).

The poet laments how the stories that once ran in her blood and revitalized her 'life-force' such as the origin of her people from six stones with tigers and animals as brothers etc. She has come to the realization that such traditions may become things of history as the new generation may fail to pass on the oral tradition, dumping it as outmoded. Nostalgia for the past makes her recount the tale of how the Ao Nagas lost their script which was inscribed on a hide that was eaten by a dog. Thus oral tradition began, narrating their stories.

So when memory fails and words falter
I am overcome by a bestial craving
To wrench the thieving guts
Out of the original Dog
And consign all my stories
To the script in his ancient entrails (SFTOL:13).

"The Deer and the Tiger" introduces the readers to the most common tiger folktales. As the story goes, the tiger requested for a little grass from the deer's grazing patch. To the utter surprise of the deer the tiger began to explain that he had become a vegetarian. Yet, the deer kept his distance in suspicion despite the tiger's varied reasons. At the end the deer picked up courage to shout out:

Go find another patch

> Yon turn-coat,
> Do not encroach
> On my territory
> That's just enough for me (SFHAT:7).

In "Soul-Bird" Temsula writes: 'There is an ancient Ao-Naga belief that when a person dies, the soul takes the form of a bird, more specifically a hawk...The sighting of hawks soon after a person's death is considered to be a good omen signifying that the transition is complete and that it is the last appearance of the loved one on earth' (SFOL:14). In the poem "Soul-Bird" the child observes a hawk soaring up into the sky as the ritualistic prayers are offered. The bird keeps circling above the mud heap over the burial site 'emitting unearthly sounds.' The grandmother tells the child confirming the transition:

> See that keening bird in the sky?
> That's your mother's soul
> Saying her final good-bye (SFOL:15).

In "Rumour" the poet presents a humorous poem about the rumour surrounding the death of God. The irony is that the centre of attention is the insignificant creatures like the little bird and the ants. The poet brings magic realism into poetry by which she mingles realistic treatment of a subject with supernatural and bizarre elements. It is an excellent weaving of realism, fairy tale, myth and fantasy. The speaker asks a little bird if God is dead. It simply flew away saying 'Who knows the truth/ Anymore?' (SOMM:37).

But the little ant didn't pay heed to the narrator. It hurried away shaking his 'spindly legs' to share the news with his colleagues. Soon the rumour had spread among the ant community 'God is dead.' The protest procession of ants led to social consequences. People got involved in various activities. The vendors began putting up stalls. Schools were closed. Officers left their jobs. Life came to a standstill as the Government declared a holiday confirming the rumour of God's death. There was total commotion everywhere. The procession led to political debates and there was total condemnation of the Government, the ants and the birds. The little bird was surprised at the turn of events and muttered:

God is now really dead,
Or worse still
He simply does not care (SOMM:40).

The poem can be interpreted in multiple ways. It has a message for every one. Children find it a perfect fable. Adults find in it social criticism and how rumour mongering can lead even to the death of God. Social instability can be brought about by political conniving and evil machinations of people.

Temsula proves herself to be a hill poet with several references to mountains and rocks (Das: 2007:60). "Stone-People from Lungterok" is a folk based poem. Lungterok refers to the six stones found in Chungliyimti village in the Ao area. According to myth six human beings burst out of six stones (*Lung* meaning stone, *terok* meaning six). Of these there were three males and three females (TANOT:79).

Lungterok,
The six stones
Where the progenitors
And forebears
Of the stone-people
Were born
Out of the womb
Of the earth (STTTS:49).

They were a people 'poetic and politic, barbaric and balladic.' They were the ones who found water and fought fire. As in folklore, the poet goes on to describe the features of the stone people. They were potters, weavers, planters, growers, hunters, carvers, singers, lovers and heroes. They were polyglots who spoke language of birds and animals. They were also a romantic people who knew the mood of the sun and the moon. They believed that the stars were pure souls looking after 'bereaved hearts.' In their religious yearning they worshipped unknown spirits. They also believed in the life hereafter and held the view that the spirits of the dead hovered over the earth in various forms until they passed in to the world hereafter crossing a passage across the waters.

"When a Stone Wept" is based on the same myth regarding the forebears of the Ao Nagas. It is believed that big stones give birth to small ones and grow to bigger size and give birth to other small stones. These are found in certain landscapes where no life exists. As these stones dispersed in all directions, one of them rolled down to a mossy bank. A west bound stone asked her to join him on his further quest, but she refused the offer and stayed on. Though he had left her next morning she felt his strange presence within her. As she became mother to man and little stones, she began to search for her man who made her Stone-Mother. When they met again he disowned his responsibility of begetting 'the little nuisances.' He callously told her not to blame any passing he-stone for her begetting stones. Disgusted by his response when she returned to her mossy bank, she found all her little stones gone from her home.

Searching for them she approached the wind and rain if they had seen them. Getting no answers, she sat crying in the fading sun. The moon suggested her to seek the help of the sun who 'burnt into her with all his might.' She agonised in pain as a 'gash tore through the side.' Seeing the Stone-Mother splintered in agony, the stone-children gathered around her. With her stone-children she returned to the graveyard of the earth where no elements could disrupt their life together.

> Chanting her litany of curses
> 'May the wind and rain, sun and moon
> From this blighted patch be forever barred
> Which failed to protect an abandoned mother
> And her hapless children (SFTOL:45).

"Nowhere Boatman" relates how it is believed by Ao Nagas that the souls of the dead have to pay the boatman who ferries them across from the land of the living to the land of the dead. And the story is narrated how the nowhere boatman carried the souls of the dead 'on the river between/ To irreconcilable worlds' (SFTOL:18). The boatman keep narrating how his riders make the queries as to how long he has been ferrying people across. But no one has asked him about his own origin. He sees himself as 'A soul without a status/ Fated to ply' his trade.

"A Tiger- Woman's Prayer" is a folk poem based on the Ao Naga belief that people have tigers as companion spirits. The tiger woman narrates how her grandfather's tiger-soul came to take control of her. She prayed that she be able to cross the place beyond the sun like the others so that she could 'raise a rainbow there/ Against our composite tears' (SFTOL:21).

"The Other World" is based on a Sangtam Naga legend about a beautiful girl named Momola whom the fish-king loved. Her mother promised to give her in marriage to him provided he gave them plentiful fish harvest. When the mother failed to keep her promise the fish-king threatened to send a great deluge. Eventually Momola was given away in marriage to the fish-king and she became a big fish with a white spot on her forehead. But Momola longed for her former life where 'human live, love and die.' To satisfy her longing she often cruised along the bay to watch human children play. But her dreams are shattered when she hears people point her out spotting her white mark on the forehead. She has no choice but to return to the waves to prevent her fish-king from causing floods (SFTOL:27-30).

"Night of the Full Moon" is a Naga myth about tigers that gather together to pay their homage to their king who is the largest among them. They offer him the best animals they have hunted in tribute. During the assembly a voice of a young tiger was heard denouncing the old system, demanding democracy to replace monarchy. The king decided to abdicate but the question remained who will lead the subjects? It was decided to hold an election to choose a leader. But problem arose when they discussed the matter of electing a leader. They had to elect the king himself as the people's leader.

> If we do not elect him
> Where shall we hunt?
> He owns all the land! (SFTOL:35).

Poems of Reflections

Temsula makes random reflections on incidents and situations in common life. "In the Morning" celebrates the beginning of a day with its 'newness/ Of dreams/ Not yet gone wrong.' The morning retreats with 'the life-giving sun' that leads the day to its end. The day-night revolution continues as 'the song/ To be sung/ In the morning' continues to give hope to the poet.

"Distance" is a poem that muses on distance in relationship that can shatter human relationships between fathers and sons, mothers and daughters, as 'Distance/Is/ What cannot meet'

(HTT:17). Her reflection takes the readers through the mystery of the world that has become a 'strange place.'

> Where people are
> Exiled in their own land
> And imprisoned in their own minds (HTT:18).

She becomes very grave in her reflection as her thoughts are turned to a world that is getting fragmented by 'National policies' and human made walls that divide people into 'haves and have-nots,' and 'tribal enclaves.' Ultimately the world becomes a 'strange place.'

"Musings During a Sermon" is a humorous reflection on the monotony of eternal life in heaven where one has to be bored with a life of eternal 'NOW' where present continues to be with no past or future.

> Heaven must be a monotonous place
> With only the present continuing,
> ...
> There is no yesterday
> No tomorrow
> Only the NOW
> Stretching into eternity
> ...
> Ah, for me, a life of diversity
> Deliver me from an eternity
> Of uncurious monotony (STT:24-25).

"Mirror, Mirror" is an introspection in which the poet analyses her reflection on the mirror.

> I look into the mirror
> And see a face
> Which now parodies
> The one that I once knew (STTTS:31).

Going back on memory lane she realises that earlier she had far better contours and firmer intent of youthful grace. The poem ends in wishful thinking.

To counter
Lost landscapes
And degenerated visage?
Is this compensation?
And my only consolation? (STTTS:32).

The poet reflects on 'Time' and its mystery in "Time." It is natural for man to try to steal time out of bound norms. Somehow time keeps getting pilfered from routine living. And all the truants we play with time to steal time finally leads to the realization that:

We were running out
Of TIME
With nothing
With memories
Of our petty thieveries (STTTS:40).

Temsula's "Pain" is a personification of pain squatting on her breast and having 'sardonic mirth' over her misery. The excruciating pain makes her hate him. Anxiously she hopes for the day when her pain would cease to trouble her.

But till then
This familiar fiend
Sits squat
On my breast
Still (STTTS:20).

Temsula has several other thought-provoking reflections in "vacant Places," "Night Watch," "Old," "loneliness," "Parting," "Despair," "Timeless," "Eclipse," and the like.

In "Vacant Places" she probes into vacant places of her soul with hollow echoes and a dying memory (STTTS:22). "Night Watch" takes note of fears that take shape in her mind during the night which leads to wakefulness (STTTS:23). In "Old" the poet refutes the saying 'old is gold' and states that old age is full of aches, loss and desolation (STTTS:24). "Loneliness" is a poem that ends paradoxically as the poet finds that it is a dreadful state of being one has to undergo. The poet asks 'Death/ Or loneliness,/ Which would you,/ Prefer?' (STTTS:27). Ultimately the reflection leads to death when all loneliness end as 'The dead/ Are not lonely' (Ibid.27).

"Parting:" is a poem that reveals human experience of parting as a feeling which is real a 'it is for ever' (STTTS:35). "Despair" according to the poet squats in the core of his lonely soul. She denies him supremacy by despising and defying him by seeking 'every passing joy' (SOMM:33). "Timeless" reflects on how time drains life out of life. Finally the poet realises how she is trapped between her mortal time and eternal timelessness (SFHAT:29-30). In "Eclipse" the poet sets herself in contrast with the 'mighty one.' God's infinity as the great core of power and centrality, comes in contrast to her finiteness as a satellite at the periphery. She finds herself as a 'tiny solitaire/ Entrapped within the circle/Of my dark desire.' (SFHAT:37).

Conclusion

"My Last Song" is a fitting conclusion to Temsula's repertoire of poems written over a period of almost three decades. She will cease to write her last song when she is broken and maimed; and when she fails to take note of the little things that daily occur such as: laughter of children, chatter of women, rainbow and the fall of raindrops, the colours of flowers, twitter of birds, a baby's smile, a puppy's wag and appeal of mutes. The poet feels that her singing will have no meaning if these little things cease to be and prays:

> May it never happen
> That I should stop singing
> Before I cease
> TO BE (STT:62).

In "Wishes" the poet expresses her longing to find expression in poetry giving form to 'Poems/That lie/ Unwritten/And of the beauty/That dies/Unrevealed' (STTTS:25).

In "Where is the Time?" The poet speaks of the brevity of time in contrast to the many songs she longs to sing for her beloved. Like the metaphysical poets she wants to turn 'all time/ Measureless' being united with the beloved soaring 'On the chords/Of the primeval song/ Which transcends the universe' (STTTS:39).

Her oeuvre has been a unique contribution to the poetry from Northeast India with its multi-dimensional writings on themes ranging from nature to various human sensibilities, marked by lyrical and melodious expressions. Her poems are rather tightly constructed with ironic overtures. At times she takes recourse to romantic tone with colloquial outbursts. Her motifs of ancestral heritage and oral tradition render her a unique poet of the ethnic traditions and sensibilities of the Northeast India.

References

Ao, Temsula. 1988. *Songs that Tell.* Calcutta: Writers Workshop. (Abbreviated : STT).

——.1992. *Songs That Try to Say.* Calcutta: Writers Workshop. (Abbreviated : STTTS).

——.1995. *Songs of Many Moods.* New Delhi: Har-Anand Publications. (Abbreviated : SOMM).

——.1999. *The Ao-Naga Oral Tradition.* Baroda: Bhasha Publications. (Abbreviated :TANOT)

——.2003. *Songs from Here and There.* Shillong: NEHU Publications. (Abbreviated : SFHAT).

——.2007. *Songs from the Other Life.* Pune: Grasswork Books. (Abbreviated : SFTOL).

Ben-Amos, Dan. 2006. "Folktale". *Folklore: Critical Concept in Literary and Cultural Studies.*Ed. Alan Dundes. Vol. III. New York: Routledge.

——.2007. "The Idea of Folklore." *Folklore: Critical Concept in Literary and Cultural Studies.*Ed. Alan Dundes. Vol. III. New York: Routledge.

Das, Nigamananda. 2004. "The Poets of Nagaland Writing in English." *Mosaic of Redemption: Essays on Poetry in English from North East.* Cuttack: M.G. Publications.

——2007."Matrix of Ecology." *Ecology Myth and Mystery: Contemporary Poetry in English from Northeast India.* Eds. N.D.R.Chandra, & Nigamananda Das. New Delhi: Sarup & Sons.

Irigaray, Luce. 2003. "The Bodily Encounter with the Mother." *Modern Criticism and Theory.* David Lodge, Nigel Wood. 2nd ed. Delhi: Pearson Education.

Kerridge, Richard. "Environmentalism and ecocriticism." *Literary Theory and Criticism.* Ed. Patricia Waugh. New Delhi: Oxford University Press.

Morton, Timothy. 2007. "Environmentalism." *Romanticism: An Oxford Guide.* Ed. Nicholas Roe. New Delhi: Oxford University Press.

Showalter, Elaine. 2003. "Feminist criticism in the wilderness."

Modern Criticism and
Theory. David Lodge, Nigel Wood. 2nd ed. Delhi: Pearson Education
The Holy Bible. Revised Standard Version. London: Catholic Trust Society. 1966. (All Biblical references taken from this edition).
Tolan, Fiona. 2006. "Feminism." *Literary Theory and Criticism*. Ed. Patricia Waugh. New Delhi: Oxford University Press.

(8)

Many Worlds of Robin S. Ngangom

Nigamananda Das

At twenty-four
I invited myself to Bohemia,
The kingdom of Art,
where people never grow old,
was my affable neighbour....
With cargoes of sand and mortar
Mammon came to inspect the city.
He cut down the remaining trees....
Morning papers like watered- down milk
hawk the same bland items:
rape, extortion, ambushes, confessions,
embezzlement, vendetta, sales, disappearances,
marriages, obituaries, the usual (2006:65, 67-68)

The lines above indicate the obsessions and concerns of Robin S. Ngangom.

Robin S. Ngangom, a prophetic Meitei from Manipur has made Shillong, his haven of soul's solace, and his poetry, nostalgic outbursts of search for roots. His quest for identity is revealed in passionate rumination of the history of the tribal traditions of Northeast and various provinces of the Northeast are reflected in his many momentary reflections. The city of Imphal, the valley of the rivers, Imphal and Nambul, has a long heroic past. Since the Pre-Christian era, the land is famous for its heroic heritage. Manipur has a glorious contribution to India's freedom struggle. So from the time of the Mahabharat up to the World War II, the land has had a glorious heritage. The poet mingles the past with the present and repents for the land's present outcast state under the heinous insurgency or militancy. His remembrance of the history and mythological past makes him an explorer of a prophecy of the similar glorious future:

> red-ruined bricks, forgotten rivers and
> neglected freedom fighters of World War-II
> bring to mind
> a king who tried to evade a prophecy
> only to be bitten by a snake-god and two lovers
> coming from different communities
> loving each other across the banks
> of a dividing river
> in a small land-locked valley (1988: 12)

The memento of World War II, the heroic exploits of the Manipuri women, and soldiers, bring to the mind of the poet, the myths of the *Mahabharat,* that of Babrubahan, Uloupie, Chitrangada and Arjuna. The mythological records of the Manipuri dynasty predate the Christian era. According to the myth, Chitrangada's forefather, the Hindu sage Marichi was born of the limbs of Brahmã–the creator of the Universe, who himself arose from the naval lotus of Lord Narayana, the Protector of the Universe. Chitrangada was the only daughter of the old king Chitra Vanu. As Chitrangada had no brother, she was coronated as the Princess of Manipur. When Arjuna was in Manipur during his travel he fell in love with Chitrangada in the valley of Imphal and thus Babrubahan was born of them. Babrubahan attended the *Aswamedha yajna* organised by Yudhistir at Hastinapur. Prior to the *Aswamedha Yajna* when Babrubahan was travelling with the horse of the *Yajna,* he showed his heroic exploits. After the *Yajna,* Babrubahan returned to Manipur with the Vishnu Salgramsila which Yudhistir daily worshipped, and a large number of Brahmins, and established a Hindu kingdom in Manipur, the capital of which was Bishnupur near Imphal. The temple of Lord Vishnu established by Babrubahan on the banks of the Loktak lake is still existing. The place is called Bishnupur and the residents, Bishnupriya Manipuris, who are the lover and followers of Lord Vishnu. The great grandson of Babrubahan named Pakhamba or Pahangpa or Jabista was first ruling Hindu King of Manipur (Gogoi 2004: 1).

During the Christian era, the descendants of a Tartar colony belonging to the Mongolian stock, which emigrated from the north-west borders of China started ruling in the land of Manipur. Their language is closely allied to those of the Kuki tribes which border them on the south (Gait 1984: 269). This tribe known as 'Meitei' tribe established their rule over the land in 33A.D. and the first known Meitei King, Nongda Lairen Pakhangba was coronated in 33 A.D. in the Kangla Fort, the seat of Manipuri culture (*The Assam Tribune*, Nov. 21/2004:1). Between 33 A.D. and 1714 A.D., forty seven Meitei kings ruled over the princely state of Manipur (Gait 1984: 269). The historic Kangla Fort situated at the heart of City of Imphal occupies 236.84 acres of land. All the Meitei kings ruled the land from here. The Britishers occupied this fort in 1891 A.D. (ibidem). The province of Manipur is named as *Kangla Men* after the name of the Kangla Fort (*The Telegraph*: Nov. 21/2004:1).

Robin Ngangom heard the legendary tales of Manipur from his grandmother. He even knew how the negro guerillas of the allied forces "nearly molested an aunt" (1988: 12) during the World War II and how his countrymen "ran in panic/across hill slopes and rice fields/many perished" (ibidem) when bomb fell on the Manipur valley. He is proud of the glorious past of the land and is confident that his Meitei race will not perish in spite of the turmoils of time. While remembering his nostalgic past he recurrently remembers these in his poem:

> Only the war was not our war.
> Our race will not perish
> We have learnt pleasure
> in lieu of a barbaric past,
> at cockcrow one morning we found
> Ourselves belonging to a nation. (ibidem)

The moments of his nostalgic past are dots of myth for him. In a decade-long absence of him in his motherland he has been obsessed of the loss he incurred in ostracising himself from his favourite hillock "Singjamei". He thus remembers a new year's day when he went there with his elder brother:

> Standing there on your hillock
> Strewn with flowers and boyish dreams,
> and a shrine to the benign goddess. (ibidem 15)

Robin considers the quest for identity as a beginning of a new consciousness. He finds pleasure in rumination of the glorious past of the land:

> Let us only speak of what reached our ears:
> In Kangleipak once upon a time
> the royal beast of Kangla bit his tail
> and the land lay snug within his coils
> and there was no dearth of mundane things
> fish was as cheap and in the fields
> ears of rice danced to the rhythm of the soil.
> From the minstrel's song at the dead of night,
> We heard winter yarns of warrior kings,
> men who assumed the land and the women no fear,
> of men with untiring sword-arms
> We were sung of extra-terrestrial maidens
> descended to earth and lost: *Ingallei* and *Kombirei*
> elusive wild flowers, falling before anyone
> Could wear them, telling all in destroying love
> We destroy ourselves (ibidem 22)

Recurrently he is reminded of the past of the land and of generations of sufferings of groaning men and slaves:

> We speak of a mythic time
> ......
> Instead of pages of heroic deeds or undying love,
> We read parchments written in blood, our history
> stained by illicit love and betrayal;
> We found our alphabet buried with the shrunken heads
> Of enemies, ghosts who died long ago laughing
> at the attempts at civilization.
> Just outside the ramparts of the city of arts,
> not dances, music or literature
> but generations of groaning men and slaves
> (ibidem 22-23)

Drawing from folklore, Robin narrates a legend of love that was enacted on the banks of Loktak, the place named Moirang. It was Khuman Khamba, a poor orphan of Moirang who loved the princess Thoibi. One day he revealed it to Thoibi and then their "love reached every lip of Moirang" (ibidem 28). Khamba then incurred the ire and rage of the King Chingkhu Naha Tellheiba and the crown prince Chingkhuba and was consequently killed. Khamba's love was a true love that could not solemnize:

> Khamba the orphan, the tall silent one,
> Khamba of the bamboo-groves
> who possessed nothing
> but the princess he loved (ibidem)

Meghalaya, the poet's present haven, has attracted him to her myths and folklore. Meghalaya is called a land of seven huts (*Hynniew-trep*). The poet addresses his haven in nostalgic memoir of love relating it to his motherland Manipur and his blood-relations there:

> Seven Huts of my solitude, my first love
> Your rain, your wind, searched my face for signs
> of guilt when I first disembarked; a fugitive
> fleeing from ties of blood and desire (ibidem 29)

In Khasi *Hynniewtrep* means seven huts. It is said in Khasi myth that "the ancestors the Khasis are heavenly beings belonging to 16 families, who descended on earth from time to time to enjoy earthly pleasures by alighting from a tree. Once while seven of these families were on earth, one of the beings, succumbing to earthly desires, chopped down the connecting tree. The seven families were stranded on earth. Hence the seven huts. The Khasis call their hills the land of the Seven Huts (ibidem 33). Indian mysticism in multiple realizations is mythical. Here a child is likened to a child-god like the mystical plays of Lord Krishna in His childhood, a woman to an all powerful goddess like Durga and so on. Even if a woman is looked down upon for her behaviour, that is mythical because in Indian mythologies the woman class has been divided into four types or groups according to their nature and behaviour (viz. *Padmini, Sankhini, Hastini, Chitrini)* and in a misogynic approach they have been undermined in terms of their strength, intelligence and moral ability which were weaker than the men-class for a long period in the history of civilization. In some Indian mythologies the woman is compared to a *sudra* or a *chãndãl* and at many places she has been hailed as mother, all-powerful, kind-hearted, etc. Robin in his poem entitled 'Existence' has made a mythic exploration of his own habit at and understanding of the situations and surroundings:

> Before rice and water are wrested
> from this two-day life,
> before the resources of endurance run dry
> chided by a ravenous existence
> I ventured out in search of things
> yet hidden from me.
> Why I was ever born I sought to know (ibidem 52)

His inability to access the mystery surrounding the nature of women leads him to say:

> I wanted to know women,
> what lies beneath that mystical exterior,
> But in this too I was defeated (ibidem).

From his surroundings he names several exponents which appeal him spiritually and mystically:

> For all my unanswered questions
> I still love that tenacity
> of the child-labourer who carries his crucifix in a light playful mood.
> I love that perseverance of the pine saplings
> in the face of the saw and the axe, and
> the generosity of slender-hipped grains.
> I admire the tramp who filled his empty stomach
> with water and slept ravished by the roadside,
> the charity of those who have so little.
> The wisdom of children also amuses me.
> (ibidem 52-53)

He explores the greatness of 'woman' by saying:

> I consecrate all my lines to her
> and she just walks across them.
> She is the kind of being
> I will search through myths of despair. (ibidem 54)

Panoramic nature brings before his mind's eyes its myths and the poet's heart is excruciated by the present day poor state of the land of his birth, *Kangleipak:*

> How can we sing of moonlight on hills,
> of lotuses in the lakes, of the misty rain,
> of legendary lovers and bardic rivers,
> or of endless rice-fields?
> ....
> In Kangleipak we do not think
> of the past or a future.
> We only make sure our thinking
> has some semblance of sanity,
> .....
> In this small patch of land,
> forgotten by history, isolated by nine ranges,
> in ignorant bliss Kangleipak lives.
> Once prime land, beneficent and fabled
> and now play-ground of black marketeers,
> haven for fortune hunters where
> none misses a heart-beat
> as you feed money, sell honour, peddle justice
> (ibidem 69-70)

In two of his poems, the poet deplores the sad fate of a legendary lover named Manik Raitong who faced the Syiem's (King's) wrath and his sad death.

> How sad is the lot of my friend Manik
> spilling his heart
> from the seven mouths of his flute.
> Even though he has dared to wear
> the flower of the syiem (1994: 21).

According to the "popular Khasi story of star-crossed lovers, U Manik Raitong, an orphaned youth, had an illicit affair with the king's (Syiem's) wife. When the affair came to light the king ordered U Raitong's death. An accomplished musician, U Raitong planted his bamboo flute in the earth before his immolation. It is believed that the bamboo flute took root." (ibidem 22):

> Because life falls like petals
> and death comes when least expected
> none remembers the passing of Manik Raitong
> and how he planted his bamboo flute
> for earth to play music in spring. (ibidem).

The poet remembers the generations of ancestors and is worried about the lost heritage and the 'myths of famine and pestilence' (ibidem 47):

> What is tradition and our history
> but death with a long memory?
> For how long will we make
> our forefathers walk as ghosts?
> To-day with grief sitting on our hearts.
> We will sing of clouds that do not come home;
> We will sing the songs of those
> banished in the mountains,
> We will drink deep from bamboo mugs
> and wipe memory from our lips.
> ......
> the hill's night sang to us,
> but concealed its myths
> Of famine and pestilence. (ibidem 46-47)

A sojourner in Shillong, Robin feels guilty for stealing the peace of the permanent residents of the place of his sojourn and for being ignorant of the myths of the land:

> We have seen hunger flowering
> from bamboos in the villages.
> We wanted peace for ourselves
> by stealing the peace
> of these gentle hills.
> Who cares to know about their dreams?
> Who learnt the language of this land?
> Who can tell me its myths?
> I'm saddened to know nothing of this land.
> (ibidem 52)

Significant changes in international politics find mythical explorations and lamentation in Robin's poetry. His once-favourite place Myanmar attracts his attention to her past and present. With 'democracy weeping in its tropical forests' the land has been floundering in nightmares. He calls it 'a mad country' due to its troublesome condition at present:

> Listen, my love,
> to Burma's story, once a pearl of the East, now
> the base mental of democracy, democracy the white
> man's cross we carry, causing its students and priests
> to mourn the fate of their native land, to sing
> its fugitive songs around the world, hoping
> the songs will preserve fragile sanity in a mad country.
> (ibidem 72)

The poet like 'a poet-explorer, from equatorial distances who was marvelled at its strange gods' (ibidem 71) has been very favourite of the land and its myths. He is reminded of his childhood days when he visited Myanmar and has been nostalgic of its beauty and glorious landscape:

> That country where I return in memory to faint journeys
> of childhood, where the serpentine roads
> of the great war again send me to its twilight borders,
> to its fair women with long hair and sandalwood breasts,
> its modest rice-fields and hills rain-sieged,
> and great monasteries old in wisdom,
> that journey was made sometime ago
> as only memory would allow. (ibidem 71)

At the failure of socialism in Russia, prevalence of utter misery and poverty in Moscow, Robin breaks down and laments for the devastation of the great culture, art and poetry. He opposes the "democracy's gospel/(that) has been heard in Russia's churches" (ibidem 53) and says:

> I wanted Russia to remain suffering
> from its Steppes to Siberia,
> looking for truth in its own breaking heart,
> not listening to the whispers of the west. (ibidem)

With the death of socialism [with the deafening heavy metal of the west/be sung at Leningrad as improvised anthems (ibidem 54)], he sorrowfully deplores the death of the rich aesthetic exercises there:

> The West breaks out into beatific smiles.
> But how terrible that Russia
> Will no more offer great art,
> Will write great poetry
> Which will harass the conscience
> Of the earth. (ibidem 53)

Recurrently reminded of his Meitei ancestry, Robin laments how his race is "cursed, to be turned/into a blind and deaf people/ worshipping new gods of greed/and narcotic death" (ibidem 59). He identifies his race as 'the companions of *Poireiton'* (ibidem 58). *Poireiton* is a mythical ancestor of the Meiteis. Exploring his ancestry, he says:

> Centuries of dusty sleep
> lulled as into fitful deceit.
> We are the children of the dead,
> the speechless people,
> heirs to artifacts broken pots
> and dwelling in the caves of oral myths.
> (ibidem 58)

In the ancient times the clan of Meiteis headed by *Poireiton,* having discovered fire and being proficient in its use, wandered in quest of a beautiful spot on this world until they found Manipur, "the hill-girt valley" (ibidem). These "men free from disease and death" (ibidem) settled in this valley, spread generations and through their heroic deeds established themselves as an arrogant warrior race and since then have been fighting till to-day:

> One day arrogant they waged war.
> Losing then won and brought heads of enemies
> washed blood-stained swords in virgin waters.
> Their descendant still fight today–
> with shadow-warriors. (ibidem 59)

Since the earliest times no significant change has occured in their habits, 'a lottery of souls is held here everyday' (ibidem 63) and with the strength of elephants they have been still revolutionary to establish their claims:

> Nothing has changed in this land
> The boys with earrings
> enter hair-dressing saloons
> and set their hair with dirty combs. (ibidem 62)

Meghalayan legends haunt his mind sporadically and draw his sympathy. The pitiful conditions of poor sufferers appeal him recurrently. In a poem entitled 'At Noh Ka Likai's', he remembers the cruelty in the legendary tale after which the waterfall and leap has been named as 'Noh Ka Likai'. Ka Likai, a young widow with a girl child, remarried. One day, her husband in a fit of jealous rage murdered the child, and cooked and served her flesh to the unsuspecting mother. After discovering the heinous act, Ka Likai jumped to her death from the edge of a waterfall. The poet feels how injustice has been done to Ka Likai and still today she has been weeping there. He consoles Ka Likai that the ancient laws of nature will provide her with justice:

> My love, today the gods are dead
> Yet do not weep.
> The ancient laws of nature
> will dispense truth. (ibidem 61)

In his tribute to Pacha Meetei (1943-1990), a Sahitya Akademi award winner and fine writer, describing Pacha's contributions, he hints at Manipur's mythic grief where death is callous and the land has been weeping for ever (1995: 125). Manipuri and Mizo affinity of cultural heritage and their division, the Mizo mythical life, Mizo folk-hero *Chhura* and simple, serene Mizo folk-life are alluded to in Robin's verse addressed to a woman from South-eastern hills (Mizoram):

> In you, woman, from southeastern hills
> all your memories gather into trembling hopes
> taking us back to a time before they gave us
> religion to divide us, before the actor priests
> who laboured for their own redemption, mouthing

the name of god among benighted heathens;
a time before science, civilized laws and
rock music, a time in the memory of gods.
Before coat and before nylon, bare-bosomed time,
time of the puan and story-telling cloak,
the streaking motif caught on fabric, the
eloquent bead encircling your slender neck
(ibidem 127).

Before Christianity came to the Lushai hills, the Meiteis and Mizos were close to each other in their religious faiths. The religion divided them; but in spite of that 'the bare-bosomed time', 'the time of the *puan*' (Mizo loin cloth) and 'the story-telling cloak' are still alive in the racial memory. Again speaking of the racial affinity between Mizos and Manipuris, Robin addresses the woman reminding her of the Mizo folk hero, *Chhura*:

Woman, from the land
of *Chhura,* our roots suck from the same
liquid tongue. Because of these
shared dreams and waters, none knows
you like I do, I who can love the
twin syllable of your name in silence. (ibidem 128)

Like Mamang Dai of Arunachal Pradesh, Robin regards all transactions of life as myths:

We are but shadows of the great spirits
who come from myth,
and are but shadows themselves.
.....
But slowly they fall into place,
these shadows immovable like foundations
filling the emptiness with indistinct
memories of birth, of the pure day
of holding hands, of the first fight
to earn boyhood, and clothes bought
on a feast day, the painful flight
of the maiden kiss still hovering
in the air, of uninvited loneliness
and the sincere joy of fornication,

of happy illnesses and feet that move
wind a mind of their own. (1999: 55-56)

As Chaucer exposed the bare realities of his contemporary religious society in an early period of the development of English poetry, Robin, among the bards of Northeast, reveals the reality in the poor's sufferings and preacher's mask:

..... The
right and wrong have become synonymous,
and citizens garland only the thieves.
The man of god merely chants the
sanctimonious burlesque of prayers,
while the poor remain cold and naked
the preacher is warm and fed. [2000(a): 38-39]

Sikkimese and Tibetan myth, mystery and ecology also find place in Robin's poetry. He feels nostalgic in the landscape of Gangtok, being reminded of a mother's lap:

beneath the veil of the Himalayan sky
until you lift us on your maternal lap
of flowers and stone, Gangtok. (2002: 94)

At the wooden palace gate of Chogyal, he gets a flash-back of the royal history of Sikkim and about the king's men punishing the hardened criminals:

who are the artisans of wood that left
no names on the palace gate of the Chogyal?
A misty forest looks up the face of a sheer drop
where the king's men punished hardened criminals
tied up in sacks, by pushing them off this cliff,
so the stories insinuate. (ibidem)

He also celebrates the glory of the Rumtek Buddhist monastery, situated at a high altitude in Gangtok and that of Karmapa who fled Tibet and reconstructed the excellently beautiful monastery which is also a significant seat of learning. Here there is constantly heard the intonation of monks' deep drone of prayer songs. Viewing the surrounding scenes, Robin is dubious of the motto of Buddhism:

> But what does one seek from the illuminate
> if the wayward mind must be conquered first?
> A grimy gap-toothed Tibetan comes begging
> while young acolytes scurry to fetch water,
> as the world of appearance marked time.
> Adornment, renunciation, ego, alms,
> where is there a life without desire? (ibidem 95).

In a poem entitled "City of Baked Clay", a term which is the English version of the word 'Itanagar', the capital city of Arunachal, the poet alludes to a land of myths, a land of song and dances [2003(a): 29]. The Meghalayan legend of *Noh Ka Likai* is referred again by highlighting the mythic greatness of the place:

> Once old gods came to play
> in these hellish gorges, they
> of white beards and resounding laughter,
> once, before the sad young god came
> to cloister your heart. And we came
> to say goodbye for the summer here. (ibidem 30)

Momentary impressions have very often influenced Robin to break out into emotions. Sweating under the summer heat, laziness and "desire not to meet anyone" (2006:27) in the long afternoon are some of the obsessions Robin ponders over and as such he feels:

> Sometimes I'm certain
> that I was nothing other than months
> ripped from a former calendar (ibidem)

Robin Ngangom truly represents the Northeast India as he has explored the myth, mystery and ecology of the various provinces of the region in his poetry.

Works Cited

Gait, Sir Edward. 1962. *A History of Assam*. Gauhati: LBS Publications(1984 Rpt.)

Gogoi, Nilutpol. 2004. "Chitrangoda's Clan": *The Assam Tribune*, dtd. 14th Nov. Sunday Reading(1).

Ngangom, Robin S. 1988. *Words and the Silence*. Calcutta: Writers Workshop.

..... 1994. *Time's Crossroads.* Hyderabad: Orient Longman.
..... 1995. "Poems". *Indian Literature:* 168 (July-Aug) ed. K. Satchidanandan. New Delhi: Sahitya Akademi. (125-128).
..... 1999. "Three Poems". *Indian Literature.* 190. (Mar-Apr) ed. H.S. Shiva Prakash. New Delhi: Sahitya Akademi. (54-56).
..... 2000(a) "Three Poems". *Indian Literature:* 197 (May-June) ed. H.S. Shiva Prakash. New Delhi: Sahitya Akademi. (37-40).
..... 2000(b). "Four Poems". *Chandrabhaga:* 2. ed. Jayanta Mahapatra. Cuttack. (25-31).
..... 2002. "Seven Poems": *Indian Literature:* 211 (Sept.-Oct.). New Delhi: Sahitya Akademi. ed. N.K. Bhattacharjee. (93-101).
..... 2003 (a). "Seven Poems". *Chandrabhaga:* 8. ed. Jayanta Mahapatra. Cuttack. (27-38).
..... 2003 (b). "Five Poems": *Anthology of Contemporary Poetry from the North-east.* ed. K.S. Nongkynrih etal. Shillong: NEHU. (149-155).
....2006. *The Desire of Roots.* Cuttack:Chandrabhaga Society.
The Assam Tribune. 2004. November 21 (Sunday) (1).
The Telegraph: Nov. 21/2004:1

(9)

The Poetry of Dayananda Pathak: Beyond His Note of Melancholy

Priyanka Sarmah

Dayananda Pathak is one of the well-known writers, writing both in English and Assamese. He has authored about twenty books in Assamese. They include translation of Shakespeare's plays into Assamese, critical works, biographies and a couple of edited works. He has also authored a few books in English. They include a critical work on the plays of G.B. Shaw, and one on Sankardeva, the great master of Neo-Vaishnavism in Assam. *Coral Island* is his first book of verses. *Golden Deer* is his second book of poems.

Coral Island is Dayananda Pathak's first attempt at versification in English, and one of the prominent characteristics that runs through all the poems in this volume is the note of melancholy. Melancholy, gloom, despondency or pessimism have been a common feature and distinctive trait of most romantic poets and this we find in Pathak's poetry also, but unlike the romantic poets he does not seek to escape from the real world. He is more like Mathew Arnold who could not find repose in anything. We find the elegiac spirit in Pathak to be very strong and this spirit is an outlet of his natural melancholy over the mournfulness of mortal destiny. His sensitiveness has made him anachronistic. His poetry is an anguished cry of desperation and frustration at the spectacle presented by modern city life in its various ramifications. His poetry expresses his profound sorrow at the exploitation and injustice rampant in modern society and the transience of human life and worldly joys. In the 'sick hurry' of modern city life the poet seems to be seeking deliverance but no deliverance came. The themes of Pathak's poems in this volume are world, life, love, loneliness and the pain of living. In dealing with these themes, there is an undercurrent of a pessimistic world-view.

NOTE OF MELANCHOLY IN THE THEMES OF PATHAK'S POEMS:

In Pathak's poems we find a note of sincerity and genuineness of an experience deeply felt. The first poem of the volume titled 'coral island', deals with the theme of mankind's history being a 'gory tale' and civilization 'a farce'. The poem that deals with this theme begins with the breakdown of electricity symbolically enough and goes on to emphasize man's dark past and dark future.

Darkness inside,
electricity has failed tonight
my blood circulation stopped,
all the arteries lay dead,
society stands blocked,
the midday sun stands adamant,
the time lay dormant.
Your history a gory tale, (Coral Island)

Life for the poet is a sad experience and this is beautifully expressed in the poems 'Diamond' and 'Naked Shell'. We are born into this world as pure and innocent as flowers. But with age and experience we lose our innocence and at the end of our life, there is nothing left but sad memories.

Phantoms of death
looms large in your face
Life exists no more
only sad naked shells remain. (Naked Shell)

In the poems 'Love of a Nihilist' and 'You Are Angel No More', he emphasizes not on beauty but on death.

Dear, you are angel no more.
What you are then?
A biological species of mankind,
and
A woman,
Top to toe. (You are Angel No More)

In the poem 'Love of a Nihilist', the emphasis is not on beauty derived from the harmony of proportions but of death which leads to the beauty skeleton being housed 'in anthropology laboratory'. He shows a link between beauty and sadness in these poems and this is possible because of his awareness of mutability.

I can count your ribs,
bones-two hundred and six.
That specimen skeleton
of Anthropology laboratory. (Love Of A Nihilist)

THE USE OF NATURE IMAGERY IN EXPRESSING MELANCHOLY :

Poets utilize different aspects of nature as metaphors to feelings. Man and nature are bound together on Earth. It affects us in every way. When the sun glows the human heart also glows, so the use of nature is apt in reflecting human emotions. Pathak also in some of his poems uses some aspects of nature as metaphors for his feelings. In the poem 'Time' he uses 'fog' and the 'cold of December' as metaphors for the pain and suffering of human life, while sunshine is used as a metaphor for hope.

Kissed by thousand deaths
stands midway
amidst December pain
and lukewarm light.
An eerie concentric fog
shrouds my being
and my estranged soul
desperately seethes
for a speck of Sunshine (Time)

In 'Naked Shell', man's old age is compared to a naked shell thrown on the ocean beach.

a lonely shell
thrown on the ocean beach (Naked Shell)

In the poem 'Peace Gently Percolates', the darkness and stillness of night is used as a metaphor for the pain enveloping the poet. The bitter rainy evening in 'Memory of a Rainy Evening' stands as a metaphor for frustration and depression.

> It was a bitter rainy evening
> on a great festive day,
> marring all mirths,
> channels of life dried up.
>
> (Memory Of A Rainy Evening)

He expresses a kind of Wordsworthian nostalgia in 'Nostalgia'—

> you painfully left behind
> in the garden of yellow jasmine? (Nostalgia)

The first poem 'Coral Island' is the place where the poet cannot find any life. To him it is a dead place. It stands as a symbol of hopelessness which he feels for mankind. There is a lot of nature imagery in the poem 'Journey' which are used to show the positive aspect of human life. In the poem 'Being One With You' the poet compares the meeting of two lovers to two rivers, who come together and continue to flow towards their common destination to the ocean bed.

> You and me,
> two rivers meet at a point
> and walked along for the ocean bed,
> our final destiny. (Being One With You)

There is the use of darkness and light in some of Pathak's poems, which helps in bringing out the themes of the poems. In 'Coral Island', the breakdown of electricity, leaving everything in darkness is significant. In the poem 'Switch off the light', the poet feels the pain of living, and thinks it 'manageable, bearable, livable' only in the enveloping darkness.

> Darkness is beautiful
> like black gold.
> It covers the truth
> Makes life manageable
> bearable
> livable (Switch Off The Light)

The image of the 'desiccated plant' is repeated in two of his poems, 'Coral Island' and 'Switch off the light'. It stands as image of death and dying

I am chilled to the marrow
to deadly numbness
like the desiccated plant. (Switch Off The Light)

MELANCHOLY IN THE LOVE POEMS OF PATHAK :

The poems like 'Catharsis', 'Holiday from love' and 'Let us seal our hearts', have love as the theme. In these poems, the poet not only suggests the ecstasy of being in love, but also the pain of being left alone. Love is a universal emotion and is sought after by everyone as it makes our life whole and complete. It is both timeless and, in too many instances, transient. The pain caused by love is universal and this is the pain which comes out sincerely and poignantly.

Love came through you,
and pain too,
melody of love
through you came that fading smile,
morbidity and satiety
the remnant of beduin love
and
you cruelly left me
at the foothill of catharsis. (Catharsis)

STYLE AND VERSIFICATION IN PATHAK'S POETRY :

In dealing with his themes the poet has employed a style and versification noted for originality of expression and imagery. He exploited fully the inherent flexibility of the language for his purpose. He has chosen to write in free verse and this has enabled him to make the rhythms of his lines appropriate and integral to the subject matter. Sometimes he resorts to the staccato style of writing. This seems to be deliberate, for the life that he sees around him is a jerky one, full of stresses and strains and of the pain of separation like in the poems 'Time' and 'At Thirty'.

The cruel stamps of Time,
In your face one can see

the expression of subdued pain.
Now you are thirty
with fine health
Beyond this what?
What next? (At Thirty)

PATHAK'S POETRY MELANCHOLIC, NOT DEPRESSING :

Though 'melancholy' many a time has been associated with sadness, despair, sorrow and depression, but it is not the same. It is a complex emotion, which is present in some of our aesthetic responses to our natural environment. Melancholy invites aesthetic considerations to come into play not only in well defined aesthetic contexts, but also in everyday situations that give reason for melancholy to arise. In Pathak's poetry, the note of melancholy not only comes out in well-defined aesthetic contexts, but also in everyday situations like in the poem 'City Bus'. The jam-packed bus, traveling by which, is quite painful is to the poet, a miniature form of the modern world where existence means compulsory pain and suffering.

Jampacked city bus on a busy road,
A world in miniature,
Makes one feel
The anguish
And the pangs of existence
And compulsions. (City Bus)

Melancholy is a complex emotion. But the complexity of melancholy is in the fact that it is fascinating in itself and on further thought it may be considered also as an aesthetic emotion. This dual character of melancholy is what makes it different from sadness and depression. There are both negative and positive aspects in it, which alternate, creating contrasts and rhythms of pleasure and these aspects combined with the reflectivity making it a refined emotion. Melancholy also involves other shades of emotions like love, longing, yearning, or missing something, as well as feeling nostalgic or the emotion that accompanies reminiscence and even dread. All these shades of emotion are there in Pathak's poetry along with his note of melancholy. One of the most distinctive aspects of melancholy is that it involves reflection. Pathak is a serious and sensitive man fully alive to the world around him. What he has seen has made him, more often than not, sad and shaken to the core and like many conscientious man of his generation he seems to be disillusioned by what modern life presents. He seems to be in search of something beyond the noise and glitter of the phenomenal world. His poems can be taken as a quest for some kind of faith and hope, and this quest is itself something remarkable. The poems bring out his note of sincerity and his genuineness of feeling. They embody an experience deeply felt and reflected on. Though the poet feels the pains of living and can only manage to live in enveloping darkness, yet, he hopes—

> peace gently percolates
> the stillness of the night. (Peace Gently Percolates)

The experience of life, though sad and painful for the poet when he contemplates in a state of creative awareness, however,—

> turn into pristine emeralds
> into moments of graceful bliss. (Emerald)

Perhaps this 'pristine emeralds' will in years to come save the 'lone soul' that—

> desperately seethes
> for a speck of sunshine
> for some fragrant light. (Time)
> having been
> lashed by century's pain
> kissed by thousand deaths. (ibidem)

These poems end in an optimistic note and confirm the poet's feeling and reflection that there is still hope for mankind, all is not lost yet. The strength and beauty of Pathak's poems are found precisely in their honest grappling of despair and faith, and in the sense that the struggle between the two is perilously close. Despite his doubts and griefs, something in Pathak is persevered in the form of hope. His search for hope and faith led him to create poetic landscapes which are highly charged, often lovely, sometimes frightening. Like Dickinson, he honours the beauty, terror and mystery of existence.

EXISTENTIAL DARKNESS OR MELANCHOLY IN PATHAK'S POETRY :

There are hints of existential darkness in Pathak's poetry. Existentialism as we know is not dark or depressing. It is about life and fighting for life. Existentialism assumes that we are best when we struggle against our nature. This is what we find in Pathak's poetry. We find happiness and sadness, dark and light, life and death etc. in his poetry. For him happiness is fleeting and we are mortals. He is aware of mankind's unhappiness but he still has hope and faith and this is expressed in his poems. Though we know man is mortal and all his endeavors are meaningless, we should not stop living. We should value our existence and at the same time try to make it meaningful. The dissolution and devastation of socio-ethical and politico-economic values of the post-modern world have disheartened the poet to a great extent but he has not given up hope.

I know where my future lies—
It is in the coral island
Our bones and ribs consummate
and make the coral island
for the children a fertile land. (Coral island)

footsteps of the newborn time,
the thrills of eternity. (Let Us Seal Our Hearts)

Would they lead to
a costly diamond
after history's
cruel sedimentation? (Diamond)

There is both yearning and sadness in his poems. In his poems bliss joins suffering as part of the soul's reality. He reflects upon the complications presented by the world and realizes that a man has to work and live within the compulsions of life, but he still has faith and through his poems he searches for that faith and hope beyond the chaos and dazzle of this unique world. Despite all the nearly unendurable elements of life, the poet feels that when there could have been nothing, there is still something. This is a great mystery. There could not have been love, kindness and beauty if there is nothing. In the end, faith and poetry is not separable for the poet. Indeed, his poetry can be taken not merely as an expression of faith but a means toward faith. His poems on patriotism like 'Motherland', 'Let Us Wake' and 'In Loving you' is a confirmation of this faith—

> I have heard you pant
> shriek and rot.
> this nevertheless, is my motherland
> I can die for. (Motherland)
>
> But dear, let us be real,
> Masters of realities,
> Never to sleep for dream,
> Never to walk in our sleep.
> We cannot sleep—
> Let us see
> What is beyond
> Beyond what we see. (Let Us Wake)

CONCLUSION :

The note of melancholy which is there in Pathak's poetry is essential; it is this note of melancholy which makes it so relevant to the contemporary world. The poet's job is to tell the whole truth and nothing but the truth and Pathak put into the words of his poetry those feelings we all have that are so deep, so important, and yet so difficult to name. The poet is a successful academician, a writer and a man with family. Yet in spite of all these blessings, a ground note of darkness and suffering runs through his poems—one that tempers, complicates and finally enriches them. This shows his sensitiveness and his alertness to the world around him. We should not judge him as a poet of melancholy. Beyond the shades of his overt melancholy there is a craze for peace, happiness and calmness. Road to peace is tortuous, but the same ends up in peace beyond the veneer of chaos and confusion of modern life. There is the desperate quest for something that makes life bearable and livable and perhaps we should focus on those points. We can conclude by saying that his poems are thought provoking and are relevant to all ages and places because what is true of one age is true of another.

Works Cited

Pathak, Dayananda. *Coral Island*. Guwahati: Sabinay, 1998.
.... *The Golden Deer*. Guwahati: Lawyers' Book Stall, 2007.

(10)

The Poetry of Kynpham Sing Nongkynrih

Nigamananda Das

Kynpham Sing Nongkynrih is a worshipper of Mother Nature. Cherrapunjee is his Innisfree. Meghalaya's rivers, lakes, forests, fairies, hills, stone and nature's bounty find recurrent depiction in his poetry. Though he published late, his forerunners have not described the nature and environmental degeneration in sufficient quantum as he has done. The cutting and burning of forests, digging mines have distorted the bosom of nature. So he has reacted vehemently against these activities in his poetry:

> The barren hills
> that bear the pockmarks
> of miners and a foolish people
> that burn and cut at will,
> looks as unremarkable
> as half-naked little brats. [1992(a): 24]

Kynpham(1964-) who teaches English in North Eastern Hill University, Shillong, is a poet, writer and translator. He was awarded a 'Fellowship for Outstanding Artists 2000' by the Government of India. He also received the first North-East Poetry Award in 2004 from the North- East India Poetry Council, Tripura (2007:i). He has travelled abroad and received accolades there for his poetry. His poems have been translated to some other Indian languages also.

He has sympathy with the nature and in his poems everywhere he gives a fond description of the graces of nature:

> The breeze, however,
> prowling between spells of furious wind,

stole up from the brooks
to meet me on the hills
and whisper its sympathies on the golden grass.
[1992(b): 18]

The cold climate of his place has been symbolic of the degeneration due to the negligence to the natural environment in all shapes. Thus to share the sufferings of the Mother Nature, he himself has decided to live like *fungus* and thus he says:

That is why I keep like fungus
to this cold and dark interior
and in everything that I do
it is only the fungus that shows (1994:57)

The persona is agonised by the strange ways and things which are alien to his land. He is upset with these:

For how long can we go on
living like wind blown thistledowns?

....

like flowers, only strangers
strange ways have come
to bloom in this land.(1998:53)

The decorations with bamboo on the occasion of the Prime Minister Gujral's visit to Shillong upset him. He shows how nature is exploited by the human beings for futile purposes:

When Prime Minister Gujral
planned a visit to the city
bamboos sprang up from pavements
like a welcoming committee.

...

only bamboos watched in silence
too used to antics of men [2000(a):55-6/2000(b): 73-4]

He considers the sufferings of and atrocities on the hills' tribes as a kind of ecological erosion. As such he justifies the insurgency reared by the tribes as a protest against their movement towards extinction, which is a way of quest for revival:

Somewhere in a forgotten little corner of the world
a hill tribe of one million, fearful of its extinction,
waged an arms insurrection against a nation of billion[2003(a). 30/2003(b):162]

With the identity of the biodiversity of his land of birth, the poet establishes the identity of a Khasi exposing the cultural ecology of the Khasis:

A Khasi is a man, who once a year,
Sport a muga-mulberry turban,
an eri shawl and is seen *en grande tenue*
at *weiking* or *pomblang*
who once a year, speaks of these great festivals
and the teachings of his great ancestors.
who once a year, says "to Know Man,
to Know God, to Earn Righteousness" is our faith.
But this, only once a year. [2004(a): 29]

Cherrapunjee is Kynpham Sing Nongkynrih's Innisfree. He has a number of poems on Cherrapunjee, Shillong and places in Meghalaya and India. Khasi legends and folklores find ample exposition in his poetry. In "A Homily", the poet describes the Khasi legend that the peacock was husband to the Sun, but then he left his wife and his heavenly home, dazzled by the flowers of the mustard plant on earth:

the Khasi knows
how once my very lustre
became the songs that ensnared
the majesty of birds,
the peacock, husband to the Sun,
who left his loving wife's heavenly home [1992(a): 15]

Legends about the falls of Cherrapunjee and the practices of Khasis have been narrated in his Cherrapunjee poems. He addresses Cherrapunjee as his mother:

Cherra, dear *Meikha*
Crowds have sung for you,
Competing Sunday bells

tolling abroad your pulchritude
those foamy-white cascading ornaments,
Your roaring falls;
those leafy green dresses
your musical forests. (ibidem 20)

"*Meikha*" in Khasi, is a paternal aunt, but it is used here in the sense of a mother. The poet writes about *Lalyngngi,* which in Khasi, means orchid. It is supposed to be a very beautiful woman who missed the cultural dance of creatures as she was much pre-occupied with self-beautification (ibidem 21). The poet addresses Cherrapunjee in several poems and refers to his love for the place. It is his Utopia:

But goodbye dear Cherra,
and your rain, good-bye.
I'm off to Shillong,
for my life is yonder,
though my love is here. (ibidem 23)

He refers to the falls of Cherrapunjee and the legends related to them. The *Noh Ka Likai* falls is named after the woman, Likai, who committed suicide there (ibidem). There is a *Dainthlen* falls where a serpentine monster named Thlen, who ate human beings, was killed and cut up (ibidem 26). *Sngi Thiang/Snioian,* literally sweet sun, is the name of the Mawsmai falls, in Cherrapunjee, which is named after the woman, *Sngi Thiang. Khoh Ramhah,* which means the giant's basket, is a conical rock formation and a tourist spot in Cherrapunjee, connected with the legend of *Ramhah,* the giant, the legend of *Suid Tynjang*–a lame demon who is believed to live in precipitous jungles and is known for its shrieking and howling. Tribal gods, demons, hills, streams, falls, places and the environing greenery find lucid verbal depiction in Nongkynrih's poetry.

Like Robin Ngangom, Kynpham Sing Nongkynrih in his latest writings reveals his love for places and myths and mysteries related with the places. Besides Cherrapunjee places in Meghalaya, and in a recent poem entitled 'Agartala Nights' he exposes his momentary impressions alluding to the significance and brief history of the place. About his love for the place he says:

I could stay forever in this warm town
of grey dust and chaotic rickshaws
learning lessons as from a book of fables. [2004(b): 51]

Tripura, and its capital city, Agartala, are seething cauldrons of the activities of the Bangladeshi refugees. The customs and Tripuri heritage are at a very bad state. The Tripuri race is festering with great wounds of hate, struggle and rage. The Tripuri tribes being driven by the Bengali refugees are living in hills and jungles. As such Agartala which literally means 'empty space' has really become empty. So says Nongkynrih:

> Agartala, empty space, should I declare
> such is the fate of all empty spaces? (ibidem)

The poet shows his sympathy for the Tripuri tribes and encourages a reawakening in their society:

> Supplant their customs, reduce their palaces
> into lowly assemblies and tourist destinations
> Herd them to the mainstream, drown them there.
> Let them emerge from the jungle only to sit
> on their haunches on the caked-mud of Bishram Ganj,
> hawking vegetables as in *Luri Lura.*
> Then raise a fence on the border
> fence out rebels and migrants (ibidem)

Luri Lura, the chaotic animal fair in Khasi folklore (as a suggested measure for Tripuris' coercive involvement in the local politics and other works to drive away immigrants), the palace of the last Kokborok Raja, Birbikram Kishore Manikya built in the middle of lake Rudijala at Melaghar, the haunches on the caked-mud of Bishram Ganj, a roaring Kokborok waterfall, which is seeker of antique souls and songs of a sad Bishnupriya are some allusions that expose Nongkynrih's interest in the history, myth, folk life and heritage of Tripura. He also mingles myths with ecological concerns showing his reactions to the contemporary living conditions of the peoples in his land of birth and proving his responsibility as a sentinel of time and cultural clime:

> I asked a learned man.
> He quoted scientific reasons
> spitfiring them one by one.
> Global warming, charcoal burning
> the ozone layer, polythene bags,

ecological imbalances, Jaintia coal mines
timber trade, jhum cultivation
West Khasi uranium and on and on.
But religious men were convinced
the world is too riddled with sin.
Hindus have gored too many good Samaritans.
Christians have forced too many conversions
and cocksure Seng Khasi should not
have ascended our holy mountain, Sohpet Bneng.
[2004(b): 49-50]

As a nature poet and spokesman of tribal issues Kynpham recurrently tries to raise the identity question. He may not be an activist; but his concerns as a conscious citizen show that he is worried about the ecological crises of our times and the crises pertaining to the land of his birth. He is worried about both the deep and shallow ecological principles and as such we can call him an ecofeminist.

He finds mystery in the very existence and motto of the hill tribes. With the myth of Sisyphus he traces the mystery of their absurd living:

Sisyphus eternally rolls his rock
to the mountain top from which it eternally rolls down
again [2003(a):30]

The very motto of the tribes' living is mysterious. They dream impossible dreams and are unaware of many of the grinding realities of the life:

Their motto:
to dream their impossible dream,
to fight the unbeatable foe,
to bear with unbearable sorrow
to run where the brave does not go.... (ibidem)

A mystery lies there in identifying a Khasi in the Meghalaya hills. So to the question, "How do you spot a Khasi?", the poet traces a strange answer:

Not by his mother tongue since
too many mothers and fathers

have rendered his tongue truly macaronic,
his features truly *olla padrida.*
Not by his dress since
he is truly universal
not by churches or temples since
he doesn't have any.
Not by his religion since
They would simply label him "non-christian,"
Not anymore as 'a red-mouthed demon' since
Kwai strain has afflicted everyone.
Not by his *syiems* since
they rule like commission agents
and serve at the pleasure of scoundrels.
Not by his leaders since
They are the scoundrels [2004(a):28-9]

The Khasi identity is revealed/celebrated once a year at *Weiking* or *Pomblang,* i.e., the Khasi religio-cultural dance festivals.

As against what Kynpham says, it is said: "There is in the Northeast an uneasy coexistence of paradoxical worlds such as folk and the westernised, virgin forests and car-choked streets, ethnic cleansers and the parasites of democracy, ancestral values and flagrant corruption, resurgent nativism and the sensitive outsiders' predicaments....As chroniclers of their subjective realities, the poets of the region do reflect in their poetry this "world of eerie contradictions" even as they explore their own mindscapes and the many-layered complexities of human relationships"(Sen 2005:43-4). He is still writing observing the world surrounding him. His future poetry is expected to reflect more about his theme, concepts and techniques.

Works Cited

Nongkynrih, Kynpham Sing. 1992(a). *Moments.* Calcutta: Writers Workshop.

.... 1992(b). *The Sieve.* Calcutta: Writers Workshop.

.... 1994. "Two Poems". *Indian Literature*: 164. Nov-Dec. New Delhi: Sahitya Akademi.(57-8)

.... 1998. "Three Poems". *Indian Literature:* 186. July-Aug. New Delhi: Sahitya Akademi.(52-4)

.... 2000(a). "Four Poems". *Indian Literature*: 197. (May-June).New Delhi:Sahitya Akademi.(53-7)

.... 2000(b). "Four Poems": *Chandrabhaga*. 1. Cuttack. (72-78).
.... 2003(a). "Three Poems": *Chandrabhaga* 7. Cuttack. (26-32).
.... 2003(b). "Five Poems": *Anthology of Contemporary Poetry from Northeast*. Shillong: NEHU. (156-164).
.... 2004(a). "Six Poems". *Indian Literature*: 221(May-June).New Delhi: Sahitya Akademi. (23-29).
.... 2004(b). "Four Poems". *Chandrabhaga*. 10. Cuttack. (47-53).
....2007. *Around the Hearth: Khasi Legends*. New Delhi: Penguin Books.
Sen,Geeti.ed.2005.*Where the Sun Rises When Shadows Fall: The Northeast*: *IIC Quarterly*, Monsoon Winter. New Delhi: India International Centre.

(11)

Naga Folk Narratives: A Bird's Eyeview

A.J.Sebastian sdb

Oral narratives are generally classified into myth, legend and folktale. Myth is believed to be true; legend purports to be true while folktale is untrue. Myth derived from *mythos* in Greek concerns supernatural beings beyond time and space. Legend is derived from *legenda* in Latin implying identifiable personalities in time and place, having extraordinary qualities and often interacting with supernatural beings or forces. In folktale fantasy reigns as it deals with fictional characters in time and place. (Ben-Amos 2006:255).

Folktale is universal as it exists among all peoples of all ages. It is handed down traditionally by word of mouth or in the written form by group of people whether literate or illiterate. These tales which exist in the memory of people cannot easily be recognizably categorised. Students of the folktale are primarily concerned with the origin and dissemination of tales as well as the folktale as an art. As an art form it concerns the conditions of folktale telling such as by the kind of people that tell tales, circumstances of the telling, the reception of the audience, the way they are handed down, and the stylistic effects of this oral art (Shipley 1993:124-5).

According to the great scholar Grimm the same folktale types are scattered over most of Europe and Asia and often far beyond. Theodore Benfey is said to have opined that the original home of all folktales is India. But most anthropologists and scholars agree on the universality of the ideas in the folktales as these come from dreams or rituals. Recent scholarship recognizes the unique history of each folktale and seek to apply the historical-geographical method (Ibid. 126). Since folktales are fictional and irrational narratives these could be interpreted at different levels : psychoanalytically, anthropologically, or literally. Psychoanalytically folktale is considered a cultural or universal dream fantasy which expresses suppressed emotions of individuals and society. Anthropologically folktales reflect a society's view of itself as these express their fantasies, mirroring their culture and history. Literary interpretation of folktales brings to focus Ethnopoetics and folktale criticism (Ben-Amos 2006: 263-66).

Story telling and folktales have been an integral part of Naga society. However, only in the recent past, these oral narratives have been rendered into written form. This paper is an attempt to assess a selection of folktales in the literature from Nagaland as storytelling will never cease to exist. These folktales deal with a variety of themes. There are the Tiger Stories, Tales on Man and animals, Spirit stories, Tales of Love and Marriage, Head hunting stories, Bird stories, Creation Tales, etc.

From the psychological standpoint certain preoccupations and fears in a family makes the children experience such fears in their fantasies though they overcome them in reality. Hence folktales have got a psychological impact on society. Anthropologically the stories narrated are representative of the fantasies of people who present their popular themes. It is also believed that folktales present opposite picture of things as they are and reflect unconscious wishes and family tensions. Therefore this is where the folktales can be analysed to examine the inner working of people in traditional societies. The folktales also have the function of entertaining and instructing people (Ben-Amos 2006:264-5).

Tiger stories

The Tiger Stories are very common among the Nagas showing the communion of man and beast. Psychologically it could be the spirit of valour their forebears wanted to put into the psyche of the children, that is shown through the tales. Today we are very concerned about protecting flora and fauna. Since Tiger has become an endangered species and the campaign to save the tiger is growing day by day, such folktales of man-tiger relationships can have its own role of educating society in ecological values.

The story of "Three Brothers" speak of the time when the Tiger, the Spirit and the Man were brothers who lived in perfect harmony. The Tiger was the eldest, the Spirit in the middle and the Man the youngest among them. After their father's early demise, the trio had to take turns to keep company to their widowed mother. The Tiger demanded his mother to play all the time with him making her sick and weak. The Spirit was very unkind to her when his turn came. It was Man who looked after her the best. The Tiger longed for her death as he had the evil design to devour her. Knowing this, the brothers sent the Tiger away to the forest. Eventually the mother died and when the Tiger returned he was prevented from enquiring of her. Then the Man tricked the Tiger with what he dreaded most – fire and trumpet. While the Tiger was asleep, Man tied a burning mat to his tail and trumpeted to drive the beast away to the forest. Thus the Tiger began to live in the forest and the Man in the village (FTFN: 7-8).

The tale centres on the concept of the brotherhood of man-beast-spirits. The harmony is disrupted by evil scheming. Cruelty inflicted on the mother by the Devil and the Tiger is central to the story in which Man is the only consolation to the mother. The lesson the story intends is the need to show love and respect to one's parents and how man began to live in a community.

"How Tigers Came on this Earth" is a tale that recounts the story of the boy who developed the filthy habit of scratching his sister's legs with his sharp nails when they worked in the forest. When the beleaguered girl complained to her mother about it, she tricked the boy to fetch water with *yungjai* (bamboo water carriers) with holes which kept him busy filling throughout the day. When a crow teased him for his leaking bamboo containers, he came to know of the trick played on him. Infuriated he ran to his mother asking her to breastfeed him as in childhood. While suckling he tore off her breast and ran off to the forest and was transformed into a tiger (FTFN: 45-6).

The story calls attention to the mother who takes corrective measures to protect her daughter from ill-treatment meted out to her by her cruel brother. It is the duty of a mother to find appropriate solution as the mother does in the case though she has to pay a heavy price for it.

A Lotha folktale about "The Cunning Man and the Foolish Tiger" shows how a man named Echu cheated a tiger and drove him into the forest. One day as Echu went through the forest with a rope to tie his mother up, a tiger met him and asked him to tie it up instead. Later experiencing excruciating pain it asked Echu to let loose the rope, but he refused. The tiger begged the passers by namely a deer, bear and other wild animals to untie the rope, but none dared to help. One day as Echu returned that way with two oxen the tiger requested him to untie the rope and agreed to have the oxen tied to his back. Echu did so and cleverly made a frightening sound which drove the oxen go mad with fear and made the tiger groan in pain and run away to the forest never to meet Echu again (FTFN:190).

The story reveals the adroitness of man in controlling the tiger and establishing his superiority over all creatures.

Animal-man-spirit relationship is furthered in other tales such as "The Weretigerman." It is the tale of Tsaricho, his father and grandfather who came under a spell and became half-men-half-spirits and were turned into tiger-men (TWC: 75-80).

Man and animals can never be separated in the life of the tribals as the following story unveils. They love their animals for rearing and yet hunting is part and parcel of traditional life in the villages as if fulfilling the biblical prescription, 'Be fruitful and multiply, and fill the earth and subdue it; and have dominion over the fish of the sea and over the birds of the air and over every living thing that moves upon the earth.' (Genesis 1:28).

The story 'Invention of Fire" revolves around men and animals who lived together as friends. They dried all their food in the sun as cooking was unknown. One day the men and the animals decided to invent fire. The party that invents it first will be allowed to cook and eat the other party. The Tiger took up the lead among the animals, but his effort was in vain. Man took a piece of wood, split it half way on one end and put a piece of stone in between. He held the device under his foot and took some thatch grass and placed it in between. He took a cane and swayed it in circular motion and made fire by friction. Man thus succeeding in inventing fire and could catch animals and cook for his food. From then on man and animals became enemies and failed to understand each other (FTFN:47-8).

Spirit stories

Stories of Spirits taking possession of humans is common among the Nagas.

Temsula Ao introducing her folk-based poem "Soul-Bird" writes: 'There is an ancient Ao-Naga belief that when a person dies, the soul takes the form of a bird, more specifically a hawk...The sighting of hawks soon after a person's death is considered to be a good omen signifying that the transition is complete and that it is the last appearance of the loved one on earth' (SFOL:14). In the poem "Soul-Bird" the child observes a hawk soaring up into the sky as the ritualistic prayers are offered. The bird keeps circling above the mud heap over the burial site 'emitting unearthly sounds.' The grandmother tells the child confirming the transition:

> See that keening bird in the sky?
> That's your mother's soul
> Saying her final good-bye (Ibid.15).

A similar story is narrated in "Hawk of the Dead." As the belief goes that spirit of the dead hover over their homes bidding farewell once again to the bereaved ones who throw water up into the air (PFN:136-7). These stories of after life is universal as the concept of transmigration is found among the tribals.

"The Silver Dzüli" is a folk-based tale of Thesuohie who was possessed by his warrior father's spirit and longed for union with the spirits. The tale concludes:

... On clear winter evenings, when the clouds hold no rain, you can see the spirits of the warriors chasing each other across the skies. On such evenings, the village people gather to watch the spirits of Thesuohie and his father. The two always rise together from the east, conflagrate in the winter skies and then softly die in the far west. And on nights such as these, the wind whistles in the bamboos; and then mothers gather their children to their bosoms and keep their fires burning all night long (TWC:88).

A Chang folktale is narrated about "The Villagers and the Devils" in which children in the village used to be carried away by evil spirits. An old man tried to trick the spirits by putting a child on the floor with a thread attached to it. Later he found the thread drawn to the forest and into a hole. While sleeping in the forest that night the devils came to carry him away to their abode as well. While trying to drag him into the hole the old man raised his legs preventing them from their plan. When the villagers heard of it they came to dig out the evil spirits from the hole. Thousands of insect like spirits flew out. Finally an old devil came out who was told by the villagers to leave them for good and he agreed to go to Dikhu river where devils are believed to inhabit (FTFN:180).Can evil spirits be driven away? Spirit stories are essential to make people believe in the supremacy of man for his survival. Psychoanalytically it is to be understood as the helplessness of man who is the victim of evil spirits as the people have to appease them for survival. Such stories can remove fear out of the community as evil spirits are given a place of their choice away from human habitation. The story probes into basic sexual motives that if distorted can lead to crime and destruction. The miraculous ending of the story continues to instruct the populace about violence inflicted on oppression of helpless women and children.

"The Greedy Man and the Water Spirit" is the story of the man who went with his friends to put poison in the river to catch fish. While diving into a deep pool in the river he reached a dry sandy area. There he found a water spirit sitting beside a hearth made of three human skulls. The spirit gave him a dried fish and warned him never to dive into the river. He returned with the dry fish and shared with his friends. Desiring to have more of the dry fish he dived again to the pool in the river, never to return again (FTFN: 12).

Tales of love and marriage

The Tenyidie folktale "The legend of Sopfunuo" is the story of pretty Sopfunuo married off to a Mao boy who eventually drove her out of his home along with her little child, due to jealousy and suspicion. While wandering in the forest they were killed by evil spirits and were turned to stones. Being told in a dream, her father arranged to drag the big stone which was Sophunuo. But due to a thunderstorm the stone pulling was halted. Meanwhile a villager had a dream message from Sophunuo, 'How dare you take me leaving behind my baby?' This is how the two stones of Sophunuo and her baby were dragged to Rüsoma village where it is believed to be growing ever after (FTFN:22-23).

"The Beautiful Damsel" is the story of a pretty damsel in a village who was pursued by many, seeking her hand in marriage. Her parents were so greedy they wanted her to be married off to a very wealthy man. Even the angels were enamoured of her beauty. It happened that an angel came in the form of a very handsome and wealthy youth seeking her in wedlock. Her parents consented. Dreaming of a very comfortable life she began the journey with her husband. They walked for days but never reached their destination. Days, months and years passed - meanwhile two children were born to them. Being unhappy with her marriage she decided to return to her village. One night when all were asleep she walked away to her village where she reached after walking for several days. She was married to a man of her choice and lived happily ever since (FTFN:5-6).

The story is a lesson on greed for wealth that can be destructive and it leads to unhappiness even if it is from an angel. Man can find happiness only in his own environment and simple lives.

"Nuzhüü" is a Tenyidie folk poem which narrates the pathetic story of a woman brought into a village to be married off. To her utter surprise she finds her husband to be a very old man. She becomes very unhappy and wants to leave, but respecting the tradition of marriage she goes on with her life. As her child grows up, he gets very attached to the village and is happy to stay on. The mother stays on for his sake. Still she continues to live unhappily and is ready to give away her 'bride price' of cattle and chickens besides the ornaments in compensation for her leaving her old husband (ACPN:231).

In "Adzügweü" a lover addresses his beloved as they are contemplating marriage which is a cultural tradition. They look for dreams and good omen as 'marriage is not a trivial thing.' Though she has promised to marry someone else from far Sehuja, she is willing to break that engagement to marry her lover as she has not yet been bought with money. However the marriage fails to take place as he does not propose to her. However, she keeps waiting and yearning for the beloved for a long period of time. Finally , unfulfilled in her dream love, she is married off to another man. Hence the woman laments:

> I went to the woods with my parents
> All the day long I waited for you to make your suit\
> But my waiting was in vain and I returned to the village
> With not a word passed between us
> ...
> I stood far off and gazed on my beloved's place
> "Who might my beloved have married?"
> Thus I wondered and remorse came upon me afresh (ACPN:231-2).

Often in stories concerning marriage a woman is a helpless victim as she is sold of at a bridal price and yet in certain stories the woman has the freedom before marriage to decide on her partner. These tales show how societal traditions are passed on from generation to generation by oral tradition.

Head hunting stories

There are tales about head-hunting prevalent among the various Naga tribes revealing how each tribe has shown its valour in the battlefield against it's enemies. Psychoanalytically these could be interpreted as expressions of strong emotions of a society.

A story is told of how head-hunting began among the Nagas. Fighting was unknown to them as they lived a peaceful life. It happened once an orphan boy brought a piece of wood from the forest on which he engraved a human figure. He decorated it with animal hair and tied it on a bamboo and placed it by the pathway. Seeing the human engraving on the pole, people suggested that it would look very beautiful if human heads could be kept likewise dangling by the roadside. From that time onwards people began to kill each other and thus began the practice of head-hunting (FTFN:29-30).

"How Man began to Cut off their Enemies' Head" narrates the story of warriors who returned after warfare. As a proof of their victory over the enemies they began to bring a part of the dead body. In the beginning they brought knee-caps of their victims. Later they began to bring heads along with the upper limbs. But this became a heavy booty for them to carry. One day a warrior saw two red ants engage in a deadly fight and the stronger one cutting off the other's head and carry it to its hole. He took the cue from the ant and began the practice of chopping only the heads of enemies to take home as trophy (FTFN:140-1).

Bird tales

Bird tales prevalent in the Naga society draw our attention to the mythological idea of the oneness of man and nature. These stories show the undeniable relation between man-and birds.

The Zeliang tale on an orphaned step-daughter tells the story of a poor girl who was illtreated and unfed by her step-mother. While pounding rice one day she sang her lamentations seeking her mother's soul to take her to the nether world and was transformed into a Nzuina (a dove-like bird). Her father, step-mother and step-brothers came to call her home from the forest, she was unable to return having been transformed into a Nzuina (FTFN:127-8).

There is a Konyak tale about "The Pact between Men and the Sparrows." Once upon a time a group of boys and girls used to gather in a cave and spent time in singing and playing games. One night the unmarried boys and girls were divided into two groups to sing and dance. As they were competing with each other a big stone appeared and closed the mouth of the cave. Their friends outside failed in their efforts to remove the stone for them. Then it happened that a flock of sparrows came that way who were requested to assist. The youth promised as reward that they would be allowed to eat paddy and corn in all the fields of men. The sparrows agreed and they flocked together and in a great rush pushed out the stone. That is why the sparrows have the privilege to eat paddy and corn (FTFN:168).

"Kaso Apfu" is the story of a man named Kaso who killed his father accidentally. It happened that one day Kaso's father wanted to test his son's bravery while cutting bamboo in the jungle. He had kept his spear very close in case of attack from roaming tigers. To test the boy's alertness the father threw a twig and instantly the boy threw his spear thinking it to be a tiger. Mortally wounded and as he lay dying the father promised to come every year in the form of a cuckoo bird to tell Kaso of seed sowing time.

Creation tales

According to an Ao Naga creation myth, Lijaba, the all powerful among the gods, first created a few plains and a few valleys and surrounded them with hills. But his creation was abruptly stopped by a huge cockroach came from nowhere and raised alarm that enemy soldiers were marching on to his territory. Being disturbed in his creation, the god Lijaba, completed the task haphazardly, and made his escape. That is why the Ao area is believed to be hilly with few plains, valleys and rivers (TANOT:78).

"Stone-People from Lungterok" is a folk based story referring to the six stones found in Chungliyimti village in the Ao area. The six stones represent the three men and the three women who were the ancestors of the Ao tribe who emerged out of the earth in that village.

Lungterok
The six stone
Where the progenitors
And forebears
Of the stone-people
Were born
Out of the womb
Of the earth (ACPN : 213).

Among the six humans there were three males and three females. The men were Longpok, Tongpok and Longjakrep. The women were Longkapokla (Lendina), Yongmenala and Elongse. Tongpok married Elongse; Longpok married Longkapokla (Lendina); Longjakrep married Yongmenala. The three men are said to be the patriarchs of the three main Ao clans: Longpok: Pongener clan; Tongpok: Longkumer clan; Longjakrep: Jamir clan (TANOT: 78).

Animal tales

"How Dog became Hornless" tells the story how the dog and the goat were great friends. The dog had beautiful horns of which the goat grew jealous. Once they found a woman putting some rice powder on the pounding table. The dog desiring to eat it put away his horns. The goat took the opportunity to request the dog to let him put the horn on his head. The dog agreed and the goat took it and ran away making the dog hornless for ever (FTFN:15).

It is interesting to know how there arose a war between the animals and birds. The bat remained neutral. When the birds asked him to join them he refused saying that he was an animal. When the animals requested him to be part of the, he excused himself claiming to be a bird. He was too cunning to join the victorious side after the warfare. Now it happened that the warring parties reached an accord preventing the war. Now the bat went to the birds to join their party. They refused to admit him into their company. He went seeking admission in the fold of the animals who threatened to kill him. Helpless he ran for his life and was ever ashamed of showing his face during day time (FTFN:55).

It is to be noted that the oral fictional tale gives the storyteller total freedom provided he/she tell tales that please keeping to the limits of local taboos. A folktale is passed on from one storyteller to another for generations and they go beyond language boundaries.

Animals and birds have close association with man and they are often anthropomorphized. At times men become beasts and birds. The tales are of different categories such as adventure stories, journeys into the other world, narratives of marriage, sexual adventure and so on.

The ordinary folktales that deal with human beings and their adventures are very numerous among the Nagas. Some of these tales are laid in a highly imaginative time and place and a land filled with supernatural creatures.

There are stories of spirits and fairies; some are harmful while others helpful. There are witches, devils, water spirits, supernatural guardians of the mountains. Belief in spirits is also very common among the tribals. It is to be kept in mind that the folktale tradition flourished among the Nagas in the past when the 'Morung' (Dormitory) system was in vogue in the villages where young people spent the night together recounting tales. The stories thus narrated had a moral influence on the young as well. But with modern lifestyles such storytelling times are no more.

Through these tales one is able to know the culture and tradition, beliefs and sensibilities, superstitions and taboos, mind and art of the various Naga tribes.

Reference

Ben-Amos, Dan. 2006. "Folktale". *Folklore: Critical Concept in Literary and Cultural Studies.* Ed. Alan Dundes. Vol. III. New York: Routledge.

Shipley, Joseph. 1993. *Dictionary of World Literary Terms.* Delhi: Doaba House.

The Holy Bibile. Revised Standard Version. London: Catholic Trust Society. 1966. (All Bibilical references taken from this edition).

Works Cited

Ao, Temsula. 2007. *Songs From The Other Life.* Pune: Grasswork Books. (Abbreviated : SFOL).

——.1999. *The Ao-Naga Oral Tradition.* Baroda: Bhasha Publications. (Abbreviated: TANOT)

Department of English.2005. *Poetry From Nagaland.* New Delhi: Savio Publications.

Directorate of Art and Culture Nagaland.1989. *Folk Tales from Nagaland Part I & II.* Kohima. (Abbreviated FTFN)

Iralu, Easterine.2001. *The Windhover Collection*.Poona: Steven Herlekar. (Abbreviated: TWC)

Nongkynrih, Kynpham Singh, and Robin S Ngangom. (Eds) 2003. *Anthology of Contemporary Poetry from the Northeast*. Shillong: NEHU Publications. (Abbreviated ACPN)

(12)

The Brahmaputra Ecology

Nigamananda Das

The Brahmaputra is a very large water body, a male river, an international river(Dutta 1) and is famous from ancient times through history and mythologies. Having a very rich religious and cultural background, this river is one of world's very important river which flows through four nations of China, Tibet, India and Bangladesh. Though flows through India's Northeast it traverses provinces of Arunachal Pradesh, Assam, Meghalaya and its tributaries flows through other provinces of the Northeast. Though this river has influenced the literatures of the region, it has also influenced the Indian Writing in English from this region. In the Northeast it is known as mainly the river of Assam as it cuts through the whole province of present Assam. It is "to Assam what the Hwang Ho and Yangtse Kiang are to China, the Nile to Egypt and the Mekong to Laos, Kampuchea and Vietnam. It is both life-giver and life-taker. An entire culture spanning socio-economic and political systems, has grown around this great sheet of water" (Hazarika 1995:42). In the present chapter the Brahmaputra lore will be highlighted through the information gathered from non-fictional prose works like *The Red River and the Blue Hill* (1954) by Hem Barua, *Strangers of the Mist* (1995) by Sanjoy Hazarika, *The Brahmaputra* (2001) by Arup Kumar Dutta and "The Brahmaputra: muse, metaphor, source of life"(2005) by Sanjoy Hazarika.

The Brahmaputra Myths:

'Brahmaputra' means son of Brahma, the god of creation. The river is known by so many names that no such river of the world is known. But the name 'Brahmaputra' was first mentioned in a much later work, the *Kalikapurana* written by an anonymous poet of the region around the 10th century A.D. This work also refers to the masculinity of the river. It is one of the few masculine rivers of the world. About the reasons of the masculinity, it is said, "...the foremost being the sheer size of the river, the power of its flow especially during the rains, the muscular currents which eternally ripple across its anguine body the magnificence of the terrain through which it wends its majestic way....according to Hindu belief rivers which flow from east to west are Nads (except Narmada), while those which flow from west to east are Nadis."(Dutta 6). The most ancient name of the river is 'Lauhitya'. In the remote past the name not only referred to the river, but also to the territory through which it flowed.

In the Sabha Parvan of the *Mahabharat* it is mentioned that Bhima in the course of his expedition to the east reached the Lauhitya region and compelled the Mlechcha kings and dwellers of the seashore to pay taxes. In the chapter nine of the Sabha Parvan, Lauhitya is also mentioned in the sense of a river. In chapter nine of the Bhisma Parvan also it is referred as a river along with the names of other rivers. In the *Markandeyapurana*, Canto 58, Lauhitya is mentioned in the sense of a specific area. In the same and preceding canto, Bharatavarsha is depicted as east-facing tortoise resting upon Lord Vishnu, various regions being shown distributed over different parts of its body. Lauhitya and Pragjyotisha as Assam was known in ancient times, lie side by side on the face of the tortoise (ibidem3-4). The Kurmavibhaga section (14.6) of the *Brahatsanhita* also refers to Lauhitya and Pragjyotisha as two different but contiguous lands. Lauhitya lying west of Pragjyotisha comprised what is now Bangladesh, though a portion of it might have been within Pragjyotisha during the reign of Bhagadatta, the Kirata king. Sage Palakapya in his *Hastyayurveda* mentions that his birth place was the hermitage of sage Samagayana, which is located near the Lauhitya sagara. It is mentioned in the *Vayupurana* that the river Lauhitya was a place for pilgrimage and holy for parents' death anniversary rituals. The *Brahmandapurana* (1.51.11) tells of the river Lauhitya which arose from the lake Lohita. In the Buddhist *Charyapadas* belonging to the region, the *Charyapada* is named as *Lauhityapada* of Lauhityadesh (ibidem 4-5).

In the *Raghuvamsa* (mid-fourth century) of Kalidasa, it is mentioned that Raghu crossed the Lauhitya in order to conquer

Pragjyotisha. The other sources of the same story are Kalhana's *Rajtarangini,* the *Mandasor stone pillar inscription* of Yasodharman (525-35 AD), the *Apshad stone- inscription* of Aditya sena (672 AD), the *Pascim Bhag CP Grant* of Sricandra(10th c. AD) and *Tezpur copper-plates and Parbatiya-plates* of Vanamala. Lauhitya in Sanskrit means river of blood or the red river. The word is supposed to have been derived from Austric Lao-Tu or Tibeto Burman Ti-Lao which means 'clear water'. The name has both mythological and literal connotations. The *Kalikapurana* means the name 'Lauhitya' due to the river merging from the Lohita lake. It is also associated with the great Hindu saint Parasurama who washed his hands in its water after committing matricide, thereby eternally staining it with blood. The same has been stated in the *CP Grants* of Indrapala that the river received the name of Lauhitya due to its water washing the mud in the form of thick blood from the axe with which Parasurama chopped off the knotty parts of the trees in the form of necks of the kings (verse: iii).

The creation myth of Brahmaputra/ Lauhitya is narrated in the Srsti-Khanda of the fifth book of the *Padmapurana.* According to it the river's gestation was in the womb of Amogha, the beautiful wife of the sage Santanu, after she had imbibed the semen of Brahma, the Hindu Lord of Creation. Amogha delivered an aqueous form at a place called Yugandhara. In the midst of the water could be seen a celestial god, clad in blue, adorned with a garland of jewels and a crown. The gods saluted the apparition and the spot became the foremost place of pilgrimage(Dutta 6). The Santanu-Amogha myth has also been narrated in the *Kalikapurana.* According to it the great ascetic sage Santanu's wife Amogha, the daughter of Hiranyagarbha, was greatly chaste. Santanu lived sometimes in Kailash, sometimes on the top of mount Gandhamadana. Once while he was at Gandhamadana, he went far away from his *ashram* to gather fruits and flowers. Meanwhile Brahma ,the creator of the universe, came on his swan to his cottage in quest of Santanu and saw his wife. Being enamoured by her beauty, He wanted to have a child by her which would benefit the world. Not recognizing Brahma, Amogha resisted His advances and declared to curse if He molested her. Thereupon Brahma returned Brahmalok after leaving his semen behind. Santanu, on seeing the fire-like semen lying on the ground, learnt of Brahma's visit and his desire. Through meditation he could learn of the Creator's true intention and requested his wife to drink the semen of Brahma and fulfil the desire of the gods. Amogha requested her husband to drink the semen himself and sprinkle it into her womb. She conceived and in due course gave birth to a watery form which in appearance looked exactly like Brahma. Santanu placed this form called Brahmakunda, in the middle of four mountains- Kailash, Gandhamadana, Jarudhi and Sambwarttaka. With the passage of time it grew into a lake, swelling up to forty miles and looking like a vast sea. Brahma himself blessed His child and gave it the name Lauhitya Ganga. Gods and goddesses came to bathe in it and drink its pure water. Much later sage Parasurama cleaved the bank of Brahmakunda and caused the Brahmaputra flow as a river. Behind this activity of Parasurama, there is the tale of his matricide and redemption in the Brahmakund. It is said that his father sage Jamadagni had a fiery temper. He married Renuka and had five sons, amongst whom Parasurama was the youngest. Once Jamadagni sent his wife to the Ganges for fetching water for his worship, where Renuka became enticed to a handsome young king Chitratha, indulged in water sport with his friends and got delay in bringing water. Jamadagni knowing about the reason of delayed got enraged and ordered his five sons to cut off their mother's head. While the four elder sons did not obey his order, Parasurama, ever obedient, picked up his axe and severed his mother's head.

Jamadagni who had divine powers and could the restore the life of his wife , could not redeem his son of his crime and advised him for severe penance and visit of holy places to and take bath there. After moving to all places except Brahmakund, Parasurama could not get any relief. Finally his dip at Brahmakund redeemed him and the bloody axe fell down from his hand. Being convinced of the miraculous sacred nature of the water of the Brahmakund, the sage made it flow to the plains with determination. With his axe, he cut a channel for the Brahmaputra first flowing into the Lohit tank. Then he cleaved the Hemsringa (Swarnaparbat) mountain lengthwise and the great river passed through the sacred land of Kamarupa before flowing into sea. Since it came from the Lohit tank or lake, it is called Lauhitya.

The Indian rivers considered feminine have been invested with sacredness. But Brahmaputra is a masculine river and its name does not occur among the seven rivers considered most sacred in India, namely, Ganges, Yamuna, Godavari, Saraswati, Narmada, Sindhu, and Kaveri. The sacredness of The Brahmaputra is narrated in the

Kalikapurana and *Padmapurana*. The Santanu-Amogha-Parasurama legend/ myth which renders sacredness to the Brahmaputra is supposed to be an offshoot of the totemistic and animistic tribal beliefs prevailing in prehistoric Assam. As in the ancient China, the original home of most of the tribes of the Northeast India, in the ancient Kamarupa or the provinces of present Northeast, virgins were offered to the river-gods. The *Kalikapurana* and *Smritishastras* attribute sacredness to the Brahmaputra as well as the Swarnashree (Subansiri), Vallava (Baroliya), Bhattarik (Jia Bharali) not only in India, but in Tibet and Bhutan. The Tibetar name of the river 'Tsangpo' meaning purifier testifies to the sanctity attributed to it.

The History of the River:

The history of Brahmaputra is the history of the region, i.e. Assam or the whole of Northeast India (Dutta 111). Francis Buchanan Hamilton in his *An Account of Assam* (1807-14 AD) dismisses the origin account of the Brahmaputra as a "monstrous fable". Yet the myth contains the rudiments of the geological truth though it was only a poetic expression of the origin and course of the Brahmaputra. The major earthquakes of the 1897 and 1950 caused massive landslips resulting in the rivers changing their courses and the Brahmaputra also underwent massive changes in its shape, size, course and the walled shape of the Brahmakunda.

Dr. John Peter Wade, who was a member of Captain Welsh's expedition to Assam in 1792-94 records the false views regarding the Brahmaputra or Luit prevailing in the region during that period in his *Account of Assam* (1800). Celebrated adventurer and cartographer, Major Renell, in 1790s propagated his theory that the Tsangpo and Brahmaputra were one and the same river and he had even drawn a map of their probable course. David Scott, the first Commissioner of Assam took much interest in the Brahmaputra and made several arrangements for survey of the Brahmaputra. The accounts of such surveys contradicted local beliefs.

The earthquakes created tremendous devastations in the Brahmaputra. An autobiographer Kiremwati mentions the scenes of flood and devastations witnessed by him in Guwahati:

> ...the Lewis Memorial Hostel located beautifully on the bank of the mighty Brahmaputra. The river was full almost

reaching the Strand Road. With the turbulent flood waters flowed carcasses of animals including even elephants and huge rolls of tree trunks, branches and leaves. Those were thrilling sights seen first time in life. Within a few days, the flowing debris were mixed with dead fishes, some even half dead swimming blindly to the bank. On early mornings, we walked along the road watching those big fishes on the bank. The Government gave orders not to eat the fish. The 15th August earthquake had created cracks in the river bed in upper Assam; and through them sulphurous chemicals gushed out poisoning the water and killing fishes. (34)

The Brahmaputra Biodiversity, Trade, Mysteries, etc.:

The Ahoms as they marched into the Brahmaputra Valley in 1228 AD from upper Burma hailed it as *mung dun chun kham* (the country of golden gardens) (Barua 12). They called the Brahmaputra *Nam-Dao-phi*, meaning the river of star-god (ibidem 6). So far as its eastern source is concerned, the Brahmaputra is bounded with stretches of summer rice and mustard cultivations, thick woods and wild ferns. As this great river runs through the valley, it looks like a ribbon in the midst of the mountain ranges. It is a very rapidly flowing river with strong undercurrents. It has a good number of tributaries. The glacier-fed tributaries on the north are the Subansiri, Bharali, Barnadi, Manas, and the Sonkosh. The tributaries on the south are the Dihing, Disang, Dikhau, Dhansiri, and Kalang. The major river of the region has two river islets in it. The bigger islet is Majuli in the district of Jorhat, which is the chief centre of the neo-Vaishnavite culture of Assam. The smaller islet named Umananda against the city of Guwahati, in the district of Kamrup is a centre of Saivite culture.

The Brahmaputra has extraordinary power. "It carries as much water as almost all the rivers of India put together. It is second only to China's Yangtze Kiang in terms of sediment it carries. One billion tons of silt flows, falls to the river bed, emerges as sandbars or islands in the heart of the river or along its flanks, rich with natural chemicals and food for farming and harvesting, as also places where cattle can be released to graze freely."(Hazarika 2005:245-6).The flood-prone area of this river valley is about 32 lakh hectares which is about 10% of the national total. In major floods as in 2004, not less than 350 embankments collapsed, causing tremendous havoc and extensive loss of lives, property damage, crop destruction and deaths of livestock (ibidem 246-7).

The Brahmaputra devastates and rebuilds with depositing silt every year. At the peak of flooding, it is 18-20 kms wide in Dibrugarh area of upper Assam. The river displaces 20-30 lakh people in Assam every year and many more in other areas. The river is very vibrant in terms of local travel, use and commerce. Every day not less than 80,000- 1,00,000 people travel on the vessels of the Inland Water Transport Department of the State government and the private ferries and boats of all shapes and sizes, ranging from dugouts and small canoes to large steel ships. About 2,000-3,000 animals are also transported as also 3,000-4,000 tons of goods everyday (ibidem 247). Thousands of crores of rupees have been spent over decades to try and control the river through embankments and other methods, but everything has failed and the river has remained uncontrollable. "In length the Brahmaputra is only the twenty-fifth largest river, but in latent energy and dynamism it is equal to any river-system in the world."(Dutta 86). During the British colonial regime and after the valley has lost its ecological glory. The historical annals written by the Muslim invaders and British colonialists are full of references to the luxuriant vegetation, dense, impenetrable jungles and the incredible faunal wealth. Deforestation for tea-plantation, growing human and urban habitation and industrialization has resulted in decimation of forests and rare animals. The British tea planters in those days routinely shot down 2 or 3 rhinoceroses before breakfast. Lakhs of birds were slaughtered. Now the forested area of the valley and hills have shrunk alarmingly. The wild animals are now to be guarded for their protection in sanctuaries. The Brahmaputra Valley has the highest concentration of such sanctuaries, like the Kaziranga and Manas National Parks, Pabha. Sonai-Rupai, Laokhoa, Orang and Pabitora wild-life sanctuaries. Kaziranga has four types of deer, wild-buffalo, rhino, and elephants among them.

The Brahmaputra river system occupies one tenth of the valley and is fed by so many tributaries. It dominates the ecology and climate of the region. The fertile alluvial soil and a prolonged season of heavy rainfall ensures the valley and the surrounding hills with an amazing array of flora and fauna. The marshy, low land areas close to Brahmaputra and some of its tributaries in the plains have a typical wetland ecosystem of savanna or grassland. The grasslands consist of an admixture primarily of *Saccharum Elephantinus* (Barotakher), *Erianthus Ravange* (Ikora), *Imperata Cylindrica* (Ulnkher). *Pollinia Ciliata* (Hankher), *Phragmites Karka* (Khagori), *Arundo Donax* (Nal),etc.

On the foot hills and hills there are tropical and subtropical forests to a height of around 2,000 metres, consisting of big and small trees and thick undergrowth of ferns, creepers and climbers. Among the trees most common are *Acacia Odoratissima* (Jotikorai), *Acacia Marginata* (Korui), *Alstonia Antidysenterica* (Dulkhuria), *Andrachna Trifoliata* (Uriam), *Bignonia Colais* (Parijat), *Butea Frondosa* (Polash), *Careya* (Kombo), *Cassia Fistula* (Sonaru), *Gmelina Arborea* (Gambhari), *Nauclea Cadamba* (Kadamba),*Spondieas Amara*(Amra), *Terminalia Hilka* (Hilika), etc. The dense jungles and grasslands possess a huge range of medicinal and herbal plants and flowers, including numerous varieties of orchids. The grasslands and forests also have a wide range of bamboo, plantain, coconut, etc. In the higher Siang- basin there are deciduous and mixed deciduous forests of walnut, oak, chestnut, pine, spruce, and rhododendron and conifers and alpine meadows at optimum heights.

In the pristine past the Brahmaputra valley was a paradise of wildlife and other part of the country could not boast such colourful faunal and avian presences. The three Asiatic species of rhinoceros- the Asiatic Two-horned or Sumatran Rhinoceros, the lesser one-horned or Javan Rhinoceros were found here. The other bigger mammals included Asiatic elephant, wild buffalo, mithun (bison), etc. Among the carnivores are found the Royal Bengal tiger, leopard, black- panther, wild cat, civet, hyena, jackal, etc. and herbivores are various species of deer such as the barking deer, hog deer, swamp deer, sambar, musk deer, etc. Among the primates are the golden langur, capped langur, and hoolock gibbon. Among the birds are present a colourful variety of cormorants, darters, egrets, herons, pelicans, wild ducks, and geese, storks, teals, kites, eagles, moorhen, jacanas, doves, parakeets, kingfishers, drongos, quails, and others. Snakes in great numbers from pythons and king cobras to banded-kraits and bamboo-snakes, etc. are seen. Some of species now need special attention for preservation as the ecology depletion is posing great threat for their survival.

The Brahmaputra ecology is multidimensional encompassing biodiversity, ritualistic, religious, mystical, mythical, historical, economic, geological, and multiple other aspects. It is as complex as its physical aspects. The culture of the entire region is influenced by this great river. It shall remain the eternal source of life, culture and inspiration for the generations to come. The writings in English produced from the region describing the river have justified to the world the importance of the river.

Works Cited

Barua, Hem (1954) *The Red River and the Blue Hill.* Guwahati: Lawyer's Book Stall, 1991.

Dutta, Arup Kumar (2001) *The Brahmaputra.* New Delhi: National Book Trust.

Hazarika, Sanjoy (1994) *Strangers of the Mist.* New Delhi: Penguin Books,1995.

— (2005) "The Brahmaputra: muse, metaphor, source of life". *IIC Quarterly*: Monsoon-Winter 2005,New Delhi, pp.244-52.

Kiremwati (2009) *Lessons from Life: An Autobiography.* Dimapur: Window Media.

(13)

In Search of Home: A. J. Sebastian's Travails in *My Travels: My Teacher*

Buddhadeb Roy Choudhury

The aim of this paper is to revisit certain pre-established, compartmentalized notions like 'home and abroad' and see whether they actually can be seen as individual entities or parts of narratives in A.J. Sebastian's *My Travels: My Teacher*. Recent debates over the ideas of 'home' and 'abroad' have drawn on the writings of Rushdie, Bhabha and Said. In fact, Bhabha's notion of 'hybridity' and Said's ideas of 'in-betweenness' can be used to re-examine the foundational aspects of the terms. I am constantly reminded of a quote from Rushdie that Meenakshi Mukherjee uses with great effectiveness:

"Home is where your post box is."

All 'homeland' are according to Rushdie 'imaginary'. In fact the idea of 'home' is inescapably rooted in one's culture and community. Given that one's own community may not be real. Similarly, given that 'abroad' is thought of only in terms of opposition to 'home', its own fictive nature cannot be overstated. Categories like 'home' and 'abroad' have been generally seen as fixed, stagnant, predefined or given categories of cognition. In a way these two terms, between them, often have important clues to a community's identity. They have been thought to be specifications one is born with and an indivisible part of an individual's identity that cannot be changed. The land in which one is born is acknowledged as 'home' and the rest 'abroad'. But Sebastian tries to redefine these categories.

Historically, it is a fact that people have always been travelling from one place to another. Departure from a place also means 'interruption in one's ideas of places'. The interruption facilitates the entrance of places in the mind that look similar, thus creating a sense of familiarity. This acquaintance builds places that change into 'home' gradually. It can thus be said that travel has aided in the creation of 'homes' at unknown places. Seen at one level, therefore, there cannot be any fixed trope such as 'home' and 'abroad'. Travel often shows how insecure such terminologies can be. 'Home' and 'abroad' are impermanent classifiers or contingent human constructs that keep changing due to, and in course of, travel. Places left behind exist in memory and turn out to be irretrievable physically for the changes that time brings in. 'Home' and 'abroad' exist in memory and can be seen as being created by imagination. There can be no fixed place designated 'home' or 'abroad' for frequent displacements have rendered these ideas useless.

Travel and travel-related stories often induce several changes in our preconceptions regarding places and people. Such stories related to mobility across borders also change perspectives. The traveler's firsthand experience often influences others' conceptions that formulate views and ideas related to people and places. Travel has also manipulated the ways of 'looking' at 'home and abroad'. Since ages now, the idea of 'home' in the traveler's mind has been influenced by the discoveries abroad. Needless to say, such stories by word of mouth have affected the preconceived notions about distant lands and cultures. Similarly, travel to distant land has drawn our attention to the multiple relocations that invest in the formation of the notion of 'home'. The discovery of America, for example, to the Christian world, was a shock that transformed thinking and helped evolve entirely new ways of looking at 'truth'. The present reading, in fact, reinstates this fact through the voice of the traveler, Father Sebastian. Here, the travels of the narrator take him to distant America in scholarly pursuits and in the process changes his ideas, thoughts and in some ways re-establishes his faith. It is indeed quite interesting to look at his maturity that is an offshoot of his journey beyond the 'seven seas'. His pursuit to comprehend the otherwise mysterious poet G.M. Hopkins engages him in a tryst with travel and helps him realize several 'truths' that were not realized earlier. *My Travels: My Teacher* shows how 'home' and 'abroad' recoil on each other and get interlocked with a fair degree of recurrence in the narrative.

Father A.J. Sebastian sdb (b.1953-) is Associate Professor and former Head of the Department of English, Nagaland University, Kohima. A Gold Medalist in M.A.(English) from Manipur University(1988), he was awarded Ph.D. in 1992 for his study on G.M.Hopkins' poetry. He undertook his Ph.D. research in collaboration with the Hopkins' Center at Gonzaga University, Spokane, USA. He also holds a PG Diploma in Psychological Counselling. An author of twelve books, his travelogue *My Travels: My Teacher* (1998) has been included among contemporary Indian Writing in English(Naik and Narayan 231). A Catholic priest belonging to the Salesians of Don Bosco, North East India, Fr. Sebastian is a very humble personality.

During his first visit to the US, the narrator carries along with him his own impressions of India. Having passed his early years and a part of his youth, he had learnt to see the customs and rituals followed in India as an indispensable part of its culture. In the chapter "To Liberty Island", where he talks of his first meeting with the Simons, a family that migrated to the US long back "With no intention of returning home", the narrator probes every nook and corner of their house to trace 'memories of home'. This is something he is overburdened with during his first few days of visit to the US, when he is constantly in look out for familiar scenes that remind him of his far away 'home' in India. During most of the time of his visit, he often looks back to India as his 'home'.

Meeting the Simons after fifteen years was a historical event. They have all migrated to the U.S. Their family property in South India has been sold too, as they are all U.S. citizens with no intention of ever returning home. The Simons own a Restaurant—"Bengal Tiger"—in a posh area of White plains, N.Y.—frequented often by celebrities seeking Indian cuisine. Suma, his sister, began to shed tears of joy—perhaps recollecting the past when we played together as kids and her feeling rootless in a foreign land, never to return to her homeland. I understood that my presence brought to her mind memories of her socio-cultural roots. Rootlessness cannot be substituted with wealth.(ibidem 14)

He has compartmentalized notions of the categories 'home' and 'abroad'. In other words, 'home' is what time takes away. In a similar manner, his use of the section "To Liberty Island" as a metaphor of freedom could be understood as one of the numerous ways to come to terms with a 'foreign culture', its affluence, seen against the greatness of 'home'. Thus, when the narrator in the chapter "To Liberty Island" comments, "Well, money could make these structures—but money cannot buy a history and culture we have in India symbolized by our monuments." (p.16). He is actually making an attempt to make a connection between 'home' from 'abroad' to compensate the gap brought about by money. Here, he goes back to India and its past to celebrate 'home'. He celebrates home to place abroad as the 'other'.

'Home' is a part of one's memory and cannot be restricted to any cultural or geographical territory. The narrator tries to reinvent his own India in America during the first visit, clearly indicating the difference between 'home' and 'abroad' as given categories of understanding. While on his visit to the Statue of Liberty, the narrator's memory flashes back the sceneries at home that he had left back to experience America. While trying to come to terms with the changes around, he tries to re-invent 'home' using numerous ways. The narrator, for example, thinks of Taj Mahal which he had visited years back and compares it with the Statue of Liberty. Travel enables him to reinvent 'lost homes', at the same time, travel expands the meaning of 'home'. We can suggest that it removes the limits of the traditional categories called 'home' and abroad', as he tries to invent similarities between the two great monuments and recollects his visits.

The concept of 'home' and 'abroad' depends and varies with one's occupation and culture. In the travelogue, the narrator, as a traveler and knowledge seeker voices his quest for knowledge through his poem (p.19), where he creates his home by means of the knowledge he carries with him. The poem is symbolic of his quest for knowledge. He envisages the link that could be employed to look at freedom and 'home' as two mutual concepts, intertwined with one another. To elaborate, the narrator looks at the statue of liberty as a symbol of freedom to link the American dream, voicing his concern for an abode that could offer a safe land to the huge mass of exiles, from across the globe, decades ago. The poem is symbolic of his quest for knowledge. The narrator can visualize a connection between knowledge, struggle, liberty and home. He can see a natural connection between home (India) and abroad (America) as a result of the struggle that went into the creation of the nation, where he had to travel in order to gain knowledge to seek emancipation and recognition. The narrator explores the connection between home and abroad by linking the American dream and the struggle to gain a permanent home in the US, with his own strife to acquire knowledge after an arduous wrestle with fate, circumstances and people. The dream of the people who came to find a safe abode in the US is symbolic of his own dream that inspires him to go to a distant land in search of knowledge and wisdom. Here, he links his idea of freedom with the Statue of Liberty. At the same time, he grows a sense of affiliation with America as home to millions of travelers, like him, and relates it to the underlying relationship between knowledge and travel, through the story of one of his Philosophy teachers. The narrator thinks of home and abroad in terms of knowledge that links both the places for him. At the same time, he is constantly making efforts to discover home at abroad. He in fact carries his home with him wherever he goes, and at times rediscovers it at different places. In chapter III, for example, he tries to re-look at his concept of 'home' to establish a tie with his 'native American brothers' when he says, "I was shocked…" the agony of a race getting extinct." (p.21). In a way, he is constantly in lookout of similarities that remind him of the 'home' left behind in India. In his attempt to familiarize things around him, he tries to re-discover 'home' at places that look similar, reminding him of the places/memories left behind. At the same time, he carries predetermined ideas that keep on recurring in his mind while traveling to places that are new and unknown.

Works Cited

Naik, M.K. & Shyamala A. Narayan. *Indian English Literature: 1980-2000: A Critical Survey*. New Delhi: Pencraft International, 2001.

Sebastian, A.J. *My Travels: My Teacher*. Calcutta: Writers Workshop, 1998.

(14)

Mamang Dai's *The Legends of Pensam* as a Travel Writing

Nigamananda Das

The Legends of Pensam is really a travel account which narrates Mamang Dai's experiences of several important moments of life. Her several visits to various parts of land with friends and relatives and narration of various episodes and legends give shape to this fantastic eco-fiction. The narrative begins with her account of flying with friends in helicopter and viewing the landscape.During the travel she has narrated history, geography,religion, legends and many tales which describe the land and her ecology and culture. The travel narrative begins telling about the mysterious land:

> The helicopter ploughs through the clouds. For a moment it lifts, then seems to take a nose dive as a current of air hits it.I wrap my arms around the empty seat in front of me.
>
> There are six of us in the ageing, struggling machine and everyone is silent or pretending to be asleep. Below us, the big river is calm, frozen between shoals and sandy flats as if locked in a trance.(3)

In chapter two there is a travel account of the narrator and her friend Mona to the village of widows and from there to different places.Travel is very much present in Adi tribe's blood.They travel long distances on foot. They travel in forests and hills to collect fruits, roots and other essentials.On the festivals they travel the road with their dance.The journey to the snow mountains in winter to collect deadly aconitum for preparation of poison is a kind of ritual.Amidst recounting of such travels Mamang narrates the Adi tribals' sense of ecology, tribal religion and ideas of Evil.

The chapter reflects Mamang Dai's postecolonial and cultural concerns about Arunachal's Adi tribe and their various travel accounts. One of the World's 25 biodiversity hotspots, Arunachal Pradesh, the homeland of twenty six tribes with one hundred and ten sub-clans, is criss-crossed by rivers and high mountain ranges running north-south that divide it into five river valleys. Siang (known as the Tsangpo in Tibet) is the mightiest among the rivers and its valley is the territory of the Adi tribe, whose religious and cultural life and postecolonial concerns form the bedrock of the narrative *The Legends of Pensam*(Penguin, 2006). Isolation has so far been the best protection for the pristine ecology of Arunachal. But Mamang through the nineteen chapters of the book upholds how the myriad shapes of pristine ecology and changes during the colonial period and the tribe's life reflect both the cosmic and toxic consciousness. The animistic faith of the people here and their co-existence with the forest ecology and natural world depict the matrix of many mysteries.

The novel combines the pristine ecology with the eroding environment of postcolonial /postecolonial (postecolonial = postcolonial + environmental/ecological) era and depicts consequences due to rapid socio-cultural changes. The importance of the role of miri/ shaman in the Adi Society, the idea of Evil and the postnatural "Toxic Consciousness" (as is evident in postnatural American Fiction of 1980s) are some of the significant concerns of the author in the book.

Memory is crucial in the tribal religion. Memory helps celebration of the festivals and performance of the rituals. After dance and songs, the dancers sit before the Shaman to listen to his sermons. He says, "We are not here without a purpose. Our purpose is to fulfil our destiny"(56-57). He continues, "In the beginning, there was only Keyum. Nothingness. It was neither darkness nor light, nor had it any colour, shape or movement. Keyum is the remote past, way beyond the reach of our senses. It is the place of ancient things from where no answer is received.... From nothingness we have come to be born under the stars, and almighty Donyi-polo, the sun and the moon, whose light shines on all equally, is the invisible force that guides each one of us."(ibidem)

From the ancient way of living to the present day hi-tech living,

Arunachal witnesses rapid ecological and cultural changes. Mamang explores the incidents and accidents and her tribe's concerns and their cultural and ecological inbetweennesses depicting the world of solitude and miracles.

Ecology, which, now-a-days, is used in a much looser sense than the scientific, presents the cultural manifestations and complex realities about anthropocentrism and ecocentrism in the postnatural world(Kerridge 536). In scientific terms, ecology is defined as the study of inter-relationships between organisms and environment, or the study of the structure and function of ecosystems or in a less technical way, the study of structure and fuction of nature(Sen 17). In the age of ecology depletion, we are concerned about homeostasis, i.e. to maintain the biological system to resist change and to remain in a state of equilibrium, which now seems to be impossible in the postindustrial, postnatural world. Broadly speaking ecology refers to the whole of cosmos enshrining both the environment and anti-environment in the world of postecolonialism. Man's imperialism over nature and his ecocidal tendencies have been paradoxical and self- destructive which have invited ecological visions translatable into social, economic, political and individual progammes of action. As such Ecology has been called a subversive science, the first law of which is, "Everything is connected to everything else"(Rueckert 107-8). This subversive science gives the much-needed support to the cause of the preservationist. As a reductionist science, it "undermines not only the growth addict and the chronic developer, but science itself"(Evernden 93).In other words it upholds the economy of nature or the concept of real wild nature as depicted in the romantic literature(Mc Kusick 200-01) as a contrast to the grim environmental threats of the postindustrial times(ibidem 199). Another important aspect of Ecology as a science is its strong connection to a history of verbal expression. "In the medicine rites of early people, shamans sang, chanted, and danced stories to heal diseases or prevent disaster, which they saw as states of disharmony or imbalance in nature"(Howarth 71).Ecology should also be understood as " a new alliance for future radical politics: postcolonial theory and environmentalism" [i.e. postecolonialism (a portmanteau term)] (Nayar 71) to address the issue of ecocide, i.e. the marginalization of Nature, waste colonialism, environmental rascism, discriminatory intellectual property rights, ecocidal "globalizing" scientific technology, the absence of Nature as a category in the theorizing of postcolonialism(ibidem) and commercialism. More importantly, " ecology can be a means for learning how to live appropriately in a particular place and time, so as to preserve, contribute to, and recycle the ecosystem."(Murphy 194)

Mamang Dai, an eco-historian, in her bioregional narrative has narrated the states of disharmony in nature in her homeland Arunachal Pradesh in form of myriad evils. Her debut novel *The Legends of Pensam* (2006) constructs a subaltern history involving Arunachal's Adi tribe, pristine animism, mysterious ecology and its tribes' profound sense and idea of the existence of Evil in numerous forms. Narrating the tribal faiths since the remotest past, she reflects how the Evil is inevitable at every walk of tribals' life and during the current years of ecocidal devastations how the Evil has incarnated in novel shapes. The novel displays and bridges the gap between the tribals' ancient and present mindsets, their innocence and experience, and narrates the elaborate rituals practiced to thwart the Evil and the roots of Evil along with the concepts in the tribal religion, the mystery of the creation of cosmos, the deity of Donyi-polo-the Sun and the Moon, and the multiple incarnations of Evil. The precolonial, colonial and postcolonial times and Arunachal's transgression through the times to the current postecolonial turmoil has beautifully been depicted. The work debates on both deep and shallow ecology, the former demanding recognition of intrinsic value in nature and the latter arguing for preservation of natural resources only for the sake of humans (Garrad 21). As a contrast to the toxic consciousness aroused by the ecocidal/ ecological disaster of postindustrial era depicted in the postnatural American fiction (Deitering 197), the pristine landscape ecology or its postcolonial metamorphosed shape evokes toxicity or psychopathy in the tribal minds in Arunachal.

Mamang Dai, the activist, fictionist, poet and journalist, is a chronicler of the Adi cultural life in Arunachal and an eco-conscious historian who has depicted the life in real situations among the serene, ferocious and mysterious mountains and valleys. Arunachal, one amongst the World's 25 biodiversity hotspots, showcases in the present narrative a profoundly mysterious and magical zone of ecology and nebulous zone of Evils.

Evil is harm-personified. It is immoral or morally bad/ devastative. An extremely unpleasant effect on people, it is connected with the Devil. It is a force that causes bad things to happen (Hornby 524). The world is the essential abode of the eternal existential struggle between good and evil.

Mamang reconstructs the animist principles and the idea of Evil in the ecology of the Adi tribals. Animism is "the belief that plants, objects and natural things such as weather" (literary ecology) have a living soul (ibidem 52). It is a belief in a power that organizes and controls the universe (ibidem). Like human rights, animism pleads for the ecology rights (ecofeminism) and animal rights. The humans smell the Evil in the huge ferocious ecology and the tribes practice the rituals to propitiate the Evil for peace and prosperity of all concerned. The Evil in the Adi culture as has been portrayed by Mamang may be classified as (i) supernatural, (ii) physical, (iii) ecological, (iv) symbolic, and (v) mysterious / magical. These evils essentialize the tribal cultural ecology.

Evils experienced by the Adi tribals have become legends and as such there are some guiding principles to deal with them properly. The *miri* (priest of *Adis*) and the experienced elderly men know many small histories about the role of Evils in afflicting the tribes. The powerful priests have very important role in the Adi society. They propitiate the evil spirits and bless the householders for peace and prosperity. The householders need to perform the rituals in frequent intervals by inviting the miris. If there is any negligence in the rituals the spirits become angry and harm the children and the householders. For good harvests, wellbeing of the domestic animals and the household, rituals and propitiation of spirits, traveling the road during the ponung festival being led by the miri are necessary. The miri has the most important role in driving away the Evil .He "is the storyteller, the healer, the rhapsodist par excellence. He sings the legends, invokes, chants and reminds. In his songs all aspects of the daily life of man are touched from guidelines for construction of shelters to the techniques of making a bow, arrows, the preparation of poison, and the origins of community hunting. If culture is what makes life worth living, then the 'miri' celebrates this in words"(Dai 1998:108). *Miri*(*Nyibu*) "is the mouthpiece of the people to communicate their grievances and suffering to the spirits and to request them for redressal- a sort of intermediary between the human and the spiritual world."(Riba 259)

The Evil is the constant obsession with the Adis. Mamang presents the *Adi* Ecotheosophy along with the various shapes of

Evils in the narrative. The central logic in *Adi* Ecotheosophy is generally explained by the Nyibu as is etched by Mamang:

> In the beginning, there was only Keyum. Nothingness. It was neither darkness nor light, nor had it any colour, shape or movement. Keyum is the remote past, way beyond the reach of our senses. It is the place of ancient things from where no answer is received. Out of this place of great stillness, the first flicker of thought began to shine like a light in the soul of man. It became a shimmering trail, took shape and expanded and became the Pathway. Out of this nebulous zone, a spark was born that was the light of imagination. The spark grew into a shining stream that was the consciousness of man, and from this all the stories of the world and all its creatures came into being. (56)

It is believed by the Adis that "the life of a man is measured by his actions and his actions are good if their origin is pure"(57). The existence of Evil is unavoidable and unpredictable. So every man has to be cautious all the time to pacify the Evil. According to the Adi belief there are numerous spirits and evils residing in the biodiversity.

1.The Supernatural Evils:

Adis believe that all agents of ecology are the abodes of spirit. The trees, forest, lake, river, place, and the like have spirits .They have harmful effects on the humanity. The supernatural evil spirits dealt in the novel are *Biribik,* the Water Serpent, *Mitimili, Dimitayang, Danki,* etc.

(i) Biribik, the Water Serpent: On a night of heavy rain, a fisherman who was all alone with his nets by the river, heard a rushing sound as the water parted and when he looked up at the tree, he was sheltering under, he saw a serpent with a head with horns coiled up in the branches looking down at him. He then ran for his life. He never recovered from the effects of that terrible vision and died within a year of wasting illness. The name of this mysterious serpent was *Biribik.* Hoxo's father had also seen this serpent named *Biribik*(9-10).

(ii) *Miti mili : Mitimili* is a race of supernatural beings. These small, quiet people first prepared the mysterious *si-ye,* that is the yeast used to ferment rice into beer. Before this race disappeared, deranged by strange visions, they gave this sacred powder to mankind warning that this sacred powder had special powers and was to be handled with respect by women only. This white powder mixed with ground ri e, roots and berries are shaped into small flat biscuits called *si-ye* cakes which when eaten make people hallucinate like mitimili race and as such are forbidden before a hunt or a journey(28-29).It is believed that a bad spirit lurking in the *si-ye* makes men go mad.

(iii) *Dimitayang:* It is the lonely spirit who stirs up the lake waters and clutches trespassing men in an embrace of ice. Every winter Adis set out on a journey to the snow mountains to harvest a precious root (the deadly aconitum) for preparation of poison arrows. They trek to the realm of silent waste and hallucinations. After collecting and packing the roots, before return, they address the mountains and air turning in every direction and bid farewell with promises to visit again. They convince the jealous spirits to permit them safe return. But once in spite of all prayers a group of Adis had to face the wrath of *Dimitayang* or some monstrous vision that devoured them in cyclonic wind, dust and cloud. When they reached home and the cyclonic danger subsided they found a dead preying mantis, which they took to be the evil spirit and performed rituals to ward off the danger.

(iv) *Danki: Danki,* the fabulous vessel owned by the *Lotang* family of *Migu* clan, was made of the strongest metal alloy. It was believed to be an auspicious gift from the gods. It had been passed down from father to son for generations in the family. One day the eldest son of the family noticed that the vessel was lying overturned in its usual place. He was surprised to see the moisture and patches of moss on its surface. Since then he was cleaning it everyday and next day finding it filled with bamboo leaves of the variety which is available only in far north hills. After such strange behaviour, the danki was afterwards split into two halves and disappeared. With that the fortunes of the *Migu* clan declined and the last son bearing the *Lotang* title who lived to the ripe age of ninety-eight had no male heir (62-63).

2. Physical Evils:

The dense forest ecology of Arunachal enshrines evils in different shapes which harm the *Adi* tribals physically and mentally. Since time immemorial these elements of danger have been source of fright for all. The tribals have been trying all the time to escape these evils in spite of which even they encounter the same evil time and again. Hunting accidents, snakes, the *si-ye* and several other small or big things including elements of nature like wind, river, treacherous paths and trees which some day or other harm them in different ways and situations are supposed to bear the evil spirits in them.

(i) Hunting Accidents:

Since the time of the arrival of firearms into Arunachal hunting has been a passion. Some times hunters are mistaken as animals by their fellow hunters and are killed. Hoxo's father, Lutor , the famous chief of the *Ida* clan was killed in such hunting accident. Many such young men were killed in hunting accidents. Interestingly in dead Lutor's shirt pocket a small fish was found. The fish was slippery and mashed and the scales stuck to his skin. There were many surmises about the existence of the small fish. Lutor might have caught it in one of the small streams for his son Hoxo. Or it might be the spirit manifestation of the Evil which caused the accident. Lekon, the husband of Pinyar also died in a hunting accident. Kalen was killed by Loma in such hunting accident. These accidents are ferocious events. Adis believe that some spirits are instrumental for such accidents.

(ii) The Python Spirit:

A tragedy that befell Karyon Togum family of Yabgo village was that Togum's son Kepi was suffering from fever for long and his condition was not improving. Kepi was taken to the hospital at Pigo, and was given tablets and an injection. But his condition did not improve for long. The child was crying and his small torso twisted stiff and unmoving. Someone told the parents to think about performing a special ceremony because it was the spirit of a snake that had coiled around the body of their son. So it was Hoxo, the nyibu, who was called to conduct the ceremony. Hoxo narrated from his vision how Togum killed a python in the timber depot in the middle of the forest. It was fact. Togum who had no experience of hunting, had killed a python which was inside the pile of logs, for which the elephant which saw it was not drawing the logs. Togum killed this terrible python with two gun shots. The spirit of the python took revenge on his son Kepi. So Hoxo had to perform the serpent ritual all night, chanting and negotiating with spirits calling them to restore the sick child. But the spirits had moved away to a place beyond recall. "They are the most dangerous ones, the ones who go away and never return", Hoxo said (24).

(iii) The Tiger/ Fire Spirit:

Pinyar, the widow, who was deserted by Orka, her first lover, and whose husband Lekon died in a hunting accident, was living all alone. Once her house caught fire and everything was burnt down. As per rule, she was banished to the outskirts of the village and had to undergo the taboo (28). This fire is generally caused by a spirit known as the Tiger Spirit or Fire Spirit. During the period of taboo when the Adi householder is banished to the outskirts of the village no one could go and eat with him/her for fear of provoking the Tiger Spirit which follows the people to their home. The angry fire spirit completely gutted twenty houses in Duyang village and the village had to perform special ritual to propitiate the angry fire spirit (122).

In the old days fire watching had been a sacred duty. All young men were expected to give their time, taking turns to stay together in the bango, the boy's dormitory, and keep vigil through the night (121). The angry fire spirit causes immense harm.

(iv) *Si-ye:*

Si-ye is the yeast which is used to ferment rice into beer. It has special powers and should be handled with respect. "There is a bad spirit lurking in si-ye that makes men go mad" (29). So *si-ye* cakes are strictly forbidden before a hunt and journey.

(v) Black Moments:

Kamur, the son of Pinyar from Orka, was well-settled in the town of Pigo, in a brick building, as a clerk in a government department. One afternoon, all of a sudden, he killed his infant daughter and younger son with a sword and started chasing his wife, who was in the kitchen, holding the bloodied sword. When she screamed and the neighbours came out, he realized what he did and then dropping the sword, he fell to the ground blubbering and weeping. He could not remember what happened. It was an evil spirit which traded his soul for that terrible hour and he had no memory of those black moments. As per the Adi belief men and spirits had been brothers. But afterwards it was a nebulous zone that divided the worlds of spirits and men.

3. Symbolic Evils:

Turmoils in the tribal world happen due to some fault/error in human behaviour or due to the negligence in rituals. When such turmoils take place, the old people of the village sit around speculating on clan titles and origins, on births, loves, marriages and spirits and ghosts. The right or wrong kind of marriage, the right or wrong kind of life, could always be traced to something in the blood. Down the line certain traits appear suddenly, in a nephew, an aunt, or a great grandson. Some blood lines are almost taboo to mention. It is due to the defect in the blood that some see visions visited by spirits, etc.

Beyond this phenomenon, there are other things, or agents which represent certain good or evil values; for example, the tooth of a tiger and a wild boar are symbols of luck and success (35), whereas the aubergine plant growing into a size of a tree with small poisonous-looking flowers, and long bloated fruit becomes a ghostly tree that creates psychopathic behaviour in people who come under it. It is believed that after sunset women should not linger by streams and rivers, because those places are visited by ghosts and spirits. Again it is believed that some people are auspicious and some inauspicious (83).

The modern times have brought in rapid changes. The inconveniences in living in the hilly terrain in Arunachal have been frustrating those who have the experience of living in the beautiful and bountiful plains. The remote land of *Adis* is disturbing the new generation. That is why Arsi being unable to raise a flower garden cursed, "Is this a place to live?...Why did our forefathers choose this place? Surely we are outcasts dumped in this bone and knuckle part of the world!"(74). This statement echoes the Mc Luhanian concept of anti-environment that urges retribalizing "the structure of psychic and social awareness... unearthing the paradoxical nature of electronic culture"(Ajayakumar 106). In ancient days crime was not committed deliberately. If anybody was committing crime, he was observing taboo or was punished. But now under extremely changed circumstances, it is difficult to control things. The postcolonial development is bringing disaster in the world of *Adis*. Due to increase in crime in forms of robbery, extortion, drug addiction and the like, the new roads are being considered great evils. " The road was bad news" (151).The roads bring "Outsiders. Thieves. Disease"(156). The theft of electric poles, the news of arson, drugs and all evils have been pushing the tribes in Arunachal into turmoil. In the era of ecology depletion, the tribals have been extremely obsessed. Out of frustration, they are no more obsessed of their ancient Evils, for which they have been nostalgic now. The ecology depletion has made them revolutionary ecofeminists. In irritation and anger they curse now: "Oh! What a place! Cursed, ill chosen, disturbed!"(168).

4. Ecological Evils:

Ecology comprises of both biodiversity and abiodiversity. Before the advent of colonizer *migluns* into Arunachal, it was only the home land of the tribes. No road links were there. High mountains, dense forest full of wild animals, poisonous snakes and insects, rivers, streams, gorges and intense valleys proved the land a difficult terrain, and its people wild and innocent. The people practiced animism, believed that everything had a soul and the spirits, if not propitiated, would harm them. Beyond that, elements of nature like wind, water, fire, sky and space have also spirits which avenge humans. Life becomes difficult because:

> It rains during the day, it rains all night. It can rain non-stop for sixty two days at a time. Not a peep of sunshine. Not a breath of wind. Every summer the tangled undergrowth clinging to the hills is swept away by the downpour, causing landslides that cut off all communication and links. (37)

The fierce hissing of rain would cover the land like the sea. It seems that the heavens brush very close to the earth. The nature displays its wilderness:

> The wild fruit born... is of unknown family, bittersweet, pungent, often misshapen and hardy, or swollen to an unnatural size. Hidden by mountains and covered by a charcoal sky the forest and rivers become battlefields ferocious with the struggle for survival. Astonishing plants with gills spring up in clumps. Delicate green shoots unfurl into monstrous fans and umbrellas with stinging hair. The wild berry covers itself with ants. Insects like miniature armadillos emerge out of nowhere and move about briskly until a flick of the broom transforms them into crumpled balls protected with green headlights. (36-37)

After the early 1800s when the first white priests, surveyors and soldiers had begun arriving in the region, rapid changes came over the landscape. The *migluns* struggled hard to make the land inhabitable for them. With the thunder of cargo trucks and bulldozers, and the shouts of men the jungle burst into flame as the mountaintops were blown off and the labour force struggled to claw their way through the rubble and drag the wretched road across the mutilated hills. There are ferocious places like the Lake of No Return, where so many airmen had lost their lives flying the Himalayan Hump during the war. About the nature of the forest a British officer wrote in his notebook: "The forest is like an animal. It breathes all around us... like a green snake out of the decaying vegetation....The trees are enormous and sinister" (52).The destruction of forests by the colonizers was politically motivated. There was an evil motive behind it of "alienating natives from ceremonies and rituals... for their replacement by alien systems"(Tripathy 101). This attempt was destined at taming the wild also. As a result of the decimation of nature, there are now no tall trees where spirits of our ancestors dwelt. With the fall of trees, they became homeless and went away leaving us unprotected (42). Other evil spirits residing in trees or hills and valleys became jealous and angry and harmed the humans. With the cutting of trees, the canopy of shelter and tradition has fallen and the wind and sun are burning our faces now. Besides that the wild rivers and mountains seem to be hungry for human lives. They are the ecological evils.

5. Mysterious/Magical Evils:

The spirits of wind, place, big trees, rivers and streams which harm the humans are mysterious and magical. Nemen, it was said, was carried away by wind and she was found dead at the water point beyond the orange trees. The ghostly aubergine plant that poisons the minds of men who go under it is mysterious like the behaviour of the evil spirits.

Myriad landscape of Arunachal and her people who consider themselves "peripheral people"(190), their living amidst many religious rituals and festivals, ancient memories, many events and incidents of life make them integral to the rhythms of ecology. Shaman's stories elaborate the truths and realities of life. He is the guardian of time and destiny. He is also the mentor of every soul and regulator of life and activities of the individual. As such he upholds the ecological vision and maintains both the deep and shallow ecology.

Adis, the followers of animism, have profound knowledge about the evil spirits, mysteries of creation and ways of nature. Exorcism, rituals for the propitiation of the evil spirits, listening to the miri/shaman about the mysteries of the creation and the old stories, legends, small histories of the land and the travel accounts of the ancestors keep them occupied in exploring the essentialism of life. The idea of Evil is the guiding principle of a cautious life that helps a tribal escape the danger at different stages of life and also enables him maintain sustainable social development and cultural integrity.

Works Cited

Ajayakumar, P.P.(2002) " 'Global Village': The Anti-Environment in Mc Luhan's Vision", *Littcrit* 53,June,(106-12).

Dai, Mamang(1998) "Reviving (Lost) Traditions".*Dailogue*. Doimukh:NEIFES,(100-08).

__________(2006) *The Legends of Pensam*. New Delhi: Penguin India.

Deitering, Cynthia.(1996) "The Postnatural Novel: Toxic Consciousness in Fiction of the 1980s".*The Ecocriticism Reader*(eds.) Cheryll Glotfelty and Harold Fromm.Athens: The University of Georgia Press, (196-203).

Evernden, Neil(1996) "Beyond Ecology: Self, Place, and the Pathetic Fallacy".*The Ecocriticism Reader*(eds.) Cheryll Glotfelty and Harold Fromm. Athens:The University of Georgia Press,(96-104).

Garrad, Greg(2007).*Ecocriticism*.London:Routledge.

Hornby, A. S.(2005) *New Oxford Advanced Learner's Dictionary*. New Delhi: OUP

Howarth, William(1996) "Some Principles of Ecocriticism".*The Ecocriticism Reader* (eds.) Cheryll Glotfelty and Harold Fromm.Athens: The University of Georgia Press,(69-91).

Kerridge, Richard(2006) "Environmentalism and ecocriticism". *Literary Theory and Criticism*(ed.) Patricia Waugh. New Delhi: OUP,(530-43).

Mc Kusick ,James C.(2007) ."Ecology". *Romanticism* (ed.) Nicholas Roe. New Delhi: OUP, (199-218).

Murphy, Patrick D.(2000). "Ecofeminist Dialogics". *The Green Studies Reader*(ed.) Laurence Coupe. London: Routledge,(193-197).

Nayar, Pramod K.(1999). "Postecolonial Theory: A New Ontopology and Radical Politics".*Journal of Contemporary Thought* (eds.)P.C. Kar et al (Summer), (71-84).

Riba, Moji.(2000) "Prayers for New Gods....The Institution of Nyibo of the Adis and Its future": *Tribal Religion: Change and Continuity*(ed.) M .C. Behera. New Delhi: Commonwealth Publishers, (257-63).

Rueckert, William.(1996) "Literature and Ecology: An Experiment in Ecocriticism". *The Ecocriticism Reader* (eds.) Cheryll Glotfelty and Harold Fromm. Athens: The University of Georgia Press,(105-23).

Sarkar, Amitabha & Samira Dasgupta.(2000). Ethno-ecology of Indian Tribes.Jaipur: Rawat Publications.

Sen, David N.(1978).*Concepts in Indian Ecology*. Jalandhar: Shoban Lal Nagin Chand & Co.

Tripathy, Jyotirmaya.(2007) "Decimation as Civilization in Colonial America: A Theoretical Overview" *JSL*, Spring,(100-15).

(15)

Four Contemporary Playwrights from Northeast India

Bhaskar Jyoti Gohain

C.G. Pai is a contemporary Indian playwright who has great passion for theatre and philosophy. Like Wairokpam Kamni Singh, he is best known for his social plays with symbolic characters. C.G. Pai is associated with Department of Gastroenterology, Kasturba Medical College, Manipur. His play *Playing At Trains* is entirely modern in spirit and form. The characters in the play are symbolic of its kind. The play centres round one main plot—story of Subbu, Ravi, Tom and Mohan's journey back home after working overseas. The play is less of action and more of dialogues. Dialogues are crisp and flaky. They are entirely functional, making for quick exchanges between characters. Monologues are also employed wherever necessary but are given as "thoughts". The style is an interesting mixture of modern English colloquialisms ("damn") and Indian words and expressions ("na"; "yaar", "pav bhaji"; "the brain goes phut"). Moreover, in the play the playwright blends both the dramatic and narrative techniques in a very meaningful way. Certain memorable moments in the past life of a character are first narrated by the character himself and then are dramatized. Acting-spots keep on shifting from place to place. Now, on a quiet railway platform with crickets' sound, now in a busy noisy street with sounds of blaring horns, bicycle bells and so on. This frequent shifting of place is made because the very nature of the play itself demands it. Nevertheless, it gives a unique touch to the overall dramatic effects in the play. Moreover, performing at various acting-spots by the day and the night enhances the pictorial quality in the play.

Wairokpam Kamni Singh from Manipur is an another outstanding theatre personality in India whose plays are widely quoted and translated into various Indian regional languages including English. He is not only a playwright but also an actor, poet and director. He is best known for his social plays with highly symbolic characters. He has won many laurels as a playwright as well as a director, both at the state and national levels. The film "Shikayat" is the Hindi adaptation of his Manipuri play *Wakat.* His distinguished repertoire includes three poems. His short play entitled *a soul, still wishing to stay alive: Hing-ning-liba Thawai* was first staged in July, 1977 at the All Manipur short play competition organized by the Theatre Centre, Manipur. It is one of his short plays that have been widely translated into differed regional languages. It is a short play pregnant with thoughts, and characters pregnant with symbolic significance. Abstract concepts are personified and are made to move and talk. The character "Thawai" is soul personified. Similarly, "Sharu-shing" is bones/skeletons personified and the character "Ashiba", the dead personified. Just like in a beast fable, here in the play also one can find birds, viz. vultures moving and talking. The play has one main plot and is based on the concepts that all the living beings in this world, whether mobile or immobile, have to accept the inescapable duty of life which is the law of nature. Dialogues are written more or less in verse form than in prose. Lines are of irregular length, long and short. They are almost written in aphoristic style and are nearly poetical in nature. The language is also highly metaphorical. The play has been originally written in Meiteilon. It has been translated from Meteilon into English by T. Bijoy Kumar.

In India, there exists almost in all linguistic regions, its own theatre traditions which in turn have influenced modern Indian theatre in many ways. All these regional plays written in respective regional languages contribute much towards the growth and development of Indian theatre. These plays are being translated into different languages including English and they exhibit apparently local colour and sentiment, besides dealing with things universal. They present the contemporary society in all its manifestations. Side by side, there are also plays written purely on the basis of the epics.

Gonesh Gogoi's *Revenge of Shakuni* is based on a story taken from the epic *Mahabharata.* On the other hand, Arun Sarma's *The*

Wolf Boy deals with the hopes and aspirations, morals and values of the contemporary society. Arun Sarma is a contemporary playwright from Assam. His repertoire includes published plays, novels, telefilms, teleplays and television scripts. He is the recipient of several prestigious awards including the Sangeet Natak Akademi Award in 2003 for his contribution to Indian theatre. He was also honoured with the Sahitya Akademi Award in 1998 for his brilliant novel *Ashirbadar Rang*. Having worked in the area of school education and broadcasting, he has also served on the the editorial board of the *The Assam Tribune* and also served as the editor of *Purbanchal*, an Assamese biweekly. His play *The Wolf Boy* is about the deprivations of rootless people. *The Wolf Boy* represents the plight of minority communities. The play has one main plot—story of a small boy brought up by wolves in a forest and his growing into a perfect gentleman under the care of a university professor of Anthropology. It is a long play in fifteen scenes. There are eight characters and each character is given due importance from the point of view of the overall development of action in the play. The pictorial quality in the play is enhanced by dress-code that suits a character's position and profession. Furthermore, music, sound and spot-light give additional dramatic effects to some specific dramatic situations. Dialogues are purely functional. The play was originally written in Assamese and was first published in *Nilachal*, a weekly Assamese magazine in the year, 1966. It was first performed at the State Drama Festival Competition, 1982. The play has been translated from Assamese into English by Ruma Phukan. The English translation of the play is purely a literal one with occasional transliteration work creeping in, in such original script words, viz, *Majani, Deuta, Shlokas*, etc. The name of the play in Assamese is *Kukurnesia Manuh*, which has been translated literally into English, i.e. *The Wolf Boy*.

Gonesh Gogoi is an another eminent Assamese dramatist who has authored four dramas: *Shakunir Pratishodh, Daxa Yajna, Harischandra* and *Kashmir Kumari*. All these plays are translated into English from Assamese. The play *Shakunir Pratishodh* is translated into English from Assamese by Prashanta Kumar Bordoloi as *Revenge of Shakuni*. The source of the play is the Indian epic *Mahabharata*, which is that inexhaustible literary reservoir from which any Indian writer can draw materials for his creative work. War forms the backdrop of the play. It is a war between Pandavas and Kauravas.

But, the central figure in the play is Shakuni-the clever uncle of Duryodhana. All the attention in the play is focused on him, as he himself once said towards the ends of the play:

> I'm the inaugurator of this devastating war and only I will draw its curtain.

The play is full of action. Dialogues in the play have a poetical quality and the style of its language is a little elevated one than that of an ordinary language. The tone of the language is authoritative as well. The play has been written in three acts. In the first act, first scene, a bard enters and unfurls the essence of the play to the audience by singing a ballad. The dramatic and the narrative techniques of the play are very skillfully handled by the playwright. Certain events and incidents that happened in the past are just narrated instead of performing them on the stage. What really attracts the attention of readers to the play is the selection or choice of the kind of story from which materials are drawn upon while keeping its relevance to contemporary society. Like Girish Karnad, Ganesh Gogoi too tries to give a contemporary meaning to an old legend as well as the facts that are embedded in the history of human experience.

Works Cited

Gogoi, Gonesh. *Revenge of Shakuni: Indian Literature* 231, Tr. Prashanta Kr. Bordoloi, New Delhi: Sahitya Akademi, Jan-Feb. 2006.

Pai, C. G. *Playing At Trains :Indian Literature* 230. New Delhi: Sahitya Akademi, Nov.-Dec, 2005.

Sarma, Arun. *The Wolf Boy*. Tr. Ruma Phukan. : *Fresh Fictions*. ed. Geeta Dharmarajan. New Delhi: Katha, 2005.

Singh, Wairokpam Kamni. *a soul still wishing to stay alive* .Tr. T. Bijoy Kumar: *Fresh Fictions*. ed. Geeta Dharmarajan. New Delhi: Katha, 2005.

(16)

The Art of Ratan Thiyam

Nigamananda Das

Ratan Thiyam is not only a pioneer theatre personality in Manipur or Northeast or India, but all over the world. His plays have been staged in more than forty cities in different countries of the world. These plays present a remarkable juxtaposition of tradition and modernity. Through the presentation of opposites and conflicts, he asserts clear message that unless the mankind resists war, halts the rat race of a frenetic existence and reverses the destruction of the planet, we live on; the fatal doomsday cannot be avoided. A staunch patriot in Thiyam voices the environmental concern, when he says, "The human race has come a long way, especially due to technological advancements, but in the course of our development, we have somehow lost touch with our emotions. The more we become advanced, the more our society is forgetting its traditions, roots and the importance of human relationship"(2008:111-12). His plays interpret the drastically changing world and the need of traditional wisdom to set the disturbed world into order. Rooted in the soil of Manipur, the plays reflect cultural matrices of the land and ecological order and disorders.

The proposed paper seeks to analyze the theatrical art of Ratan Thiyam and his four plays entitled *Wahoudok* (Prologue), *Hey Nungshibi Prithivi*(My Earth, My Love), *Chinglon Mapan Tampak Ama*(Nine Hills, One Valley) and *Chakravyuha,* in the light of ecological humanism and cultural parameters that sustain the human society.

Ratan Thiyam is an artist par excellence in theatrical production, direction and popularization. He is both an artist and activist. The theatrical art and its propagation has been his religion for quite some years. His devotion to the stagecraft and tenacious efforts to carry forward the tradition is really praiseworthy and that has bestowed upon him multiple awards making him a charismatic personality in many countries of the world. For his concerns for Manipuri theatre as well as the world theatre and concerns for human values in this decadent world of value degeneration, he can be applauded as a humanist or more particularly an ecological humanist for his profound ecological concerns.

Humanism is "based on the premise that the fullest development of the individual is an end in itself, apart from the reward of an afterlife that the intelligent satisfaction of the body is almost as important as the development of the mind, and that man can attain truth through the critical use of his intellectual powers. Humanism has been generally used to describe any ethical system which is seen as man's highest duty, the fullest possible development of human potential"(Lemon 112). Many humanists stress the need for a rounded development of an individual's diverse powers, physical, mental, artistic, moral, etc. The term "humanist" in our time "connotes those thinkers who base truth on human experience and reason and base values on human nature and culture, as distinct from those who regard religious revelation as warrant for basic truth and values"(Abrams 123).

Ecological humanism (eco-humanism) is a theoretical coinage to humanize ecology, and to give humanist/ human dimensions to ecology. Ecology in its multiple manifestations essentially refers to the physical macro-nature and the human spiritual world including all moral and ethical values that govern the human activities.

Ratan Thiyam as an artist humanist has made profound deliberations on the indigenous traditional knowledge and exercises of eco-humanism in his plays. The present paper is an attempt to expound his strategies in his plays to humanize ecology.

The first play in his *Manipur Trilogy* entitled *Wahoudok* (Prologue) is a play of four scenes which explicates the creation myths as per the Metei traditional folklore and mythology. How the Universe was created out of the Void with the very first utterance of the first Word by the Almighty and this complex world continued expanding exploiting the bounty of nature and how exploitative activities of the human mortals have brought about disasters and have dragged the whole humanity into difficulties. The play is profoundly prophetic in tone and it links myth with reality.

The Almighty Lord cried "*Hoong*" and out of the black void of space appeared the gaseous halo of seven colours and He with the help of the gods and goddesses went on creating the various agents of this universe. The Mother Goddess hinted at Her sons to create humans limb by limb in the image of the Almighty. As human civilizations flourished, wars, diseases, and scarcity of food led to political and economic difficulties. With the suffering of human beings, ill feelings among themselves spread.

At this juncture in the third scene appear seven *Maichous,* the prophets, who predict the future of the civilization:

> Man will turn into beast; man will stop loving man, man will devour man. Fire breathing out from the mouths of the rich nations with sufficient arms and military power will start burning the weaker nations. Fortresses will start fighting one another. Fire will start burning with earth as wick and water as fuel. Killing and wanton murder, arrest and kidnapping will happen more frequently, news of wars and devastations will reverberate in all the four directions and eight corners. Wrong pens will start scribing on departmental scrolls forcibly; the purse of the dignitaries looking after the departments will start bulging. (Thiyam 2008:11)

The predictions depicted/ envisioned by the seven *Maichous* are characteristic of the environmental apocalypse in different epochs. The prophets by their apocalyptic prophecies have warned the civilizations about the ecological disasters that would pose dangers for the civilizations. Thiyam by presenting the same has played the role of a prophet. He has also provoked the mankind to look back to the history of civilization to learn how to behave with the nature and to maintain both the physical and spiritual ecology for the benefit and good future of the civilization. The play enshrines a wide spectrum of human evolution right from the birth of the Universe based on the myths of the *Meteis* to the modern times, divided into four distinct episodes: the birth of the Universe, the creation of living beings, the outset of human civilization and the modern times.

His play entitled *Hey Nungshibi Prithivi*(*My Earth, My Love*) hovers round the ecological crises due to the wars, attacks and harmful human activities in degenerating the ecology. The history of mankind unravels horrendous images of the past devastations. The history of Manipur is a witness of the seven year Burmese devastation, when thousands of people being tortured mercilessly were dragged away as slaves and hordes of children had been suffocated to death with the smoke of burning chilies. The Germans packed lakhs of people in concentration camps and made them starve to death. To exchange killing of their five hundred thousand people at Stalingrad, the Russian soldiers raped fifty thousand German women. To retaliate the Japanese attack on Pearl Harbour, the Americans dropped atom bombs on Hiroshima and Nagasaki causing immense ecological disaster. The genocide during the Khmer Rouge regime in Kampuchea is also the utmost disturbing accident in human history.

The history is crippled with atrocities on women, children, animals and life sustaining biodiversity. So there have been attempts at different times in the past and present eras to negotiate peace and prosperity. In the play, seven sisters, (celestial nymphs) weave a cloth, the traditional symbol of love, peace and honour, in a loom for offering to the Almighty with a prayer to put a stop to war and bring peace to the Earth. History is personified as an old man. The nymphs assuming the shapes of birds and human incarnates fly around the world and specially to see the demolished Ottoman bridge on the Neretva river built by Suleyman, the Sultan of Mostar. The image of colossal Buddha at Bamiyan, and appearance of Mother Teresa to accept the discarded baby are symbolic of man's awareness of ecological humanism, which has sustained the religion and life in this world.About the play says Ratan, it "is a poem by birth, a collage of many thoughts and a presentation of contemporary ideas without a conventional plot-a document of a restless society and its political turmoil where the sufferers are only poor people."(qtd. by Gardner 111). Prof. Chuck Berg praises Thiyam for his minimalist staging infused with wonderful tale. He says: "Thiyam, by reframing the issues of modernization through the lens of his native culture transcends the usual polarized terms of the globalization debate by means of the poetics of Manipuri speech,music,movement and myth."(124)

His play entitled *Chinglon Mapan Tampak Ama* (*Nine Hills, One Valley*) refers to the glory of the culturally rich Manipur, the mystical land comprising of nine concentric ranges of hills encircling a valley.

Invoking the evil spirits and propitiating them for the peace and prosperity of the denizens is a way to realize the Deep ecology. This play of three scenes presents the cultural traditions of the land in propitiating the Evil in the animist principles. The seven wise men awaking from the ominous dream, go back to slumber again to dream of the same with pressing intensity. Time is personified as a demon that brings in the Evils which need propitiation for allowing better future for humankind. In the second scene the Seven Wise men wake up again to see their dreams turned into reality. Genocide, political instability, venality, unemployment and extortion by unlawful elements have disrupted the land. So the wise men come forward to protect and save their people from the miseries. In the third scene the seven wise men call upon the celestial nymphs and the mothers to help them write a new book of knowledge drawing upon the ancient scholars, ancestors and preceptors, who have been the pillars of wisdom. The completed book contains the wisdom of freedom, peace, religion, politics, economics, human rights and responsibilities for the present times. The seven wise men leave behind the book of knowledge for the younger generation.

In the epilogue the mothers relate to their children the glory of the past, the evergreen world of nature along with the unwelcome changes of the recent times. Symbolic lights are lit on the hill tops and valleys to enlighten and remind the people of their past glory.

In his interview taken by Kavita Nagpal and Geeti Sen, Thiyam has asserted the goal of writing plays by telling: " ... a production needs to relate to the making of history: to the political situation, to religious factors, to socio-economic conditions. The sufferings of human beings became the theme of some of my plays-..."(2006:227). In his play *Chakravyuha* he has exemplified the crisis of spiritual ecology that is rampaging today's world by employing the myth of Chakravyuha from the *Mahabharat*. The killing of Abhimanyu, the greatest youth hero of the Mahabharat war by the Kauravas by flouting all the norms of war, is a great crime. Nobody could resist Abhimanyu, the son of the greatest Mahabharat hero Arjun and Subhadra, the sister of Lord Krishna, and he created utmost havoc in the Kaurav camp through his irresistible valiance. To destroy this evergreen ecology of cosmic and earthly power the *saptarathis* (seven great heroes of the Kaurav camp) violated the norms of war and all at a time attacked him after killing the pilot of his chariot and making him weaponless and helpless. So this greatest youth hero of all the times and wars in his last words before breathing the last uttered the following words which remind all the generations to shun the blind egos and criminal use of power:

> Adieu, O mother earth. And you humans full of carnal desires, jealousy and corruption....As I leave for the last time I look at you, my mother earth....
> O great Kings and emperors of this world, ensconced under canopies of power....But you have polluted this fair and pure earth with your blind egos and criminal use of power....The search for truth will remain unfulfilled.(1998:51)

Arjun in the second scene before narrating to Subhadra about the secret and difficult way of entering the Chakravyuha and the related *mantras* hinted at the maladies in this world against the humanism:

> Where there is no affection amongst brothers, relatives and kinsmen; where corruption and selfishness are consecrated; in this world of disfigured human nature, he will be another addition. (ibidem 30)

Subhadra also expresses her concern over the characteristics of time:

> In this age, when truth has started changing into falsehood like a chameleon changing colour, those of us who have reached middle age will meet the same fate. I don't know how the future generations are going to survive this age where fiends operate in human disguise.(ibidem 31)

The prologue of the play presents the evolution of theatre as the fifth veda and evolution of all Vedas and human sciences, thereby presenting the essence of literary eco-humanism and the value standards. So the Sutradhara recites the critique on the human sciences and humanism as the essence of exploration of Self and realization of human responsibility in sustaining the ecology and guarding its maintenance:

Jagraha pathyamrigvedat samabhyo geetamevacha/
Yajurvedadabhinayan rasanarthavanadapi/
Vedopavedaih samvaddho natyavedo mahatmana/
Evam bhagavata srishto brahmana sarvavedina.(ibidem 5)

Dedicating his *Manipur Trilogy* to his parents Ratan Thiyam has claimed that it is his parents who have baptized him in the religion of humankind. So Thiyam, the artist humanist is an explorer of human values through the enactment of his thoughts depicting human activities and concerns and realizing human responsibility towards maintenance of ecology in its several manifestations providing utility to mankind. In his understanding the concept of eco-humanism enshrines respecting both Deep and shallow ecology as well as spiritual ecology.

Works Cited

Abrams, M.H. *A Glossary of Literary Terms.* New Delhi: Cengage Learning India, 2005.

Berg, Chuck. "Indian Show proves worldly": *Capital Journal, 4 Nov.,* 2006: *Manipur Trilogy*,pp.123-25.

Gardner, Lyn. "Review of *Nine Hills, One Valley*": *Manipur Trilogy,* pp. 110-11.

Lemon, L.T. *A Glossary for the Study of English.* New Delhi: OUP,1974.

Thiyam, Ratan. *Chakravyuha.* Calcutta:Seagull Books, 1998.

—. *Manipur Trilogy.*Guwahati: Wordsmith, 2008.

—. "Re-inventing Tradition in Performance": *IIC Quarterly.*New Delhi:IIC, 2006.

(17)

Mitra Phukan's *The Collector's Wife* vis-à-vis Arundhati Roy's *The God of Small Things*: A Comparative Study.

Narendra Tiwary

Mitra Phukan and Arundhati Roy are celebrated women novelists in Indian English literature. They belong to different regions of India. Mitra Phukan is an Assamese. Arundhati Roy is a Malayalee. But both of them have certain common features as novelists. Mitra Phukan's *The Collector's Wife* has been written against the background of the state of Assam. In her novel *The God of Small Things,* Arundhati Roy has presented the picture of her own state Kerala. Suffering of women forms the core issue in her fiction. Both the novels deal with postcolonioal socio-political issues of the respective states. The issues are personal as well as public; local as well as universal. Thus, a comparative study of the novels *The Collector's Wife* and *The God of Small Things* is essential and interesting.

In *The Collector's Wife,* Mitra Phukan has described the life-story of Rukmini Bezboruah . Rukmini is the wife of Siddhartha, the District Collector posted at a small town Parbatpuri in Assam. She is English-medium-educated and teaches literature at the local college. Outwardly, she seems to be happy. Being the wife of an IAS officer, she enjoys social respect. She lives in the big beautiful bungalow on the hill above the cremation ground. Thus, her life looks well-settled and safe, unaffected with toil and turmoil of the common folk below the hill-top. But her life is not as elegant and peaceful as it looks. In reality, she has the experience of resting at a high place with volcano beneath which can erupt any moment and engulf the so-called kingdom and her life.

Mitra Phukan describes the socio-political situation during the Assam Students' agitation of the 1970s and 1980s. It began as a movement for self – determination but being misdirected has developed into a full blown insurgency. There is chaos and confusion everywhere. There are always some incidents of kidnapping, extortion, murders, and killings in the town:

> Every week, reports of fresh incidents of extortion or looting, or of gunning down unarmed citizenry, appeared in the papers. One or the other of the many terrorist, or pseudo-terrorist outfits that the district teemed with, unashamedly claimed the "credit" for these incidents within a few days. (2005 : 81)

Rukmini, the protagonist of the novel, is affected both ways – directly and indirectly – in her personal and social life. Her husband Sidhharth remains busy in maintenance of law and order in Parbatpuri. For both of them, social responsibility has been more important than the personal one:

> Over the last eighteen months in crisis – ridden Parbatpuri, Rukmini had visited many homes to offer condolence, sympathetic visits to victims and relatives of violence and extortion. It had always been the same. The ring of mourners, always emphasized their own mental, and even physical agony when they had come to know of the injury or bereavement. Indeed, during the condolence visit, they almost always focused on their own trauma. (ibidem 237)

In discharging social responsibilities, both Siddhartha and Rukmini forget their personal responsibilities, i.e., to have a baby for themselves and an heir for the family. In a state of chaos and confusion, Siddhartha, popular for his honesty and sincerity as an officer, is found dishonest in his personal life. He makes secret physical relations with one of the colleagues of Rukmini. Rukmini is proud to mention to Manoj Mahanta that Siddhartha is "very finicky about the demarcation between government property and private ownership" (ibidem 102) and at the same time shivers at her growing disloyalty to her husband . Though Rukmini is faithful to her husband, she has illicit relations with her old friend Manoj Mahanta . Unfortunately, Manoj Mahanta is kidnapped and in a search operation led by Siddhartha, both of them are killed. Thus, the story of the novel *The Collector's Wife* ends on a tragic note.

In her review of *The Collector's Wife,* Rebecca Sultana says,"The novel reveals how the private space can be appropriated by the public as we discover the personal enmeshing into the political with tragic consequences" (www.thedailystar.net / 2005 / 04 / 30 d 50430202129 . htm). In conversation with David Barsamian , Arundhati Roy expresses similar view about her novel *The God of Small Things* as a book which connects the very smallest things to the very biggest . Whether it's the dent that a baby spider makes on the surface of water in a pond or the quality of the moonlight on a river or how history and politics intend into the most intimate relationships between people – parents and children, siblings and so on." (www. progressive.org/mtvr401.htm)

The God of Small Things deals with love story between Amu and Velutha. Ammu is born and brought up in a highly respectable Christian family of Kerala. Outwardly, all the members in the family look happy and satisfied. But reality is quite different from appearance. There is suffocation inside the house. Ammu avails chance to visit Calcutta. She happens to meet a Bengali boy. In order to escape suffocating atmosphere of the family, she marries him. But this marriage does not prove to be successful. After being blessed with two children- Estha and Rahel, she divorces him and comes back to Ayemenem – her parental home. Here, she suffers insults and humiliation as a divorcee in a traditional Hindu family. She feels unbearable pain when her children are hated and humiliated by everybody in the family – even by maid servant Kochu Maria. Velutha , an outcaste known to her since childhood, shows love and affection to Estha and Rahel. His love for her own children draws her attention towards Velutha. This attraction develops into illicit relations between Ammu and Velutha. Thus, they break "love-laws" (1997 : 33) and become victim of political forces in society.

Comrade Pillaai is a CPM leader of ruling party in Kerala. Velutha is an active card holder member of Communist party in India. But he does not come forward to help Velutha. Rather, he becomes instrumental in tragic end of Velutha's life at police station in Kottayam. Ammu also dies at Bharat Lodge at the age of thirty-one only.

Both the novels, *The Collector's Wife* of Mitra Phukan and *The God of Samll Things* of Arundhati Roy suggest the omnipotent and omnipresent role of history and its forces in human life. In *The God of Small Things,* Ammu marries a youngman in Calcutta without the consent of her parents . She is a Christian and her husband is a Bengali Hindu. Again, she divorces him and comes back to Ayemenem, her parental home along with her children – Estha and Rahel. Worst of all, she falls in love with Velutha and has physical relations with him. Both of them are outcastes. An outcaste cannot rebel against social traditions and break its laws. If he/she breaks the laws, society has no place for him/her. Baby Kochamma believes:

> ...that a married daughter had no position in her parent's home. As for a *divorced* daughter (-), she had no position anywhere at all. And as for a *divorced* daughter from a *love* marriage, well words could not describe Baby Kochamma's outrage. As for a *divorced* daughter from a *intercommunity love* marriage – Baby Kochamma chose to remain quiveringly silent on the subject. (ibidem 45-46)

In patriarchal society, women have to keep promises in many ways. In *The God of Small Things,* Ammu breaks her promises by marrying a person outside her caste and community without the consent of her parents and again divorcing the same. She is found disobedient to her parents; to her husband; to her caste; to her community etc. In *The Collector's Wife,* Rukmini also breaks her promises as she fails to give birth to a baby. She disappoints her in-laws, her husband and herself as well. A married woman must be a mother. She has an obligation to give an heir to the family. She has an obligation to her husband and herself as well. If she fails, she is a curse to family, to her husband, to herself and to society also. She is looked down upon in society. Above all, she loses confidence, love and respect of her husband. Rukmini has respect in the family. But she is aware of her responsibilities as a daughter-in-law. Mitra Phukan describes how Rukmini is beset with the usual feminine concerns – a pressure to conform and be the ideal wife:

> Siddharth was an only son, and the burden of producing

> heirs rested on her shoulders. Or rather, in her dysfunctional womb. Looking at her, of course, nobody could say that this vital organ was flawed. But her waist – hip ratio, as promising, visually, as some fecund, prehistoric mother goddess's, hid the fact as revealed by the tests, probes and scans taken by the white – coated, bespectacled, Dr. Rabha, that it would be difficult for her to produce *any* heir, male or female. These days, Rukmini was always burdened with the feeling that she had been unable to fulfil her part of a social contract. That she had not kept a bargain. That she had reneged on a promise of vital importance. (2005 :53-54)

Both Mitra Phukan and Arundhati Roy have new historicists' approach to life. They think that history and its forces determine human life. In classical tragedies, destiny plays an important role in life. In case of Rukmini and Ammu, history and hegemonic forces are responsible for tragic stories in their lives. This is the tragic vision of both the novelists. History is the witness that women have always been the victim of men. Even the husband treats his wife as a woman only. He fails to provide a life of dignity in the family or society. He does not hesitate to exploit her honour and reputation for his self and petty interest. A woman has to qualify several tests in order to prove her faithfulness as a wife. Her reputation is always in question whereas a man seems to be free from any kind of stigma in life. When a woman is in trouble, father, mother, brother, sister and relatives act merely as agents of history and leave her to suffer alone. Society fails to appreciate the predicament of women where she becomes helpless and is compelled to break the social norms. As minute observers, Arundhati Roy and Mitra Phukan have tried to draw attention to such situations and champion the cause of women.

In the novel *The God of Small Things,* Ammu is deprived of higher education because Pappachi considers it as an unnecessary expenditure (...) for girls. Because of dowry, he is unable to find a suitable husband for her. When she finds a husband for herself, she is treated as a disobedient child. The family finds an excuse to sever all relations with her. Ammu is disappointed to find her husband a drunkard. He agrees to the proposal of Mr. Hollick to leave his wife with him in order to save himself from being dismissed from the job. For the drunkard husband she is no better than an article to be pawned as when he is in trouble. Her feminine sensibility revolts against this abject humiliation. She divorces her husband and comes for shelter to her parental home where she was born and brought up. She becomes an object of pity and humiliation. As a mother, her heart bleeds when she finds her children mistreated even by the maid-servant of the house Kochu Maria. Her mother cries within when she feels the miserable condition of her twins: "Like a pair of small bewildered frogs engrossed in each other's company, lalloping arm in arm down a highway full of hurtling traffic" (ibidem 43). The novelist comments : "While other children of their age learned other things, Estha and Rahel learned how history negotiates terms and collects its dues from those who break its laws" (ibidem 55). Her father does not believe that an English man can covet another man's wife. His brother Chacko comments that the twins – Estha and Rahel are indescently healthy.

In a similar situation, Chacko enjoys confidence in the family and respect in society. He also married an English lady Margaret Kochamma and she divorced him. Chacko has a daughter Sophie Mol. Sophie Mol is the centre of attraction of everybody in the family because she represents the parental authority. In this situation, Velutha shows love and affection to Estha and Rahel. Ammu feels obliged. She is drawn towards him and compensates with physical love.

In Mitra Phukan's *The Collector's Wife*, Rukmini is an obedient daughter and obedient wife. Her's is arranged marriage. She is married to Siddharth, the District Collector. Rukmini is not a revolutionary girl. She is not a revolutionary wife as well. Her husband is not a drunkard like Ammu's husband. But he is equally careless in respect of his wife. Ammu's husband is not a responsible husband. But the wives of both the husbands have to suffer social humiliation and insults because of their carelessness and lack of personal concern. Siddharth is popular as an honest officer. Rukmini is proud of him for his honesty. He shows his loyalty towards the government as an employee. He shows his responsibility towards the public of his sub-division where he has been posted as an administrative officer. But he cannot spare time for Rukmini. She joins as a lecturer in local college not because she likes it but because that is the only option left to her in her short stints as the DC's wife in a small town. At home, she has no work to do. After many years of her marriage, she has not been able to become a mother. Although Rukmini enjoys social respect, she is an object of criticism in society. She is fortunate that her in - laws have no complain but they are impatiently waiting for a child from Rukmini. Her mother-in-law always takes a chance to remind her: "Have you decided yet about fertility pills?" she asked, after talking the other things for a few minutes.

Rukmini unconsciously fingered the amulet that she wore around her neck. "No ma, not yet. Actually Siddharth and I haven't really talked I mean, discussed the whole issue properly. But don't worry –we'll come to a decision soon…."(148)

Sidhharth is as careless as Ammu's husband. But Rukmini's husband, Sidhharth, is a responsible officer as the District Collector. He shows all concern for the people of Parbatpuri. But Rukmini remains excluded from his responsibilities. He does not think that he has his obligations towards her. If Ammu suffers because of her husband, it is his ignorance. But suffering is the lot of women. It does not make any difference whether the husband is literate or illiterate; educated or uneducated. In *The God of Small Things,* Pappachi is one of the most respectable among the Syrian Christian people of Ayemenem for his human concern for all. But his wife Mammachi does not come within this purview. To humiliate her was his routine work. Even physically, he used to assault her:

> Every night he beat her with a brass flower vase. The beatings weren't new. What was new was only the frequency with which they took place. One night Pappachi broke the bow of Mammachi's violin and threw it in the river.(47-48)

Pappachi is not different from Kathakali men who beat their wives, "even Kunti, the soft one, with breast" (236). Siddharth is one of those males who have least concern for their wives. Siddharth does not beat his wife. But his neglect of Rukmini is no less than physical torture of Mammachi or Ammu or wives of Kathakali men. Mitra gives a feminist touch to the sufferings of Rukmini for her fault that she desires to be a mother:

> She had suffered silently through all the prying and probing, as male gynaecologists – her doctors had all been male – had studied her womb, her vagina, and her ovaries. She had tried to be as impersonal as the doctors and technicians themselves, when she lay on the hard

> tables, being examined by humans or by machines. But she had always felt a sense of violation after each examination, each test. It was irrational, she knew, yet she could do nothing to prevent these feelings from crowding her mind as she pulled up her panties, and re-arranged the pleats of her sari after each examination. (83-84)

In fact, Rukmini is not barren. Dr. Rabha is a family doctor. He is working at the instruction of Siddharth. Dr. Rabha, as directed by Siddharth, convinced her that she was unfit to become a mother. Every married woman wishes to be mother. It is the highest prize of her life. If she is denied of motherhood, it is the worst curse for her. The reason is known to Siddharth of playing such a cruel trick. He betrays Rukmini as a husband and exploits her faith and confidence in him. He has illicit relation with one of the colleagues of Rukmini. He has time for all whom he wants to meet. But he maintains his dignity at home. For him there is no difference between his presence in the office or at home. Although Rukmini, the wife of an IAS officer, she looks as helpless as Ammu or any other woman is in patriarchal society. In utter confusion and disappointment, Rukmini moves out in a car for fresh air and for a change but she happens to read few lines in a magazine:

A young couple (-) looking for a female ovum donor. Applicant should be of good complexion and below thirty years of age.(86)

Rukmini is already thirty-five years old. Like Ammu, she begins to think about herself. In *The God of Small Things,* Ammu is called *Veshya*. She begins to think how the *Veshyas* were sometimes clean shaved and compelled to walk on the road. In *The Collector's Wife,*

> Rukmini closed the magazine as well as her eyes, and leaned back against the hot plastic seats. Her back was already damp with sweat, and she could feel her flesh sticking clammily to the seat behind her. Ignoring the unpleasant feeling of being velcroed to the plastic, she tried to imagine the advertisement that they, Siddharth and she, would frame if Dr. Rabha ever told them that an ovum donor was the only chance for Siddharth to father a baby who would be legitimately his in the eyes of the law. (87)

Siddharth is quite unaware of the mental agony of Rukmini. He does not want to feel as well. Rather, he enjoys having seen Rukmini pulled up her panties, and re-arranged the pleats of her sari after each examination because it was his own creation. Rukmini not only disliked but also hated the repeated medical examinations in order to activate her fertility. She always 'felt a sense of violation after each examination' which was really a kind of emotional violence mercilessly and deliberately to faithful and innocent wife by intelligent husband.

Both Rukmini and Ammu are the victims of careless and irresponsible husbands and conservative society. A woman must obtain motherhood. Preferably, she should be blessed with a son. Second, she must not be away from her husband or be a divorcee. If she fails to keep her promises in either case, she is only considered responsible and hence remains unwelcome in society. Society takes it for granted that such a woman is a sinner and she cannot be allowed to go to heaven after her death. But a man is never found guilty in the event of not fulfilling the agreement as a husband and to his wife.

Obviously, Rukmini and Ammu are answerable to their families and society as well. In the *Mahabharata,* one of the classics of *Hindus,* Kunti had to take the responsibility of bearing children because Pandav was forbidden to co-operate with her. In order to have an heir to the throne, even king Dasarath had to accept three queens in marriage. Siddharth has no time to share the problems of Rukmini. Nor does he care if she is away from home even till late hours at night. Rukmini has social respect as DC's wife. As a teacher, she gets intellectual satisfaction. That is, however, a forced option for her. In the absence of motherhood, she is denied of her own social respect. In personal life, she is deprived of the most important satisfaction as a woman. Arundhati Roy puts the same question in her novel *The God of Small Things*. Mammachi is aware of 'Men's Needs'(258) but it seems that in her opinion 'Women's Needs' do not exist at all. Siddharth, like Chacko, satisfies his own need but he does not think about Rukmini. Unlike Chacko, he, of course, is not seen objecting to his wife in this respect. Thus, Rukmini and Ammu both are put in situation acting against themselves,

In the bathroom, Ammu realises that she is still young in age and spirit. She has not yet reached thirty. Rukmini is always made to feel that she is already thirty-five years old:

And that time was running out. As Dr. Rabha had so kindly pointed out, thought Rukmini with some annoyance. Did the men have no sensitivity?

> Still she knew, who better than her biological clock will soon begin to wind. In different words, Renu Bezuboruah had said the same thing as Dr. Rabha. The womb matures faster than the brain, reflected Rukmini.... (84)

Rukmini further reasons:

> Women at forty-five were nowadays in peak physical condition. Only their wombs showed signs of ageing. And intellectually as well as emotionally, and also, almost always, financially, weren't forty-five year old women better able to cope with the demands of new motherhood than girls barely out of their adolescence ever could? (85)

A divorcee or a woman without children should not be neglected in the family or the society. She is also a human being like any other men. She has feelings and emotions which need to be satisfied. If 'Men's Needs' need to be satisfied, so is it with women's needs. If men cannot lose their dignity after divorce, women should also be given the same opportunity. Women are not simply a child bearing machine. They can contribute to family and society in many ways. If they are not given proper honour, they can bring chaos in society. They can challenge the traditional values and assert their identities. They have their sustaining vitalities and they have proved themselves. Indian English novelists have always been highlighting women issues in order to maintain order in society.

Mitra Phukan and Arundhati Roy have also taken up the issues of women. They emphasise the old values to be reviewed. Women should not suffer social discrimination on the basis of sex and gender. There has been social and political revolution in order to provide women status of honour and dignity. However, weaker section of society is still weak and those in power are still dominant. This is a postcolonial issue.

As postcolonial novelists, Mitra Phukan and Arundhati Roy deal with postcolonial problems. The issues prevailing during precolonial period were found to continue with the colonizers and even after their departure. Colonizers established their colonies with a human face and expressed their commitment to replace their traditional values with human values. But subordination and oppression of outcastes continued in colonial style. The colonized countries held colonial power responsible for all the social evils like social discrimination on the basis of caste, class and gender. The colonizers left but colonialism continues in different forms and at different levels.

Siddharth is the District Collector of Parbatpuri. The District Collector and other officers of independent India seem to be representatives of colonial power in stead of the officers of Indian Administrative service:

> The DC's bungalow at Parbatpuri was a legacy of the days when the British had administered the district from residences-cum-offices perched on hillocks that lifted them, symbolically as well as literally, high above the native 'masses' below. The town of Parbatpuri was liberally strewn with several of these hillocks that reared up suddenly from the plains as though for the express purpose of providing places for the rulers to live. Each major functionary of the town lived atop his own little eminence, from which he surveyed the world below as Shiva might, from Mount Kailash. (18)

Mitra Phukan suggests that after departure of the colonizers, India became an independent country. Power came into the hands of Indians. British Government was replaced by the Government of India. British officers were replaced by Indian Officers. However, no remarkable change is noticed before and after independence. Indian officers hardly show any interest in common people and their problems. They hesitate to freely mix with people below their rank and file. Therefore, they prefer to attend the club and get relaxed from worries and anxieties of life. Even at home, Siddharth used to maintain his official dignity and behave as an officer with his wife, Rukmini. But he used to be a normal human being at the club free from official style:

> It was only in the Parbatpuri Club that he seemed to relax somewhat and the worry lines seemed to become

> fainter as he laughed and smiled with a cold drink in his hands. Perhaps, it was banality of the jokes or the tritness of the conversation there that refreshed his mind, thought Rukmini. Or perhaps it was the fact that the club was one of the few places where he could shed his official persona.(82-83)

Mitra Phukan highlights 'colonial mimicry' and 'hybridity' in Indian culture. British people wanted to make Indian people like themselves in culture, civilization, fashion and style. However, they did not like that the native 'other' should really be like the European 'self'. They wished 'sameness' in the natives but not without 'otherness'. Thus, the natives, in the process of adoption, could only 'mimic' the master. As the colonial power could not create the image of the 'self' nor could they allow the colonized to stay in their native state, it resulted into *hybrid* products of negotiation – "both political and cultural – between the colonizer and the colonized" (Das 2002: 223). Thus, *hybridity* shows the position of *in-betweenness :* "adoption" Englishness and "original" Indianness (Nayar 2002 : 200).

In *The Collector's Wife,* Mitra Phukan has nicely presented the postcolonial picture of Assam. All the important characters in the novel including Rukmini are interesting examples of colonial mimicry and hybrid culture. They are proud of Indian culture and fashion. But they love to be unique in European style. Siddharth is an Indian Administrative officer. But he enjoys his life as British officers at hill-top. He prefers to maintain reservation in public as well as in personal life. But he finds himself comfortable at club and believes in extramarital relationship. It reveals his dual personality. Rukmini is a descent lady. Unlike Siddharth and other ladies of her status, she feer like enjoying the company of common people. But English literature has been her favourite subject. Because of neglect and carelessness of her husband, she revives her old friendship with Manoj Mahanta. She remains away from home and without hesitation she enjoys company of Manoj Mahanta. She earnestly desires to be blessed with a child. But her Indian sentiment does not allow her to take the help of science:

> Taking the fertility drugs would be, thought Rukmini, like placing her body completely in the hands of science.

> The child, when born, *if* born, would be as much the offspring of Dr. Rabha and the white-coated technicians who operated the machines and the laboratory equipment, as it be hers and Siddharth's. The private act of conception would become a scientifically – conducted laboratory experiment .(84)

However, Rukmini, though not deliberately, has extramarital relation with Manoj Mahanta and becomes pregnant.

In *The God of Small Things,* Pappachi is always seen in three-piece suit. His family is highly respectable among the Syrian Christians of Kerala. He, however, shows faith in social discrimination on the basis of caste, culture and community. Ammu divorces her husband in order to save her chastity. But she falls in love with Velutha and indulges in sexual pleasures with him. Estha and Rahel revolt against teaching English at home. But they enjoy Englidh film *The Sound of Music.* Chacko admits with repentance that:

> ....they were a *family* of Anglophiles. Pointed in the wrong direction, trapped outside their own history, and unable to retrace their steps because their footprints had been swept away. (52)

Both the novels *The Collector's Wife* and *The God of Small Things* abound with the notions of "affirmation and contestation", "desire and repulsion" at different levels and in different forms. This is one of the key-notes –the note of 'ambivalence' in postcolonial literature. Thus, Arundhati Roy and Mitra Phukan deal with the themes of 'mimicry' 'hybridity' and 'ambivalence' and they are appreciated as Postcolonial novelists.

As postcolonial novelists, they deal with all the social and political issues present in society. Arundhati Roy deals with issues of caste, culture, religion, unemployement, communism, naxalism, capitalism, etc. Mitra Phukan has also same concern for the similar issues. In her novel, *The Collector's Wife,* she dwells upon the issues of insurgency, student's agitation, illegal migration, kidnapping, extortion, murders, killings, etc. Both of them deal with the local issues. Mitra Phukan has presented the situation of Assam during the 1970's and 1980's whereas Arundhati Roy shows her concern for Kerala.

In the novel *The God of Small Things* Arundhati Roy has presented the problem of unemployment and exploitation of unemployed youths by giving false hope of employment:

A jeep with a loudspeaker drove past, blaring a Marxist Party Song whose theme was Unemployment. The chorus was in English, the rest of it in Malayalam.

> No vacancy! No vacancy!
> *Wherever in the world a poor man goes,*
> No no no no no vacancy! (269).

Frustrated from the Communist Government of Kerala, a group of people think that *Inquilab* is the only solution:

> The man like a knot gave baby Kochamma his red flag as a present. 'Here', he said. 'Hold it'. Baby Kochamma held it, still not looking at him.
> 'Wave it', he ordered.
> She had to wave it. She had no choice. ... ...
> Now say *Inquilab Zindabad!'*
> *'Inquilab Zindabad',* Baby Kochamma whispered.

Like Arundhati Roy, Mitra Phukan has also nicely presented the social picture of agitated Assam:

> With each new incident, the previous ones that had caused such furore, were all but forgotten. It seemed to Rukmini that the people of Parbatpuri had a memory recall of only a week or, at most, ten days. The latest horror was discussed and commented upon from every possible angle. But when a fresh atrocity burst upon the town, the previous incident was forgotten with a promptitude that never failed to amaze her. Spine-chilling incidents of six months ago were now dim and hazy in the collective memory of Parbatpuri.(82)

Amidst such confusions and commotions, love-story springs up. In *The God of Small Things*, Arundhati Roy presents love-story between Ammu and Velutha. Ammu could not compromise with her feminine chastity for husband to save his job 'being looked after'by Mr. Hollick, the white officer in the tea garden. She, however, offers all that she has is in the possession to Velutha. Her sacrifice is for her children. When she is under trial in the court of History and its hegemonic forces, she says:

> 'Because of you!' Ammu had screamed. 'If it wasn't for you I wouldn't be here! None of this would have happened! I wouldn't be here! None of this would have happened! I wouldn't be here! I would have been free! I should have dumped you in an orphanage the day you were born! You're the millstones round my neck!(253).

In *The Collector's Wife,* Mitra Phukan describes the love-story of Rukmini and Manoj Mahanta. Society and family expect from her a child. This is the law of History that a woman must be a mother to prove her identity. She wants to share her problems but Siddharth has his own problem as an officer –

> Never a talkative person, he grew almost taciturn now, at least when he was with Rukmini. Sometimes thinking that it would help if he talked about his work, Rukmini tried to draw him into a conversation about his day, on their occasional evenings together. But he never opened up. Perhaps he was unable to. (82)

Mitra Phukan shows suffering of Rukmini because she is not a mother. She earnestly desires that she were a mother. Ammu curses herself that she had been a mother. Studied together, both of them suffer because they are women. In patriarchal society, women are born to suffer. In both the cases, it appears that men have no responsibility to share with women. In quest of attaining her motherhood, Rukmini is compelled to have extramarital relationship with Manoj Mahanta. She becomes pregnant and brings happiness for the family. For Rukmini, as in the case of all women, happiness is temporary. Unfortunately, Siddharth is killed in his attempt to save Manoj Mahanta from kidnappers. Manoj Mahanta is also killed by them. Mitra Phukna describes the psychological condition of Rukmini:

> She hadn't been aware that the tears had come. Tears for two men. One who had died, not knowing that he was going to be a father. And another who had been prepared to be a father to an unborn child, not his.(348-349)

Similar is the situation of Ammu. Ammu had to divorce the father of her children – Estha and Rahel. Velutha, who gives love and affection of a father to her children, is killed at the police station. In both the cases, politics plays an important role. Velutha is the victim of politics of caste. Ammu is the victim of patriarchal politics. In order to hasten the tragic end of Ammu and Velutha, the state, the church and the family join to-gether. Rukmini, Siddharth and Manoj Mahanta are the victims of directionless and misguided politics in Assam. The students agitation in Assam began as a movement for self-determination. It is given a wrong channel of insurgency, kidnappings and extortion. As such, political instability becomes the order of the day. In Kerala, Communism and Christianity both stood for social equality, social harmony and human values. The communist Government of Kerala forgets its mission and its leaders like Comrade pillai not only fail to support but he also plays the politics of caste. In the church, social discrimination has safe shelter. Women, children and outcastes are tortured and humiliated. In North-eastern states women are supposed to have better edge compared to other states of India. Assam and North-Eastern states are said to be the place of worship of women or the place where woman is worshipped. To be precise, Kerala is patriarchal and Assam is matriarchal state. Ammu marries by her choice. Rukmini's marriage is arranged one like that of Pappachi's and Mammachi's. Siddharth represents the state. Pappachi represents Christianity. Rukmini is meek, submissive and obedient to traditional values. Above all, she is more or less financially independent. Ammu is revolting, disobedient and breaker of love-laws and traditional values. Suffering, however, remains an integral part in the life of Ammu and Rukmini as well. The story of Rukmini and Ammu leaves a pessimistic note about the fate of women. In a review of *The Collector's Wife,* it has been remarked, "The final denounment is horrifying and yet true– for there can be no other 'end' to such a tale, where the personal is so densely interwoven with the political"(Blurb). It is applicable to *The God of Small Things* also. This is, however, true that both the novels are free from pessimistic tone. Rukmini, though meek and submissive, proves that she can be mother independent of her husband. Ammu also proves that a mother can play the role of father.In short, both of them prove that women have sustaining vitality.

Mitra Phukan's *The Collector's Wife* and Arundhati Roy's

The God of Small Things have many common points of comparison and analysis together. Both the novels can be read in the light of New Historicism and Feminist theory of literature. New Historicism is based on the assumption that a literary work is the product of the time, place and circumstances of its composition. Both the novels deal with postcolonial and feminist issues which can be read and interpreted in its social and historical context.

References

Das, Bijay Kumar. 2002. *Twentieth Century Literary Criticism*. New Delhi: Atlantic Publishers.

Nayar, Pramod K. 2002. *Literary Theory Today*. New Delhi: Prestige.

Phukan, Mitra. 2005. *The Collector's Wife*. New Delhi: Penguin Books.

Roy, Arundhati. 2008. *The God of Small Things*. New Delhi: India Ink.

—— 2001. Interview by David Barsmanian, dtd February <www.Progressive.org/mtv 0401.html>, pp.1-7.

Sultana, Rebecca. 2005. "The personal enmeshed with the political" www.thedailystar.net/2005/04/30d50430202129.htm pp.1-2.

(18)

Mitra Phukan's *The Collector's Wife*: A Study in Technique

Nityananda Pattanayak

The social and political upheavals in Assam during the 1980s and early 90s gave impetus to a group of creative writers in the state to capture the volatile experience in words. Mitra Phukan is one such writer whose *The Collector's Wife* (2005) is written against this backdrop of social flux and political unrest. It depicts the myriad problems afflicting the state during the period like influx of foreigners, growth of "ethnic consciousness" dividing people along we/they, ours/theirs, rise of insurgent group and the incidents of killing, kidnapping, extortion, repressive measures taken by the state power to annihilate "rebels", flood problem, falling standard of education etc. However, the work is not a mere commentary upon social and political developments of a people. In it is densely interwoven the cultural and moral issues confronted by an individual, her condition in the vortex of events, her emotional make-up as conditioned by these and the question of relationship between man/woman and husband/wife. By putting her female protagonist in the context of her (protagonist's) domestic environment conditioned by traditional values and contemporary situations, the novelist subjects her to explore her identity.

Rukmini, convent educated, wife of the Chief Administrator of a district living in the sprawling bungalow atop a hillock prefers a part-time job of a teacher at a local college to overcome her loneliness and boredom arising out of her childlessness and the protective ring thrown around her due to her position. A woman about to cross her fertile period, she is under tremendous social and family pressure to bear child. Her husband Siddharth surrounded by "Deaths, Murders, Kidnappings" fails to attend to the physical and emotional needs of Rukmini. Rukmini suffers from a wounded ego, cries for freedom from the "claustrophobic confines of her immediate circle" and conceives from an "other" man under a compelling circumstance. She also finds out her husband Siddharth continuing physical relation with one of her colleagues, not as "prettier, nicer" as her. Towards the end, when everything becomes known to each other, in a quiet moment under the cover of darkness, in their bedroom, both spill out their helplessness, realize how under the sickening circumstances they were misunderstood by each other. So the aim of the novelist is not only to reflect the events taking place in the contemporary society but also to explore the individual personality by setting situations on them, to show the vulnerability of an individual in the midst of volatile social and political conditions and her frantic search for equilibrium in life.

How does the novelist present the story of an 'injured' wife's search for an equilibrium in life in the backdrop of social flux? What narrative strategies has she adopted to present authentically the complex human emotions and problems alongside the social and political developments of the land? The nature of the story demands a third person narration as events and incidents arising out of social and political unrest cannot be narrated from the perspective of First Person nor from that of a witness agent. So the omniscience narration is adopted. Only once at hypodiegetic level the narrator takes the help of a character-Animesh Dutta- to describe the circumstance surrounding the tragic death of Siddharth and Manoj that occurred at a distance. Animesh's recounting of the incident flows in over telephone like a cinematic voice. At another point in the story the narrator takes the help of a letter from Manoj to describe his present condition in captivity to induce in readers a sense of immediate involvement and anticipation. This deviation is needed to present events dramatically so as to form a sense of immediacy.

But omniscience narration, as Wayne C. Booth has pointed out that it "will tell us nothing of importance unless we become more precise and describe how the particular qualities of the narration relate to specific desired effects" and hence "focus must be treated as an independent constituent point of view, alongside grammatical person of the narrator and access to consciousness".

Phukan's objective in devising a narrative strategy for *The Collector's Wife* therefore was to come up with a perspective which would allow her to give her work a commentary- like quality on the current social and political developments and at the same time to enable her to reflect the intensities of everyday life as experienced by an essentially vulnerable individual who fell victim to this chaos. Phukan met her objective by giving her novel the kind of omniscient narrator associated with traditional and natural mode of narration while focalizing most of the story through Rukmini, the wronged wife, a victim of her husband's apathy and negligence due to prevalent social uncertainty and violence. Thus Phukan takes full advantage of the flexibility offered by omniscience narration and at the same time retains privileges of the first person narrator. She has used external focalization to enable us to see Rukmini from the perspective of others like Rita and Priyam who watch her discomfort when three ladies at the wedding reception pass unsavory comments on her. But what is important here is the use of internal focalization to get readers involved in Rukmini's life by taking them into her mind, thereby ensuring sympathy for her and understanding her problem. For example, when at the suggestion of Manoj Mahanta, Rukmini desires to escape from the "claustrophobic confines of her immediate circle" (134) by opting any profession in a big city away from her husband's protective shelter in small towns a train of thoughts run past her mind,

> Suddenly she wanted to leave Parbatpuri, and all the various mofussil towns that she could see stretching drearily ahead of her till Siddharth got his seniority and was able to work in the State Secretariat in Guwahati, which in itself would be no big jump, anyway. She wanted the excitement that leaping into a new life would bring. To bus it to work, to rub shoulders cheerfully with fellow humans, instead of traveling always in a cocoon of isolation. To fashion, if not immortal poesy, then at least a few lines of attention-grabbing copy that would launch a new product. So what if the product was only a mediocre washing powder? Without her inspired lines, the product would have sunk without a trace in the Great Indian Marketplace. Or to be a journalist, with, perhaps, her own column, for which her readers would wait impatiently, so that they could then say to others with an

> air of authority, "But Rukmini Bezbaruah says..." To be able to influence the thinking of so many people, to make her readers sit up and take note of her point of view... She wanted to get away from the endless rounds of shooting, kidnapping, extortion, activities that were slowly draining away the life blood of all who lived here. She wanted to wake up every morning in a place that was vibrant with energy. So what if it was polluted and overcrowded? She was fed up anyway with sylvan greenery behind which bristle acres of AK-47s. She wanted to talk of something new and different,... She was tired of all this, tired also of trying to have a baby with a husband who, in the past so many weeks, had not even touched her, let alone slept with her. (162-163)

In this passage Phukan blends third person narration (She wanted the excitement that...), free direct speech (which now in itself would be no big jump, anyway), direct thought ("But Rukmini Bezbarooah says..."), free indirect thought (So what if the product was only a mediocre washing powder?) and employs an accelerated narrating pace. The passage is dominated by free indirect discourse where frequent switches between future (To bus it to work, to rub shoulders cheerfully with fellow humans), present (instead of traveling always in a cocoon of isolation) and past (a husband who, in the past so many weeks, had not even touched her), create the illusions of having access to the mind of a woman whose thoughts slip out from a "cocoon" of 'isolation' and romp about in the future life of freedom. The shift of perspective from the third person observation to that of first person participant helps us to know the train of thoughts in the character flowing freely without being hampered by the presence of the narrator. The narration dramatizes the thought and impressions of the character whose heart cries to escape from a "cocoon of isolation".

Equally effective Phukan is in chapter twenty where she has used very often this perspective to reveal the complex human emotion and feelings. Here we come across Ruknini's startling discovery that she is carrying the foetus from an "other" man, her joys and excitement at the discovery that she would no longer be castigated as a barren woman. Here we find her pain and anguish at the sudden discovery that Siddharth who always gives her the impression that he is burdened with weighty matters even to the point of having no time to share bed with her is having physical relation with an "other" woman in his bed room. Here also she discovers how vulnerable she is physically as her driver-cum-bodyguard is a member of a terrorist group. She realizes how Siddharth's manly appearance or his authority fails to give her necessary emotional and physical security. A good number of passages in this chapter employ the perspective of Rukmini to reveal authentically and superbly feminine sensibility, e.g. in the passage beginning with "This wasn't fair...," (278). Rukmini poses so many questions to herself that they have no possible answer. Rukmini's mind is in ferment when while searching intensively a meaning to her identity she is tossed between social morality and justice to her. The passage is full of Indirect Discourse, and has a series of questions. It has fragmented syntax, staccato phrase that take us direct into the mind of the protagonist. It reveals her mind about man-woman, husband-wife relation, about a wife's position in the society and family circle.

However, at some critical points in the plot this kind of perspective is conspicuous by its absence. If Phukan had employed this perspective at some other crucial moments in the life of Rukmini as when she was subject to humiliation by three ladies at a marriage reception for her infecundity or in the aftermath of her sex with Manoj, it would have been more rewarding. Moreover, at the close of the narrative the voice of the author becomes louder than the voice of the narrator. It seems the sensitive author pushing aside the narrator pops up and acts like a propagandist. It would have been more pleasing if she had been suggestive remaining in the background.

Time, physical time, moves in order in the novel. Public referents of time- advent of spring with the cooing of the cuckoo, then the month of April and the "mid-May heat of the day" (68) and then the rainy season when the Red River is in spate and colleges in Assam open after the summer vacation, i.e. early August- are seen moving in the narrative in order. The action in the novel takes place hardly in a time span of six months. How does the novelist explore an individual personality with such a complex vision set against a social and political criss-crossed with problems that remain unanswered, 'for there can be no other 'end' to such a tale', in such a condensed time? The novelist has introduced subtly a few discrepancies of time into the story that help her to offer a near complete picture of the protagonist at a critical juncture of her life.

There are two discrepancies – one anaelepse and the other prolepsis – in the story. They are placed at crucial points in the plot and inform us of character traits and motivation. An external anaelepse occurs when, at a passionate moment, lying on bed with the 'other' man in a closed half-dark room at the Ranijan Tea club Rukmini goes back to her hostel days. Her mind drifts "into a dream-like state" when she remembers how even an illustrated text of the Kama-Sutra "had not excited her at all" during her adolescence period. But now with Manoj she is surprised at the "suddenness of her passionate response" and realizes that the presence of "the hidden, surreptitious nature of the passion" (143) in her which she had never exhibited even when with Siddharth erupts when finds proper environment. The present when contrasted with the past reveals the extent of sexual gratification and psychological satisfaction that Rukmini derived in her union with Manoj. This also informs suggestively the consummation of their sexual act.

A prolepsis occurs almost in the middle of the narrative that informs us of the narrative that informs us of the extent of Rukmini's desire to run away from the "claustrophobic confines" of "Parbatpuri, and all the various mofussil towns that she could see stretching dearily ahead of her" (162). This temporal shift by way of hope is a kind of Rukmini's wish fulfillment where she imagines the experience of "something new and different" and the "thrill of a faster paced life" than the "gossip about fellow teachers, or fellow club members or about the latest killing or the latest extortion demand" (163).

The novelist celebrates another time – an inexpressible sense of fulfillment akin to Timelessness. When Rukmini and Manoj are set to do the act for a new life to come, for a great fulfillment "Time stood still... everything receded into the background" (141). But even when the news of death of Siddharth and Manoj come in time moves on – "the ticking of the clock, louder than before, was the only sound in the room" (336), lest caring about the mundane affairs of the world, the death and destruction. The narrative contains some variability of duration in the story and the length of text devoted to it. A formal introduction scene between Manoj and other teachers including Rukmini takes long two pages while the manner of his death is reported only in a few words. It is because Manoj alive was to play a more important role in the life of Rukmini than Manoj dead.

The events and incidents are so arranged in the narrative that nothing seems superfluous, each contributing to make the plot compact and each carrying forward the action to a closure. The novel begins with an incident in the life of Rukmini. "Hurtful comments" passed on her at the wedding reception of her colleague Rita, Rita's discomfiture, Priyam's "abrasive attempt at sympathy" and temper of Rukmini rising – all drop hint at the course of action to follow. A little earlier in the same scene Rukmini's meeting with Manoj Mahanta foreshadows their relationship. The first chapter also drops hints on the foreign national problem, ours-theirs dichotomy, kidnappings, killings, extortions going on in the land. Thus there is a psychological build up, an end focus, in the first chapter in which the reader can piece together the things to follow.

Succession of events in the plot is governed by what Cobley says, "the chain of causation which dictates that these events are somehow linked and that they are therefore to be depicted in relation to each other". Rukmini's quick acceptance of Manoj's offer for an outing, her meek surrender to him at the club house are due to Siddharth's lack of concern for her and his failure to satisfy her longing for love and sex. Their physical union also arouses our curiousity to know what would happen next considering the incompatibility between Rukmini and Siddharth. The novelist also contrives an incident where Rukmini is hit with a stone thrown by the agitators so as to prepare the ground for the detection of her pregnancy. After building up a situation for leading the plot towards a climax, a scene is presented where the doctors examining injured Rukmini declare of her likely pregnancy. Immediately after the doctor's confirmation, when Rukmini is searching a way how to face Siddharth on the matter, a scene is placed where she discovers the sex bout of Siddharth and Priyam. The scene is here necessary to make Rukmini overcome her guilty feelings and prepare herself to face Siddharth with full confidence and determination. Even the incidents like ghastly killing of Deuri or Mitali leaving Parbatpuri have not been devised superficially, but to tell about the prevailing law and order situation in the land and also to bolster Rukmini's courage to face the realities of life. Again, the final incident is not melodramatic because it prepares the ground for the protagonist to reach an equilibrium, to discover herself in the scheme of life. Hence the closure of the narrative is not super induced, rather a form proceeding since the novel is "a tale, where the personal is so densely interwoven with the political." (postscript)

Chance, co-incidence, accident and the like play significant roles in creating conflicts and bringing resolutions, moving action toward the denouement. Manoj's accidental collision with Rukmini at the market place that prepared the ground for them to build intimacy, unanticipated raining on their way to the Hatibagan Tea Estate that forced them to take shelter in the Ranijan Tea club where they indulged in sex leading to the pregnancy of Rukmini, the injury sustained by her due to accidental hit of the stone resulting her to get hospitalized where her pregnancy was suspected, unexpected arrival of Rukmini at the bungalow catching Siddharth and Priyam unaware, sudden gunfire from the insurgents killing Siddharth on the spot are some of the situations built on liberature model that determine the course of action. Thus realism and elements of romance interplay, one meets the rational satisfaction and the other emotional pleasure, one involves objective and artless causality and the other inexplicable things in life. These fictious elements, however, do not stand in our way of deriving aesthetic pleasure from the story. As Burner puts it: the act of "telling a story" cannot simply be understood by interrogating the illogical principles of sense and reference contained in the act, (instead) we interpret stories by their verisimilitude, their truth likeness or more accurately their life-likeness.

Elements of mystery and premonition that remain present in the story create suspense. The suspense that how Rukmini would face Siddharth after the detection of her pregnancy was sustained for long. It was resolved with her sudden discovery about Siddharth's infidelity. The section where Rukmini found Siddharth in action is packed with suspense and excitement. Eerie silence engulfing the sprawling bungalow was suddenly punctuated with a "sound, slight but unmistakable" that "made the back of her neck prickle." Earlier the feeling of Rukmini, who with the streams of visitors coming to her to inquire about her injury "began to feel as though there had been a bereavement in the family, that she was perhaps a recent widow" (216), worries the reader to think if something terrible was not going to happen to her?

The plot leaves a permanent gap – for how long Siddharth and Priyam were in intimate terms? Nothing in the plot gives any hint of it. But the gap is not crucial or central to the narrative because its concealment does not affect the process of the protagonist's 'becoming'. There is also a temporary gap when the identity of Mukul Madhav is kept withheld for a considerable time weaving all kinds of mystery around him.

The action of the novel moves out of Parbatpuri only once, to Ranijan Tea Club; that too, when the place failed to usher a new life, fulfill the protagonist's sense of completeness. The story time is hardly six months. It is rather a splendid feat of the novelist to present complex human emotions and intricate social and political situations in such a limited space and time. If the action of the novel had taken place against a vast space and time the focus would not have been sharp, triggering every possibility of the technique getting muddled. The use of limited space and time in a novel is supported by J.W. Beach when he stresses on the short period of time for bringing dramatic quality to a work of fiction.

Apart from creating a host of background characters to realize a sense of society in action, the novelist has drawn a handful of characters who what William Harvey says are ficelles. Priyam, Manoj, Nandini, Mitali are such characters who create "perspective of depth". These characters have been created and better delineated than any other background characters to serve a purely mechanical role in the story, to offer a symbolic value to the protagonist. Nandini and Mitali are there to help Rukmini find an equilibrium in life, to discover her inner strength and her identity. Priyam is another ficelle who acts as a foil for Rukmini how to extricate herself from the dilemma. Thus the major characters in the novel have been contrived as opposites to each other. Siddharth is a perfect opposite to Manoj. He is reserved in his speech and action when with Rukmini. He is a queer cold abstraction of a man for her. But Manoj is articulate, vigorous, bubbled with ward feelings and swayed with instinctual way of living. Unlike Siddharth, he is considerate towards her, attends to her emotional and biological needs. "Manoj grinned back at her. His brown eyes looked carefree and young, unlike, Rukmini couldn't help thinking, Siddharth's, which always gave the impression that he was burdened with weighty matters, even while watching a sitcom on TV." (111). However, Siddharth's character often treated negatively is given another dimension when on Rukmini's candid confession that she needed the "deep friendship", "companionship" of Manoj to escape from the sickening atmosphere he said, "I have always felt that you've coped marvelously "with the loneliness at Parbatpuri" and "all those other district towns that I was posted in". The voice is genuine, welled from the core of the heart and the "Revelations" sounds clear.

Phukan's art of using environment as a means of delineating character, crisis or conflict in human relationship is to be noted. To give two examples, one external and another internal, will serve the purpose. Rukmini and Manoj share a common idiom when observing through the open window of the bungalow the "purple hills fleshed with a luxuriant growth of vibrant, deep-hued greenery". They gazed at the hills. She realized, "...she could look at them now without the sense of unease that had haunted her earlier". Nature in its luxuriant growth "now does not look as intimidating as they had a few weeks earlier" (201). When this external environment reveals their common taste and common temperament, description of an internal environment suggests obliquely how Siddharth who was once full of vitality and artistic temperament turned sapless under the degrading social and political environment. The repeated mention of a large canvas hanging on the drawing room wall across which is painted three "horses (who) galloped joyously, their muscles rippling with vitality", a painting made by Siddharth evokes the sense that how once he, too, was lively, joyous, imaginative and full of sexual vitality, but the tumult events of the land robbed him of all vibrancy.

Naming is an art that many novelists follow to delineate character traits: "fictional names do seem to be meaningful". Phukan has named the protagonist and her male counterpart after two prototypes for ironic treatment. Rukmini, the wife of Sri Krishna had many wives and beloveds. But Rukmini, the protagonist is childless and is to long for her husband's love. Siddharth, too is the other name of Buddha, who though was unattached to family yet was above worldly pleasure or cares and anxieties. But Siddharth in the novel has taken the burden of "holding a fortress against a long and heavy siege." This ironic treatment sheds light on the modern day human beings.

To delineate the character of Rukmini explicitly, Phukan has taken the help of her fantasy, used the device of psychological realism. She has depicted a scene in which Rukmini has been shown "leaning back against the hot plastic seats" while turning over the pages of a magazine and imagines "the advertisement that they, Siddharth and she, would frame if Dr. Rabha ever told them that an ovum donor was the only chance for Siddharth to father a baby who would be legitimately his in the eyes of the law" (87). The fantasy placed here at a critical juncture in the plot- after Rukmini took all possible medical help and is now poised to take supernatural help for conceiving- acts as a device to probe into the hidden motives and submerged wish of the character, to "find out the hidden life at source."

Rukmini's existential dilemma and her moral awareness are focused by adopting the technique of psychological realism. Even though Manoj's companionship gives her immense pleasure yet, simultaneously, a part of her mind goes on saying, "...going out with a strange man. Like a date, almost, only worse, because you know practically nothing about him. What will Siddharth say?" (101) and later she sometimes wondered "if she would be able to face Siddharth" (159). Even after finding warmth in Manoj she has a soft corner for Siddharth. "His feelings seemed to have atrophied. Perhaps it was the nature of his work that had deadened his emotions and passions. After all, who could not be affected by having to deal with... deep seated disquiet all around? It was self-preservation, perhaps, which had caused him to grow a protective shell around himself, a shell which now excluded even her." (202). This double consciousness in Rukmini focuses on her inner conflict arising out of her struggle between her frantic effort to get herself extricated from loneliness and her desire to uphold family values.

What catches the immediate attention of a reader while going through the text is the free use of some Assamese words. Phukan's preference for certain content words in Assamese to their English equivalents is aimed to give her novel a regional flavour. The use of the word Baideo for elder sister and mention of some articles like mekhela sador (traditional dress used by Assamese women), riha (a kind of yarn produced locally), anchal dupattas (dress used by girls), phulam gamosa (embroidered napkin that carries cultural significance), bindi (sticker used by women on their forehead) without finding their English equivalents are repeatedly used in general types. However, some others like *bota, japi,* etc., associated with the Assamese culture and *nimbu-pani* (lemon water) are mentioned in italic type. Words like samsan (cremation ground), mali (gardener) are used both in general and italic type. However, some words commonly used in Hindi heartland like dhuti-punjabi, aabir, puri-aaloo have been used in italic type, though the dress materials like anchal-dupattas are used in general type. As the narration shifts to tea-garden areas we notice the change in register. The novelist uses the words like *bistiwallahs, turkies, gorey log* etc. used frequently in garden areas to evoke local atmosphere. The choice of language by Phukan reminds one of Henry James' observation on *Adam Bede,* "one writes the novel, one paints the picture, of one's language and of one's time."

The nature of the theme demands a grim and somber form. However, when a tragic note runs long in a narrative, the reader develops a kind of suffocation from where he tries to escape. Phukan with her use of ludic language in the narrative provides this relief, without affecting the overall form of the novel. For example, before a turning point in the plot, the novelist, with the use of ludic language, lightens the atmosphere, thereby preparing the reader to enjoy the suspense that is to follow.

The bags that were hoarded under mattresses were a source of constant friction between couples. While housewives congratulated themselves on having succeeded in squirreling away so many of these, husbands disliked the crackling sounds that disturbed their sleep every time they turned. Worse, the sound distracted them at critical moments whenever they made love. The town's husbands, therefore, were staunch supporters of Arnab Chakravarty's campaign against the use of plastic carrybags. (33)

The language used here is not sarcastic, it is not used to satirize anybody. It is aimed at giving pure delight. A serious artist as she is, Phukan attends to her style meticulously. She loads her narrative with similes, metaphors, symbols and other figures of speech that help her make the meaning explicit. For example, the similes and metaphors used in the first chapter are most befitting to the occasion of a wedding reception. The are commensurate with the intensity of the situation and add to the carnival atmosphere of the occasion. Some metaphors like "The wedding venue was an island of light" or similes like "Rukmini was carried along like a leaf on a stream" (40) are aimed to create a sense of exaggeration while others like "Her eyes, ringed with too much black and blue were as hooded as an underground don's" when read together with the earlier sentence, "Rita's normally clean-scrubbed face looked not like a college lecturer's but a somewhat desperate street walker's" (5) are for arousing irresponsible smile. However, as the narrative progresses the number of similes and metaphors dwindles, appropriate to the changing tenor of the story.

Enjoyment of a work is derived very often from guessing things little by little. Symbols and metaphors used in *The Collector's Wife* heighten the significance of the work. They represent the hidden cause. The rain and jackfruit mentioned in the eleventh chapter are two plain symbols that have been used to represent fertility. A powerful metaphor is placed almost in the beginning of the narrative. In chapter three, Manoj and Rukmini collided at the market place causing the spill out of pink cotton panties carried by Rukmini in plastic bags over the pavements, "the round tins of mackerel... rolled to a stop in the mud" and eggs lay in heap inside their bag, slowly oozing yokes and whites onto the pavements". (36) The metaphor compels the reader to anticipate the sexual collision between the two. Suggestive language like "A well-fed cow ambled across the road a little way ahead,... the sky had become overcast with heavy bellied black clouds..." (129) when Manoj and Rukmini were driving to the Ranijan Tea club, or "A dog, well-fed, with a healthy shine on its white and black coat, crossed her path. Further down, a cow nibbled at the grass on the verge, her calf near-by" (266-267) when Rukmini was troubled after witnessing the scene of sexual act between Siddharth and Priyam conveys the tenor of the story more "luminously, and generally with a perception of delight."

The cremation ground is a *leitmotif* in the text that informs about the death and destruction to follow. The unusual detail and various types in which it is mentioned—cremation ground, *samsan,* samsan- warns of something horrendous would likely to follow. "A large image of Kali stood to one side of the entrance... Little children played under the watchful eyes of the skull-draped, scimitar-wielding Kali, unperturbed by the processions carrying dead men and women on pallets" (22) is echoed in "The lively scene was presided over by the Goddess of Death, whose statue, blue-black and dark, menacing and huge, stood at the far end of the park. Garlands of skulls were entwined around her neck, and hung down her naked body. One of the grinning death's heads was positioned over her pubis. Red tipped breasts thrust themselves out aggressively... while her hair was long enough to cover her buttocks, streamed anarchically behind her." (268-269). Immediately after this there is the mention of the bungalow of the Chief Administrator of the district. "The house was screened by trees, but Rukmini was certain that if the branches were lopped off, the bungalow would be as visible as Kali" (269). This motif forebodes the text, the text encourages him/her to start integrating the information. With the movement of each narrative unit s/he forms an idea about the way the narrative will close.

Phukan constructs her sentence according to the demand of the occasion. She uses long-winded, verbose sentences when she offers nature description. But while informing about gruesome incidents, she uses short, choppy, staccato sentences in separate paragraphs to heighten the grimness of the situation. For example to describe an incident of extortion, kidnapping and killing of a tea-garden manager and his wife the sentences run as below:

> "Both the Manager and his wife were tied to the bedposts before being shot."
> "There was a demand for money some days ago. Five crores.
> I believe."
> "The wife was raped before she was shot. Repeatedly. In front of her husband!" (26)

The same breath-holding narration is noticed at the time when drowning of Manoj Mahanta and his captors is described.

The sudden loss of one man was too much for the equilibrium of the boat. It flipped, tipping the others into the water below. Screams fading into nothingness. Dark heads bobbed once or twice on the river. Hands, clawing desperately at the air, moved rapidly down river, swept swiftly away.

The racy narration builds up suspense and arouses excitement.

Phukan's persistent emphasis upon describing minute details of nature is a significant aspect of her art. Her meticulous attention to every small things of nature surrounding Parbatpuri lends touch to the physical reality of the location. It also helps to form the attitude of the characters, e.g., in chapter twenty, on page two hundred sixty-two, the soothing effect of the surrounding calmed down the troubled mind of Rukmini who was passing through emotional turmoil after witnessing Siddharth and Priyam at compromising position. However, the same effect is not always achieved. Sometimes, Phukan's tendency towards reproducing nature scenes is carried to an excessive degree, so that the description fails to succeed in organic narration. Such descriptions seem hanging loose on to characters or situations. To cite examples, the journalese of Phukan in describing the fury of the Brahmaputra during the rainy days (261) or offering the view of the hills and the river (263) are like romantic, decorative description of nature. They are neither related to character delineation nor to the elaboration of plot or theme.

To arrive at the conclusion Phukan's effort and success, except minor aberrations, in combining structure, character and style into meaningful wholes in *The Collector's Wife* holds the promise of a great artist in future.

Notes and References :

All the textual references in brackets are from *The Collector's Wife* published by the Penguin Books India in 2005.

Wayne C. Booth "Distance and Point of View", *The Theory Of the Novel,* ed. Philip Stevick (New York: The Free Press, 1967) 91.

Wallace Martin, *Recent Theories of Narrative* (Ithaca, NY: Cornell UP, 1986) 146.

Paul Cobley, *Narrative: the New Critical Idiom* (London: Routledge, 2001) 5. qtd. in Cobley 220.

Joseph Warren Beach, *The Twentieth Century Novel: Studies in Technique* (New Delhi: Kalyani Publishers, rpt. 1988) 159.

Gregory Currie, *The Nature of Fiction* (Cambridge Univ. Press, 1990) 129.

E.M. Forster, *Aspects of the Novel,* (1927: New Delhi: Atlantic Publishers, 1995) 53.

(19)

Gender Discrimination in Easterine Iralu's *A Terrible Matriarchy* and Shashi Deshpande's *The Dark Holds No Terrors*

A.J. Sebastian sdb

1. Introduction

'World over girls have proved themselves to be as smart and successful as boys. And yet in may societies especially in the developing countries they are discriminated from the time of their birth and are frequently reminded of the things they are not allowed to do. Often there is great rejoicing when a boy is born as he is considered an insurance and support for the family. He is to inherit the patrimony and continue to propagate the family lineage. Many women are disheartened when they give birth to a girl. In some traditions when a baby girl is born, it is announced" "The servant of your household is born" ("Gender Discrimination." http://www.childreninneed.com).

Feminism is a way of looking at the world, a framework or lens through which other issues can be examined. The basic premise of feminism is that societal structures are based on a false assumption that men are superior to women, and that this state of society is unfair and unfounded and causes gender oppression. Feminism, like women, is not homogenous. There are many, many offshoots of feminism which hold different theories about the nature of gender inequality. A mainstay in feminist theory is patriarchy, a relationship of power existing between men and women in which men are in control of socio-economic political power and women are subordinate. Patriarchy is the root of gender oppression ("Feminism." http:// thinkinggirl.wordpress.com).

Theories of gender oppression go further than theories of gender difference and gender inequality by arguing that not only are women different from or unequal to men, but that they are actively oppressed, subordinated, and even abused by men ("Contemporary Feminist Theory."http://highered. mcgraw-hill.com).

The gender discrimination portrayed in Easterine Iralu's *A Terrible Matriarchy* and Shashi Deshpande's *The Dark Holds No Terrors* come as a challenge to the widespread belief in gender inequality that exists in a male dominated society.

2. Lieno, a victim of Matriarchal mores

In *A Terrible Matriarchy,* Easterine draws our attention to a particular form of matriarchal control in her society that perpetrates gender inequality. She also points out that women themselves have their due share in committing violence against the girl child.

The foundations of Matriarchy are maternal authority and women's Superiority Complex. From the moment of birth, men are taught to defer to maternal authority. Men who marry usually find their wives expecting the mantle of maternal authority to be simply handed over to them by and from the man's mother without missing a beat. It sometimes takes many battles for a man to make the point to a new wife that she is his spouse and equal, not his mother. Women who stubbornly insist on being slow learners on this issue set up oppositional and adversarial positions which often will poison the marriage over time. Women expect to be able to make the rules and simply expect men to obey them. When feminists realized that they were about to overthrow women's own matriarchal power base with their initial anti-marriage and anti-motherhood stances, they did an abrupt about-face and embraced motherhood even more fervently than they had rejected it just a few years before. Matriarchy depends on shadow power. It must deny its power and function from the shadows. All matriarchal power stems from the maternal role and maternal authority, and the power to grant or deny sex ("Confronting Matriarchy." http://mensnewsdaily.com).

The novelist has very realistically portrayed matriarchal hegemony. She has acknowledged that "the little girl is a combination of many little girls. Some girl readers have told me, 'I am that little girl, I was mistreated because I was a girl-child' Some girl-children have suffered more abuse than this one in the story" (Easterine. e-mail. 14 January 2010).

Some of her personal experiences have also surfaced in the story as she acknowledges: "I put together my experiences of school and growing up to piece Lieno's experience into a typical childhood experience. I was bullied at school as the youngest in my class, she is bullied at school... *Dielieno* actually means, *errand girl,* so it is a name that designates what the status of a girl-child is, she is considered good for running errands and looking after the house. Nothing very wrong with that but grandmother's way of raising her harshly and preferring the male-children I felt was wrong and I have seen that in many families" (Easterine. e-mail. 14 January 2010).

In the novel Easterine looks into the various aspects of matriarchal assertion in manifold ways, challenging the commonly held feminist point of view. The story surrounds the five year old Dielieno, only girl child and youngest of the five children. Sometimes she felt unwanted and took for granted that she was an after thought since her parents often made her wear the leftover clothing of her brothers. Though growing up as the darling of her family, at the tender age of four and a half, she knew that her grandmother didn't like her when she refused to give her a much desired chicken leg. She was told, "That portion is always for boys. Girls must eat the other portions" (*ATM* 1).

Lieno observes how her mother lived a very unhappy life, living in utter dread of the granny who never appreciated anything she did. When Lieno's mother sent her elder son to fetch water, she was told by grandma to send the girl instead, as she held the view that no man is to carry water. Grandmother always boasted off how she began to work when barely four and insisted that "The girl must be made to work at home. Don't let her run about with her brothers any more. That is not the way to bring up girl-children" (4).

Lieno was always referred to as "the girl" by her granny, denying her any individual identity. When she asks her mother why she is never called by name, her mother shrugs off saying that she is someone special to grandma. But when she is called so even after two years, she picks up courage to speak up: "Grandmother, my name is Dielieno, remember you gave me my name? Why won't you call me by my name?" (4). With a stick in hand, she got a grim remark from the granny warning her not to be cheeky. The grandmother literally treated her like an "errand girl" as her given name *Dielieno* meant - a name granny herself had given, implying her to be a non-entity in the midst of her brothers.

Lieno had great fun sitting in the lap of Uncle Atu when he came to visit grandma. When she started climbing on his shoulders, she was caned by grandmother saying, "Girl, what do you think you are? A monkey?... I've never seen such a badly behaved girl" (5). When uncle defended her being only a little child, grandma retorted that no decent girl climbs up a man's shoulder. Being hurt, Lieno kept away the whole day and expressed her hatred of grandma to her father showing her bruised calf. Though angry, her father only said, "It is for your own good, your grandmother would never do anything to you that is not for your welfare... She only wants to raise you to be a good woman" (6). But she wasn't convinced as it got ingrained in her soul that grandma hated seeing her enjoying herself and wished that the old woman died. Lieno's mother became pale on hearing her pathetic story and asked if granny ever mentioned "bad blood." When she nodded, mother made her promise never to mention it to anyone.

One day Lieno overheard her parents discuss their plan to send her to live with the grandmother who lived a lonely life. Though mother remonstrated with her father, he had his way saying, "Mother was right. You are not raising her properly. She will leave tomorrow for mother's house" (10). Shocked by the decision, Lieno went to bed dreaming of holding her grandfather's hand. Suddenly the face changed to be grandmother's, who shook off her hand with a stern look as Lieno woke up with the fear of the inevitable.

When she reached grandmother's home to stay, Lieno was told to keep away from her as she might have brought germs from her home. She ordered Bano to bathe the girl in icy cold water. Hardly she had put on some clothes to warm herself up in the bitter cold, she was directed by the old woman to fetch water.

At the house, Lieno was given various tasks such as fetching water, stacking firewood, making grandma's bed, gathering the chickens at sunset and counting them. When Leto came to visit grandma after three days, Lieno clung to him, but granny sent her to bring sweet potatoes for her brother. Granny showed her usual affection for the boy, however he felt embarrassed and excused himself to go and cut firewood. However, she made him promise to visit again and she would cook many dishes for him. The young girl recalls: "It amused me the way my brother had to extricate himself from grandmother's clutches. With some revulsion I recollected that she was going on like a young girl with him, vying for his attention and bribing him with good food. The meat that hung on the spiked bamboo was not for us. It was for Leto and all my brothers" (18). Lieno's fear of granny grew day by day as she picked on her with silly things.

When her parents visited after six months, Lieno was delighted to sit in her mother's lap as long as she could, but was chased by the grandma to bring tapioca. As mother introduced the topic of sending Lieno to school, grandmother spoke of her days when girls didn't go to school but stayed at home to learn household duties and went to the field. Her father put in his opinion for the first time ever in front of his mother: "Mother…You mustn't think we don't respect your views on the subject. We took this decision for Lieno because she is a bright girl…Of course, she will continue living with you and helping you in your house. And of course, we want to listen to what your decision is on this" (23). They couldn't do anything without her final decision on the fate of Lieno. However, from the following day she could go to school with her best friend Vimenuo. But grandmother didn't like Vimenuo's folks, considering them descending from bad blood.

Grandma was never happy about her schooling and kept telling Lieno's mother, "I really don't know what it is your generation sees in school. Your children are not being taught the skills of life because they are too busy studying. I was doing such a good job of teaching the girl to work…It was difficult enough. She has a stubborn streak to her. Now you come with all these plans for school. She will completely forget all I have taught her now" (37). When the father spoke of the poor performance of his sons, grandma began defending them saying that they would be alright as they are to be taught to be manly:

> In my father's day, boys never did any work because they had to look after the village and engage enemy warriors in warfare. The household that did not have a male heir was considered barren. They were always in constant danger if there was a war. The women would only have one man to protect them. That is why we love

> our male children so much and we give them the best of food. And we should (37).

Little wonder why grandma picked on Lieno when she returned late from school after special tuition to learn how to read and write. Feeling frustrated at the beatings and scoldings heaped on her, she wanted to know from Bano why granny hated her so much. Bano had the usual litany: "She doesn't hate you…she wants you to be a good girl. It's her way of bringing you up to be a good woman" (39).

Lieno's teacher Miss Sobu became pregnant with the Drawing Teacher's child which made grandmother very cynical and angry, because such teachers teach bad things to children. Grandmother found only two kinds of people in the world as Bano recounts: "In the first group are those who are upright and go to church regularly and come to all the community gatherings. The others are those who do not go to church regularly and are fond of drinking and whose daughters sometimes get pregnant before they can get married. She is convinced that only those in the first group will get to heaven and the rest will all go to hell" (81). As a matter of fact grandma disliked pretty girls presuming them to go wrong sooner or later. Hence Lieno could never hanker for pretty dresses as long as she lived there. She began to understand why her mother though pretty, never wore any good looking dress.

When Lieno was nearly eleven years, grandmother began to stare at her for something she didn't like. She enquired from Bano, "Has she got the curse yet?" (130). At bedtime, Bano explained what the curse meant when girls reached their puberty. Grandmother's fear was that girls would become pregnant if they mingled with boys. The young Lieno discussed the matter with her friend Vimenuo and became scared of the curse and was prepared to eat most bitter gourds to prevent the bleeding.

Finally, on her thirteenth birthday she got the curse, bringing along with it her embarrassment and fear of being found out by schoolmates. Having her mother as a role-model "... a girl's core gender identity is positive and built upon sameness, continuity, and identification with the mother" (Showalter 320). The girl as she matures to adolescence and adulthood, is embarrassed by her sudden physical growth. She finds herself very different from the boys of her age making her afraid and ashamed of her womanhood.

Lieno was delighted to pass the Matriculation examinations with a second division. Being the smartest for studies in the family, Leto volunteered to sponsor her college education. When her father referred the matter to grandmother, she pointed out very religiously that, "... a woman's role is to marry and bear children...That is her most important role. Men don't like to marry educated wives. Then, if you find no one to marry you, you will be alone in your old age and have no one to bury you...See what a terrible thing it is not to have children to bury one?" (*ATM* 206). So saying she wanted them to reconsider their plan of college education for the girl. But the tide turned to Lieno's favour and she could pursue her dream.

Lieno kept wondering how her father and her folks kept slavishly respecting grandmother's rigid views. "I had myself never learnt to feel anything of the sort and always wondered how father and his siblings could be so devoted to her. They tried to fulfil her every wish. They quoted her constantly and it irked me that they would expect their spouses to be awed by her wisdom and her philosophy of life and try to abide by it" (271). No wonder she continued to be more domineering than ever in advanced age. Lieno kept to her personal opinion as a young educated girl of twenty one, though her mother tried to tell her to be less harsh in her opinion of grandmother saying, "I know you were unhappy in her house but she was trying to teach you to become a good woman. Men don't like women who are aggressive and outspoken. They like their wives to be good workers. You are a good worker, Lieno, but you must try to be more docile" (271-2). But when Lieno began to let out her suppressed bitterness at the way she was treated as a child being bathed in icy cold water at her bidding, counting repeatedly chickens in the dark etc, mother was shocked. She merely argued that all these granny did to Lieno because she was a girl not a boy. However, she always felt being punished for being born a girl and wished she was not a girl.

To calm down the girl her mother sat beside to explain the crux of the matter:

> Your grandmother was the eldest of the children. She grew up in the village and moved to the town only when she was married. When she was young she lived through a very hard time. In the village, widows without sons lost their husband's property to other male relatives. So

> she understood that it was very important for a married woman to produce as many male offspring as she could... But people were unkind and mocked those who could not produce male children... I think your grandmother looks at her sons and grandsons as a kind of insurance and she is inclined to take a very conservative attitude towards your brothers by pampering them as she saw other boys being pampered in her childhood. (272-3)

Mother further pointed out that grandmother's attachment to boys is due to her need to be looked after in old age. Grandma always thought that women had to depend on men as they were weak. Mother advised Lieno to be sympathetic to a weak old widow who sought to secure the loyalty of her sons and grandsons. Grandma grew up in a society where women pushed their men to go to war as they would be safe under such good warriors. Instead of hating her, Lieno is prompted to understand grandma's predicament and forgive her. In her sober moments, Lieno realised that if she refused to forgive grandma, she would herself end up being embittered. Slowly she began to understand how a deep sense of insecurity led grandma to hold on to her views and convictions. From then on, Lieno's fear transformed into pity as she understood grandma trying to buy love. She resolved to be kind to the old woman. Meanwhile Bano brought news that grandmother was bedridden and immobile. When Lieno and her mother were by her bed-side, Lieno uttered, "Grandmother, it's me, Lieno, I want to say that it is okay, I forgive you for being harsh with me" (280). The soothing words of forgiveness made grandma's immobile face beam with a hiss and tears welled up in her eyes. Grandmother cried her tears, displaying her grief, before she passed away that night.

Foundations of Female Power has been grandma's strength and stay throughout the novel. It is built on, a) Maternal Authority through Moral Power, b) Control of the Education/Socialization system through Indoctrination Power; c) The Rescue Reflex through Victim Power, d) Emotional Terrorism and Violence – through Intimidation Power ("Confronting Matriarchy." http://mensnewsdaily.com).

It is relevant to reflect on the statement of Luce Irigaray: "It is also necessary for us to discover and assert that we are always mothers once we are women. We bring something other than children into the world, we engender...love, desire, language, art, the social, the political, the religious... and we must re-appropriate the maternal dimension that belongs to us as women" (Irigaray 420-1).

Easterine's use of the narrative through the innocent eyes of Lieno is similar to that of Jhumpa Lahiri in her narrating the story of Hema and Kaushik in "Once in a Lifetime" with Hema's first person narration through her 'innocent eyes.' Likewise, Lieno takes the readers through her life, stage by stage through her innocent eyes. We enter into the world of discrimination meted out to her in the name of tradition by an autocratic grandmother.

3. Sarita, a victim of Patriarchal hegemony

In *The Dark Holds No Terrors,* in her fight for survival, Sarita, the protagonist, comes out of the patriarchal society, dispelling the darkness of female bonding and oppression. She is haunted by her mother who condemned her when she was unable to save her brother from drowning. When the mother dies, her anguish doesn't cease to exist. She leaves her home to look after her aged father, more as an escape from her sadistic husband who oppressed her physically and mentally. Though she tries to forget her past, she is haunted by the past – her childhood oppression under her tyrannical mother, her marriage to Manohar (Manu) and her children, the way her gentle poet husband turns a dreaded maniacal oppressor when she overtakes him professionally as a successful doctor and her leaving him. Her angst finally make her go beyond the shackles of dependence on others to evolve a meaningful life for herself, asserting her self sufficiency as a woman.

The novel is centred on a patriarchal system in which a girl is expected to live under male hegemony. She has no identity of her own. Sarita's struggle for survival begins from childhood when she is discriminated for being born female. "One is not born, but rather becomes a woman. It is civilization as a whole that produces this creature which is described as feminine" (Beauvoir 295). Her father keeps to his patriarchal attitude and is indifferent to her struggle against all odds and frowns when she returns home, separated from her husband. She is left to struggle on her own being victim of a callous system since, "Man can think of himself without woman. She can not think of herself without man. And she is simply what man decrees...She appears essentially to the male as a sexual being. For him she is sex... absolute sex, no less. She is defined and differentiated with reference to man and not she with reference to man and he with reference to her, she is the incidental, the inessential as opposed to the essential."(534)

This study focuses on the merciless attitude of Sarita's mother who herself being a victim of the patriarchal hegemony, continues to perpetuate it, taking it on the young girl. She proves the paradox of life when one perpetrates what one suffers and hates. When the accidental death occurs, she is blamed: "Why didn't you die? Why are you alive and he dead" (*DHNT* 14).

She recalls how from early life she was a victim of discrimination as her brother was given all care and attention. Being a girl, on her birthday there was no puja performed. She felt neglected as her brother was the centre of attention. After Dhruva's death, all celebrations ceased to exist as she didn't count as a person. Often she is reminded about her destiny as a woman to be married off:

> Don't go out into the sun.
> You'll get even darker.
> Who cares?
> We have to care even if you don't. We have to get you married.
> I don't want to get married.
> Will you live with us all your life?
> Why not?
> You can't
> And Dhruva?
> He's different. He's a boy. (45)

The angst simmering deep down in the psyche of the mother is one of getting rid of the girl to a prospective man who wouldn't reject her. The girl is looked upon as a liability until married to be a subservient wife and property of her in-laws.

When she began her menstruation, Sarita experienced the most inhuman treatment of all as though a curse had come upon her: "It was torture. Not just three days when I couldn't enter the kitchen or the puja room. Not just the sleeping on a straw mat covered with a thin sheet. Not just the feeling of being a pariah, with a special cup and plate by my side in which I was served from a distance, for my touch was... Pollution. A kind of shame" (62). Ignoring her feminine identity, her mother makes her ashamed of herself telling her: "You're growing up" she would say. And there was something unpleasant in the way she looked at me, so that I longed to run away, to hide whatever part of me she was staring at... A kind of shame that engulfed me, making me want to rage, to scream against the face that put me in the same class as my mother" (62).

She continues to grow in her loathing for her femininity as a shameful "dark, damp and smelly hole" (62) and hated herself being a discarded woman. She had to accept the unacceptable: "Things fell, with a miraculous exact exactness, into place. I was a female. I was born that way, that was the way my body had to be, those were the things that had to happen to me. And that was that" (63).

She was made to feel different from her brother who was the darling of the family. She was told to dress modestly and never to parade her femininity in front of males at home. Though acknowledge to be a sexual being, she is warned, "You should be careful now about how you behave. Don't come out in your petticoat like that. Not even if it's only your father who's around" (55).

To liberate herself from her worthlessness, she qualifies herself to be a doctor. But that too was a façade under which she took shelter: "They were all props, I decided later, to help create and maintain the necessary image. For by then I had learnt it too, to create an image of myself for the world, to live within it, hiding my real self so resolutely that at times I forgot myself it was just a facade (88).

However, after her marriage to Manu, her sufferings continued unabated with more and more of physical and mental torture from a man who suffers from inferiority complex. He turns out to be a maniac suffering the pangs of sadism since she is professionally superior to him. Unable to endure him, after fifteen years of wedlock, she decided to return to look after her father. Though frowned upon by her father and alienated from husband and children, she continues in her thirst for power, becoming self centred day by day. She could no more blame her destiny as a woman being ill-treated by her mother, husband and society. To recover her self respect she had to face the grim realities of life and find solution to her existential dilemma.

She comes to the realization that she can get recognition in a patriarchal society only in her old age after she had surrendered her identity in marriage. She is respected as a mother but her identity as a daughter and wife have been hacked, thus repressing her identity as a woman. By then she has become a passive victim of the system and continues to perpetrate the evil she herself suffered. Helplessly the victim becomes the victimiser- and the circle of oppression continues. Sarita's mother had been such a victim of society who suffered in her childhood. Her mother was deserted by her husband, and had to bring up her two daughters. Sarita's mother had thus a difficult childhood being raised fatherless in the home of grandparents. Her mother suffered her predicament in silence. As a child, Sarita's mother absorbed her mother's predicament and herself began to feel the sense of insecurity. Her anguish of being abandoned turned her to exercise overt authority over her children. She became antagonistic towards Sarita being born a girl- a burden inherited. She directed a venomous persecution of the girl, disregarding any mother-daughter intimacy. The mother never allowed any freedom of expression to the child as she grew up, nor bothered about her feelings as a child:

> 'Why are you so late?'
> 'We went for a walk!
> 'A walk? Such a long? Don't you know it's dark!'
> ...
> I kept silent and that enraged her even more.

'Can't you talk? Am I so much below your notice? You can talk to your friends for hours, but you can't speak a sentence to your mother. What am I? Am enemy?'

'Is it such a crime to go for walk?' I burst out 'walk? Didn't you think you could have helped at home?

There are the vegetables to cut, the buttermilk to be churned. When you're working, I never ask for a bit of help. I slog the whole day all by myself. But to go for a walk...'

A huge anger filled me making me almost blind. What about me? It was my birthday. Did she remember that other girls had gifts and smiles and festive meals. While I? (170).

The mother forgot even Sarita's birthday, in her determination to rule with her feminine vision, establishing her full control. Sarita's mother kept up the traditional practice of disseminating gender discrimination, rearing a girl child as per patriarchal mores. It is psychological that the mother victimises her daughter the way she was victimised. Such women are never evil per se, but have become victims of the social conditioning under patriarchy, which they continue to perpetuate like a programmed robot. Her bitter past is transferred to the child by excessive control through persecution mania. Such women suffer from "Matrophobia"... the fear of one's mother or of motherhood but of becoming one's mother. But where a mother is hated to the point of matrophobia there may also be a deep underlying pull towards her... An adolescent daughter may live at war with her mother yet borrow her clothes, her perfumes (Rich 62).

Such mother hatred leads to identification with the mother as she grows up to be a woman. This perhaps will continue to rule Sarita unless she, being an educated woman, rises above gender discrimination to break loose from the sins of the past. Self realization comes when she utters, " because there's no one else, we have to go on trying. If we can't believe in ourselves, we're sunk." (*DHNT* 220). Taking stock of the situation, she takes responsibility for her existence, deciding to return to her own home, living by societal mores.

4. Conclusion

Girls in both the stories are made to feel inferior and worthless in comparison to their brothers, declaring them second rate, thereby limiting their opportunities. Deep poverty and gender bias against women don't let them develop their potentialities. Added to it physical and emotional abuse keep them from being themselves. The status of women is central to the health of any nation in its social and economic progress. Unfortunately female children are most defenseless against the trauma of gender discrimination. The following obstacles are stark examples of what girls worldwide face. But the good news is that new generations of girls represent the most promising source of change for women—and men—in the developing world today. Education of women is essential to ending gender bias and discrimination. Girls' education also means comprehensive change for a society ("Gender Discrimination." http://www.childreninneed.Com).

Lieno's bitterness is transformed into forgiveness for her grandmother, understanding her social dilemma during a period of Naga history when a male was deemed to be the warrior protector of the family. Such convictions of the older generation are to be understood in the backdrop of the socio-cultural growth of a society in transition.

Sarita, on her part, prepares herself to accept her predicament and live a meaningful life as per social norms. She begins to understand her mother's pathetic situation in an androcentric society, where silence was her only option. Her discrimination of her daughter resulted purely from societal pressures to which she had become herself a silent victim. Both Lieno and Sarita, in the course of time are self-educated enough to arrive at their own solutions to their predicaments. In their own ways they attempt to liberate themselves from the shackles of patriarchal and matriarchal hegemony.

A Terrible Matriarchy and *The Dark Holds No Terrors* pose probing questions to all and sundry to care for children, irrespective of their gender identities, acknowledging their preciousness as gifts of God. The novels make a clarion call to all men and women to play their responsible role in bringing about social transformation by doing away with all forms of gender discrimination.

Works Cited:

Beauvoir, Simone De. *The Second Sex*. trans. H. M. Parshley. London: Vintage, 1997.

"Confronting Matriarchy." http://mensnewsdaily.com/2009/11/17/confronting-martriarchy -and-the-false-premise-of-feminism.

"Contemporary Feminist Theory."http://highered. mcgraw-hill.com/sites/0072817186/ student_ view0/chapter13/chapter_summary.html).

Deshpande, Shashi. *The Dark Holds No Terrors*. New Delhi: Vikas Publishing House, 1980. Abbreviated *DHNT*.

Easterine. e-mail to the author. 14 January 2010.

"Feminism http://thinkinggirl.wordpress.com/feminism/

"Gender Discrimination." http://www.childreninneed.com/magazine/gender.html.

Iralu, Easterine. *A Terrible Matriarchy*. New Delhi: Zubaan, 2007. (Abbreviated: *ATM*).

Irigaray, Luce. "The Bodily Encounter with the Mother." *Modern Criticism and Theory*. David Lodge, Nigel Wood. 2nd ed. Delhi: Pearson Education, 2003.

Rich, Adrienne. *Of Woman Born: Motherhood as Experience and Institution*. New York: W.W. Norton, 1976.

Showalter, Elaine. "Feminist criticism in the wilderness." *Modern Criticism and Theory*. David Lodge, Nigel Wood. 2nd ed. Delhi: Pearson Education, 2003.

(20)

Abhiyatri : The Story of a Rebellious Woman

Basavaraj Naikar

Nirupoma Borgohain (1932—) is a very important Assamese short story writer, novelist and journalist. A prolific writer, she has published thirty-three novels and novellas, twelve short story collections, eight essay collections, five translations, a travelogue, a children's novel and an autobiography. She has received several prestigious awards like the Swasti Award from Bangalore, the Tirumahalamba Award from Nanjangud, The Basanti Devi Award and the Barua Award of the Asom Sahitya Sabha, the Pabitra Saikia Award and the Central Sahitya Academy Award (for *Abhiyatri* in 1996) for her significant contribution to Assamese literature.

Born in Guwahati in 1932, she was educated in Cotton College, Guwahati and Calcutta University, Calcutta. A double post-graduate in English and Assamese, she worked as a Lecturer in English at various colleges and as editor of *Saptahik Sanchipat and Chitrangada.* Presently she is a column writer for several weekly and daily newspapers of Assam. Among her many novels, some like *Anya Jiban (Another Life), Iparer Ghar, Siparer Ghar (The House of this Side and of That) and Din Prati Din (Everyday)* have received special attention from readers and critics.

In the present article an attempt has been made to discuss *Abhiyatri* (1995), which won the Central Sahitya Academy Award in 1996. The novel is based upon the rebellious life of Chandraprabha Saikia (1900 -) who happened to be a spirited freedom fighter of Assam and who defied the norms of patriarchal society. There is a good deal of similarity between Nirupama Borgohain and her protagonist, Chandraprabha as far as their courage, rebellious and restless creative life is concerned. That is exactly the reason why novelist has succeeded in giving a very authentic picture of Chandraprabha Saikia.

Nirupama Borgohain is a writer with vast experience of Assamese life. She has been both the sweet taste of success and the bitter taste of humiliation. As she declares, "Truth has been my credo. I have never flinched from speaking the truth" (*The Telegraph*, 16 March, 2002). But surprisingly the path of truth is full of obstacles. She has braved many obstacles in her personal life and career and lived a life of strong convictions. Being a woman, she has depicted various aspects of Assamese life from a woman's perspective. She has depicted many women characters very authentically because only a woman can understand the heart of another woman. Most of her novels and short stories are based on real models of life. "I have seen life from a close distance. And all my character are drawn from real life. Sometimes 'she' is my servant's mother and sometimes she is a person who lived in my in-law's village. Moreover, I limit my writing to my experience" (*The Telegraph*, 16 March, 2002). Her honesty and conviction are evident in her words. In her themes, she is very realistic, but in her style she is poetic rather than dull and sentimental. Though a woman-writer, she is happily free from inhibitions, but never bordering on the pornographic level like Shobha De. She has focused her attention on the victimization of Assamese women by the patriarchal male dominated society because of her natural sympathy for the female gender. But she does not wish to be called a feminist writer. On the contrary, she wants to be considered as a humanist writer: " I am a humanist. But sadly enough, most women in our society are battered and bruised at every step of their life. Being a woman myself I can't remain detached and it shows in my writings" (*The Telegraph,* 16 March 2002).

Nirupama Borgohain started her writing career as a schoolgirl. She has been known for her depiction of the harsh realities of rural life as well as those of the sophisticated or middle class urban life, from a woman's perspective. Her novel *Anya Jibon* (Another Life) has received special attention from readers and critics for the way it delineates the plight of women living under the (literal as well as metaphorical) yoke of male tyranny. In another significant novel, *Iparer Ghar Siparer Ghar* she portrays the dislocated life of a poor and beautiful woman, who is driven to prostitution by her harsh fate. She has thus enriched the Assamese literature thereby contributing to the wealth of Indian literature. Her contemporary consciousness, feminist perspective, realistic style and keen observation of life lent a special charm to her writings. She can easily be compared and contrasted with other women writers of India like Amrita Pritam, Kamala Das, Mahasweta Devi, Indira Goswami, Triveni and so on, for the realization of the principle of unity in diversity in Indian literature and culture.

Abhiyatri, honoured with the Central Sahitya Academy Award in 1996, happens to be very significant novel containing all the aforementioned qualities of the writer. Nirupoma Borgohain has justifiably chosen a woman character as the protagonist of her novel to counterbalance the male-protagonist of male writers of India. She has depicted the life of Chandraprabha Saikiani characterized by the struggle for women's rights around 1920s, long before the modern feminism made its way into India became fashionable. The novel is biographical in theme, realistic in style and balanced in its overall approach.

In *Abhiyatri,* Nirupama Borgohain offers a picture of the evolution of Chandrapriya's personal life from childhood to death. The narration is relatively brief and brisk, concentrating on the main events of Chandrapriya's life. One of six daughters of Ratiram Majumdar, the headman of the village, Daisingari Chandrapriya has a strong desire to be educated. Her younger sister Rameswari also has the same desire – a desire not commonly cherished by girls in the Indian patriarchal society of the early twentieth century. Even as a small girl Chandrapriya has an intense awareness of the restrictions imposed upon her gender – i.e. femininity – by the patriarchal Assamese society. Both Chandrapriya has and Rameswari takes great pains to go to the school at Kathalmuri by wading through slush and by being bled by the leeches. They have to undergo a good deal of physical discomfort in order to acquire some knowledge. "For some time now the two of them had been giving a kind of revenue in blood to the leeches who lined up on the muddy and watery path to the shrine of learning. Some times Chandrapriya felt like tearing her hair and raking her face. Why did God have to give her the itch for learning? Look at the other slush to become a lady-pundit. By now her girl friends had pasted the label of lady-pundit on her. She also walked around with other epithets clinging to her, such as 'tree-climbing Tom' and 'bandit-queen'" (p.1).

Both Chandrapriya and Rameswari want to be educated. Rameswari dreams of becoming a doctor. For girls to be educated in 1920s was neither desirable nor fashionable in the patriarchal society of Assam. It was in that context that Senipriya, sister of Gangapriya was educated and became a school teacher in the government middle school at Bhakigaon and even doled out a gift of education to Gangapriya's little children. Although Gangapriya is herself illiterate, she takes keen interest in the education of her daughters. But Ratiram Majumdar, who represents the patriarchal society, has his own difficulties with his daughter's education. The village school teacher draws the attention of Ratiram Majumdar to the daily struggle of the girls to reach the school. "But then he saw that the poor things had to practically swim to get along, all his pleasure was gone. The pundit was amazed that they do this every day to get to school. So he says, what's the point of navigating this flood to go to school? I've been wondering – how did we make a big slip here? Our kinsfolk and friends all tried to talk us out of it, but we wouldn't listen. Take you, you though of making scholars out of them. Well, who's going to marry them after they get all puffed up with scholarly pride?" The education of girls like Chandrapriya and Rameswari is problematized by the lack of facilities like proper roads or vehicles and by the lack of value for it in the marriage market.

Chandrapriya and Rameswari become conscious of their gender with all its distinctiveness and limitation right from their school days. They acutely feel the gender difference imposed by the patriarchal society of India. Chandrapriya mutters like a small volcano to her sister. "Boys and Girls - the way folk go on about boys and girls, boys and girls – I'll go nuts, really. It is as if God used gold and other precious metals to fashion boys out of, and cheap clay to mould us girls" (p.8). They wonder as to why even God created this gender-discrimination between boys and girls in the human society. They question even the difference in the dressing habits prescribed for men and women. They feel that their *mekhelas* (petticoats) are very inconvenient for the free movement of their legs. They slip off everything and just wrap their *mekhelas* around their breasts, dive into water and enjoy the sport. Chandrapriya curses her dress and longs for a male dress. "Isn't it much trip over all the time?" (p.8). The restrictions imposed upon the feminine gender by the patriarchal society are interrogated by Chandrapriya and Rameswari right from their childhood.

The relation between feminine gender and education in the patriarchal society is foreground in the novel. It is very ironical that girls who are keenly interested in education are positively discouraged from pursuing it whereas boys who may not be really interested in it are encouraged to pursue it. When Chandrapriya and Rameswari return home from school with their limbs and garments bespattered with mud, their father boils with fury, "Hey, what a sight you make at this hour. People will get scared if they see you, thinking you are some kind of demons. Did you go to study or to frolic mud and water? From today you don't study anymore, don't you ever think of going to school again" (p.11). Ratiram Majumdar orders them to stop going to school and help their mother in the household work. But Dharma, the younger brother of Chandrapriya is not really interested in going to school or acquiring knowledge. But yet his special right remain unchallenged. Chandrapriya is really puzzled by the double standards recommended by patriarchal society in the case of boys and girls.

Chandrapriya happens to be a very sensitive and imaginative girl. Sometimes she has terrifying dreams and feels depressed afterwards. But on the whole, she is a girl budding with a lot of gusto for life. When she is busy with the household work of helping her mother, her luck seems to have turned. One day, Ratiram Majumder cheers his daughters by his words, "Sick of you and other one's sulking, I went to the headmaster of Daisingari School. He has agreed to take you in" (p.27). Chandrapriya and Rameswari are simply overjoyed at the unexpected turn of their luck and prospects of continuing their education. Chandrapriya not only finishes her education at the their luck and the prospects of continuing their education. Chandrapriya not only finishes her education at the Daisingari school, but also starts a school on her own in order to help the girl to be educated. She interrogates and disagrees with the patriarchal society, which discourages women to have the formal education for several reasons. Illiteracy thus happens to be a common disqualification of Indian rural women in general. But Chandrapriya resists the patriarchal injunction by not only having her own education, but also by helping other girls having their education under her tutelage. She has a missionary zeal and works in her school of bamboo poles without any salary. She believes in the view that education can liberate women from all the restrictions imposed upon them by the patriarchal society. Not bothering about the salary, she wants to concentrate her attention on stimulating the rural girls to be educated. "I'm simply focused on expanding the school and whetting the girls' appetite for learning " (p.31). Even as a young girl she exhibits the qualities of a social reformer. She wants to open the window on the world. As she explains to Dandi, "We must keep ourselves informed about important national and international events. Just let this school of mine become a viable concern – I'll create a small library and will also keep newspapers" (p.33). Her dream of beginning a small library of books and newspapers is, obviously, symptomatic of her concern for womankind.

Chandrapriya improves her school gradually. The number of pupils also increases as days go by. Although she started her service without salary, she is now given a salary of six rupees per month by the local board. She has trained her pupils in such a beautiful way that she easily earns the appreciation from the school inspector Nilakantha Barua. He exclaims, "Well, it is remarkable that despite being a girl of thirteen you show such an inclination for studies" (p.37). Chandrapriya expresses her feministic views about the equality of sexes, "sir, with respect, I think that there is only some biological difference between a boy and girl, which need not prevent a girl from doing what a boy can do" (p.37). She also tells him how she had earned a medal with a portrait of George V embossed on it for doing well in her school. The school inspector, who recognizes the hidden spark in her, helps her to continue her education by recommending her to the Mission School at Nagaon. Chandrapriya feels simply ecstatic about the unexpected turn of her luck. Chandrapriya and Rameswari wish to begin a new life by having a new identity by the change of their names to Chandraprabha and Rajaniprabha respectively.

When she joins the school, her rebellious nature asserts itself. She does not tolerate any kind of injustice anywhere. The Mission School in which she has been studying is run by the Christian missionaries. The encounter between Hindu and Christianity is one of the consequence of colonialism and has both the positive and negative aspects attached to it. When Chandrapriya stays in the hostel and notices the high handed behaviour of the warden, Miss Long she rebels against it. "I can't take her prejudice ways anymore. What a hypocrite this woman is. She forces us to read it for her enlightenment, she does not like to be forced by Miss Long to do so. Similarly she dislikes the conversion of poor girls of villages into Christians with many enticements. Once after coming to know the plight of a Hindu girl housed in the storeroom of the hostel, Chandraprabha organizes a strike by the wards of the hostel against the warden, Miss Long. Initially Miss Long exhibits her pride and prejudice. Chandraprabha threatens, "We hear that you've put a girl inside the storeroom just because she wouldn't be converted to Christianity. If you don't retract your decision, we'll not do the Bible class today"(p.43). As Miss Long talks insultingly about the poverty of Indians, Chandraprabha retorts, "Madam, I can't believe that you're taunting us, the children of the very land whose air you are breathing, whose food and water has sustained you. If you don't withdraw your insulting remarks, we'll launch such a movement that you'll have to scamper away to your native country instead of happily running a school here"(p.44). She enthuses the pusillanimous Hindu girl till they bond together and wrench victory from the authorities. She beams with a sense of satisfaction.

In 1920s there was some turbulence in the political life of Assam as also in the other parts of India. The Civil Disobedience Committee met at Tejpur and was graced by the presence of leaders like Motilal Nehru and Ballabhbhai Patel. Chandraprabha, who is a very sensitive lady, observes the socio-political life around her with great curiosity, because of her social concern. At this time, she gets involved in a love, indulges in self-pity. On the contrary, she wants to dedicate her life for the social service. She tries to channelise her frustration through reformative activities.

As Chandraprabha remembers her past days spent at Tejpur, one may easily see her qualities of leadership and social concern. For example, when she leaves the primary school at Nagaon and joins the middle school at Tejpur, she gets the support and blessings of Paramananda Agarwala and Amiya Das. She is slowly initiated into public life by Jyoti Prasad Agarwala by being made the supervisor of the girls, wing of volunteer youth. She is pleasantly surprised by the turn of her luck. Jyoti Prasad Agarwala "said that he intuitively sensed Chandraprbha's leardership qualities" (p.51). It is indeed a great honour for a lady coming from rustic background to be accepted by the dignitaries of Tejpur. Sometime later, she is selected to give the keynote address at a drug prevention meeting. The Headmistress of Tejpur Girl's Middle School, Chandraprabha overcomes her shyness and makes a very impressive speech. She describes opium as "devil's dust" and castigates the drug-pushers and drug-users. "Chandraprabha ended her speech with something like a roar. There was another roar as the throng came out of the raptness and greeted the young women's debut into public life with thunderous applause" (p.52). Kiranmoyi Agarwala is so happy that she rests her hand on Chandraprabha's forehead and admires, "Saraswati, my dear, you lighted up everything today as if with a moonbeam. You were true to your name, Chandraprabha – the radiance of the moon. Here are my blessings: You'll be a great leader and bring a smile to the wan faces of the women of Assam" (p.52).

Chandraprabha's speech is followed by Acharya Prafulla Chandra Roy's. In his speech he highlights the achievement of prose writers in Assam as early as sixteenth century. Likewise he echoes Mahatma Gandhi about female education. "You must not neglect women's education. If the female race – half of the population is enslaved by ignorance, national progress will be a stillborn child" (p.53). Acharya Prafulla Chandra Roy's concern for female education acts as a mirror to Chandraprabha's own, helps her to concretize her reformist philosophy of life. The nationalist movement inspires her to a great extent. She is simply thrilled to hear the speech by Mahatma Gandhi in Tejpur. She is deeply influenced by Gandhiji's ideas of *swadeshi,* his disapproval of superstitious and obscurantist practices like child marriage and polygamy. After the speech Gandhiji sits down and writes an article called 'Lovely Assam' in which he pays great tributes to Assamese women: "The Assamese women weave dream of angels in cloth, they are born weavers" (p.56). Deeply inspired by Mahatma Gandhi, Chandraprabha and her colleagues burn the foreign-made cloths and manage to buy the khadi cloths which are very expensive. She joins Kiranmoyi Agarwala and others and starts a Mahila Samiti. She propagates Gandhiji's message in the villages, encourages them weave cloths and become part of the Non – Cooperation Movement. She even takes up the responsibility of helping the destitute women by providing the Singer sewing machines to them.

As days go by, Chandraprabha takes more and more interest in the socio-political activities. On Jyoti Prasad's suggestion, she trains about twenty women for the parade on horseback during the 1921 Ryot Conference at Chariduar. She imagines each of her "women as a deity like Durga, inhabiting the heavens" (p.58). Her image is growing in the society rapidly.

Chandraprabha, though rebellious by nature and intolerant of injustice whenever she confronts it, is a young lady with a deep passion and biological desires. When she is teaching in a Middle School at Tejpur, she happens to meet a young man called Dandinath Kalita, who appreciates her literary taste and talent. She falls in love with him in spite of the impossibility of marriage between them according to the traditional norms. She being a lowborn cannot marry her highborn lover. But still their passionate love gravitates them mutually. "So for two years they experienced hell and paradise, ecstasy and frustration, in alternation" (p.55). The lovers experience the joy of love and frustration of caste-difference. Finally their love bears fruit. The premarital love plunges her into a metaphorical hell. As she grows aware of her pregnancy, she returns to her native village, Daisingari. "Chandraprabha left Tejpur before the shape of her body heralded a new birth. At Daisingari, Atul was born" (p.59). The birth of a baby born outside wedlock is not appreciated or approved by the patriarchal society of Assam. She is subjected to slander, disparagement and isolation. Ironically, her niece, Rukmini also gives birth to a baby. But the difference between the two is the one between illegal and legal. "She got the news that a boy was born to her niece Rukmini. Whereas the birth of a boy had everyone's face with shame, this birth had become an event of rejoicing" (p.59). Rukmini's own mother was a child mother. "The irony of a child-marriage taking place in Chandraprabha's family at a time when it was publicly rolling against the practice skewed her innards" (p.60).

When swinging between gloom and gladness in family matters, Chandraprabha keeps on observing the political life of the nation, which is not very cheerful at the moment. Because of the violence at Chaurichaura Gandhi has put a stop to agitationist programmes. She also observes the sharp ideological difference between Mahatma Gandhi and other political leaders like Subhas Chandra Bose, Jawaharlal Nehru the elders like Motilal Nehru, C. R. Das, Lala Lajpat Rai and C.N. Sharma.

By this time, Chandraprabha's creative urge begins to assert itself. She plans to write her first novel. Chandraprabha does not allow her domestic responsibilities to suppress her creativity. With great perseverance, she completes her autobiographical novel *Aparajita (Unvanquished)* running into 343 pages, which is autobiographical. Her mother does not understand and approve of her creative urge, as it is not materially useful.

Poverty happens to be a very depressing aspect of Chandraprabha's family. Her brother Dharma has turned out to be a wastrel and no help can be expected from him. Her younger sister Rajani skims a small amount of her scholarship to send to the family. It is exactly during crisis that she is offered a teaching job at a girls' school in Kaljirapara. The offer turns out to be a godsend for Chandraprabha. Her love affairs with Dandinath Kalita had added to her difficulties in life. In addition to poverty, she has to suffer the social stigma in the society at every phase of her life. Her illegitimate motherhood has created a great personal as well as social problem for her. She loves Dandinath passionately, but she cannot marry him for caste reasons. She pines for his company day in and day out. She does not enjoy the pleasures of having a proper family. She is so sensitive and understanding by nature that she even sympathizes with Dandinath for his helplessness in the matter. When she hears the news of his marriage with a girl called Kamal under the parental pressure, she exercises an extraordinary control over her emotions. Kamal also happens to be a sensible wife of Dandinath, who accepts Chandraprabha as her 'elder sister' and communicates with her regularly.

Chandraprabha is considered as a 'fallen woman' by the patriarchal society of Daisingari village. "The atmosphere of the village was conscious and hostile, home was dull and melancholic"(p.64). The villagers are contemptuous of Chandraprabha as they do not like to be counseled by a fallen woman. Chandraprabha's unmarried motherhood becomes a subject of gossip in 1920s when the modern radical feminism was not yet fashionable in India. (Unmarried motherhood in1980s has been hailed as an achievement by the modern feminists.) Chandraprabha has to be very bold to face the hostile patriarchal society. When she joins the school at Kaljirapara, people taunt her about her illegitimate child, Atul. Initially the women of the village, who are part of the patriarchal society, plan to insult her. "By then the news of her appointment and joining had spread and the mothers had tutored their children to haul abuses at Chandraprabha. As she made her way, she felt as if she was splashed with venom from both the sides. The children hooted and jeered, and called her obscene names. The women mostly stayed in the background, but one of them came forward to shout: 'Wretched woman! Now she'll drag our girls down to the pits'" (p.66). But as days go by, people are reconciled to her condition and let her alone. Chandraprabha's 'scarlet' past become insignificant. A liberal gentleman called Gopinath Medhi offers shelter of his home to Chandraprabha thereby preventing her from traveling the rugged path with her son Atul from Daisingari to Kaljirapara. Chandraprabha puts up with all this insult and inconvenience with an extraordinary courage, which simply admirable.

Chandraprabha's rebellious nature asserts itself whenever she sees some injustice done to somebody. Once she sees a low caste girl waiting near a temple well silently. She asks the girl as to why she doesn't get the water. Greatly amused, the attendant replies, "She can't touch the water because she's a low caste. She is waiting for some one of a proper caste to come and fill her pitcher"(p.67). The attendant further clarifies that they can't allow the low caste person to contaminate the water of the well, which is used by the high caste people of the temple. Chandraprabha blasts the attendant to her heart's content. She then goes to the abbot of the *Kirtan ghar* and secures the right for every one to draw water from the well. To celebrate her victory, she collects a few low-caste girls, marches them towards the well and arranges for a communal drawing of water. Then her face beaming with the broadest smile. She says, "From today, this water is really pure."(p.68).

The love affairs between a high caste man (Dandinath Kalita) and a lower caste girl (Chandraprabha) is not approved by the patriarchal society. It becomes a subject of gossip. But sensitive people do not make any fuss about it. Gopinath Medhi "had also spread the information that Chandraprabha was secretly married to Dandinat Kalita at Bhairb temple, Tejpur. But there were social obstacles to their living together. Dandinath was high caste, while Chandraprabha was of a lower caste. At the same time, there was a hope that Dandinath would one day be able to accept Chandraprabha as his wife and Atul as his son"(p.69). He wants to stop the wagging tongues. But unfortunately it is not possible. For example, when Chandraprabha takes Atul to the convention of Sahitya Sabha, some women innocently asks her about the child's father, she explains the story of her life boldly and calmly: "With the utmost naturalness in the world, Chandraprabha unfolded her history of single motherhood. The gathering was stunned into silence. Afterwards, when Chandraprabha went to bathroom with

Atul, the women spoke up: "It seems that we women are our worst enemies. Have you paused to consider that the other partner in this scandal is leading a happy married life, while Chandraprabha is carrying the burden of shame?"(p.72). Though rational men and women understand Chandraprabha's predicament, the orthodox ones continue to wag their tongues. "It was amazing that Chandraprabha was not bowed down by grief, and went around proclaiming her illegitimate motherhood so defiantly. She herself was a child-widow. Now she was a beautiful woman, who was stranded in life, with no hope of fulfillment of any kind. And her presence was supposed to cast a shadow on holy rituals and social occasions, so that she was isolated and ostracized"(p.73). The same patriarchal society, which looks down upon a widow or a single woman, also looks at her temptingly. "Yet the widow was not safe either. Men's lascivious attention was frequently attracted by her full enticing figure"(p.73). Only a widow can understand a widow. When they form a procession to go to the convention, Chandraprabha sees a widow lagging behind. Chandraprabha grabs her by the hand and drags her to the front. At this tears well up in the widow's eyes. Chandraprabha wants to give a new confidence and dignity to the widow, who is suppressed by the patriarchal society. After her widowhood, she had almost come to terms with the annihilation of her social identity and was in the habit of shrinking in public. Now suddenly this stigmatized woman was threatening to open up new horizons for her"(p.73). Chandraprabha, thus, helps the widow to have a new confidence in herself and not suffer cast-off feeling.

After Rajani Kanta Bordoloi's speech against opium and alcohol and for the emancipation of women, Chandraprabha is angry to notice the segregation of men and women under the pandal. She is irritated to see the women sitting in the enclosures like caged animals and listening to the speech on literature. She therefore, yells, "My sister, why are you crouching inside like captured vermin? If you have any pride at all, if you don't think it's your god-given right to stand on the same footing as men, then do stand up for that right, and break free from this cell, this cage!"(p.74) Chandraprabha struggles hard to bring the shy and illiterate women out of the restrictions of the patriarchal society.

Though Chandraprabha fell in love with Dandinath Kalita in a passion, she could not marry for communal reasons. She is thus compelled to remain an unmarried mother and a single woman.

Although she is quite bold to face the contingencies of her life, Dandinath Kalita doe not have the willingness and courage to defy the norms of the patriarchal society. Yielding to the parental pressure, he has married Kamal. It is tantamount to betrayal of his beloved Chandraprabha. Though she is deeply disappointed by her destiny preventing her marriage with her love, she never hurts or taunts or insults him. This is because she not only loves him deeply, but also understands his helplessness and the circumstantial imperatives. She is very unlike the modern radical feminists, who shout at abuse, hurt and insult the lovers, who shy away from inter caste marriages because of their helplessness in the patriarchal situations. To understand is to pardon. As she understands Dandinath Kalita's predicament, she sympathizes with him and takes entire burden of the social stigma on herself. She has to bear the great responsibility of rearing her child, Atul to be a fine human being.

An unmarried mother living away from her lover to be a burden to her parents. Chandraprabha's father Ratiram Majumdar grows anxious about her future. Although Dandinath Kalita has not been able to marry Chandraprabha, he keeps on sending a little money to her almost regularly, for her expenditure. In spite of his marriage with Kamal, Dandinath Kalita and Chandraprabha being star-crossed lovers, pine for each other. But alas, the patriarchal society does not allow them to be united legally. He writes plaintive as well as passionate letters to Chandraprabha and wants to know if she would forget him. After finishing the letter, Chandraprabha presses it to her breast with desperate ardour and thinks inwardly about the dilemma of love. "My heart's monarch, is it so easy to forget you? If I could banish you from my memory, perhaps there would be some peace in this weary soul. But our love will cross the frontiers of forgetfulness itself and mortality simmers on. It's a strange thing this love that you are bounded to. It's madness, an intoxication. It is a compound of unendurable pain and absolute bliss, dearest"(p.70).

Again unlike a modern emancipated woman, Chandraprabha does not go to the extent of searching for another, richer or better lover for emotional or biological satisfaction. Unlike a modern feminist, she never says that she cannot control the itch between the thighs. On the contrary, she boldly accepts the sneers and jeers of the patriarchal society.

Just Chandraprabha defies the norms of patriarchal society in the matrimonial matter, she defies the norms in other aspects also. For example, cycles are ridden only by men and not by women in the Indian society. But Chandraprabha defies this norm and rides a bicycle for frequents. The people of her area are surprised by the sight of a lady riding a bicycle. They express their sense of surprise as well as contempt for her. "Oyee, just look at that Look. Look at that female riding a bicycle. O, no, now I've seen everything . A female creature on a bike! Of course, this female is abandoned – what else do you expect from her?'"(p.75). Not heeding the wagging tongues, Chandraprabha continues the bike riding, as it is necessary and convenient for her to cover the long distances on the narrow and looping roads of the villages where she tries to organize womenfolk.

Chandraprabha questions the norms of patriarchal society about the dressing habits of women. Even as a small girl, she finds her *mekhela* very inconvenient for easy movement of legs. Once she and her younger sister Rameswari swim in the pond and find their *mekhelas* very cumbersome. They, therefore, question as to why they should wear them compulsorily. "Getting up to go and making heavy weather of wearing her sodden, cumbersome *mekhelas.* Chandra cursed her dress and said, 'Isn't it much better to wear a dhoti like the boys, something you can hitch up as high as you like, and something you don't trip over all the time'"? (p.8). This simple tough indicates Chandraprabha's interrogation of the sartorial segregation of male and female genders imposed by the patriarchal society. She defies the dress codes enjoined upon the gender by the society.

Although Chandraprabha could not marry Dandinath Kalita for practical reasons, she loves him deeply. She remembers him in her lonely moments and pines for him. Once when her memory becomes very intense, she writes a passionate love-letter to him: "Dearest, (she wrote), Lay down your head on my lap, love and lend me your ears for a moment, Didn't we devour the hours together, and didn't it seem that we would flow into one another with our endless talk? What happened to all that? What are you doing on the other side of silence? Here, at this moment, I am all-alone in the night. Didn't we come together again and again, on such nights, which were strictly our own? Now every part of my body is aching for one blink of life? Can I see you once more? Why do things that seemed everlasting – you, the warmth of your body, your loving chatter - now mock me with their absence? One day you came to me wearing the mantle of a beggar and you courted me, saying that you'll lie prostrate at my door. Now I am on my knees. I have no shame. I crave your caresses all over my body. But what about you? You incomparable, don't you? Then why do you have to care about this miserable spectre? Send me word, and I'll hack my own limbs off, one by one...."(p.64-65)

Dandinath Kalita has been sending some money to Chandraprabha as and when he can. But his gifts are accompanied by reprimands about her new attachments with male friends and her extravagance. "Darkness shrouded Chandraprabha as she thought about those accusatory paper missile"(p.78). In spite of the fact that Dandinath Kalita has no legal control over her, Chandraprabha still loves and respects him and takes his advice seriously. After the death of Ratiram Majumdar, Chandraprabha's mother warns her when the latter wants to go Bajali to participate in a political programme: "Go if you must, despite the state you're in. But don't get too intimate with those young men, and don't spend nights with anybody and everybody. Tongues will wag"(p.88-89). The mother articulates her fears about the scandal-mongering habit of people in the patriarchal society. But Chandraprabha does not bother about such gossip. Being young and lonely, she longs for male company. She thinks that nobody has a right over her body or mind. "During calmer moments when she was all by herself, Chandraprabha had to admit that the company of young men made her tingle. Dandinath Kalita had accused her for a long time that she established quick intimacy with the males she met. But when she remembered Dandinath Kalita's charges, she erupted inside. Even if I lose my head when I see men, what right have you to accuse me, she thought. There is no desire of your that you have left unfulfilled. But you don't spare a moment to think about me, for whom no gratification of any kind is possible"(p.89). Chandraprabha, obviously, thinks of asserting her sexual and emotional identity.

Chandraprabha remains devoted to her lover Dandinath Kalita although she could not marry him. Because of her passionate love for him, she keeps on writing letters to him now and then and enjoys receiving letters from him. She has preserved his old letters in a chest with great care and reads them nostalgically at her leisure. "There was, however, a box crammed with Dandinath Kalita's old letters into she could dip to quench her thirst. For her, this old and rusty was a chest of treasures. Here lay hidden the great Assamese writer's heart's offerings made at his most ardent moments"(p.95). She takes out a letter at random from the pile and reads it with deep love. The letter contains nectar and venom. The lover chides her for numerous moral shortcomings, but still sings "If from the straight, narrow path/You should ever stray/Then for you, to my lord/I'll pray/And pure portrait/I'll preserve in my heart"(p.95). Chandraprabha plants a soft kiss on the letter and clutches it to her heart.

The plight of an unmarried mother is very pitiable. Although Chandraprabha is bold enough to face the unsympathetic patriarchal society, she finds it difficult to take care of her child, Atul because of her socio-political preoccupations. Atul feels the conspicuous absence of his father because of the wagging tongues of his school fellows." It was becoming impossible for Atul to study at school in Daisingari. He was having to face barbs from his malicious little school fellows, who heckled him about his invisible father"(p.96). Chandraprabha has to give a psychological strength to Atul by preventing him from a sense of forlornness.

Dandinath keeps on sending some money to Chandraprabha whenever she is in trouble and enquires after his beloved son. But Atul cannot understand why his father lives far away from him. He has a crisis of identity and asks his mother for clarification. "Sometime ago Atul had suddenly asked her: 'ma, don't I have a father? All my friends- Harish, Kali, Tarun- have fathers. Do you know, ma when the boys quarrel with me, they call me a bastard? What does that mean, ma? You are not a widow, are you? No, you are not a widow like Khagen's mother. Her forehead is bare, but you wear sindhoor. Then my father is alive. But where is he?'"(p.108). Chandraprabha has to answer the disconcerting question. She grows angry at her peculiar condition. "Chandraprabha felt like smashing her head against the wall. She became livid with rage thinking about Dandi. It was his journey of life with such a severe social handicap" (p.109). She has to satisfy Atul with her camouflaged answer, "My precious darling, when your father doesn't stay with you, then people called you a bastard. Your father stays very far away. He is imprisoned there, and he has been unable to come to us by breaking his chains"(p.109). The innocent Atul is easily satisfied by the story and fantasizes about the chains that bind his father.

As days go by, Chandraprabha tries to forget her personal frustration by canalizing her emotion in a creative way. She dedicates herself more and more to social work activities, the women's organizational work. As a result of their constant fight, the Cotton College – the premier institute of Assam starts admitting girl students. Because of the financial pinch, Chandraprabha has to work and even earn her livelihood. At present she has been serving as the Headmistress of Mahjerapara Balika Vidyalaya at Krishnanagar of Nadia district in the State of Bengal. But the authorities of the School Management "were demanding that she sign a declaration to the effect that she would not take part in any agitational activities against the government. Although she needed the job for money and the nearness of Atul that it ensured, Chandraprabha would not sign. And so the axe had fallen at last"(p.113). Consequently she is terminated from service. Jobless, she returns home for a brief while. But there also she is shocked to learn that their ancestral land had been mortgaged to Seniram by her younger brother Dharma. As days go by, she takes every bitter experience in her stride. The positive result of their activities movement give her a sense of satisfaction. When she visits Guwahati, she is received very warmly by her well wishers like Swarnalata Saikia and her daughter Pushpalata, Dr. Bhubaneswar Barua and his family. They proudly inform her that a girls' hostel has been constructed at Cotton College. "Another milestone was thus created after the right for girls to study at Cotton College was won. When Chandraprabha viewed the hostel, she felt her heart brimming over with contentment…."(p.114).

Chandraprabha's vista of socio-political activism goes on widening day by day. In 1936 she is summoned by the Congress Party to campaign for the party nominee for the Legislative Council election. She, therefore, goes to Barpeta, riding her bicycle and canvasses for the Congress candidate enthusiastically.

In spite of her private hell, Chandraprabha plunges into political action. When the smouldering independence movement catches fire again, she begins to work for the nationalistic cause. She forms a committee called the Organization for the Succour of the Distressed and makes the members go from house to house and collect donations. When she goes to Bajali, she argues boldly with a *daroga,* but is finally arrested by the British Government on 27 January 1943 when she has a meeting with women in the Harimandir of Pathsala. The police start dragging her. She asks them not to drag her, as she is willing to go with them. "But the policeman paid no heed to her word and kept on dragging her. Seeing this, the other women became infuriated and started to pull Chandraprabha in the other direction. A few women became so excited that they got hold of her *mekhela* and *chadar* and started pulling. As a result, Chandraprabha was suddenly almost stripped in public. Meanwhile the women started scuffling with the police in earnest. Many women rained blows on the police and swiping off their *topees,* trampled on them. The police also laid about them with their batons, injuring a few"(p.129). She is made to walk to the Police Station. The Assistant Inspector "was in a nasty mood over the incident in the temple, and seeing Chandraprabha, gave her a resounding slap and shoved her to the ground. Chandraprabha crashed down on the hard floor and hurt her hand. Despite seeing that Chandraprabha was hurt, the Assistant Inspector did not show any signs of remorse. In fact, he chortled as he stood over her"(p.129). Then they make her spend the night in the lock-up. None can fail admire the mettle of the strong willed Chandraprabha who is not at all afraid of anyone and who is ready to undergo any suffering mental or physical.

When the police van that is taking Chandraprabha to Barpeta, stops near Pathsala Railway Station, there occurs a bomb blast very unexpectedly. The soldiers who are present there and everywhere because of the World War II, try to arrest an innocent boy. But Chandraprabha who is a fighter for justice, dissuades the soldiers from arresting the boy. Then Chandraprabha is taken to the jail at Barpeta, which is like a hell-hole. But interestingly enough, she happens to meet her son Atul also there as he is also connected with the independence movement. At Guwahati jail also she fights the authorities against the discrimination between higher class and lower class person in treatment. Her humanitarian approach is wrongly branded by people as 'socialism.'

After serving her term in the Guwahati jail, she returns home to face dreary domestic problems. By now Atul has grown into a young man and has passed his B.A. degree from Cotton College in 1946. Time has brought about inevitable changes in her looks. "A rather sad looking middle-aged woman with graying hair and lined and furrowed cheeks stared back at her from the mirror"(p.134). But she quickly reconciles herself to the ageing process in order to resume her reformative mission. Consequently, she reactivates the Mahila Samiti, with the support of Induprabha and Dr. Barua. Then they hold the fifth conference of the Asom Mahila Samiti at Kumar Bhaskar Natya Mandir, Uzanbazar, Guwahati. They decide to fight against untouchability, the greatest bane of India. "Many proposals were adopted at this conference. One that was very close to Chandraprabha's heart was the resolve to extirpate untouchability. The resolution was immediately tested. "Low-class women delegates served food to upper-class women who ate without demurring. Seeing the vision of Gandhiji translated into reality right before her eyes, a lump came into Chandraprabha's throat. This was the moment of fulfillment that left her contented at every pore of her being"(p.135). She keeps on counseling the rural women to give them a new confidence about themselves.

Chandraprabha starts a magazine entitled *Abhiyatri* (which means 'pioneer') to serve as a mouthpiece of the Mahila Samiti and to propagate the Gandhian principles. Her son, who is a chip of the old block, discontinues his postgraduate studies, plunges into social action and becomes an assistant editor of a daily newspaper called *Asomiya*.

Chandraprabha continues her social work even after India achieves independence. She and her companies fight against untouchability and illiteracy, to rehabilitate the destitute and the fallen women and open child-welfare and childbirth training centres all over Assam. Because of her strong convictions and bold action Chandraprabha is popularly described as an 'iron maiden.'

Once there was a big earthquqke in Assam in 1950. Chandraprabha busies in the relief work, along with Usha Das and Miss P. Rasul. But on the way they have to cross two rivers, i.e., Khablu and Subansiri. By the time they reach the bank of Subansiri, the last ferry is cancelled because of some mechanical trouble. Hence the three women have to spend the night in a reedy hut of the boatmen and partake of the ordinary meal of rice and *dal*. Chandraprabha advises Usha, "Usha, if you commit yourself to public life, you'll have to meet these inconveniences in their stride".

Chandraprabha writes a detailed history of the Mahila Samiti for the benefit of posterity. After the independence of India, she joins the Socialist party. She also becomes the President of the All India Assam Peasants' Conference and targets being dissatisfied with the faults and contradictions of the Socialist Party, she returns to the Congress party and contests for Bajali constituency in the 1957 State elections. But unfortunately she, the first Assamese woman candidate, is defeated in the election. That is because politics requires tact and cunning people. But Chandraprabha's candour has to cost her about five hundred votes. Though temporarily disappointed by her defeat in the election, she soon forgets it and dedicates herself to the service of Mahila Samiti.

By this time much water has flown under the bridge. On hearing the news of the death of her unofficial husband, Dandinath Kalita, she removes the *sindhoor tilak* from her forehead. She thinks that she has become truly independent now. But time has its adverse effect upon her health. She has started suffering from gastric ulcer. Never bothering about her ill health, she lends her support to the Orphan Welfare Centre concerned about destitute women of various types and rural women. As Girija describes, "The woman has consecrated her entire life to the welfare of suffering women of all kinds! What has she not put her hand to? Eradication of untouchability, rehabilitation of 'fallen' and abandoned women of society, the establishment of welfare centers for mothers and children, the service of *harijans,* prohibition of drinking and alcohol-you name it. I shall remember how defies the gender difference and discrimination perpetuated by the patriarchal society.

Chandraprabha in her capacity as the President records all the amelioratives of the regional Mahila Samiti. The document runs into about a hundred pages. The cover page contains a photograph of Mahatma Gandhi flanked by the messages from the Mahatma and Binoba Bhave. The Mahatma's message reads:" The Samiti does not need any blessings; its own work is enough." Binoba Bhave's message reads: "The souls of men and women are on the same level. Therefore a woman has the strength and ability that a man has." The messages of these great men testify to Chandraprabha's greatness as a social activist and as a woman with a will who defies the gender difference and discrimination perpetuated by the patriarchal society.

Now Chandraprabha realizes that she has reached her seventieth year. She has not been keeping well for the past few years. Her gastric trouble worsened. She becomes more and more conscious of death. She wants to spend a little more time with her dear ones. Atul has bought a second-hand car and moved to a new house. Chandraprabha has a sense of fulfillment now. She is also happy to note that Atul is contesting the election as a Congress candidate from Guwahati. But she is admitted to the Chatribari Mission Hospital at Takaubari as she has reached the last stage of cancer. Atul becomes sad and helpless, but as the irony of life would have it, he wins the election and becomes a member of the Legislative Assembly of Assam. Chandraprabha, in spite of her sagging health, feels happy about her son's political victory. But she advises him to follow the moral path and dedicate himself to social service; "Son, your victory erases all the pain of my life, all of it. Now a great burden is on your shoulders. You must not betray the people who made your triumph possible. Have the people in your heart always; never think about your interest. And corruption! Avoid that demon, my son. And one more, think – never to become a minister. The seat of minister is slippery; it's so very easy to slide from it into corruption and depravity. Once in that den,you'll forget all about the people"(p.164). Chandraprabha's advice to her son is a model to be followed by all the politicians of modern India.

Chandraprabha's secret desire for fame and glory is more than fulfilled when she hears the news that she has been awarded the Padmashree. In spite of her ill health, she wants to receive it from the President of India on 24th of March. She asks Atul to make arrangements to send her to Delhi. Atul assures her that all the arrangements have been made. 6th March happens to be Chandraprabha's birthday. Atul goes to her bed and finds her unconscious. "Silently and alone he digested the irony of the supine creature's ardent desire to go all the way to far off Delhi to collect her reward. Another great irony was in store. On her birthday Chandraprabha died"(p.165). Thus ends the life of a dynamic woman who fought for justice and gender-equality and against gender-discrimination, illiteracy, ignorance and exploitation all through her life. Chandraprabha who fought for the emancipation of women all though her life was finally liberated from the mortal world itself. That she should die on her birthday itself seems to be a big irony of her life. But her death is preceded by a sense of fulfillment. Her life has been quite meaningful simply because she has led a bold life of strong convictions.

Chandraprabha has braved the patriarchal society by leading the life of an unmarried mother. The growing age has brought a great tolerance in her. "She was not completely spared from sarcastic remarks, but an older and hardened Chandraprabha was now inured to such remarks, and they could not lacerate her any longer, the way they did when she was young and vulanerable"(p.134). She has the satisfaction of motherhood in spite of the inimical patriarchal society. She is happy to see that her son Atul passed his

B.A. degree from Cotton College in 1946. "Despite Dandinath's urging, Chandraprabha had refused to destroy the seed in her womb. Now the seed had budded and flourished. Living in a hidebound and unforgiving society, she had thrown down a gauntlet – she was going to make a man of her boy. And now the dream comes as true as the light of the sun and the moon"(p.135).

There has been a change in Atul's psychology over the years. He is no longer an innocent boy trying to break the chains that bind his father. Having becoming an adult now, he understands the predicament of his parents. Although he loves and respects his mother, he does not appreciate his father for his lack of courage in matrimonial matters. Chandraprabha wishes that Atul should meet and talk with his father, who is eager to see him. But Atul flatly refused to do so. "Chandraprabha felt that now Dandinath would yearn to see Atul. But Atul was implacable regarding his father. After Atul's matriculation Chandraprabha had timidly suggested to her son that he should meet his father. Then quite normally obliging boy stiffened at the suggestion and said in a steely voice: 'If I have to go to Dandinath Kalita, why don't write me a certificate attesting that I am his son, mother? Otherwise how will he recognize me?' It was pointless to try and change Atul's attitude now"(p.136). Chandraprabha who has been fighting with the patriarchal society cannot fight with her own son who has internalized the patriarchal code in him. He seems to be very angry with his father for betraying his mother and for not meeting him earlier. Chandraprabha narrates it to Induprabha, "Indu, father and son met for the first time today, but there was no union, no reconciliation!... Indu, Atul's father suddenly arrived from somewhere while I was not at home. At first Atul did not even recognize him. Of course, he had never seen his father. When Atul asked this stranger about his identity, he said with a bent head:' I am your father, son. I am Dandinathe Kalita.' Indu do you know how Atul reacted to this revelation? He became agitated and said in a flinty voice: "All your life you hid this identity and now you have come to me in secret, wearing this identity. You may leave, I'll never call you father'"(p.148). Chandraprabha feels sorry for both her lover and son simultaneously. She sympathizes with her lover who has for being insulted so blatantly by his own son. Chandraprabha cries about her strange plight, but Indruprabha exhorts her by highlighting her courage and perseverance. "Actually, you are Suryaprabha as much as you are Chandraprabha. Surya diffuses its life-giving warmth throughout the world and burns and banishes all foulness and diseases from the world. That's what you have been doing. Who knows better than me? Under your sunny influence, Atul Saikia is a worthy member of this society today. When his father saw what his son had become, his old heart had swollen with pride – I'm sure off that. In a way, you defeated him by accomplishing what you promised to do, but he must have enjoyed this defeat. Any father would.Induprabha not only consoles Chandraprabha about Atul's rash behaviour with his father, but also tries to highlight Chandraprabha's achievement.

Days go by, Chandraprabha immerses herself in her social activities. Atul grows into a responsible young man, gets married and settles down in life. A few years before Atul gets a son, Dandinath dies. "God had freed her from another shackle. A bizarre bondage this was, not sanctioned by society, yet unbreakable and singly perpetual. But it was indeed"(p.153). When Chandraprabha hears the news of Dandinath's death, she removes the *sindhoor tilak* from her forehead and tells Induprabha, Indu, my forehead is unmarked today. I am truly independent now"(p.154). She shed tears and feels sad about not having been able to see him before his death. "Indu, as he lay on a hospital bed in Dibrugarh, he wanted to see me once last time. But I didn't know until it was too late"(p.154). But Atul does not show any response to the news of his father's death. "Atul responded to the news of Dandinath's demise with a wry smile. His father was gone forever, but he did not feel bereaved" (p.154). Atul never feels any attachment for his father as the latter always remained as a phantom on the fringe of his consciousness. He is not enough to understand the dilemmas of his father and mother, because he is still a hot-blooded youth.

Atul is really surprised by his mother's behaviour. Although Chandraprabha defied the norms of the patriarchal society by falling in love with Dandinath Kalita and by leading the life of a single woman and unmarried mother, she never goes in search of another man for her biological satisfaction, emotional, social and economic security. On the contrary, she compromises with her situation and continues to believe that Dandinath is her husband, although not recognized by the society. That is reason why Atul is puzzled by his mother's assertion. But she often showed herself to be such a spineless, submissive creature too. On the one hand she was continually on the warpath for women's rights and she played a life-long role of the servile, devoted wife, even when the honour and recognition of wifehood was denied to her. It is true that Chandraprabha, in spite of being a rebellious lady in so many respects, lived like a devoted but unofficial wife of Dandinath, simply because she loved him too deeply.

After the death of Dandinath, Atul shows some signs of maturity as he has crossed the age of thirty. He seems to have understood the mystery of life and the importance of human bondage. "Although Atul's feelings were often incinerated by his mother's bizarre relationship with Dandinath, he himself established a bond with that person in an oblique way. However, that was after Dandinath's death. Atul showered a lot of affection on the daughter of Dandinath's widowed daughter Punya. When the girl was married at Tejpur, Atul went to the wedding with Bina to give his blessings. That was the first time Atul had entered the house of his father. He was now above thirty"(p.154).

Chandraprabha's father Ratiram Majumdar happens to be a village chief. Ratiram and Gangpriya had eleven children of which eight were girls. But now only three girls are alive. Ratiram Majumdar, a believer in the patriarchal values, initially does not wish to educate his daughters beyond the high school level. But after being convinced about the daughters' persistence and ambition, he yields to their demand and sends them to school and college. He wants to educate his son, Dharma as he is a boy but ironically the boy does not show any inclination for learning. The gender-expectations of the patriarchal society are reversed.

As Ratiram Majumdar grows old, he is worried about Dharma's truancy and irresponsibility as well as general financial problems of the family. Chandraprabha has to take responsibility of helping the family financially as much as she can. She, therefore, works in schools in different capacities. In spite of her own personal problem of facing the stigma of being an unmarried mother, she has to take care of her parents also. Being unmarried, she has no home of her own, but has to stay at her parental home forever. Though Dandinath could not marry her, he keeps of sending money to her now and then. Chandraprabha tries to console her father not to worry about the family. But after a few years, Ratiram Majumdar dies. Consequently his family becomes forlorn. Chandraprabha tries to hold the family together. But Dharma, the prodigal brother disappears from home after secretly mortgaging all their land to Seniram, the moneylender, for three thousand rupees. This is shocking news to entire family. Dharma has left them all in midwaters as it were. Chandraprabha writes to her sister Rajani that they must struggle hard to reclaim the land. She goes to Guwahati and files a case against Seniram, but the court dismisses the case. Chandraprabha and her mother are deeply frustrated by the defeat in the legal case. After a few months they hear the news that Dharma has married a girl in Shillong. But they are unhappy about his not sending them money that he had escaped with. After some time Rajani and Chandraprabha pool together three hundred and sixty rupees to liberate their land, but all their efforts culminate in failure. The land is lost forever. Thus Chandraprabha and her mother and sister have to face the problem of financial insecurity, all because of the carelessness and irresponsibility of her younger brother, Dharma.

Chandraprabha was happy about her younger sister who was admitted to the medical college who later became a doctor. Rajani married a man called Prafulla Dutta and led a happy life for some years. Chandraprabha was happy about her sister's happiness. But alas! It did not last long. There is a very unexpected turn in Rajani's life. Prafulla, who wants to help Chandraprabha and her mother by arranging for the sale of mustard seed, has now become a *tantrik*– a demon worshipper by a strange quirk of his fate. Not only that. But he has made his wife Rajani also his consort and disciple. Cosequently Rajani, having come under the influence of a *tantrik* guru-cum-devotee, begins to dislike Chandraprabha and hate her husband. Prafulla Dutta, therefore, writes to Chandraprabha about Rajani's insanity. Now Chandraprabha has the double sorrow of seeing her sister's insanity and hearing the lamentation of her mother. Rajani labours under the illusion that she is an incarnation of the goddess Kali. Chandraprabha brings Rajani home and tries to push her into medical practice in order to wean her away from the *tantrik* path. But the effort turns out to be rather futile. Rajani embarrasses a surgeon in the Barpeta Civil Hospital boasting about it: "But he does not realize that he should prostrate at my feet constantly, licking my feet-like-red-lotus"(p.122). As Rajani curses the absent surgeon obscenely, Gangpriya starts wailing loudly by clasping Rajani to her breast. "Chandraprabha stood stock-still and speechless observing the absurd tragicomedy where the mother's crying struck up a bizarre concert with the daughter's howling laughter"(p.123). That a talented young woman's career should have such a tragic climax is indeed pitiable.

Chandraprabha has to bear the sorrow of her sister's madness and of Prafulla's helplessness. "He started ranting that it was just his foul luck to marry a girl like Rajani. Not only was she a lunatic, but she was also an adulteress, a creature with no mortality. Prafulla's accusation was not baseless. Rajani goes around with an uncouth educated character from Daisingari. If anyone says anything, she charges him or her with obscenities and threatens violence. So Prafulla left us. Now I alone am responsible for Rajani, once again. But the trouble is, she can't stand me either. She accuses me, in her broken, madwoman's language that I have always been her worst enemy, and I have been careless and extravagant with money and bled white and finally destroyed her. Imagine the toll this is taking on our mother"(p.124).

After some time they learn that Rajani died in rather sordid circumstances. Rajani had become illegally pregnant and died after giving birth to a dead child. "One day they learnt that after giving birth to a dead child in a peasant's hut on the bank of a small stream, Rajani had followed her child out of this world. When Chandraprabha reached the spot in one breathless dash, she saw that her precious darkling kid sister Rajani, the first female gynaecologist of Assam, was lying all bloodied beside her stillborn baby, her face pressed to the damp earth"(p.137). Rajani's strange life was an extraordinary blend of glory and shame. But no vestige of glory attended her exit from this world. Because of Rajani's shameful and pitiable end, Chandraprabha and the rest of her family lose all peace of mind and are on the verge of insanity.

In addition to being a rebellious lady with a restless soul, Chandraprabha has an inner urge for creative writing also. In spite of all odds and inconveniences of domestic life, she cultivates her talent for creative writing. "Apart from weaving cloth at home, Chandraprabha also started spinning a narrative, a novel named *Aparajita* i.e. *The Unvanquished.* Before this she had sent a few articles here and there, but she was pouring everything into this novel. This was to be an autobiographical novel. She kept up an unflagging pace while writing this novel, recounting her agonies, tribulations and also her triumphs over these misfortunes" (p.61). Her urge for creative writing serves two purposes: one, to articulate her inner feelings thereby achieving a sort of catharsis; and two, to attain a literary immortality in the world. Creative writing may be pursued by male writers without much difficulty, but not by female writers so easily. The special burden of domestic life acts as a great hindrance to the practice of creative writing to a woman. Like Virginia Woolf, she needs not only a room of her own, but also a chunk of time or leisure for herself. Chandraprabha's creative pursuit is sometimes disturbed by the tearful clamour of her little son, Atul. But in spite of all these obstacles, she goes ahead with her writing, which is really very admirable. "Sometimes she peeved and exasperated herself. Chandraprabha flung away her pen. It seemed that women's talents and aspirations were doomed to be throttled by the coils of domesticity. Yet, one day she made the stunning discovery that she had churned out 343 pages of the novel"(p.61). Chandraprabha continues her writing in spite of all the hindrances and inconveniences. Her writing is not appreciated even by her own mother who asks her, "How much longer will you keep on at this stuff, wasting all this ink and paper?...Can you feed yourself or the little one by writing like this?"(p.61) But Chandraprabha persists in her creativity and completes the novel, but there was no publisher. The market for writers was crushingly disheartening. Even an established writer like Dandinath was not getting any returns" (p.64).

Chandraprabha's writing of her debut novel at a very young age is admirable. But unfortunately it is not published by any publisher. The publishing scene in India was very bleak at that time. She has started her second novel also, but does not have the necessary enthusiasm to complete it. Though unhappy about Atul's missing his father, she tries to bring him up properly. "In this lacerated and sorrow struck state of mind she had started another novel which she called *The Last Haven*. But she stayed tenaciously hopeful. Perhaps a breed of appreciative feaders would begin to sprout in Assam, and among other things, they would enjoy the intimate, autobiographical aspects of her novels. "Chandraprabha also got solace from the fact that one of her stories called 'The Sad Wayfarer' had been published in the inaugural issue of a magazine called *Abahon*"(p.96). Though not being able to finish *The Last Haven,* she begins to write another novel, which she entitles as *The Ancestral Home*. She continues to write her novels and stories to ease her restless spirit and satisfy her creative urge.

When working as the Headmistress of Mahjerpara Balika Vidyalaya at Krishnanagar, Nadia district in the State of Bengal, she starts writing another novel called *Gauri-Shankar*. Chandraprabha has contradictory experiences of joy and frustration in her publishing ventures. "*The Ancestral Home* was published in the year 1937, her first extended piece of writing to be transcribed to the printed page. However, the sweetness of this success was shadowed by the memory of the failure of *The Unvanquished*. She has wrung the earlier work out of her bitterest grief and her most intense joy. But there had been no takers. *The Ancestral Home* she had dedicated to her rustic father, who had the vision and the gumption to do an unheard of thing like educating a girl-child"(p.118). The novel evokes some praise in critical circles and brings some satisfaction to her. But she feels discouraged by the lack of publicational opportunities in Assam. As Chandraprabha confesses to Padma Kumari Gohain, "Lack of time never prevents anyone who has the will, you know. It is just that I don't have a publisher who can publish my writings. You know how difficult it is with writers in benighted Assam" (p.141). Though literature and social activity are complementary to each other, Chandraprabha has decided not to publish any more literary works. She tells Padma Kumari, "Your words drip with logic and reason. But I am despaired of publishing any more books in my lifetime. I'll be content if I can keep *Abhiyatri* on its feet" (p.142). In 1947 Chandraprabha has started amagazine called *Abhiyatri* (which means 'a pioneer') a mouthpiece of the Mahila Samiti. She writes the editorial for it regularly. She runs it continuously for seven years until her gastric ulcer and financial problems compel her to stop it. "Her *Abhiyatri* got stopped after sailing for seven years. The subscribers did not pay up, and she accumulated debts in the press" (p.155). Chandraprabha's story as an editor of a magazine is representative of that of innumerable editors of small magazines even now in India.

Chandraprabha makes up her mind and writes the history of the Mahila Samiti. "As she completed the history of the Mahila Samiti, Chandraprabha's pen and mind flitted from place to place. Golaghat, Jorhat, Haflong, Tejpur, Mangaldoi, Dibrugarh, North Lakhimpur, Tinisukia, Garo Hills, Nagaon, Hakema, Sibsagar, Barpeta—these places hurled their rich memories at her. These memories had to be sanctified, enshrined in print"(p.158). While writing the history of the social activities of the Mahila Samiti, she psychologically relives the past and nostalgically experiences both the sorrow (of her private hell) and satisfaction of having done some selfless public service. She had identified herself with the Mahila Samiti totally and does not expect any reward of recognition from it.

But her desire to get her novels published remains unfulfilled. "She had actually applied to the Congress government for a loan to publish her works, but the appeal fell on deaf ears"(p.164).

Thus *Abhiyatri* succeeds in giving a picture of one of the rebellious women of Assam and remains one of the classics of Indian literature.

Works Cited

Borgohain, Nirupama. *Abhiyatri,* (Tr. Pradipto Borgohain) New Delhi: Sahitya Akademi, 1999.

The Telegraph. dtd. 16 March 2002.

(21)

Liberty/Equality vis-à-vis Corruption : A Study of Homen Borgohain's *Pita Putra*

Nigamananda Das

This article examines a vital aspect of Indian democracy in reflecting on liberty/equality in human society along with the rampart corruption that exists therein. John Stuart Mill in his essay " On Liberty"(1859) demarcates the appropriate region of human liberty to " the inward domain of consciousness, comprehensively the liberty of conscience, the liberty of thought and feeling; absolute freedom of opinion and sentiment on all subjects, practical or speculative, scientific, moral, or theological."(108). Secondly, according to him, the principle requires liberty of tastes and pursuits, of framing the plan of our life to suit our own character; of doing as we like, subject to such consequences as may follow, without impediment from our fellow creatures, so long as what we do does not harm them; even though they should think our conduct foolish, perverse, or wrong. Thirdly this liberty allows the individual freedom to write without harming others (ibidem). Locke is of the opinion that all men are equal by nature and they have equal right and their natural freedom and can not be harmed by the will or authority of any other fellow being (Dahl 1991:85).

In 1776, the authors of the American Declaration of Independence announced: "We hold these truths to be self-evident, that all men are created equal, that they are endowed by their creator with certain inalienable Rights, that among these are Life, Liberty, and the pursuit of happiness."(Dahl 2001:65).The moral judgement upholding equal claims to life, liberty, and happiness and other fundamental goods and interests is called the principles of intrinsic equality. Violation of the principles of liberty and equality gives birth to corruption putting the citizens into crises. The democracy in our time has been challenged by multiple layers of corruption which have produced unnecessary concerns and tensions for the citizens.

In a democracy the citizens are entitled to a number of fundamental rights. Democracy helps people to protect their own fundamental interests. The human liberty and political equality can only be assured to the citizens by the democratic government. In the same way the democratic government can provide maximum opportunities for persons to exercise freedom of self-determination and for exercising moral responsibility (ibidem 60). Thus democracy is instrumental to maximum feasible freedom and this freedom can be achieved in three ways: (i) general freedom like rights to free expression, political organization, opposition, fair and free elections etc.,(ii) freedom of self-determination: to govern oneself by laws chosen by oneself in association with others, i.e. to obey collective decisions binding on all members of the association; (iii) moral autonomy : to be morally autonomous is to be self-governing in the domain of morally relevant choices (Dahl 1991:88-91).

Democracy fosters human development. It has failed in the story of the two generations of the post-Independence India as is depicted by Homen Borgohain in his Sahitya Akademi award winning novel *Pita Putra* . The two generations of Assamese society caught in the tumultuous wake of India's transition to Independence represent the tenure of Sivanath Phukan, a prosperous landlord of Mohghuli village and his children. Sivanath, as the chronology in the novel proves, was approximately born in 1895 or 1896 AD. In August 1942 he was forty six or forty seven years old (21). He was such prosperous a landlord that one fourth of his villagers rented his land as sharecroppers. He was a principled man, did not tolerate corruption, and was honest and truthful to his core. He believed in aristocratic values. As all villagers were his tenants and below his rank and status,he always maintained his dignity. During the pre-Independence era even, he was aware of corruption and ill-doings of Reba mahajan and the village surveyor, Keshab Handique known as Keshab Mandal. Sivanath had three sons namely Gourinath, Kalinath and Lakshminath and two daughters namely Rambha and Savitri.

Sivanath like his village friends was very ambitious about India's independence. He was aware of the corruption, black-marketing and hoarding activities of the wholesaler Reba mahajan, who entered the village during the Second World War. He was also trading in opium and liquor. He was a hated enemy of the Congress Party workers and a right hand man of the officer-in-charge of the thana(police station). Though he was the symbol of corruption for the Congressmen during the pre-Independence era, he could manage to become the President of village Congress committee after India's independence through money and management tricks.

Sivanath was elated and much aspirant for the new time after the Indian Independence. India became independent and democracy prevailed. But in the aftermath the results which the freedom fighters or the common men aspired did not come true. It resulted in extreme misery, nepotism, corruption and all forms of evils. The novel depicts two worlds: "one is the external world of action and events of Mohghuli and the other, the largely inner and private world of the central character," Sivanath Phukan (Bormudoi ix).

The characters instrumental in the external world who stand for corruption are Reba mahajan, Keshab Mandal, Kanak darji, Biswa Hazarika MLA, thana OC, school inspector, corrupt excise officials like Suren Mahanta, etc. They were the obstacles for people's equality or liberty. As a contrast to this external world which was a part of the country's democratic system, the personal world of Sivanath presents turmoil. Sivanath, though, enough learned in literature, cultural values and contemporary way of life, was conservative and orthodox. His narrow aristocratic view of life resulted in turmoil in his personal life. His narrow views did not allow any liberty or equality to his children. The inalienable rights of life, liberty and happiness were not allowed by him to his sons. The sons could not enjoy the liberty of thought and feeling, freedom of opinion, sentiments, tastes and pursuits. Sivanath loved his eldest son Gourinath the best. Gourinath was studying engineering in Guwahati. One summer vacation when he was at home, his sister Rambha discovered a love letter from his suitcase. This came to the knowledge of Sivanath and he declared to disinherit Gourinath. Sivanath had his own dreams for his son. According to him, "Marriage was not just a personal choice."(89).Again opposite to his choice, Gourinath's would-be wife Urmila belonged to scheduled caste. So against all threats of Sivanath, Gourinath wrote to his father from Guwahati after the summer vacation declaring his firm decision to marry Urmila. He even was prepared not to receive any kind of financial assistance from his father for his studies. In his letter to his father, Gourinath pointed out certain attitudes of Sivanath which are opposed to the democratic principles:

> I know you are liberal in your attitude. Despite spending your whole life in the conservative social set up you have tried to nurture a modern outlook through your readings....Do you remember that occasion when the head of the Garmuria 'sattra' came to visit our village? He must have talked about untouchability ... Prabhat's father had challenged you...saying, " Siva, you declare that you are against untouchability and the caste-system. But can you...bring a girl from a low caste as your daughter-in-law?"...So my decision to marry her should be a challenge to prove your idealism(92).

Sivanath cut off his son Gourinath from his life. His youngest son Lakshminath, being involved in bad company remain addicted to wine all through his life, challenged him, attacked him and remained his lifelong enemy. His middle son Kalinath, learning from his elder sister Rambha about Lakshminath's attack on his father, left his studies and came back home to take care of his parents and family property. He also wanted to free the village from the bad effect of the liquor business, which had spoiled the local youths, thereby pushing the village economy and future into utter misery. After independence the first gift Mohghuli got was the Local Broad road which connected Mohghuli village to the town. Gradually a few traders from town appeared in the village for starting their business . A young muslim- Fazal Ali who came from the town to open a small shop of paan, betel nuts, bidis and the like, turned his shop into a liquor den. Even one day a few young men saw Binod sharing a chicken curry cooked by this muslim shop keeper. It spread through the village because Binod was several times ostracized by the villagers for beating his innocent wife and for being involved in anti-society activities.

It was Kalinath who could realize the liquor business in the village spoiling the youth. He visited his childhood's poor friend Dibakar for his assistance in his mission of reforming the village by stopping the liquor business. In Dibakar's house Kalinath encounters Dibakar's beautiful humble sister Bohagi. Bohagi steals Kalinath's heart and mind and Kalinath thereafter frequents Dibakar's house every night due to his enticement to Bohagi and for his mission. He earns ill-reputation due to that and even becomes a subject of discussion among the youths of the village whose interest of drinking was hampered by Kalinath's action against wine addiction prevention.

One evening there took place a fierce fighting and bloodshed in front of the police station among the drunkard gamblers. There was nobody to control it. Kalinath appeared there and went straight to the OC to complain. To his utter surprise he found the OC in his drinking session with his friends including the Congress President Reba mahajan, VDP Secretary Kusha Chutia, high school teacher Nanda Saikia, the doctor and the lawyer. The OC did not pay any heed to the complaint of Kalinath and on the other hand threatened him to throw into the lock up. Finally announcing Reba mahajan, Nanda Saikia, Memera and Bhogmon as his witness, Kalinath came back from the thana. The OC calling Memera to him narrated false charges against Kalinath that he was drunk; He visits the characterless sister of Dibakar of the Samua village who could dare to indulge in sex with the SI during daytime in the dark dak bungalow for a teacher's job in the LP school etc., etc. and he would one day puthin in the lock up. Memera informed all these to Sivanth , which put a full stop to Kalinath's visit to Dibakar's house every night and his love affairs with Dibakar's sister Bohagi. Though declared to marry Bohagi, he could not as Bohagi's poor family was much below his status and his father Sivanath did not allow it.

Similarly Rambha was ugly looking. Though Kanak thikadar proposed to her , Sivanath turned down the proposal as Kanak's father was a servant in Sivanath's household. Sivanath also believed in untouchability. The villagers belonging to Kaivarta or fishermen community were lowcastes. They were not allowed seats in Sivanath's house. Savitri brings *tamul* for Katia and throws the same at him without giving in his hand.

Sivanath disinherited his eldest and youngest sons, could not arrange marriage for his daughter Rambha and Savitri and became completely obsessed by the economic and social changes of the time. As he was astonished with the behaviour of Keshab Mandal in relinquishing government job and joining freedom struggle at the beginning, the truth about Keshab Mandal's character was also revealed afterwards. Keshab Mandal left the government job to become a disciple of Gandhi, took part in the Quit India Movement of 1942. Then he surrendered at the police station when warrant was out for him. He spoke to Sivanath , "ahimsa is my motto."(14). "Satyagrahis do not fear anything. That's their first lesson."(ibidem). But the same person after independence turned to his previous state of deceiving people as he deceived many people even after receiving bribes when he was the surveyor. When the dike was washed away and the whole village was flooded and the fishermen being poor people were starving he created discrimination and deprived them of the relief goods. He was even encouraging the liquor trade and had taken money several times from the excise official Suren Mahanta for the election campaign of Biswa Hazarika ,MLA and for his own expenses. The election process was not free and fair. He signed the application prepared by Kalinath during the anti-liquor campaign for the transfer of Suren Mahanta and on the other hand immediately sent his men to Suren Mahanta to arrange with Biswa MLA so that Mahanta's transfer would not take place. He with his corrupt friends did not even attend the anti-liquor meeting organised in the village.

The corrupt practices of Biswa MLA, Keshab Mandal and Reba mahajan prove the corruption rampart in the democratic system in India immediately after the establishment of the democracy and withdrawal of the foreign rule. This also shows that the oppressive foreign rule was just replaced by the peoples' rule or democracy, but with no reform, on the other hand with more oppressive system. The school inspector in the pretext of giving a job of LP school teacher to Bohagi, invites her to the lonely dark dak bungalow, where he tries to rape her. The thana OC threatens to entangle Kalinath with false cases and destroy his career. Kanak thikadar enthused Lakshminath to drink more and more by providing him food and drink in order to disturb peace in Sivanath's house and marry his daughter Rambha for establishing himself soundly in the society. This shows corrupt contractor's strategy in stealing away happiness of his fellow beings for his own selfish designs. At the behest of Kanak also Lakshminath was visiting his father and family members recurrently in drunken state and abusing them demanding his share of the property or some amount of money for his drinks.

To get Suren Mahanta transferred from Mohghuli village to free the village from liquor malady, Kalinath went to Shillong. Back from Shillong he wanted to stay with Soumitra, his friend, son of Dr. Mukherji. Soumitra was a brilliant student. .His father wanted that he (Soumitra) would become an IAS officer. But in the mean time he has become a revolutionary of social change, a leader of self-determination. He goes out in morning and comes back home at night in a drunken state. So Dr. Mukherji attacking the youthful dream of Soumitra says, " Wasn't it Nirad Choudhuri who said that the idealist young Indian starts his life as a disciple of Marx and ends up in later life as a disciple of Ramkrishna Paramhansa."(193). That night Soumitra and Kalinath debated for a long time. Kalinath could find the frustration in Soumitra and his design of self-determination.

Soumitra said to Kalinath, " I've been suffering from insomnia for sometime now and have to take sleeping tablets"(195). Then he became irritated when Kalinath attacked him by telling, "These rebels who came alive in liquor parties are false idealists"....We Indians want to make shortcuts to everything. But there is no shortcut to revolution"(197).

Soumitra becomes irritated to listen to Kalinath. In his excitement he says, "In this unfortunate country, the problem of liquor is but a small one compared to more pressing problems ....So do you think you can bring in change in the society through the so-called democratic means?...Remember, I too want democracy. But a democracy that gives birth to a crude animal like Biswa Hazarika, a democracy that does not allow punishing the greatest enemies of the society is not the one I believe in. I want a democracy where those trampled by society will rule. I want a democracy that will free these poor people from economic and political slavery. And to achieve it the only path is revolution through an armed struggle....We will fight in the hills, in the forests and the lanes of the cities. Come, join us. You have experienced enough of the justice doled out through the democratic process....Come along with me."(198-199).

Sivanath in spite of his status and social dignity faced challenges of time. During the first planting season after the dike was constructed, the villagers did not care to ask him his land for share cropping. He could not tolerate this liberty of the villagers (96). During the first Bihu Celebration after the independence, Sivanath was disturbed and anguished to see the change in schedule of the visit of the Bihu team. The huchari party should logically start from one end of the village. But it always started from Sivanath's house as his was the wealthiest and most respected family in the neighbourhood. But after the independence before Bihu it was decided in a meeting at the namghar that "since now all people are equal after the independence, the Huchari should start where it should have done all along- from one end of the village."(50).So Sivanath and his wife became upset and they did not wait for the huchari team and assigned the responsibility to their servant Nakul. The Huchari team was insulted as Nakul kneeled down for the ritual blessing. The team on the spot declared the excommunication of Sivanath's family. This was unprecedented in the history of the village. As Sivanath was disturbing liberty of the villagers, he faced the disciplinary action by the mob.

Mahatma Gandhi was a strong influence on Sivanath. Prior to 1921, Sivanath was supporting the armed struggle for freedom. His ideal was Sabyasachi of *Pather Daabi*.

But he "found Mahatma's call for ahimsa and the symbol of the spinning wheel so different and innovative that he stopped mid-track. Even his favourite writer, fiery Ambikagiri was now a pupil of Gandhi and the strain of his poems turned from exonerating radical armed struggle to one of the moral resistance."(24). Even Kalinath once pondering over the teachings of Gandhi, doubted if the evil can be rooted out from this world. It is a mystery and it can not be wished away (158). " Non-violence or ahimsa and satyagraha to Gandhi personally constituted a deeply-felt and worked-out philosophy…his view is no different from the one of the most celebrated liberal arguments for tolerance- the meta-inductive argument of Mill's *On Liberty*….According to Mill, and according to Gandhi…truth is never something we are sure we have attained. We must therefore be made modest in the way we hold our present opinions, and we must not impose our own conceptions of the truth on others."(Bilgrami 4160). Though Sivanath was a follower of Gandhi, he was not true to the afore-said concept. He was imposing his views strongly on his children and did not allow them any freedom. So the novelist comments: "The values Kalinath and his friends learnt told him that he should go against his father's dictatorship. In a false alter of aristocracy his father had sacrificed his children one by one"(162).At another place it has been commented: "Indian parents seldom like to give any freedom to their children, nor do they like to see them mature preferring to keep them under control"(148). Though he was liberal in opinion about the untouchables, he could not sacrifice for them. He helped the untouchable Kaivarta tenants of his neighbourhood and sympathized with them. But he did not allow Gourinath marry Urmila who belonged to a scheduled caste family. Like Gandhi's view/advice to the untouchables "Some of them are addicted to habits of drinking and gambling of which they must get rid"(Anand 138), Sivanath was recurrently advising his untouchable tenants like Katia. Liberty and equality has been recurrently debated and multiple layers of corruption unraveled in the pithy discourse of the novel. Liberty, equality, corruption and mismanagement of the democratic system are the major issues here.

Incidents narrated in the novel happen between 1912 and 1972. Sivanath's son Kalinath who tried his best to prohibit liquor from his village Mohghuli to reform the society, was unsuccessful in his venture due to the intervention of corrupt MLA Biswa Hazarika and corrupt excise officials. But through his moral consciousness and endeavour he could become a minister after 1972 elections. His friend Soumitra, whose parents aspired that he would become an IAS officer, through his involvement in bad company of false revolutionaries of self determination and his constant addiction to liquor spoiled himself, joined the Naxalite movement, and being arrested by police, was in the Tezpur Jail, when he was informed that his friend Kalinath became a minister after winning the Assembly election of 1972.The novel provides a good analysis of the democratic system in India and peoples' confusion over its principles and the consequences.

Works Cited

Anand, Mulk Raj. *Untouchable*. New Delhi :Pearson Longman,2007.

Bilgrami, Akeel. "Gandhi, the Philosopher": *Economic and Political Weekly*, Sept.27,2003, pp.4159-4165.

Borgohain, Homen. *Pita Putra*. New Delhi: NBT, 1999.

Bormudoi, Anand. "Introduction": *Pita Putra* .New Delhi: NBT, 1999,pp. vii-xi.

Dahl, Robert A. *Democracy and its critics*. New Delhi: Orient Longman Ltd., 1991.

——. *On Democracy*. New Delhi: EWP, 2001.

Mill, J. S. "On Liberty": *The Liberal Tradition* .ed. Allan Bullock and Maurice Shock. Oxford: OUP,1967, pp.108-115.

(22)

Yeshe Dorjee Thongchi's *Sonam* : A New Historicist Perspective

Juri Dutta

Yeshe Dorjee Thongchi, a recipient of the Sahitya Akademi award in 2005, published his first novel *Sonam* in 1981. Thongchi's novels generally deal with the traditional cultural life of Monpa and Sherdukpen tribes of Arunachal Pradesh. *Sonam* is no exception in this regard. The novel centres round the Brokpa tribe (a section of Monpa), a community owning the Yak herds. The family system of he Brokpas, where a woman is socially allowed to marry more than one man is the custom in which the story of the novel is rooted. Such a unique system is called *khor depka* by the Monpas. In the Monpa society polygamy and polyandry are socially permissible and we can trace the trauma, agony and conflicts of the characters of the novel resulting from such a system due to which the universal man-woman relationship is affected. The setting of the novel against the backdrop of the Dirang and West Kameng's customs and culture of the society where the domestic yak-oriented economy is the mainstay of the locals.

This paper is an attempt to situate Thongchi's *Sonam* in the time to which it belongs, as well as to see it as the reflection of the collective beliefs, social practices and cultural discourses that must have shaped his views and motives as expressed in the novel. One also needs to observe his concern in depicting the life and society of the characters of that particular time.

New historicists believe that literature is not independent of economic, social and political conditions and therefore, not subject to timeless criteria of artistic value. In a given historical moment, different modes of discourse such as law, theology, morality, philosophy, literature, art, and architecture are not autonomous, but the constitution of a given cultural field and of some ideological codes that order all discourse in that particular culture. A literary text, therefore, is always subject to the particular conditions of a time and place. Thongchi's *Sonam* is also subject to the particular conditions of a time and a place—the time being the middle half of the 20th century and the place is that of the inhabitance of the Brokpas (the Dirang and West Kameng Districts of Arunachal Pradesh). Thongchi himself has said that he has tried to draw the picture of the Brokpa tribe and the polyandry system prevalent in the society (in his preface to the revised edition in 2005).

A new-historical essay will place the literary text within the 'frame' of a non-literary text in the sense that it can very often be seen bringing together the theme or subject-matter with one or some historical document. Peter Barry has mentioned Stephen Greenblatt, a prominent new historicist in explaining the concept as:

> He [Greenblatt] draws attention to the marginalization and dehumanizing of suppressed other (Grady) usually by starting an essay with an analysis of a contemporary historical document which overlaps in some way with the subject-matter of the play (1995: 173).

Apparently, *Sonam* deals with no historical happening or document but reflects the culture and society of the Brokpa tribe of Arunachal of a particular time. Having stayed among these people at Tawang the novelist has seen, met and interacted with them from very close quarters and thus *Sonam* is not only a literary text with a triangular love story but a social document of the Brokpas. This reminds us of Louis Montrose's oft-quoted definition of New historicism as a combined interest in 'the textuality of history and the historicity of text' (Murfin and Ray, 1998: 243).

New Historicists never subordinate the historical documents as 'context', rather they analyse these as co-texts (ibid). In the novel *Sonam*, Thongchi has not used any particular context but the entire novel is a co-text of the traditional beliefs, rituals and culture of the Brokpa tribe and the story of the love and hatred, the ecstasy and trauma of Lobjang, Sonam, Pema Wangcu and Tsering Drema.

A literary text, for the new-historicists, is an interactive component within the network of institutions, beliefs and cultural power-relations—practices and products which constitute what we call history. The novel *Sonam* can also be read as a convergence of different beliefs, power-relations, cultural practices, and ideologies of a particular society. *Sonam* begins with the description of a robust young shepherd of the Brokpa community coming back home from the Choksum hills to the Sakteng village. With the progress of the story, Thongchi introduces us to a variety of social customs and traditional beliefs as well as the lexical and cultural world of the Brokpas. The livelihood of Lobjang (the main character) of rearing Yaks and going to far off places like Tawang, Bhutan, Kalaktang, Rupa, Dirang to sell or barter ghee, mar (milk fat), churpi (a type of cheese made from milk), and sheep-wool gives the idea of an actual Brokpa man with an animal farm away from home. At the very outset of the novel we are introduced to a traditional belief when Lobjang thinks of bringing his wife Sonam to his farm and staying there together.

If Sonam was taken to the farm and they start living as husband and wife the sanctity of the place would be violated. Any physical intimacy with the wife would incur the displeasure of the Sungmu, the household deity of wealth, whereby good fortune would forsake the place and epidemics would break loose upon the animals of the farm. (15)

"Ideology", as explained by James H. Kavanagh (1995) "is less tenacious as a 'set of ideas' than as a system of representations, perceptions and images that precisely encourages men and women to 'see' their specific place in a historically peculiar social formation as inevitable, natural, a natural function of the 'real' itself" (310). Lobjang does see his and wife's social roles as inevitable and natural and he does not envisage the possibility of any change.

The traditional life of the Brokpa society is reflected throughout the novel by the mention of various words which are restricted to that community. The words like *chupa* (people or the Panchayat), *aara* (wine), *gorbu* (vessel to take food), *nasang* (permanent host and friend), *nekar* (pilgrimage), *duntsang* (the dancing and drinking to celebrate an occasion), *saksoiban* (to bow down), *Rimpoche* (the abbot, who is posted at Tawang Monastery by his holiness), the Dalai Lama from the reincarnated Lamas, *Drapa* and *Anei* (hermit and nun), *thekasam, boitang* (a Tibetan coin), *mone soreten, sanraji* and so on take us to a world Thongchi has seen, lived and communicated with.

For Yeshe Dorjee Thongchi, a Buddhist by religion, the tendency to look at things from a Buddhist viewpoint is reflected in *Sonam* as in other novels too. We, therefore, get references to the Gompa of Tawang, the second biggest Buddhist temple of Asia, of Lama and Rimpoche, of *drapa* and *anei* in the novel. Moreover, one of his famous novels *Saba Kota Manuh* (2004) is set against a ritual of the Monpa tribe and the love between a reincarnated Rimpoche and a man who slices dead bodies into hundred and eight pieces as a ritual. The society and the characters of Thongchi's novel *Sonam* reflects his own beliefs, ideals and views as seen through an insider's eye as well as through the eye of a Buddhist. Thongchi has confessed, "In various matters, the Monpa tribe and the Sherdukpen tribe to which I belong there are lots of similarities" (In the preface of *Saba Kota Manuh*).

Again, we can read Lobjang's departure for the Tawang gompa (Buddhist Monastery) along with his children, Rinchin and Tashi to make them *anei* and *drapa* (nun and hermit), as the reflection of the novelist's deep faith in Buddhist religion or his belief in Gompa as the ultimate solace for an anguishing soul. Here, we see hardly any difference between literature and history, between literature and reality, between literature and culture or social customs, tradition or belief. "New-historicism insists upon a different methodology, a cultural criticism that refuses to see literature and history as two distinct entities since such differentiation is a product of our own phenomenological cultural conditioning." (Panja, 2002, 197).

The novelist is successful in drawing the picture of a tribal society while describing any incident in terms of traditional beliefs, superstitions and cultural system. When the tiger which kills many of Lobjang's animals and of others cannot be killed, then the people of the village are frightened and start believing that it is not a tiger but some spirit who has come to take revenge for some misdeed of humans. Moreover there are many rituals, including worship of traditional deities for the cure of Sonam's disease, the Lama's and priests' ways of looking after Sonam to cure her disease and putting *boitang* (Tibetan coin) in Sonam's mouth immediately after her death. Thongchi has noted in an article, "I have framed my writings on the characters, and the atmosphere among the various tribes and tribal people of the hilly region of Arunachal" and "I have presented the colourful lives, social customs and cultures of different tribes of different districts of Arunachal Pradesh" (2006: 9). It is obvious that in the novel *Sonam* too, though the novelist ascends artistic height, it can also be seen as commentaries on Arunachal's tribal life, specially the Brokpas. To quote Murfin & Ray:

> New historicist critics assume that works of literature both influence and are influenced by historical reality and they share a belief in referentiality, that is a belief that literature both refers and is referred to by thing outside itself. (1998: 240)

New historicism does not pertain to a school or to a coherent theory of cultural history. Instead it designates a fairly diverse body of scholarship with some common attributes. And varied influences of different modes of criticism such as Feminism, Marxism, Foucault's concept of power and history, Althusser's concept of ideology have shaped new historicism as a mode of study with considerable diversity and disagreement among individual exponents of it. However, such influences have widened the concept of new historicism. Taking into account such a broader outlook, it can be said that the New Historicist belief is that the human subject is the ideological product of power-relations in a particular society. We can say, that the author of *Sonam,* the characters within the novel and even the audience/readers the author writes for, are 'subjects' produced and positioned by the play of power and ideology within the discourse of a particular era.

It is due to the 'power', the power that the men of the society like Lobjang enjoys, that we see him acting according to his whims. He blames Sonam for all the problems in his life and even when he is invited to have a meal with her, he refuses. It is power that Lobjang uses to exercise his will in the lives of his wife and their children. It is he who makes Pema Wangchu a *Khor depka* for Sonam and took both his children to the Tawang gompa to make them *anei* and *drapa.* However, the fact that the same sense of power that Lobjang enjoys can also ensnare him in its own trap is proved when he is unable to go to meet Sonam. His beloved wife, even when she is acutely ill.

Sonam is basically about the sorrow and agony as well as the love and hatred among the three main characters caught in a love triangle. It has been mentioned that the main theme of the novel centres round the social system where a woman is allowed to marry more than one man. Apparently it seems that the women enjoy more freedom in such a society, but while going through the novel, one discovers that it need not necessarily be so. The community is not only male-dominated but abounds in ideologies and beliefs helpful in gender construction. Polyandry and polygamy are permissible in Lobjang's community and we hear him talking to his wife to get another groom for her in a matter-of-fact manner. When he discovers Pema Wangchu, let us bring him into our household" (21) and "If you are not interested in Pema Wangchu let me look for another boy. Tell me is there anybody else that you would like to be a co-husband to you?" (22)

It is clear that Lobjang is not at all worried to share his wife with someone else. But at the same time the intention behind such a proposal is questionable. Polyandry is prevalent in the society of the Brokpas to which he belongs and he is so constructed by the ideologies and beliefs of his society that even such an idea of sharing the most cherished woman of his life does not create any trauma or agony in his mind. Instead he is happy to get a man who would help him in his household activities. Lobjang, being the male 'subject' of the society has the 'power' to decide and Sonam has to accept it in spite of her doubts and uncertainties.

The New Historicists focus attention (within both text and co-text) on issues of patriarchal structures and their perpetuation. Peter Barry has mentioned Louis Montrese's essay '*A Midsummer Night's Dream* by constantly insisting on Elizabeth's difference from other women. "Thus Elizabeth's rule was not intended to undermine the male hegemony of her culture. Indeed, the emphasis upon her difference from other women may have helped to reinforce it"

(Barry 2002: 181).

In *Sonam*, patriarchy is prevalent in the society which is reflected in the character's opinions in different situations. The strong note of patriarchy prevalent in the society is based reflected in Lobjang's faith on an age old belief of violating the sanctity of the farm by Sonam's coming there and staying together with her husband. In Lobjang's words we hear the bias of a typical patriarchal man when he was alone and going to Pema Wangchu's house:

> Women are like dogs, whoever pats them on their back-they will meekly follow him and will snarl and snap at him who once in his life speaks or behaves badly. (86)

His male ego does not allow him to go to Pema Wangchu's house to have his meal in spite of the invitation of his wife Sonam. And he refuses Pema Wangchu's sister and had dinner in Tikoroi's house. (102)

The most significant aspect that deserves to be mentioned about the novel is the writer's addition and extension of some ideas and chapters in the new edition of the novel in 2005. Thongchi has tried to justify the changes:

> At the time of writing the novel, I did not have much knowledge about the traditions and rituals, customs and culture of that society. Polyandry is a practice of the Brokpas (the yak owning community) and such a practice of marrying more than one man is called *khor depka* by the Monpas. Due to my ignorance the words like Brokpa, *khor depka* etc. were not used in the novel.

But the changes in the new edition of the novel go far beyond the inclusion of words from the Monpa society. A new-historicist reading of the novel forces us to concentrate on the significant changes brought about by Thongchi in the new edition. As Murfin and Ray say:

> [...] new-hisoricists follow a set of basic scholarly procedures. These procedures... assume that new historicists will study a literary work's 'point of origin' via biography and bibliography (241).

We can analyze Yeshe Dorjee Thongchi, a top-level bureaucrat, an intellectual, a progressive member of Arunachalee society while focusing on the new ending of the novel. The situation can be compared to what Stephen Greenblatt has pointed out in case of Shakespeare's indecisive self at the death of his son Hamnet whether to follow the Catholic rituals or to be loyal to the Queen and the Protestant belief of the abolition of purgatory. While discussing *Hamlet,* Greenblatt has pointed to the struggle between the Protestants and Catholics (Gewertz). Greenblatt notes that Shakespeare's eleven year old son Hamnet died in 1596 shortly before his father began to write *Hamlet.* It might have been possible that Shakespeare's Catholic father urged his son to have prayers and to perform the rituals. As the rituals of purgatory had been abolished by the ruling Protestants, Shakespeare had a dilemma—whether to risk punishment by praying for his dead son or obey the law of the land. This anxiety regarding one's obligation to the dead, Greenblatt suggests, lies behind Hamlet's indecision about whether or not to obey his father's ghost and take revenge upon Claudius. (ibid.)

The first edition of *Sonam* concludes with Lobjang's departure to the Tawang gompa along with Rinchin Jangmu and Tashi. But the progressive being of Thongchi is no longer happy with the same conclusion. He feels the need to speak more about *khor depka*—about the age-old tradition of the Brokpas whereby a woman is allowed to marry more than one man. We can hear him expressing his own belief towards the end of the novel through the mouth of Tsering Doima:

> My sister warned me not make the same mistake made by her. She advised me not to get involved with another man to encourage *khor depka* (128, new edition)
> And
> We won't live as Brokpas anymore. We will go to Tawang and buy some land or cultivate. If we remain Brokpa, I will not always be able to accompany you. I will be compelled to perform *khor depka* again with someone else. (ibid)

Being born to the Sherdukpen society which is very close to the Monpa society, Thongchi has observed the Brokpas from close quarters. In the first edition of the novel, he was happy to portray life as it is. But in the new edition he felt the need for its extension—showing Lobjang's repentance of his action and his willingness to act according to the wish of his dead wife Sonam. One discovers a new urge in Thongchi to reform society.

Sonam is a text that lends itself quite easily to a new-historicist framework of study as it is a novel rich in socio-historical connotation. It is the kind of novel that problematizes the differentiation between fiction and history.

References

Althusser, Louis. 'Ideology and Idelogical State Apparatuses' in *Lenin and Philosophy and Other Essays*. London. Verso. 1971.

Barry, Peter. *An Introduction to Literary and Cultural Theory.* Manchester. Manchester University Press. 2002.

Borgohain, Homen. (ed). *Satsori.* 1-15 March 2006. Guwahati: Saraighat Publishers.

Eagleton, Terry. *Literary Theory: An Introduction.* New Delhi: Maya Blackwell. 2000.

..... *Marxism and Literary Criticism.* London: Routledge Classics. 2000.

Kavanag, James H. 'Ideology' in Lentricchia, Frank and Thomas McLaughlin. (ed) *Critical Terms for Literary Study.* Chicago. University of Chicago Press. 1995.

Ryan, Michael. *Literary Theory.* Oxford: Basil Blackwell. 2002.

Thongchi, Yeshe Dorjee. *Sonam.* Nalbari. Journal Emporium. 1981(2005).

..... *Sonam.* Trans. Mridula Barooah. Guwahati. Spectrum Publications. 2001.

..... *Saba Kota Manuh.* Guwahati.

Murfin, Ross and Supriya Ray. *The Bedford Glossary of Critical and Literary Terms.* New York. Bedford Books. 1998.

Panja, Sharmistha. (ed) *Critical Theory: Textual Application.* Delhi. Worldview Publications. 2002.

Veeser, Aram. (ed) *The New Historicism.* London. Routledge. 1989.

(23)

Ecology and History in Mamang Dai's *The Legends of Pensam* and Easterine Iralu's *A Naga Village Remembered* : A Comparative Analysis

Nigamananda Das

India's Northeast is one amongst the World's 25 biodiversity hotspots and 17 biodiversity heritage sites. Ecologically rich as it is, the literary genres from the region explore the flora and fauna and the mysterious ecology and expose eco-consciousness of its people and other ethnic realities. As such the ecological writings are canonical as they expose the postcolonial ecological erosions. So far the Penguin India has published more than half a dozen fictional works of authors from various provinces of the Northeast. These works explore the ecology and history of the region. The paper aims at analyzing an Arunachalee writer, Mamang Dai's novel *The Legends of Pensam* (Penguin, 2006) and a Naga writer Easterine Iralu's *A Naga Village Remembered* (2003), comparing their ecological and historical concerns. These first generation post-colonial first novels in English from the two different provinces of the Northeast showcase to the world some unknown chapters of India's history and ecology.

As a contrast to the "toxic consciousness" (Deitering 202) represented by the post-1980s postnatural American novels, the novels in English from India's Northeast, especially *The Legends of Pensam* by Mamang Dai and *A Naga Village Remembered* by Easterine Iralu explore the ecology and history of their respective regions which have remained unexplored in writing till date. Mamang Dai, an ecopoet and fictionist from Arunachal has mixed history with ecology and ecotheology to provide the readers with a recipe of unique taste, that reflects an inbetween place in the mountains of Arunachal Pradesh. A former civil servant, now turned journalist, Mamang interprets the "hidden spaces of heart where a secret garden grows" (vii). Her exploration of ecology in the tribal world of Arunachal has mostly been restricted to her own community of Adis. She says, "Like the majority of tribes inhabiting the central belt of Arunachal, the Adis practise an animistic faith that is woven around forest ecology and co-existence with the natural world" (i).

The Legends of Pensam evokes the "toxic consciousness" in presenting a comparative exploration of the past. The situations and surroundings of the past were completely different from what we are in. The fictionist in the prologue voices the same :

> We make no comparisons now. The river cuts through our land as before in its long journey to the sea. In spring the red flowers still blaze against our sky. But the old people now, the few of them alive, turn slowly in their sleep as the fires burn down to a heap of ash. In the middle of the night a bird swoops low and calls out in a wild, staccato note. The thatch rustles. The bamboo creaks. *The darkness is full of breath and sighs* (italic mine).

The paragraph above presents a few contours of ecology. It presents nature in broader sense. It may be the total cosmos and beyond and it depicts the chasm between the past and present. That chasm depicting *darkness is full of breath and sighs* (italic mine) in nostalgic, chaotic, toxic and significantly disturbing. We feel that we had something better in the past which we have lost now. As such our mind is occupied in a constant comparison between the experiences felt and the present feeling.

Divided into four sections, the novel consisting of an intricate web of nineteen stories, presents the history of a tribe which comprises a "moving tribute to the human spirit" (blurb). These stories are like legends narrating incidents or accidents relating to popular figures in the Adi clan of Arunachal. The stories depict "pensam" (inbetweenness) of several kinds. The very first legend "the boy who fell from the sky" speaks of Hoxo who saw "a green wall of trees and bamboo, and a green waterfall that sprayed his cheek and washed the giant fern that seemed to be waving to him (7). "The colour green always soothed him. It was the colour of escape and solitude" (8). The legend concludes in informing that Hoxo's father, Lutor, the famous Chief of the Ida clan was killed in hunting accident leaving behind his widow wife and son. Before changes came in shape of post-colonial encounters, life in the tribal world though seemed to be very difficult and uncertain, was happy, meaningful and magical.

In the tribal world of Arunachal, the mysterious prevails plentily. A married woman would become a widow at any time. Nature and spirit, even evil spirits played games with human life. The story titled "Pinyar, the widow" reveals how Pinyar who became a widow before she was twentyfive years old. Pinyar in spite of oppositions from her parents and relatives fell in love with a man named Orka from a village beyond Siyum hills, far to the north of the country (26) and bore a son named Kamur from him, but the marriage failed and Orka left her taking his son Kamur away. Pinyar remarried a man named Lekon and became widow in the third month of her marriage as her husband Lekon was struck down in a hunting accident. Her lonely life was again threatened when her hut one day was accidently caught fire and turned into ashes and that removed her to forest seclusion as per their tribal tradition. Her son Kamur who was well settled with a government job, two sons and an infant daughter was accidentally in trouble oneday due to a trance like fit that invaded his soul and made him mad so that he killed his infant daughter and one son with a rusty *dao* and attacked his wife who fortunately survived due to intervention of the neighbours.

The mysterious/magical trance which troubles most human in the tribal world is believed to be from two or three sources of intoxication. These sources may be rice beer which is prohibited for the hunter before his hunting expedition,or the spirits and some trees having evil spirits boarded on them. About the rice beer and the race of miti-mili it is said :

> Once upon a time, there lived a race of supernatural beings called miti-mili. These small, quiet people were

> the first to make mysterious si-ye that is the yeast used to ferment rice into beer. Before the miti-mili race disappeared, deranged by strange visions, they gave this sacred powder to mankind, and a strong belief grew that si-ye had special powers and that it was something to be handled with respect. Only women were allowed to handle it, and Pinyar herself made the best si-ye cakes. She mixed the white powder with ground rice and roots and berries and shaped it into small flat biscuits. ... they are strictly forbidden before a hunt or a journey. ... 'It makes men hallucinate, just like the miti-mili race. But sometimes some households forget to observe the rules, and then our men die in the forests' (29).

About the peculiar trees which have magical powers that intoxicate, human minds and make them commit sins, it is said :

> People talked about the peculiar trees of the place. They remembered the aubergine plant that had grown to the size of a tree. Nobody could recall who had planted it or when. It bore small poisonous looking flowers that grew into long, bloated fruit, menacing and shiny. It was a ghostly tree and no one dared to cut it down. Kamur had sometimes been seen under that tree at odd hours, doing nothing in particular (31).

The guardians of history speculate on the troubles in the tribal surroundings and feel that there is something in the blood or some spirits and ghosts or marriages (right or wrong) that are responsible for these accidents (ibidem).

Narration of ecology and ecocriticism "involves a deliberate act of prestidigitation, a problematic process in which an identity is projected onto nature" (Head 235). Again [Lawrence] Buell's 'aesthetic of relinquishment' actually involves the need to imagine 'non-human agents as bonafide partners', and in his discussion of 'Nature's Personhood' Buell considers how, in environmental law, our identity can be assigned to nature 'to engineer a change in the legal and ethical status quo by a discursive innovation frankly announced as fictive' (ibidem).

Mamang Dai through her chain of stories called "legends of Pensam" has asserted an identity of Arunachal and its tribes by associating the tribal life and activities with nature. Everything happens here in the bosom of nature. The natural surroundings and human and nonhuman transactions assume unlimited dimensions. Ecology encompasses all human and non-human transactions in all the spaces. Mamang mixes history, ecology and ecotheology/ecotheosopy to give an understanding of the total tribal ecological and historical tradition in Arunachal, especially her own Adi Tribe. The novel contains several paragraphs on the ecology – types of landscape and related traditions which Mamang calls "small histories" (36) :

> Everyday I saw clouds dropping lower and lower like ominous waves. The hills were blue, their outline rimmed in black, and the trees were still. Soon, the first fat beads of water would tear the giant leaves of the wild yam. Then fierce, hissing rain would cover the land like the sea.
>
> At such times it seems the heavens brush very close to the earth. The wild fruit born of this union is of unknown family, bittersweet, pungent, often misshapen and hardy, or swollen to an unnatural size. Hidden by mountains and covered by a charcoal sky the forest and rivers become battlefields ferocious with the struggle for survival...(36-37).

The ecology of Arunachal was unknown to the other world up to the nineteen century. "The first white priests, surveyors and soldiers had begun arriving in the region almost two hundred years ago, in the early 1800s. Since then people from other worlds had come and gone, though the only records of their journeys are the stories that the older men and women remember" (37-38).

After the whitemen's entry into this fantastic ecological paradise, changes have been rapid. The early decades of the 20th century witnessed great upheaval. In 1911, a British political officer set out from the plains of Assam on a mission to explore the course of the river Siang flowing through the territory of the Adis. He was Noel Williamson, with twenty years of experience in dealing with the tribes in the hill tracts of the country. But unfortunately an angry Adi struck him down in the village of

Komsing. It developed into massacre where Williamson, his tea garden doctor friend Dr.Gregorson, fortyseven sepoys and coolies were killed. The three men who survived told the world what really happened. News of the massacre sent shockwaves across colonial India and resulted in punitive expedition of 1912, which become known as the Abor Expeditionary Field Force. A memorial stone to Williamson was unveiled, where it stands now even looked after by the villagers as the British had instructed (48).

In the midst of the dense natural surrounding there exists the tribal theology/theosophy which is also ecological. Prior to the advent of Christianisty into this ecology, there was the traditional tribal religion, which still exists. The Arunachalee tribals believe in the Almighty Donyi-polo, the sun and the moon (57). The priest chants verses, tells tales to the folk who sit before him to listen. He explains, "We are not here without a purpose" (56). And adds :

> Our purpose is to fulfil our destiny. The life of a man is measured by his actions and his actions are good if their origin is pure. From nothingness we have come to be born under the stars and almighty Donyi-polo, the sun and the moon, whose light shines on all equally, is the invisible force that guides each one of us. All life is light and shadow; we live and we die, and the path of destiny is the quest for faith (57).

Again about the whole creation/ecology the priest says:

> In the beginning, there was only Keyum. Nothingness. It was neither darkness nor light, nor had it any colour, shape or movement. Keyum is the remote past, way beyond the reach of our senses. It is the place of ancient things from where no answer is received. Out of this place of great stillness, the first flicker of thought began to shine like a light in the soul of man. It became a shimmering trail, took shape and expanded and became the Pathway. Out of this nebulous zone, a spark was born that was the light of imagination. The spark grew into a shining stream that was the consciousness of man and from this all the stories of the world and all its creatures came into being (56).

Mamang Dai mixing memory, desire, history and religion with ecology provides a real picture in fiction. The work is a landmark in postcolonial writing and being the first English novel from Arunachal Pradesh it is very important work in Indian English Literature.

Easterine Irulu's *A Naga Village Remembered* is also the first novel in English by a Naga writer. The book being a historical account of the proud Khonoma village and the Battle of Khonoma (1879-1880) and the activities of the American Baptist Mission and the first converts, also depicts the ecology and history of the hilly terrain and the faith of its people. Consisting of fourteen chapters, the novel presents a detailed account the Battle of Khonoma and bravery of the Angami tribes of the village and the surrounding hills. In the introduction to the book the novelist gives a description of the village as is given below :

> Khonoma nestles amid mountains that are as high as 7,000 feet, a little village on a small hillock, cradled by gaunt mountains which form a natural fortress. Hidden from human view by this natural fortress of mountains, Khonoma can be seen from only one direction in the Northern Angami region between Meriema and Chieswema. Though her size of 500 houses was rather average among Angami villages, her fame spread far and wide as a warrior village. Her warriors of the Semo, Thevo and Merhu clans hardly numbered over a thousand at any given time in her history. However, Khonoma's protectorate extended in every direction, to the Southern, Northern, Eastern and Western Angami and Naga villages. To her north, there was some Sopfuma villages of the Shepoumaranth region who lived under protective alliances with Khonoma. Still further to the north, Khonoma's fame spread as far as the Maram and Anal regions on the borders of the Manipur kingdoms. On her north-western borders her name was respected all over the Zeliangrong region right up to the forts of the Kachar kingdom. On her south-eastern borders, Khonoma's fame was known through villages under her protectorate. On her northern borders, she had alliances with many villages. The kingdom of Manipur too knew of Khonoma's fame and had at one time sent Manipuri

> soldiers to guard the Semoma clan while they built their first fort. The King of Manipur had even sent his troops to assist certain clans in the village in their wars against their enemies. As for the plains of Assam to her west, Khonoma was a constant thorn in Assam's flesh for the repeated raids of head hunting and booty hunting (xi).

The first British expedition to the Naga Hills was led in 1832 AD by Captain Jenkins and Captain Pemberton. The second expedition took place in 1849, when the British Govt. learnt that Khonoma had aided men of Mezoma opposed to the Government. After attacking and suppressing Mezoma, they attacked Khonoma to quell what they called "Khonoma defiance". Houses of the Thevo clan and Merhu clan were burnt (xii). The third attack came on the 10th December, 1850, in an expedition led by Captain J. Butler and Major Foquett, Lieutenant Reid and Lieutenant Bivar. In October 1879, Deputy Commissioner Damant was killed at Khonoma. The Kohima garrison was shortly attacked by men of Khonoma, Tsutuonuomia clan, and warriors of Viswema, Chedama, Secuma, Jakhma, Zotshuma, Piphe and Tsiepama. The garrison survived a long siege and then prepared for another assault on Khonoma. The final expedition on Khonoma was in November, 1879 (ibidem).

Surrounded on all sides Khonoma was attacked on 22nd November with troops of 3369 soldiers. Greatly outnumbered by the British Army, the men of Khonoma retreated to their impregnable mountain fort and the battle turned into a siege of the tough little Angami village for four months. On 27th March 1880, a treaty between the representatives of the British Government and the elders of Khonoma brought conclusion to the conflict.

The cold night, hills and hillocks, festivals, animistic faiths and the Naga resistance to the colonial rule and the history of the battes form the bedrock of the novel. The festivals are integral to the hill ecology, e.g.,

> On the last day of the festival the villagers followed the two young children appointed to perform the *rhoutho* ritual of seed-sowing.
> At the fields, the elder pronounced the blessing ... "My

> paddy may you grow up well, though the weeds are abundant, my paddy do you grow around the tree stumps and boulder. It will be the food of generations, the food of wartime, grow bent over with full husked grain" (66).

Both the writers are conspicuously concerned about the history, ecology, ecological theosophy and the turmoils of time against their respective animistic faiths. The two novels are significant additions to the tradition of Indian English fiction and to the ecocritical "toxic consciousness" as they refect the degradation of pristine virgin ecology.

Works Cited

Dai, Mamang. *The Legends of Pensam.* New Delhi: Penguin Books, 2006.

Deitering, Cynthia. "The Postnatural Novel: Toxic Consciousness in Fiction of the 1980s": *The Ecocriticism Reader.* Ed. Cheryll Glotfelty and Harold Fromm. Athens : The University of Georgia Press, 1996, (198-203).

Head, Dominic. "Ecocriticism and the Novel" : *The Green Studies Reader.* Ed. Laurence Coupe-Oxon: Routledge, 2000, (235-241).

Iralu, Easterine. *A Naga Village Remembered.* Kohima : Ura Academy, 2003.

(24)

Outliving Turbulence: An Analysis of *These Hills Called Home*

Rupam Gogoi

India is a land of diversities. Varied people, varied culture, numerous languages and dialects, ethnic groups together form the Indian national identity. Yet secessionist voices cannot be avoided and the quest, more often than not assume violent propositions. The Nagas started their movement for a homeland in the mid 1940's. The legendary leader Phizo even declared independence in 1956, albeit unsuccessfully. Negotiations to bring peace to this war zone began more than 50 years back and in the 1960's highly honoured mass leaders like Jayprakash Narayan, Bimala Prasad Chaliha and Reverend Michael Scott began their tryst for peace. Nagaland has traversed a long route since then but not much has changed. Though violence is nothing unheard of in the Naga hills, the people have not forgotten their common legends, history and unique culture that would ultimately bind them as a race.

As the title of the book *These Hills Called Home* suggests, the ten short stories incorporated in it portray the life and times of the people whose life is unimaginable beyond the beauteous and the bounteous Naga hills. Terrified at the massive-scale crackdown on militancy that often land the common man in trouble, and battered by the fast changing social, political, economic and even cultural scenario, the Nagas search for a root that would keep intact the identity of their race. Temsula Ao has given us a picture of Nagaland afflicted by militancy, shocked by the excesses of the armed forces and sucked by a class of hypocrites and opportunists. But, what blurs all these is the tryst to create something durable face of devastation and hopelessness the creative spirit cannot be masked for very long. Creativity requires zeal and not merely passionate forebodings. The people portrayed in the book, if not wealthy, are never beyond the sway of creative urges. Sentila of 'The Pot Maker' is a classic symbol of the fact that satisfaction might not necessarily spring from works involving less labour and more profit. Her creative urge gets more steadfast as opposition from her mother increases and back breaking labour intensifies.

The concept of 'Home' is what the writer has emphasized in these short stories. In context of *These Hills Called Home*, the concept of home is not restricted to an individual household but its periphery widens to encapsulate all the hills adorned by the industrious and simple living Nagas. Insurgency—if the rebellions talked of abundantly in the book might be called—is in search for an independent homeland for themselves. This argument might be a bit out of place and harsh to the so-called mainstream for whom secessionist activities ransack a well ordered 'Home', that is the nation. Temsula Ao has given a lively description of the land of Nagas. She has immaculately expressed the beauty of the natural scenery and has described certain places thereby making an attempt to give as much information as possible about a region that is little known or not well known outside its geographical boundaries.

The dominant aspect of the book is insurgency and the lives of the people who can hardly move out of certain buzz words such as ambush, encounter, raid, curfew, enquiry and investigation. 'The Jungle Major' is a tale depicting the slow but certain spread of militancy. The story begins with a marriage that raise many eyebrows. It is tough to believe that a beauty of Khatila's charm and grace would tie the knot with Punaba. The girl's family belongs to a major clan but a string of rejections by suitors surprise everybody. Inspite of all odds they marry much to the dismay of everybody:

> But then there it was, the apparent mismatch was on, and the marriage took place in due course. (p.2)

A driver by profession, Punaba gradually gets involved in underground activities. The apparent "mismatch" is not a "mismatch" in their real life. The passionate bouts of love making while Punaba takes time off his underground activities show their attachment to each other. Freedom is Punaba's zeal but Khatila's love forms his emotional and moral base. The reign of terror unleashed by the armed forces often decimate the whole villages. The slightest of information regarding sheltering a terrorist can bring doom for all. Once Punaba is caught napping during one of the visits to his wife. Armymen reach their house and it is Khatila who saves him from certain death. When the captain comes searching he could hardly believe that the person Khatila is abusing to go and fetch water can be her husband. Punaba escapes in the guise of a servant. The underground authorities appreciate him for his planning and he rises in ranks. Khatila's "shrewd planning" goes unsung but not forgotten. However, Punaba's headlong dive into militancy is cut short as he surrenders on the appeal of his wife seeking his company. The story presents certain undefinable traits of the Nagas. They crave for freedom and fight for it but human values like love and friendship cannot be overlooked. However, we can conclude from the story that appearances can be deceptive—the apparently mismatch couple is definitely well matched.

'Soaba' is stupid in the language of the Ao. The man who is the centre of attraction in the story cannot be said to be quick witted or a nice speaker but he is definitely not an idiot in the harshest connotation of the term. In a land ravaged by merciless blood bath where people stay in constant fear of being intimidated or being harassed, Soaba is a non-entity. He is nothing to anybody other than an unpaid servant. No doubt, he himself keeps on changing his place of work but that is basically because of absence of kind Samaritans like Imtila. It is love and compassion that binds people together. The nomadic Soaba finds a shelter in the warmth of Imtila's love. Soaba's inherent innocence has been nicely shown—

> At first they did not understand what he was trying to say; but he kept on pointing to himself and saying Supiba in the garbled way that he spoke. When someone from inside the house called out Soaba, the boy began to scream Supiba, Supiba...from that time on they called him Supiba in deference to a simple mind, which in some mysterious way had sensed that there was something bad about the name Soaba that was tagged on to him. (p.14)

The interesting point here is that Supiba is the short form of 'Stupid Bastard' as made by the unschooled and innocent Soaba on listening his master call someone by that name.

The story also highlights another face of terrorism. Opportunism at its worst has been shown in the story. Imlichuba unleashes his reign of terror being backed by the government machinery. His tape recorder is the only one in the town and the music exuding from it intersects everybody. But, the louder the volume of music, the shriller becomes the pathetic shouts of the tortured brethrens. In 'The Jungle Major' we find Punaba agreeing to quit the life in jungle for the sake of his wife, but in 'Soaba' we find Imlichuba destroying his family life even though he is an important organ of the government machinery and his duty is to enhance peace by cutting down insurgent operations that according to the government has ruffled the fabric of the society. Ironically, these forces create more trouble for the common man than the underground revolutionaries. Power at its worst manifestation is ghastly. Soaba's murder is a rejoinder here. Soaba might be an idiot or a stupid for all but he is Imtila's source of hope in a world where made up appearances and show of pelf and power are the dominating traits. Soaba finds "love, protection and care" in Imtila which she unfortunately could not bestow upon her husband whose turbulent existence ultimately give way to nothingness. The gradual disappearance of Imlichuba's immaculate dress symbolizes the waning of his unbridled power just as the scene of scampering people yielding way to gun-trotting Imlichuba once symbolized his unquestioned authority.

'The Last Song' is a melancholic tale about a young girl named Apenyo whose song to mark the first day of the newly constructed village church becomes her last song. Tragedy strikes her family when she was nine-months old. The news of the illness of her father Zhamben reaches the village without giving the relatives a chance to reach him. In this geographically isolated and structurally under developed region, news travels slow, probably except the news of extortions and underground activities. Crushed between love for their brothers and sisters in jungle and fear of the warnings of the armed forces, the villagers lead a life of constant mental agitation. Apenyo's song is set against the backdrop of the brutality of armed forces. She sings in the midst of a commotion indicating terrible times ahead. Something inside her makes her sing even with danger lurking right over their heads. The singers of the choir sing alongwith Apenyo so that she is not identified and taken to task. Libeni could feel the soulful song of the girl and the necessity of stopping it immediately yet events take turn towards the worst before she could do anything. Human rights violation is often reported from India's North-East, the picturisation of Apenyo and her mother Libeni's gangrape and brutal murder focus upon the bestial qualities of the men in uniform. The new church thus becomes a symbol of devastation rather than resurrection of noble thoughts and blessed ideals. The captain takes shelter in a mental asylum—thus indicating that no sane man can escape the pangs of conscience after such spine chilling savagery.

The story brings in two aspects of the Naga society which can be visualized in almost all the tribal societies of the north-east. The first is adherence to certain old traditions and customs, even though they have adopted one religion or the other. In 'The Last Song' we can see this from the controversy regarding the burial of Libeni and Apenyo:

> The deaths of these unfortunate people were considered to be from unnatural circumstances and according to tradition they could not be buried in the village graveyard, Christianity or no Christianity... we are still Nagas. aren't we? (p.30)

They are laid to rest just outside the graveyard and the singer Apenyo is given a "song-less funeral". The second aspect is the importance bestowed upon story telling which is no less than a ritual. An old woman has been shown telling a group of children about a black December Sunday after harvests when a singer draped in an attractive attire sang for the last time as the euphoria was soon suppressed by gloom with ravages beyond human imagination littering in the whole area. The song of Apenyo attains mystical and mythical significance. Apenyo must live on and so should the song that she sang amidst chaos as if trying to show that the melody of chorus and drub the cacophony of chaos. The act of telling the story to a group of children far removed from the melody of nature assumes special significance as this is an attempt to revert to the past in order to shape their future.

'The Curfew Man' presents a pathetic picture of Satemba

caught a quagmire that engulfs all the militancy infested regions of the world. Satemba was once a constable in the Assam Police. He was a police who adorned jersey more than his khaki-coloured uniform. His shattered knee cap put an end to his career as a footballer and being unsuitable for any table job, he retires from his service. Honouring his association with the Assam Police, the authorities decide to bid him farewell by giving him all the regular pension benefits even though he could not complete the requisite number of years in service. The petty pension of Rs. 75 per month hit the family hard and Jemtila starts working as a domestic help. Her work at the SDO's house brings in an opportunity for Satemba—he is recruited as an informer. But, he could not remain aloof from the pangs of conscience. Helping the armed forces in his duty but thoughts of fall out with his struggling brethren disturbs him.

And for the briefest of moments he wondered if his superiors would give him a special bonus for helping them to capture or kill the underground leaders. But even this prospect of monetary gain did nothing to allay his misgivings. (p.40)

Meanwhile, working in the cold of the night deteriorates his wound further. The chance encounter with a stranger, very likely of the underground, further intensifies his mental agony. When the other knee cap also gives away, Jemtila appears to be the happiest being on earth. It is in Satemba's unbearable pain that she finds profound relief. Satemba's unavailability infuriates the officer and he starts searching for another curfew man. Satemba is a relieved man after abandoning this thankless job which made him suffer both physically and mentally. It is ironical that pain is the base of pleasure. But, the brutal human world is full of such surprises. It is not Satemba, the man who is the centre of attraction of the story but Satemba, the curfew man.

'The Night' is a piercing account about the fate of a girl whom the society abhorred for her two illegitimate children. Imnala was a beautiful girl and a student of eighth class in a school at Mokokchung. But youthful passions could not be controlled and she slipped into a situation which she should have avoided. A "deluge" of suitors wooed her but it was the Junior Engineer who catches her imagination. Unbridled passions of youth give way to passionate advances and ultimately a condition which no one really expected. Imnala got pregnant and the man disappeared amidst rumours that he had gone to China to train himself as a soldier in the underground army. News of his marriage with a female cadet also did the rounds. This storm had hardly subsided when Repalemba appeared into the scenario. A petty contractor who was offered small contracts as part of Government's policy to keep the youth away from underground activities, he talked with Tekatoba, Imnala's father about a probable contract which would yield much profit. Repalemba's entry shook the world of Imnala for the second time. She repeated her earlier blunder and was to be a mother of another illegitimate child.

The story is not merely about a woman who committed irreparable mistakes but is a presentation of the trends of the whole society. We get a clear picture of the customs of a society which often tilt towards men in its judgement. What however deserves mention is the resilience of Imnala to move out of these constraints to live a life of her own. The unique feature of Naga society is that the maternal uncle plays an important part in advising and escorting a girl to the meetings involving the gaonbura and other village elders to decide a case. We see that if a child is not given the father's name, he is not entitled to be a member of any clan and he becomes a sort of "non-person". Alemba could not marry Imnala but he at least showed some courage in giving his name to the unborn child and preventing his wife's party from being too abusive and violent. The term "true man" when used to Alemba might seem to be a bit out of place but considering the nature of the society, the title cannot be said to be without any worth. A resurgent Imnala vows to be a woman of substance but she is bound to face immense mental hardship regarding her status as an unmarried mother in a society which punishes the likes of her but the Alembas escape the scrutinizing eyes of the society:

> ...she would have to face and bear the scorn and abuse of Alemba's wife and the censure of society whose balance of justice always tended to till against the woman. (p.54)

'The Pot Maker' is much removed in its theme from the other stories. 'The Night' has minute trace of the underground but this story lacks any such observable trait. It is about the preservation of a tradition, an art at a time when the youth is slowly but surely moving away from it. The art is tough to sustain and financially not very lucrative yet it must not be lost. This tale is about Sentila who takes up the creative art of making pots and in this process not only gives vent to her creative spirit but saves an art from being thrown into oblivion. Even the frustration that punctuates the noble deed of creation is given vent in music by the propagators of the art—

> One of the old women sang beautiful folk songs while working but when something went wrong, she would substitute the words to suit her anger and frustration.... (p.60)

Arenla wants her daughter to take up weaving which would at least save her daughter from the hard life of a pot maker. But we find that she bows down and Sentila blossoms as a master craftsman. The tribal societies are characterised by passing their talents from one generation to another in order to ascertain the continuity of certain traditions, customs and art. So, that's why Mesoba, Sentila's father faced the inquisitive eyes and curious questions of the villagers. The elders of the village comment thus:

> ...skills such as pot making, which not only catered to the needs of the people but also symbolized the tradition and history of the people did not belong to any individual. And experts were obliged to pass on their skills.... (p. 61-62)

The Nagas are steadfast in the preservation of their unique culture and for this the responsibility must be collectively taken.

Another aspect of the Naga society that we find in this story is the prevalence of dormitories for young men (morung) and young girls. The girls attaining puberty stay in these dormitories under the guidance of 'Onula' or Aunty. The girls are taught and trained in the skills that are necessary for sustenance. Talents are to be groomed into perfection. Sentila's talent is nurtured and polished and soon we find her growing into an excellent pot maker. But, Arenla passes away before her daughter is recognized as a master of the craft. Sentila's pathetic cry is touching:

> Mother, I did not wish it to happen this way; it simply came to me. Please forgive me. (p.67)

Onula could guess that the two rows of moist pots are the creation of two distinct artists—one dead and the other emerging into the horizon against all odds. Sentila upholds a tradition that would certainly keep the uniqueness of the Nagas intact at a time when change is preferred over continuity. She is will power personified against preponderance of the thoughts of incompetence.

'Shadows' is a story dealing with the shadowy aspects of the underground. It is not that the revolutionaries or the insurgents are preoccupied only with their goals and ideals. Disputes and arguments often reach alarming levels. Souring relationships amongst the cadres lead to crimes as heinous as cold blooded murder. This story highlights such a brutal episode thereby raising many questions on the professed or affected humanitarian ideals of a band of revolutionaries whose aim is to save their people from the sufferings inflicted upon them by the nation against whom they have taken arms. The first few lines give us an impression of the life lived by the brave soldiers of the underground army.

> It was a sunny day. For the first time in six days, the Sun's rays had penetrated the thick foliage of the jungle. (p.69)

Travelling through such rough terrains, the twenty one volunteers are to reach China via Burma. They are to be trained there and come back to their homeland and fight for their mission. The volunteers are generally chosen on the basis of acts of bravery shown by them—the encounters with the Indian Army being a major criterion. But the north-eastern states have a problem of excesses. Representation of the different tribes and sub-tribes, clans and sub-clans often complicate matters in the political arena. This aspect of representation is honoured in the underground army also. The 21 volunteers we are concerned with display such a phenomenon with the sole exception of Imli, the son of the second-in-command of the underground army.

Imli's entry into the underground army was opposed by his father and called it his "mad pursuit". Another trait of the underground leaders can be seen here. Being the second-in-command, Imli's father always tried to increase the number of freedom fighters. However, the thought of his son joining his army saw his fatherly love suppressing his esteem and pride as a leader spears heading a secessionist movement. He wanted his son to be educated and away from the world of the insurgents. The situation does make us think about the leaders who try to include the youth as fighters yet their own siblings away from this world where uncertainity of life is the most certain eventuality.

'Shadows' is a manifestation of the dictum of 'poetic justice'. We find that Hoito planned the brutal, spine chilling murder of Imli and the reason was the rude reprimand that Imli's father gave to him in public. The ghastly murder even shocked experienced cadets like Roko and Lovishe. Roko tried to observe the rituals of the dead as best as he could. His love for young Imli was evident in his behaviour towards him and from his reaction on seeing the caracass. He could feel the pain of the excruciating death experienced by Imli. However, the underground authorities did not divulge anything. Though it was everybody's guess that Imli's murder was pre-planned yet the whole episode was closed down as an accident even though his father wept bitterly in front of one of his cadets. Hoito's disappearance and his condition on being traced point out the pangs of conscience felt by an individual on committing any crime. What 'Boy' did at the end of the story was another murder exhibiting the same savagery as the earlier one but the hunter of the earlier operation was hunted down in the second. The murder of Hoito can be said to be a discernable shadow of the murder of Imli.

The story showcases one interesting trait of the underground—the prevalence of secessionist groups within the secessionist set up. That power is corrupting and inflated ego destructive can be seen in 'shadows' Temsula Ao has tried to obliterate the romantic notion of 'revolution' as held by the youth in insurgency—inflicted region. Armed rebellion shows mirages but not the corpus:

> Whatever romantic idealism had first made him decide upon a life in the underground army had soon evaporated and been replaced by a new awareness of the ground reality. (p.76)

An Old Man Remembers' repeats an image of 'The Last Song'—the image of an elderly person sitting by the health telling the young children about the glory of their past resplendent with joys inspite of the interspersing testing times that often made them bow down to let the storm pass off. The innocent adolescent pleasures of Imtisashi and Imlikokba were cut short by the ever-intensifying operations of the marauding Indian Army. Their subsequent surrender took them out of that world but Imtisashi thought it wise to hide these things from his grandson. Imli's death changed the world of Sashi. His wife's death had already created a void, now his friend's passing away seemed to intensify his sense of loneliness. Sashi's final adien to Imli was heart rending. Imli always supported the notion of making the younger generation know about:

> ...the people's history and that they should not grow up ignorant about the unspeakable atrocities, that they, the older generation had witnessed. (p.93)

Sashi could feel the worth of the words of Imli:

> Good old sensible Imli, how right you were and how wrong I was in thinking that the bad things will go away if one does not think about them. (p.93)

Later on we find that Sashi accepted the idea of telling his story to Moalemba, his grandson and realized that:

> ...once in a lifetime one ought to face the truth. Truth about the self, the land and above all, the truth about history. (p.112)

The underground army is often romanticized. However many had to join it out of sheer compulsion. We find Sashi and Imli being forcefully recruited into the underground army:

> Soldiers we were made into and that's what we resolved to remain. (p.101)

Suddenly they became men out of boys. They did commit heinous crimes but repented for those. But we find Sashi unable to withstand the devastated face of a dead soldier who was killed while they were executing their plans. He too felt the pangs of his conscience like Hoits of 'Shadows' and the Captain of 'The Last Song'. They (Imli and Sashi) made a desperate attempt to run away from the life of jungle. However, on reaching their village they found to their surprise that the entire village was charred. The people had to take shelter in the forest at the west end of the village which was traditionally thought of to be the shelter of the spirits of the forest. Even that refuge did not remain safe for very long and the villagers including the disfigured and handicapped father of Imli had to move away from there. Once Sashi was injured during an ambush and taking the opportunity both of them surrendered with the help of the Pastor of Mokokchung with the promise that they would not reveal the secrets of the underground army to anyone.

Towards the end of the story we find Imtisashi further maturing as a wizened man. In his adolescence, the sight of a woman walking naked in the middle of a group aroused his curiosity but as he aged, he found much depth in his wife's practical explanation:

> ...the human body was not a subject for speculation or abstraction. (p.112)

The story of Sashi was not the story of an individual but of he society. He wanted Moalemba to take the best out of what he had listened to:

> You have to make what you can from what I have tried to tell you. (p.112)

His thoughts no longer ventured around the mundane, but they flew to a new horizon where he could sense better days for his people. Might be the times have changed and life has become fast and comfortable yet the youth cannot be let to forget that the voice of the soul, of conscience must be heard instead of only gratifying bodily appetites. A new dawn fraught with hopes and opportunities would light up the land which is replete with unforgettable sacrifices made by the likes of Imtisashi and Imlikokba.

'The Journey' is not about guns and violence. Tinula covers the distance between her home and Mariani and vice versa everytime her school close for or re-open after vocations in great discomfort. Walking along steep hilly jungle tracks involves danger and so they try to cross the danger zones as fast as possible. We find that Tinula tires out and has to be urged by Temjenba, her brother to walk faster. While for the young ones like Tinula, jungles are all about foliages, beautiful music of the birds and scenic beauty; but for the experienced ones like the woman accompanying them it is fraught with dangers. She knows every bit of the forests of their route and could even tell the direction into which the herd of elephants has moved even though for Tinula the forest appears the same everywhere:

> Do not worry nephew, they have already crossed our route. Look at the break in the forest to your left; they have gone to the other side away from our pat. (p.117)

After an exhausting journey, Tinula reached her school late in the night and was asked to share Winnie's bed who informed her about Herbert and his new girlfriend. This was a bit shocking for Tinula as she at thirteen had no clear-cult idea of having somebody as her boyfriend. Though her tender heart did not crave much for Herbert, yet she did expect that he would look at her.

The night dawned a new experience for Tinula. She was sharing the same bed with Winnie yet a wide gulf was created between them that night. Vast stretches of flat land and hilly terrain separated Tinula's school and her home, yet she could imagine and feel the warmth of their affection and care. The tattered blanket for which she had to struggle with her cousins appeared to her as being warmer than the soft sheets and warm bed of Winnie. The squealing piglet disturbed her sleep in the morning at her village but the words of Winnie had the same effect upon her. Her body shook for a long time in Winnie's bed yet the tussle for the tattered blanket with her cousins was a memorable moment for her. Tinula had no clear impression of Herbert but she could form an idea about Winnie of being a girl who hurt her quite intentionally. This story emphasizes upon the notion that human relationships are not determined by the distance separating people but by attitude and good nature that always binds. Two people might be quite closer to each other physically and yet be separated by a huge mental and emotional gulf.

The last story of the anthology, 'A New Chapter' is about a new class that emerged when militant activities were soaring and political equations framed and changed in keeping track with the turn of events. While the underground forces kept shifting their base in the jungles, the army established itself in the prime locations—villages and towns. While the local populace lived a life of fear and uncertainity, rumours of aristocratic life style of the army officers spread like wild fire. Many jostled to make a space for themselves in this circle. The armymen were handsomely paid for serving in this remote and troubled area. They carried out encounters to make their superiors know about their acts of courage. But more often than not they were fake and doctored with largely distorted figures of casualty. The 'army contractors' were emerging as a powerful class in the Naga social scenario:

> In short, these contractors were actually a new class of Nagas, who emerged as the third force in the power equation between the two warring armies. Both sides recognized their utility in their game and used them unscrupulously. (p.123)

Bendangnungsang belonged to a well-to-do family. His father was a proud retired government servant and his brothers were in lucrative and powerful positions in the government machinery. He started his career as a contractor supplying meat, fish, vegetables, fruits etc. to the army camps set up at interior areas. His intention in taking up this profession was to make easy money. But he had to depend upon the plains for his supply. Meat-on-hoof, fruits and fish made it difficult for him to earn a decent profit. At such a time Nungsang met Bhandari to earn profit by slightly changing the terms of his contract by establishing a good relationship with the concerned officers. For twice a month meat was to be replaced by pumpkin, squash or gourd and fresh fish was to be replaced by dry fish. Apples and mangoes were replaced by locally available fruits such as pears and plums. For pumpkins he depended upon his cousin Merenla and petty businessmen like Sattar and Karim managed dry fish for him at different points of time.

Meanwhile Nungsang tried to establish a good relationship with the underground in order to escape from paying taxes to the parallel government. He tried his luck in politics also. A dark horse amply supported by lady luck and shifting political loyalties, Nungasang became an M.L.A. Bhandari and his ilk helped him to be their representative. The pettj traders were coerced into donating for the election fund and those whom Nungsang owed money thought it better to forget the whole episode. Nungsang's symbol—a hornbill worked wonders for him. Fluttering white flags with a hornbill embossed upon it presented a majestic picture. Imkrong, who made the symbol of hornbill something to reckon with got only promises for rewards in future. However the effect he created upon the people could hardly be forgotten:

> Even years later, older people recalled that the sight of the legendary birds stirred something elemental in their racial memory and they fancied that the birds had descended from their lofty perches in the deep and dark jungles and had come to participate in the political parade with a clear message for the people. They claimed that their votes were swayed by the impact made by the sight of this ancestral symbol. (p.140)

The opportunist Bhandari was ready with his plan of making the new MLA table a bill in the house in order to get his tribe recognised as an indigenous group of the state. Pumpkin Merenla on the other hand made money by supplying pumpkins to Nungsang. Suddenly she found her stock of pumpkins rotting in the house with nobody to take them away. She sensed the hidden motives of her cousin. The family ties values by the woman carried almost nothing to Nungsang and so he quietly left this woman once he established himself in the political scenario of the state. She felt the agony that arose out of such a situation:

> Slowly and painfully she began to see that people who go away from villages think and act differently even if they are relatives. She said to herself over and over again that a fellow villager would never have treated her in this manner. (p.144)

She tried to obliterate all marks of her deal with Nungsang. By throwing pumpkins to the pigs, she began a new chapter in her life by taking herself away from the fast changing political calculations of the land. A new chapter began in the lives of Bhandari nd Merenla as Nungsang entered the alleys of power. The body whom Wati, the underground leader, introduced to Nungsang as his son later on became his son-in-law. Thus, everybody was trying to manipulate the things and sequence of events in order to suit one's own interests. Bhandari became a prominent man owing to his close association with Nungsang. As for Pumpkin Merenla, she became only 'Merenla' and had to revert back to her earlier way of life away from the selfish and unethical world of forgery, coercion and deceptive appearances.

The stories can be broadly divided into two categories—stories that deal with insurgency and it's impact upon the people and stories that emphasise upon the creative spirit of man that knows no limitation or subjugation. The people portrayed by Temsula Ao are the common people who are the worst suffers of any army operation. Heroic acts like that of Khatila in 'The Jungle Major' often goes unheard, inspite of saving a whole village from being turned into ashes. The plight of women as portrayed in the stories cannot be said to be a very encouraging one we find that they are the worst sufferers on the face of mindless violence. Mercilessly gang-raped they also are to bear the trauma of being unawed mothers and social outcasts. In the Naga society too a man is a symbol of social security as said by Imnala's mother in 'The Night':

> Remember, in our society a woman must have the protection of a man even if he happens to be blind or lame. A woman alone will always be in danger. (p.53)

In 'Soaba' we find Imtila being sidelined by her husband on attaining power. Apenyo is a pathetic representation of a woman's desire to seek melody in chaos although the results are nothing but disastrous.

The questions of home, nationality, nationhood and identity have also been discussed in the stories. The identity crisis of Bhandari is worth mentioning. He has been in Nagaland since his birth. His ancestors were rewarded with land in the land of the Nagas in recognition of their services to the British army. Yet, he cannot say with confidence that Nagas have accepted him as one of their own race and is not considered an 'outsider'. However, the Nagas are themselves divided in their notions of nationality and nationhood. While a group seeks complete separation from India, another group wants to be part of what is called the mainstream. The 'home' of Nagas is turbulent and mass resistance against the state is unparalleled in the history of independent India. History often leaves aside much for the people to recall and propagate. History might discard certain events as trivial but Temsula Ao says, "Sometimes it is the trivial that triggers the process of remembering a great loss". From this vantage point we can feel the importance of Imtisashi telling his grandson about his past is not merely a discourse on the adolescent pranks and youthful adventures of two friends and how they matured with age, but he tells the tale of a land battered and butchered yet resilient to start life afresh in the new dawn. Story telling enhances the collective memory of a race seeking answers to questions of identity, nationality and the idea of 'home'.

Temsula Ao's concern is to show violence as a scourge. It opens upon space for doubt and hatred. No civilized society can ever encourage this. The times are fast changing and people are ready to travel outside there are searching for a better source of livelihood. The heterogenous population of the towns show such a trend. Of course, a town in the area of the Aos would have an Ao majority. This trend suggests a change in the socio-economic system of the society. Violence mars development and hence it will be better if it subsides for ever and the different tribes and other people whom Nagas refer to as "outsiders" stay in peace and enhance development of the land.

In a war zone where news must travel fast, informers are an inseparable part of the government machinery. Satemba is one such informer and he is considered worthy till he can move around. The moment he is deemed useless, he is replaced. Soaba is also abused and killed without any reason. Human values are not considered on such fronts. But amidst such gloom art thrives—art transcends all. That's why we find Apenyos and Sentilas trying to keep alive certain traditions and customs that give a sense of dignity to the Nagas. The writer has delved into the heart and soul of this mighty race and shows that wisdom emanating from antiquity transform the mindset of people even though we might be residents of a global village. The sense of keeping a tradition intact can be seen in Tinula's journey up the hills where she could find some sort of elixir of life.

To opine that Temsula Ao, while negating the romantic notion of war talks of an insignificant present and a terribly gloomy future is wrong. She aims to provide her people the courage to live on with dignity, honour and self respect. The glory and grandeur of the race must be preserved for posterity. To call the homeland of the Nagas only a militancy infested zone is a misnomer. Birendra Kr. Bhattacharyya in the preface to his famous novel *Iyaruingam* (1960) has said:

> Nagas too are humans, but of a special type. Underneath the iron armour in their hearts there blossom the beauteous flowers of timeless humanity.

Temsula Ao appears to be a chronicler of a mighty race. She has been objective in her analyses and simple and captivating in her presentation of the Naga way of life. However, the issues that the writer has dealt with in this book might seem to be regional but the inherent universal appeal cannot be overlooked. Her message appears loud and clear:

> I hear the land cry,
> Over and over again
> Let all the dead awaken
> And teach the living
> How not to die.

Works Cited

Ao, Temsula.. *These Hills Called Home*. New Delhi: Zubaan (Penguin), 2006.

(25)

Ethnic Representation in Easterine Iralu and Nilakshi Borgohain: A Study of their Select Stories

Binda Sah

Unity is by no means uniformity. Meaningful unit emerges out of the realization of differences. And differences add colour to the world, make it exciting, beautiful and challenging. But one must take care that these differences should not create any indifferent sentiments and feelings. As we know, India is a wonderful land of differences, with so-called unity in diversity, but with indifferences all around, and thanks to such indifferences, there is a growing sense of ethnicity, its representation and assertion in every nook and corner of India, and Northeast is not exception to it. The entire Northeast is ethnically sensitive, and its sensitiveness finds expression in different forms in works of the writers of this region. To talk about the ethnic representation I have chosen two women writers: Easterine Iralu, and Nilakshi Borgohain. Both the writers are already recognized as representatives of Northeast: Iralu as a Naga writer with her publication of various poems, short stories and two novels entitled *A Naga Village Remembered* (2003), A *Terrible Matriarchy* (2008) and Nilakshi as an Assamese writer with her first collection of stories entitled *Streets of Fear* (2002). However, whereas Iralu who taught English at Nagaland University, has lived her life so far in Northeast and Norway, Nilakshi crossing the geo-political boundry of the Northeast is presently living in Gurgaon, Haryana, working as a freelancer. This makes the study of ethnicity a bit interesting for they live in two different social milieus. Moreover, ethnicity is a matter of experience and not just living in a particular ethnic group.

Easterine Iralu's stories are set in the ambience of tribal community life of Nagas and present a thoughtful reflection on the adherence to tribal values right from day-to-day activities to the spiritual engagement. Her stories selected for study in the paper are "Death by Apotia', and 'Suping with the Spirits". These stories reveal Iralu's colourful picturization of the tribal inhabitation, apart from highlighting the gradual shift from community life to that of the individual one. Her "Death by Apotia" is a poignant story of an accursed family; a curse that continues for four generations. Killing each male-member when they are in their spring of life, Apotia in the story is a symbol of any "unnatural deaths, deaths by drowning, during childbirth, in war," etc. (104). Under the ever-looming fear of Apotia, the story ends with the expiation of curse with the death of the protagonist, Vin, with whom the story begins and the apotia of his proceeding three generations has well been narrated to him by his maternal grand-mother. Between the accomplishment of the first apotia and its ultimate expiation lies the whole saga of an acute pain and apprehension of losing life when it just starts blooming. However, it provides a good raw material to study the people's attitude to the family accursed with apotia. In fact, the very beginning of apotia is rooted in the superstitious and supernatural beliefs of the community. Vin's great grandfather, the first victim of apotia, was killed by a boar while hunting a dear with spear, and it is natural that one may get killed while hunting. But as no reason and rational argument stands before the customary belief of the people, the death of Vin's great grandfather is declared apotia after going through the various aspects of the incidence leading to the death. The deadbody is considered to be accursed and so is given an exile burial outside the village gate. Such burial further leads to the birth of an eerie feelings among the villagers as some feel the presence of an invisible entity while crossing by the apotia burial. This superstitious faith and supernatural fear of apotia is confirmed when apotia struck the brother of the grandfather of Vin who was killed "when a muzzle loading gun went off accidently, a bullet went through his temple, killing him on the spot" (107). The apotia continues for four generations in form of some natural calamities or accidents. While executing the impact of apotia, the writer presents before us the ethnic cooperation and solidarity in form of the customary 'Peli' work. The continuation of 'Peli' work throughout all the four generations is the suggestive of the firm adherence to the ethnic values. However, the story also reveals the people's adherence to the superstitious and supernatural taboos as well.

Significantly, "Death by Apotia" reveals Iralu's art of story-telling, shaped by her awareness of fairy-tale-narration, which finds its perfection in her story "Supping with the Spirits". This story originates from the mouth of an aged midwife and unfurls through her experience with the community of spirits; the spirits having family and hospitality like that of human beings. This unfamiliar experience of the midwife changes her very notion of spirits being filthy and fatal, and provides an additional lustre to her narration of the story. Her narration is so minute and lucid that she takes the entire typographical feature of her journey to Thizama to attend a delivery case within her sweep of narration: "The road that leads to Thizama, it winds around the old helipad by the circuitous route. The other route climbs uphill upto this hillock and at this point here, a path leads down to Thizama..." (164). The tortuous journey of the midwife reveals the hardship of life in the hilly villages near Kohima. Iralu, in this story, with her keen sense of observation and lucidly tight narration, succeeds in portraying before us an authentic picture of tradition and hospitality of Naga people living in hills under the seemingly apparent story of a midwife's experience with spirits.

In contrast to Iralu's natural setting of limited range thanks to her deep concern with the projection of the community life of Nagas, we find Nilakshi's stories having a setting of wider range and a concern deep-rooted in her awareness of the oneness of human beings. It is this awareness that makes the sensitive readers delve deep inside her stories only to find themselves somewhere within them. Her two most touching stories selected for analysis in this paper are "A Local" and "A Sariwallah".

"A Local" is a story about the projection of ethnicity and identity reframation in modern heterogenous society. Through the experience of Aparajita Phukan, the protagonist of the story, the writer casts light on the pang of being questioned of one's own identity on the basis of biological feature of one's body and geographical location of one's home. The story begins amid the lush greenery of a tea-garden in Dibrugarh where the protagonist has her sojourn during her school holidays. The peaceful environment of the garden and the simple but harmonious attitude of the people executes a deep influence in shaping her personality and consciousness of her ethnic and national identity. However, once she is removed from her familiar milieu she is faced with a necessity of identity explication and assertion as well. Aparajita's experience as a student of the University of Delhi questions the very existence of a composite identity called INDIAN: "Identity as an Indian would always need an explanation" (18). It is, indeed, very difficult to define 'Indian' as it is a composition of different parts, and the Chemistry among the parts is so weak that they prefer to be identified as parts rather than the whole, and, so, despite being attached, they ever remain detached from one another. For this detachment, Aparajita feels as foreigner in her own national capital because of her so-called 'un-Indian appearance'. "Everywhere she went, everyone she spoke to, she was questioned and asked to elaborate exactly of which area she was a local" (38). She is hailstoned with a number of awkward questions regarding the region of her origin. In fact, her un-Indian appearance often lands her in unusual situations; a situation where her degree of endurance and depth of ethnicity are tested—a painful experience which teaches her to question the very concept of being local. She is reluctant to accept that she is a local only in Assam where her ancestors of Tai Ahom ruled for a period of 600 years because "Her ancestors had migrated across the Patkai hills into Assam in 1228 AD. Like most Indians, the Thai Ahoms were not the original inhabitants of India" (39). Aparajita's awareness of her ancestral invasion and inhabitation, and the history of Assam; its glorious past and pitiable present has been lucidly but protestingly expressed in the story. The agony of being marginalized and stigmatised existence is creatively used to foster a conscience which could comprehend the transitoriness of any identity framation: "Blanketing humans of any region under any particular identity can always prove to be a dangerous hypothesis" (40). And this has been proved by the unrest and separatist tendency that has beset the entire Northeast during the last few decades. The conflict among the various ethnic groups of the region can well be accounted for the frequent application of the term 'local' as well as the politics of ethnicity and identity. Sanjib Baruah in his *Durable Disorder* has explicitly brought out the true nature of Indian national identity which is often hampered by the politics of ethnicity: "ethnic politics is radically different from the politics of identity that is not grounded in homelands—the latter is often easily incorporated within a larger ideology of state nationalism"(123). If identity is not grounded in the concept of homelands, its determination is sure to be dangerous on the basis of regionalism and political boundary, and Nilakshi Borgohain is trying to convey this message through her story "A Local". Indeed, in this age of globalization and transculturalism, it is very difficult to determine where one particular individual can be considered a local. The very concept of being local is dubious and vicious as nation, region, state or ethnic territory can not be a permanent, but merely a transient category of belonging.

Both the writer and the protagonist are aware of this nature of human identity and believe that the alienation of the region from the main stream is due to the lack of proper representation as well as recognition. That the region is not recognized outside its territory is revealed in Aparajita's experience as a wife of a multinational company employee stationed in Gurgaon where she is shocked to know the people's total ignorance of the Northeast. Here the questions of her origin assume wackies propositions with questions like "Where on the earth was Shillong?", "Didn't she mean Ceylon?", "Was Assam a part of India?", "Did she know magic?", "Weren't the men from the Northeast violent, insurgent head-hunters and maneaters?" These questions baffle her as they come from the so-called most educated people, and she wonders as to who is to be blamed for it. Definitely not the people, but the administration to some extent as the writer herself comments, "The history book in their school days had almost always been silent of such a land for a long time" (40). In a nation of multifarious ethnicity it becomes imperative for the centre to address its margins properly so as to root out any discontent among the margins lent that becomes detrimental to it. The discontent of Aparajita Phukan, resulting from her sense of unbelongingness in own nation, is the product of the conflict between centre and margin, or self and other. This conflict as in the political game of power margins are made to remain margins and others is otherised further. Under such circumstances, it becomes moral obligation of the margins to assert themselves, and Nilakshi's "A Local" is a sincere assertion of her ethnicity under the purview of Indian nationality.

Here we witness a sharp contrast between Iralu's representation of ethnicity and that of Nilakshi's. Ethnicity can be represented at various levels. Iralu represents the traditional, cultural, ecological as well as spiritual aspects of her ethnicity while Nilakshi concentrates on the political perspectives of her ethnicity. Nilakshi's political awareness of her race being marginalized teaches her to recognize the oneness of human beings as every ethnic group is, in some way, marginalized in comparison to other. Consequently, she feels the agony of a man or race being marginalized and treated as alien. This humanistic sense of Nilakshi is well expressed in her story "A Sariwallah". This story is about an illegal immigrant Bholanath, a Bangladeshi, who sells sari from door to door. The sarees that he carried are symbolic: "Every sari speaks about the tradition of the region through its design" (26); 'Kancheevaran' from Kanchipuram, the 'patola' from Gujarat and Orissa and 'bandani' from Rajasthan. Bholanath's collection of these sarees are the symbolic collection of cultures and his selling of them in the Northeast, and particularly in Assam, is a symbolic act of acquainting cultures and establishing cultural link. His experience with the art of different cultures has made him a perfect man who understands humanity despite his business like mentality. The story is simply about Bholanath's skill of selling sarees to the lady narrator. In the process of demonstrating his sarees Bholanath shows such concern, patience and persuasive skills that the narrator is compelled to buy three sarees, but her inability to pay the decided amount reveals the true nature of Bholanath—a nature generally not found in the business class. He sells the sarees at a price no where nearer to its original price. The narrator is left with a mixed feeling at such nature of Bholanath, and at the end of the story, she realizes that Bholanath is not just a sariwallah, he is a man of simple human benevolence and humanity. This strange encounter with a sariwallah makes the narrator realize that humanity is not subject to any caste, community, race or region. To achieve this we just need to do simple act of human benevolence as in the case of Sariwallah. After all, it is only the humanity or human identity that is permanent because we can change our cultural identity, we can change our linguistic identity, we can change our ethnic or national identity, but we can never change our identity as human beings.

Both the story writers have shown brightness in their art. It is expected that they will shine brighter in the days to come.

References

Barua, Sanjib. *Durable Disorder: Understanding the Politics of Northeast India*: New Delhi: OUP, 2005.

Borgohain, Nilakshi. *Streets of Fear*. New Delhi: Minerva Press, 2002.

—."A Local": *Indian Literature*. New Delhi: Sahitya Akademi, June-July, 2005.

—. "A Sariwallah": *Indian Perspectives*, Aug 2005.

Iralu Easterine: "Death of Apotia" :*The Heart of the Matter*, ed. M.C. Zama, New Delhi: Katha, 2004.

Iralu Easterine: "Supping with the Spirits" : *Earth Songs* ed. K.C. Baral: New Delhi : Sahitya Akademi, 2005.

(26)

Birendra Kumar Bhattacharya's *Love in the Time of Insurgency*: A Study of Social and Political Change in Nagaland

Satyendra Prasad Singh

The invading Japanese army had reached Imphal and Kohima but held there by the British and Indian forces. Both the combatants had suffered considerable losses. The Japanese army had begun to retreat. The tribesmen of Nagaland welcomed the British and having been hostile to the Japanese, provided information of the whereabouts of the retreating Japanese.Sharengla, the Naga girl, was pregnant and wanted to live as husband and wife with Ishewara, the Japanese soldier. Since he feared that the white soldiers would shoot him like a stray dog and the tribesmen would hand him over to them, he left Sharengla and thus could not keep his promise to her.

After a long time, Sharengla experienced the war and its devastation with the frightening explosion of bombs, destruction of houses, the screams of inhabitants wanting to escape and the trepidation of the earth. Sharengla's village was devastated. Livestock scurried to escape. The church spire was licked by small shooting flames. Pieces of burning wood started to fall. Embers burned and ashes floated in the wind. Sharengla's cottage was reduced to ashes. Bombs were dropped by the planes on other villages also. The villagers were displaced by the war. Imphal was bombed by the Japanese Tojo army in 1942. Most of the homes came under the occupation of the Japanese. The Imphal valley was bombed for two years and people fled to different villages. When the Japanese started to retreat, displaced people were hopeful for returning to their homes but tragically most of the homes had been destroyed by Allied air attacks.

Modern humanitarians attacked wars. Bernard Shaw stated that romantic war was only butchery. Tolstoy objected to war because it was real and he wanted to abolish it. Shaw objected to the idealization of war. He had reservations not to war but to the attractiveness of war. Tolstoy affirmed: "There shall be no wars." (Chesterton 52). Bernard Shaw only thought: "Wars if you must; but for God's sake, not war songs." (ibidem). Birendra Kumar Bhattacharya considered war harmful to mankind and believed that problems could be solved through the Gandhian principle of non-violence. Subhas Chandra Bose allied with the Japanese keeping in view that they would assist in driving out the British. An underground movement was underway in Nagaland. Videsselie was the activist of the Indian National Army along with Phanitphang. He wanted to establish an independent Nagaland. He felt that his dream could be fulfilled through warfare. Sharengla did not accept this idea as she had experienced war and its follies. Due to the war, prices of essential goods escalated and the homes of the villagers had been destroyed. Rishang believed in peaceful progress. Gandhian principle on values attached to ends and means attracted him. Sharengla comparatively found Rishang better than Videsselie: "Peace is better than war" (Bhattacharya 27). War destroyed human dreams and had changed the face of Nagaland. The British transformed this into a military camp with airfields and the people's lives and altered substantially. The people liked to follow Christianity—the way of love and peace. Rishang felt that the Japanese were steeped in Bushido cult, the Nagas in the cult of violence, the white nations had forgotten the message of Jeshu, bringing untold misery and people longed for peace. A tragic victim of war, Sharengla had lost her chastity and her mother died of unrelieved sorrow and her father had died of a peculiar disease that resulted from war.

Phanitphang's mother, Sirala, also had bitter tone regarding war. She told Khating: "What are you fighting for, tell me? To sacrifice the little you have, for others? This killing business is terrible(ibidem 33). Khating viewed that this was not all killing. This was done to drive out the Japanese. Sirala found that the white or the brown human nature shared similar characteristics. When the war was over, Rishang told Sharengla that many worries would be over with peace. All were happy when the war ended. Dr. Brock said that atom bombs were dropped over the Nagasaki and Hiroshima, the Japanese cities. He reported: "Seventy thousand people have died a fiery death in the destruction that followed" (ibidem 52). Rishang concluded that the victor would have to repent for such wanton killing.

Ngazek believed in the traditional Nagaland. The old wit, Thisan, compared Ngazek to the Shiroi Lily. This could be grown only in the topmost soil of the hill and only in the land of the Nagas. Thisan affirmed: "Transplant it to another soil, it will stop to grow"(ibidem 34). He had the idea that Nagas required a different kind of freedom. In line of Videsselie his concept of freedom and progress was different from Rishang's. He thought that the Nagas must strive for an ethnically defined freedom and not just be a part of free India. Christianity and modern education were taking them on the wrong path. They wanted neither the white men, or the black men. They had no love for the Japanese too. Ngazek stated of ethnic autonomy: "The Nagas were happier when they were naked. We had no food problems. Our needs were few and we were able to satisfy them,... We want to live life our way. Not be ruled by foreign ideas. (ibidem 35)

Rishang and Khating believed that modern ideas could make a better Nagaland. Khating viewed that Christianity and education had widened the people's outlook. They made them free from the shackles of superstitions and parochial existence. Pettigrew and Dr. Brock had started schools and churches in the villages that spread new ideas and knowledge of modern medicine and machines. The government established modern education and built roads. These things were necessary for the Nagas.

Ngazek objected to these exposures and substantiated that these developments contributed in making of an unreal Nagaland. Khating admitted that the people of Nagaland would take time to know the meaning of progress of science, writing, communications and good government. He observed: "We can be better Nagas only by giving up our ways." (ibidem 36)

Ngathingkhui had modern ideas and allowed young men and women to select their ways and style of life. His daughter, Khathingla, studied in a missionary school. Marriages between Christians and non-Christians were common. Ngathingkhui asked the consent of Ngazek for getting his daughter married to a Christian youth, Rishang. The latter was opposed to such unions. He believed in tradition. He reminded Ngathingkhui that he was the leader and the awunga. As chieftain, he was the protector of traditional cultural institutions, the head of the village administration and all social and religious activities even though they might be performed by the village priests. The defence of the village was once the duty of the awunga and he had the task of looking after the poor and the needy, the respect of the shang. Ngazek told Ngathingkhui: "Every individual is expected to be conversant with the unwritten bylaws and social mores and, I cannot excuse you if you plead ignorance. You must do nothing that would erode the shang's prestige." (ibidem 62)

Rishang's father, Yangmaso, was also opposed to his son's marriage to Khathingla because the prestige of the shang was involved in it. Ngathingkhui said that times had changed. Sons and daughters felt and acted in different ways and parent's actions must bring benefit to them. So far as the marriage was concerned. Rishang was very saddened to defy his elders. But Jivan asked Rishang to pursue his own decision. He was of the view that every society enforced its irrational customs and ideas on its young and so an individual was left no alternative except to defy them. It was the need of the hour to move out of the narrow walls of the world and to traverse the path towards the new world. Rishang's mother was unhappy because her father was responsible for the mishap of Rishang's father. She felt that the daughter would not be free from father's sin as the effect of misdeed was carried to many generations. Jivan took Rishang's mother as a conservative not wanting any change. He asked her to permit young man to marry according to choice. Rishang married Khathingla against the system. Jivan married a Naga girl out of his caste. But pioneers in every society suffered mentally and physically for fighting old ideas and practices.

Small pox was spreading epidemically. At Phanitphang's courtyard, elders were busy in a heated discussion regarding the ethics of the vaccination campaign. Some Nagas wanted a vaccination campaign but conservative villagers led by Ngazek opposed modern prophylactic immunization. Ngazek considered the spread of the disease as the result of breaking up of the unwritten laws of society. The maiba had divided the cause due to violation by youth. A genna was prescribed for its cure.

Rishang having modern outlook opposed that taboos and genna could cure this disease but Ngazek rejected the proposal as it was against the tradition. Ngazek argued: "You cannot kill a disease by injecting the germs that are causing it. "Moreover tradition forbids it. We should hold the genna." (ibidem 47). Rishang told him that science could not be ignored.

Ngathingkhui argued that vaccination protected him during World War I when he went with the British Indian army to France. The doctor was like maiba. Kamyou might act through a germ for use one to kill another. A doctor was just the instrument of Kamyou. The war had taught many things—flying machines to herbal medicines to surviving death by violating social rules. Ngathingkhui affirmed, "If rules don't change automatically we must force the change. I am all for vaccination." (ibidem). Ngathingkhui's decision was opposed to tradition. Ngazek was totally hurt. He said: "Discipline is above everything, above my son, relatives, friends. Genna cannot cure unless you as the awunga bring the village together to ivoke it power." (ibidem). Ngazek told that taboos and genna had been with them all the time, be it with unclean or suspect food or in emergency. He viewed that the series of rituals must be observed regularly involving whole villages, shangs, households, people of all age groups, men and women, boys and girls. Finally, the assembly welcomed the vaccination campaign.

In the mean time, Videsselie was engaged in seditious activities. A warrant for his arrest was issued by the government. He wanted the Nagas to be independent through Machiavellian principle of ends and means.

During the war, Videsselie joined the INA in Singapore and returned to the Naga hills dreaming of liberation. He was raising a guerilla army to fight the British. Although the movement was called for independence but indeed it was a movement for secession, a separate Nagaland. Videsselie's wild and unrealistic dream caused conflict with the new government. His actions had divided the Nagas. Rishang, who believed in Gandhian principles, felt that India was one and the sufferings of the Nagas could not be solved in isolation. Rishang told: "Most domestic problems are settled through discussion. So there is a tradition of non-violence among the villagers. Many of them are now Christians, they believe in peace." (ibidem 131) He wanted to persuade the Nagas to abstain from violence and strife and follow the path of Jeshu and Gandhi. Revolutions were meant for change of the system. The purposes of revolution could be achieved without weapons. Since Videsselie's men were busy in collecting men, materials and arms, most of the Nagas perceived the risks involved in Videsselie's acts. So they asked Rishang to launch a campaign against Videsselie. The majority of the people disliked violence and the idea of secession.

A conference was organized at Huining by Rishang and his group. But there was stiff opposition from Videsselie's men. Envey and Phanitphang, both extremists, were engaged not to allow the meeting. Videsselie opted terrorist methods to give his men scope to intensify the the underground work and to point out to people the inferiority of Rishang's methods. Rishang was abducted by his men. His kidnapping was taken as an injustice and he became the natural choice of war-torn Nagas. He was kept in a secret rebel camp in the Naga hills. Videsselie met Rishang there. Rishang concluded that the aim of Videsselie's violent movement was to bring people to freedom. He asked Videsselie's definition of this freedom. Videsselie affirmed: "I want an independent Nagaland where a Naga can feel that he is somebody and can be his own master. Life will then be worth living." (ibidem 203)

Rishang did not want Nagas to live and die as Nagas. He wanted them to develop a complete individual transcending their limited tribal personality and inhabit as prestigious member of the great Indian family. Videsselie told Rishang that a Naga could not be made in such a way because like a tree, a humn being required congenial environment and native land for development. Rishang believed that a man's environment was the whole earth and so he should not be restricted to these hills. Videsselie argued: "These hills are the Nagas' abode. I believe that the Nagas are a separate and distinct nation (ibidem). Contrary to this Rishang replied: "You are obsessed with the idea of a separate Naga Nation."... "The Nagas are a district group no doubt, but they belong to a great family, I mean the Indian nation." (ibidem 204). He appealed to Videsselie to give up this campaign but he refused to give up his conviction. The latter fled the country after a police operation.

After the arrival of government troops in the Naga territory, the guerillas returned to the distant jungle near the Burmese border unable to carry on their activities. Peace enveloped most of the villages identified new forces working. Roads, hospitals and schools were needed to be established. War compensation was a topical issue. After the departure of the British, the Nagas were inspired to self-rule. The need of the hour was education. Schools were opened by the foreign missionaries. Their religion provided the convert a new vision of God and a new type of heaven. This was a kind of spiritual democracy in which human affairs were to be managed like the Panchayati rule considered by Gandhi. Internal conflicts would be solved and the fight against poverty and backwardness would benefit the people.

The Nagas wanted Rishang's leaderhip. Rishang discussed with the people to create strong public opinion against bureaucratic delays and administrative negligence. The people felt the need of a democratically elected administration with people's full participation for the removal of conflict. The economic and social grievance was to be solved in a new fashion.

Following a separatist course, Videsselie's men again became active in Nagaland. They came to the village at night to collect tolls, house tax and rations. They were running their own administration. The Nagas complained that the government was not safeguarding the interest of the people. Videsselie's men made efforts to begin no-tax campaign against the government. They were spreading propaganda among the villagers that they were trying to bring freedom to Nagaland in the manner of Gandhi. But Rishang inferred that the Nagas were indeed independent and the rebel's technique was not the method of Gandhi. It was the call of the time to uplift the living standard of the people.

The villagers had no roads and no modern means of communication. No welfare agency came to their help. The police was partially effective in ensuring security and peace to the village. Rishang appealed to people to approach the SDO at Ukhrul for their work in the democratic way. Envey and other rebels warned the elders not to follow Rishang's leadership. Videsselie carried the message of violence to each Naga cottage and Rishang's duty was to spread the message of peace. The peace mission asked the people to represent their grievances peacefully and to reject the violent path shown by Videsselie. The villagers disliked violence and thought of a peaceful solution to problems.

Rishang answered them in the meeting that the Nagas were not a separate nation. He told the villagers that the Nagas were as Indians as Assamese or Manipuris. They all lived in the common territory and were under the same administration. The fate of the Nagas was very much related with the lot of the country. Bhattacharya reported Rishang's ideas: "He said that Indian democracy was evolving gradually and that within a few years, the best elements of Naga democracy could be incorporated in it. He explained the idea of the Gandhian state in which the monorities too would have a legitimate voice. The illiterate, the poor, the tribal and the rural population would benefit. The Nagas too would enjoy considerable freedom, especially in the areas where they had the required expertise. (ibidem 230-231) Following procedures of a democratic polity, the villagers now liked petitioning, holding meeting and talking with the government across the table. The peace campaign assaulted the very demand of the rebels for a sovereign state.

The Nagas were attracted to the glamour of modernization. They were interested in the ideal of independence. But, freedom was not a substitute for a really good life. Love, peace, beauty and brotherhood helped to make a decent life. Violence did not end violence. To eliminate the cause of violence, a spiritual force was needed. For this, a mind was required that was always wedded to the best values of life and always ready to translate them into action.

Bhattacharya's novel creates, as the title suggests a binarism between love and insurgency, one that suggests negotiation and understanding, the other force and violence. Woven into this matrix are the opposing philosophies of Gandhi and strategic materialism, of ahimsa and authoritarianism. This novel of social commitment, of a holistic order is the voice of a civilization that seeks the triumph of values that sustains, nurtures and nourishes life and humanity.

Works Cited

Bhattacharya, Birendra Kumar. *Love in the Time of Insurgency,* New Delhi: Katha, 2005.

Chesterton, G.K. *Bernard Shaw,* Ludhiana: Kalyani Publishers, 1972.

(27)

From Separation to Reunion: A Study of *Gateway of Heaven*

Basavaraj Naikar

Bhaskar Roy Barman is an internationally published poet, short story writer, novelist, translator, critic and book-reviewer. A recipient of many national and international awards, he has enriched the realm of Indian English Literature with his creative and critical writings. *Gateway to Heaven* (2004), happens to be his debut novel dealing with the contemporary Indian life in the northeastern part of the country. The title of the novel is a bit misleading in that it suggests a romantic and ideal world with a religious dimension. But on the contrary, it is a very realistic novel, which depicts the dilemma and predicament of a writer (in this case a novelist), against the background of the contemporary Indian society. The novel assumes the meta-literary quality as it deals with the literary career of a writer and his relationship with the family and society.

The novel is set in Bengal of the transition from twentieth to twenty-first century. The characters are drawn from real life of the Bengali area. Hence the interplay of characters and events takes place against the backdrop of Bengali culture. The novelist presents the Bengali chronotope in which the protagonist is located. Arindam, the protagonist of the novel undergoes a series of very disturbing experiences, which easily hold a mirror to the Indian society in transition from tradition to modernity and from nativity to pseudo-westernization.

Arindam, the protagonist happens to be a Lecturer in Bangla and a novelist, who depends upon the publisher directly for financial support and upon the media of journalism for publicity and the readers for appreciation. Besides being a novelist, he is a sort of journalist also, who contributes articles to the Bangla magazine *Desh* now and then. He has suffered in his life due to the freedom of expression that he has exercised. Ironically the suffering is caused not by others but by his own father-in-law, who happens to be the President of a college establishment. The clash of personalities and ideologies between his wife and father-in-law on the one hand and himself on the other has led him to suffering and insecurity. "He had got sacked from his service as a Professor of a private college. He taught Bangla. His father-in-law happened to be from the Governing Board of the college Arindam had incurred the wrath by divorcing his daughter and he therefore played a major role in getting him sacked. Earlier on, Arindam had published in a leading magazine, *Desh* an article pinpointing the poor quality of teaching in privately run colleges. His father-in-law had capitalized upon this article in getting him sacked" (p.4). Thus the novel problematises the freedom of thought and expression in the Indian society governed by the philosophy of convenience.

The novel begins in *medias res* showing the protagonist Arindam residing in a room in Asit Sen's house in a village. It is only through Arindam's memory that his past trauma is revealed. "His own son, Gautam was sent away to a boarding house to study there. He was sort of snatched off him. His wife, Susmita lived separately. She was... His thoughts stopped short, for the heard a knock on the door" (p.1). As the narrative gathers speed, we learn the details of the cause and the purpose of his coming to the present village. He has come to the village and been staying in a separate room in Asit Sen's house because has divorced his wife, been separated from his son Gautam and terminated from service in a private college. His main purpose to stay in this village, far from the madding crowd of Calcutta is to write a novel about the village life commissioned by his publisher, who has advanced him some royalty for the purpose. Arindam's aim is to have the first hand experience of rural life in order to literaturise it. Though exiled from his family, he wants to convert the exile into an experience of exploring the various aspects of rural life and human nature.

One day Arindam is invited by Arati on behalf of her father Asit Sen for dinner. Initially Arindam is angry at the invitation and declines it, but finally accepts it because of the change of attitude in him brought about by his interaction with Arati. Arindam is pleasantly surprised by the fact that a ninth standard village girl like Arati has read his latest novel. "I happen to have read your latest novel, *A Slice of Life*. It has got an autobiographical flavour" (p.5). Naturally Arindam is pleasantly surprised, proud and elated to learn that his novels are being read even in such remote areas. Perhaps there is no greater reward for a writer than the appreciation by the reader. He thanks Arati for her appreciation of his novel, 'I'm glad and flattered to know you've really delved deep into it. It's true it contains a few autobiographical elements, but it's not an autobiography in the true sense of the term. However any novelist is proud to have a discerning reader like you'" (p.6). But soon Arati punctures the ballon of his ego by telling him that her boyfriend "Abhik dismissed it as rubbish... He didn't relish the novel because of its pungent autobiographical flavour" (p.7). Since Arindam is a well-known man his private life has also become a matter of public interest. Arati and Abhik try to see some connection between Arindam's divorce and the motif of divorce. We've read of a similar divorce and causes in the novel" (p.7). The main character of his novel, Shampa and Prabeer are parallel to Susmita and Arindam to the actual event of divorce in Arindam's life. When Arati and Abhik draw Arindam's attention to the connection between art (novel) and reality (Arindam's life), Arindam remembers the unhappy incidents of his life and broods over them.

The novel problematises the clash of ideologies worsened further by the clash of egos. For example, Arindam is an advocate of Indian brand of feminism and therefore attacks other Bengalis, who talk of Western brand of Women's Lib in a parrot like fashion, without bothering about the degree of its relevance or possibility of its application to the Indian society. There is thus a blatant conflict between nativist thought application to the Indian society. There is thus a blatant conflict between nativist thought and Western, hence borrowed thought. "As a liberal writer Arindam had advocated Women's Lib and had even aligned himself with the cause. He had written an article championing Women's Lib. His article demonstrated independent and different views about Women's Lib, which came into direct conflict with Western concept. His views backfired on him. The views of other members were more or less pragmatic and seasoned by western concepts. They talked parrot fashion, about Women's Lib. Arindam emphasized viewing

Women's Lib from the angle of Indian tradition. He could not..." (p.12). The ideological clash between Arindam and Susmita could have been resolved amicably if Susmita had overcome her egoism. But her egoism is supported by her father's egoism and intoxicated with money, power and influence. Her father happens to be not only an ex-Judge of the High Court of Calcutta, but also the President of the Educational Institute/Society in which Arindam has been working. Further Arindam's wife and father-in-law have instilled the career craze in his son, Gautam, who is consequently alienated from him. "Arindam heaved a deep sigh that emanated from his novel. This craze for career had estranged Gautam from him. Susmita had instilled into him the feeling that her father, his maternal grandfather, an ex-Judge of the High Court would make sure of his career, he had an immense influence with the Chief Minister" (p.20). Gautam, thus, suffers from the virus of career-craze.

Both Susmita and her father were egoistic and their egoism expressed itself in the status-consciousness. Susmita happened to be impulsive both in marrying Arindam and in divorcing him. "Daughter of an ex-Judge of the High Court, Susmita was very conscious of the status of her father's family. She even disdained Arindam's father, who was just a schoolteacher. He had suffered a lot in order to get Arindam properly educated. Arindam was a brilliant student and the father had objected to their marriage. Wallowing in the sunrays of Susmita's love, Arindam had sidetracked his father's objection. Even Susmita's father had not approved of the marriage. But he had to bow to his daughter's wish to avoid a scandal, she had threatened to elope if he did not agree to this marriage. Finally while agreeing to the marriage he had nurtured a desire to have his daughter domineer over him. His desire manifested itself fter they had been married. He had got him a professorshin at a Government sponsored college called City Arts College. Rebati Guha had gradually octopussed him through Susmita and had distanced him from his parents" (pp. 21-22). Thus Arindam has suffered a lot in his life due to the status-consciousness of his wife and father-in-law. He has been forced to be alienated from his own parents.

It is true that Rebati Guha has helped Arindam to get a teaching post in a Government sponsored college with an ulterior motive of keeping his own daughter happy. But when the clash of ideas grows stronger between the two, the enmity becomes greater. First of all

Rebati Guha had initiated the Women's Lib Movement and got Susmita associated with it. But Arindam had written an article in *Desh* against the Western bias of the Women's Lib Movement thereby irritating and insulting his own father-in-law. Again his publication of another article on the poor quality of teaching in his college creates an embarrassing situation for his father-in-law, who was on the Governing Board and whose position was endangered. The father-in-law-son-in-law relationship is overshadowed by the employer—employee relationship. Consequently his colleagues bring pressure upon his father-in-law to ask him to disclaim his two articles dealing with unpleasant truths. But Arindam, who happens to be a man of strong conviction and principles, refuses to yield to their pressure. As a result Rebati Guha expels his own son-in-law from the college by terminating his service and by separating his daughter and grandson from Arindam. Arindam is, obviously, a representative of freedom of thought and expression. He does not mind losing his job for following his own principles.

Arindam's views on Women's Lib are very realistic. Women's Lib Movement in the Indian contest is more fashionable than in the West in that it is political in nature, status oriented and city-centred. The members of the Women's Lib movement are not bothered about the rural women. "Members of the Women's Lib movement did never bother to come down to the village to liberate women from their age-old bondage to the customs of the village. To champion Women's Lib in the villages won't vouch for their political power and social status. The movement had shattered the happiness in many families. The members of the movement were not so keen on liberating women as they were on gaining their political ends" (p.25). Arindam is quite right in thinking that the women in the villages, bondaged to the age-old customs, are quite happy.

The novelist highlights the protagonist's relationship with the reviewers of the commercial literary journals. He shows how professional jealousy plays a prominent part in the Indian world of journalism. A reviewer may boost the career of a writer if he likes the latter or ruins it if he dislikes him. Similarly the editors of magazines also may play a lot of mischief by not publishing positive reviews and by deliberately publishing negative reviews. Thus journalism as one of the media becomes a weapon of helping the friends and harming the enemies, due to personal or communal animosity. This is a harsh reality of the Indian commercial literary journalism.

Arindam has suffered a lot at the hands of this media. Shankar Sur, a friend of Arindam was helped by the latter to become a staff reviewer for *Herald*. Shankar Sur has failed to become a successful novelist. Goaded by the latent frustration in his creative career, Shankar Sur writes a very harsh review of Arindam's latest novel, *A Slice of Life* and gets it published in *Herald*. When Arindam asks Kumud as to why the latter did not prevent the publication of the negative review, Kumud pleads his helplessness and attributes it to the editor's discretion. His remarks about Shankar Sur's review throw light on the psychology of professional jealousy so common in India. "I'm just a journalist. I know when a failed writer turns into a reviewer he becomes ferocious and jealous of other writers. He doles out his disappointment in his reviews and lashes out at new writers on the rise" (p.17). Then Arindam says something about the ethics of reviewing and publishing. "It doesn't behave a reviewer, a good reviewer to stress the bad side of a work. It's his responsibility to bring to light the inherent merit of the work as well. It's certainly incumbent upon a dynamic editor to see to it that impartial reviews by published in his newspaper" (p.17). But contrary to the ethics of publishing, the editor of *Herald* has allowed a negative review of Arindam's novel to be published. Perhaps his intention is to damage the literary career of Arindam. The reviewer had written that "...it was a sort of punching of his previous novels and that the novelist failed to give anything new to the readers in his novel" (p.14). The publisher is also disappointed by the review and fears that it may have adverse effect on the sale of the novel. But the review "to prove false the fear of the publisher, had increased the sale of the novel. The review might have driven book-loving people and his general readers to a curiosity to read it" (p.28). The reviewer and the editor may play mischief with the reputation of a writer, but they can never change his destiny. Far from suffering from low ebb of sale, Arindam's novel enjoys a boost of sale thereby nullifying the evil intentions of the reviewer and the editor. Not only that. The publisher commissions a new novel on rural life and pays some advance on royalty to Arindam.

It is this new assignment that has brought Arindam to the village. So far he has written novels about urban life, but now he has to explore the rural life and write about it in a realistic way. That is the reason why Arindam has come to the village and been participating in the village life, observing a variety of people, making diary-entries and reflecting on his new experiences. His experience of rural life enables him to have a contrastive view of urban life. He realizes the advantages of rural life and the limitations of urban life.

Arindam's stay at the village helps to extend his experience of rural life and knowledge of human nature. Initially he hires a room in Asit Sen's house. The daughter of Asit Sen and her boy friend and other villagers treat him with due respect because he is a famous Bangla novelist. Whenever people meet him they display their knowledge, appreciation or otherwise of his novels. Arindam feels satisfied and even elated when people appreciate his writings and disconcerted when they find fault with them. But yet he wants to maintain the balance of his mind. When Arati, daughter of Asit Sen, meets Arindam and conveys her father's invitation for dinner, Arindam refuses to accept it. But as Arati reveals her literary taste and awareness about his novels, he begins to like her and consequently accepts her father's invitation for dinner.

At the dinner party Arindam happens to meet a few guests of Asit Sen, who casualy discuss Bangla writer like Manik Bandopadhyaya and Tarashankar Bandopadhyaya and issues like interdependence of writers etc. A guest namely Amulya Datta introduces himself to Arindam and refers to the latter's ghost story and innocently wants to know if Arindam has imitated it from an English ghost story. Arindam clarifies his doubt by stating that he has not imitated an English ghost story, but drawn on two English ghost stories in writing his. Then Amulya Datta asks Arindam if the latter believes in ghosts. But Arindam confesses honestly that it is difficult to answer. He also explains that for most of the Western writers ghost story writing is a part time exercise, although they may not believe in ghosts. For many writers writing ghost stories may be an academic exercise backed up more by imagination than by real or firsthand experience. But Amulya Datta confesses that he has had the firsthand experience of possession by a ghost. Arindam learns a few more details about Amulya Datta from Arati that her father does not like him, as he is a charlatan, but yet he has appointed him to give private tuition to her Dada, who is weak in Maths. Arindam is surprised to know that a Maths techer like Amulya Datta is interested in the supernatural beings like ghosts. "Experience tells me Maths teachers are generally practical-minded. They, I know, dismiss the supernatural as rubbish" (p.52). Arindam learns another piece of information from Arati that her uncle Subal, who is unmarried, lives in the farmhouse, which is surrounded by evil spirits; and encounters them with his incantations. Arindam is rather puzzled by the news and his curiosity is aroused further. That is the reason why he enquires Asit Sen about Amulya Datta's interest in the supernatural. But Asit Sen describes Amulya Datta as a charlatan, who once witnessed a ghostly possession of a son by his own father. Asit Sen's disapproval of Amulya Datta is expressed in is words, "What has surprised me about Amulya Datta is that he has interested himself in the supernatural and is advocating the doctrine that there exist ghosts, that is, souls. It always sounds strange of a Maths teacher to talk about ghostly possession. Then Asit Sen tells him rather unwillingly that the ghost of Kalyan Ghosh possessed his son, Subir, that Kalyan Ghosh died more than a year ago. "It's strange, because it's unbelievable. It fits in well with Amulya Datta's theory. On possessing his own son the ghost of Kalyan Ghosh sent for Amulya Datta—no one else!" (p.58). In spite of Asit Sen's dislike for Amulya Datta's so called charlatanism, Arindam wants to know more about the mystery of ghosts and spirits from Amulya Datta.

Later when Arindam meets Amulya Datta in a teashop, he draws him into conversation and wants to elicit more information about the supernatural phenomenon. Amulya Datta knows that Arindam being a city-bred man does not believe in the supernatural. But Arindam wants to know more about it, although he may not believe in it. Therefore Amulya Datta tells him about a farmhouse which is haunted and which is inhabited by Subal Kundu, the elder brother of Asit Sen. He tells him further that there lives a vampire near the farmhouse, which talks to Subal Kundu in the semi-darkness of evening.

When Amulya Datta goes to Arindam's room, he is requested by Arindam to tell the story of a ghostly phenomenon that the former had read somewhere. Amulya Datta, therefore, narrates the story with great relish. According to the story a novelist from Kolkata is invited by a *zemindar* of a village to stay in his house. When the novelist comes to the village, he takes a fancy to the garden-house and insists on staying in a room of the garden-house not knowing that it is haunted by a ghost. The *zemindar* allows the novelist to stay in the haunted room. As night advances, the novelist experiences the presence of a female ghost in the room. The ghost talks with him and disappears through the wall into the sky. Next day, the *zemindar* hears from the novelist the details of his nocturnal experience and tells him that his brother's wife had drowned himself in the same pond; and that the female ghost, which talked to the novelist and disappeared in the sky was none other than his brother's wife. The ghost story narrated by Amulya Datta, obviously, arouses Arindam's curiosity.

Later when Arindam refers to Kalyan Ghosh's house in the presence of Samir, the boy friend of Arati, the latter says frankly, "It will be, I think, beneath your dignity to go to Kalyan Ghosh's house at the persuasion of Amulya sir. He is a charlatan" (p.102). Samir, who has inherited the pride of his father and is a believer in science, does not believe in the supernatural. But Arindam snubs him by defending Amulya Datta's belief, "He is not to blame for believing in the existence of the soul. He is conducting a para-psychological research. May be you do not believe in existence of the soul, but you should not deride others for their belief" (p.103).

Next time when Arindam meets Amulya Datta, he asks the latter to investigate the mystery of Asit Sen's haunted house and even encourages him to edit a journal dealing with the supernatural. Insisted by Arindam, Amulya Datta takes him to Kalyan Ghosh's house. Arindam wants to know the details of the ghostly possession experienced by Subir. Requested by Arindam, Subir confesses, "Yes, a ghost, I mean, the ghost of my father possessed me. But I did not feel the effect of the possession, though I lost control on myself. The ghost of my father masterminded me. On possessing me, the ghost of my father, so I was told, ordered Kamalbabu to send for Amulya Datta" (p.120). Arindam's curiosity being aroused, he asks Amulya Datta as to why the ghost should send for him especially. Amulya Datta replies, "The ghost of Subirbabu's father knew I believe in ghosts and he needed my help" (p.120)

To offer more evidential weightage to his words, Amulya Datta takes Arindam to Kamalbabu's house. One day Kamalbabu went to Amulya Datta's house and knocked on his door. When Amulya Datta opened the door and saw Kamalbabu panting and frightened. Kamalbabu babbled out the details of the supernatural event that he saw, "Last midnight when Subirbabu got out to urinate beneath a mango tree he shrieked and swooned. Attracted by his shriek, his wife got startled out of sleep and came out to see what had happened. Seeing Subirbabu lying unconscious beneath the mango tree she got frightened out of her wits and cried her heart out" (p.128). When Subirbabu recovered from unconsciousness, he started talking incoherently. People who had gathered there understood that Subirbabu was possessed by a spirit ghost. When somebody suggested sending for an exorcist, to their surprise the ghost in Subirbabu said, "You needn't send for an exorcist. I won't do any harm to Subir. I am the ghost of his father, Kalyan" (p.123). When people ask the ghost about what wrong his son had done to him, the ghost replied, "It will be difficult for you to understand why I have possessed him. Send for Amulya Datta. Only he can understand my problem. He is researching into the supernatural" (p.124). When Amulya Datta was called in, the ghost explained the details of its dissatisfaction further,

His voice struck me with extreme wonder. It was not the voice of Subirbabu, it was distinctly his father's.

"Do please, tell me what I'm required to do", I mumbled.

The ghost didn't reply forthwith and let a few minutes pass by silently.

The room was hushed up in an eerie silence.

After a while the ghost said, "In the funeral rites no fare was given to the ferryman to carry me across the Baitarani so the ferryman didn't ferry me across to the abode of death. I got stuck in the world of the living. I am roaming this area restlessly. I ought to have told Subir before I died that he should give the fare in my funeral rites."

But the priest ought to have told Subirbabu to give fare in the funeral rites," I said.

The ghost giggled. "He was a charlatan," he said. "Even he was not conversant with the scriptures. He didn't know one had to give fare to the ferryman during funeral rites."

"Do please, tell me, what I should do," I said humbly.

"I shall be grateful if you will make Subir go over to Kashi to give the fare to the ferryman and accompany him yourself. Then I will be released from the imprisonment in the world of the living" (p.125).

Consequently Amulya Datta obliged the ghost of Subirbabu's father by accompanying Subir to Kashi and giving the fare to the ferryman.

The news of the haunted farmhouse belonging to Asit Sen has been published in *Ananda Bazar Patrika*. This is brought to the notice of Asit Sen, but he shows no special interest in it. Amulya Datta suggests to Asit Sen to get the superstition investigated. Arindam shows greater curiosity in unraveling the mystery and makes it a part of the novel that he has been writing. He tells Asit Sen, "You know I've come down here to write a novel. I've heard of the superstition and discussed it with Amulyababu in a tea-stall. I think I should devote one or two chapters to discussing and unveiling the mystery. I hope you would have no objection whatsoever to unveiling the mystery" (p.143). Asit Sen says that he has no objection, "But I won't permit you to investigate the mystery just to expose you to blood-sucking by the vampire" (p.143). Arindam does not believe in the existence of vampires because campirism is a foreign concept and not suited to Indian culture. Asit Sen grows angry at Arindam's disbelief in his words. Finally Amulya Datta tries to pacify Asit Sen by saying, "You know we have formed an association to research into the supernatural and preternatural. The Guild, I mean, the association may be entrusted with the task of investigating the mystery. Arindambabu will help us" (p.144).

But Arindam's desire to investigate the supernatural mystery does not continue because of some unexpected event. Asit Sen, who is a politician keenly interested in the coming election, wants to start his college in the village immediately and even appoints Arindam and Amulya Datta as part time teachers in it. This temporary appointment of Arindam as a Professor in the local college gives him a bit of financial relief and saves him from the need to depend upon his publisher's royalty. As he has been making regular entries in his diary about is experiences in the village, he hopes to use the material and convert it into a novel. It is precisely at this time that he gets a letter from his publisher in Kolkata reminding him to complete his novel about the village life:

> Dear Mr. Basu,
> We have not heard from you for a long time. We have commissioned you to write a novel around the village life and given you an advance. You have not written till now to tell us how far you have progressed in writing the proposed novel.
> Your friend Mr. Kumud Kar, told me you intended to investigate a mystery that centres on a vampire, which is living somewhere in the village. He also told me that you would devote one or two chapters to treating the mystery. We appreciate your decision to incorporate two or three chapters on the mystery into your novel. We ourselves

> did read the news about the vampire. We should be grateful and obliged if you would let us know how far you have progressed in writing the novel.
> We look forward to hearing from you soon. With kind regards and best wishes.
>
> Sincerely yours
> Shyamal Baral

Arindam has not even started the novel, but the publishers reminder impels him to expedite the process of writing.

Arindam's stay in the village helps him understand the contrast between the city life and the village life. He realizes that the city people are obsessed with career, status, money, fame and social status, whereas the village people are contented with whatever they have, live in close connection with Nature and believe in supernatural things and events.

Arindam has fought for certain principles in life and consequently antagonized his wife and father-in-law. He is forced by the circumstances to be divorced from his wife, separated from his son, Gautam and terminated from his job as a lecturer in the local college at Kolkata. But, in spite of all this emotional and professional and financial suffering he does not wish to compromise with his principles. He has the courage of conviction. All these personal problems compel him to leave the city and go to a village to write a novel about the village life. He is sustained by the advance royalty given by his publisher in Kolkata. He did not yield to his father-in-law's pressure to change his views about Women's Lib Movement and the drawbacks of the College Management and teaching there. Arindam may be described as a Cordelia-figure, who speaks the bitter truth without sugarcoating it to please somebody. He has the courage to face the music of his deeds. That is why he goes to the village and lives there like a forced bachelor, being denied of the comforts of domestic life. His stay in the village is partially exilic and partially experimental and explorative.

While he has been experiencing and observing the village life, certain changes have taken place in the city, especially in the lives of his wife and father-in-law. Arindam learns about these changes from Kumud. When Kumud meets him and tells him about the declaration of the date of State elections, Arindam shows his usual indifference to political matters. But Kumud reveals some very important information about Arindam's family. "Another aspect of the development concerns your father-in-law, I mean your ex-father-in-law. It might interest you. The CM lately learnt that your ex-father-in-law had misused his power and many people complained about him. He also got to know how his craving for power had brought about your separation from his daughter. He has curtailed much of his power" (p.129). Kumud tells him further that Rebati Guha held his daughter responsible for his having been shorn of power. Arindam's past bitterness makes him say, "I don't bother about what has happened to Susmita and her father. They must expiate their wrongs. They had taken Gautam away from me. Just tell me the news about him" (p.129). Then Kumud narrates the change in the life, attitude and behaviour of Susmita, "I've not yet finished my story. As you yourself know, Susmita has inherited her father's hauteur and developed a sense of self-prestige as well. She left her father's house and put up at the house of a friend of hers. She brought Gautam from the hotel. She telephoned me to go over to her friend's house, giving her address. When I went over there she requested me to get her a job. When I asked her to request her father to get her a job, for he had still some influence left, she disdained his 'help'" (p.129-130). Kumud continues to say that Susmita has fallen a victim to such political upheaval and that he has been trying his best to help her get a job in a Government-aided college. Kumud is very keen on bringing about a reconciliation and reunion between the husband to solve. Just reconcile yourself to the changed situation and forget the past" (p.135). Arindam does not show any eagerness to do so. But Kumud wants to show him the letter that Susmita has written to Kumud and indicates the change that has happened in Susmita's attitude. "What was done could not be undone. Susmita has now understood her mistake. She has hinted in this letter at her desire to get reunited with you" (p.135). Arindam is so angry at his wife's status-consciousness that he suggests, "She had better marry another person, who enjoys her status" (p.135). Then Kumud convinces him about the need for taking care of his son, Gautam by reconciling with his wife, "Gautam is bearing the brunt of what she has done. Susmita has slid out of the slough of hauteur and unshackled herself from her father's influence. An opportunity presents itself to you to retrieve Gautam. Please don't let go of this opportunity presents itself to you to retrieve Gautam. Please don't let go of this opportunity" (p.135). Kumud tells him further that Susmita has dissociated herself from the Women's Lib Movement. "No one associated with it is serious about it. They are irrespective of men and women, criticizing the role of husbands and never delve deep into what contributes to conjugal happiness or conjugal rift" (p.136). Kumud leaves the letter on Arindam's table for him to read it later. Arindam reads the letter, notes Susmita's hint at her repentance and her concern about Gautam's future. Obviously he begins to think seriously about his wife and son and look at the domestic problem in a new light. He learns that his wife has realized the importance of her husband and family and overcome her egotism and status-consciousness. The slow changes that have been brought about in Susmita's life testify to her ripening and to her better understanding of life. The fashionable Women's Lib Movement has not been able to give the happiness that she dreamt about.

After a few days Arindam receives another letter. This time it is from Kumud, who has written about the further developments in the domestic life of Arindam at Kolkata. Arindam reads the letter with some interest,

"As I told you earlier on, I used my good offices to have Susmita get an appointment at that Government-aided College. Gautam was admitted to class IX in the High School wing of the college. At first complications had arisen over the title and guardianship of Gautam. I was present at that time. Susmita herself solved the problems. She said that Gautam's title was "Basu" and that his guardian was 'Arindam Basu'. These easy solutions surprised me and the Principal, for he knew you and Susmita were separated. But the Principal could not accept these solutions, because it was against the rule, Gautam was living with his mother at the decree of the court. I promised the Principal, I would see to it that you and Susmita are reconciled. I don't know how you will take my promise. I promised reunion for the sake of Gautam and particularly because the solutions Susmita had suggested testified to her earnest desire to get re-united with you and to how much she loves you.

Even after that the thing has come to such a pass that we can't afford to remain silent over it. Something must be done about it. Gautam has stopped going to school, because his classmates are teasing him by asking him why his parents have got divorced. He looks frustrated and is gradually getting introverted.

Think it over as a father. If something should happen to Gautam, you would yourself carry the blame and it would also affect your readers.

It is absolutely for you to decide what you will do.

Before I conclude this letter I should like to inform you of an interesting thing, which might interest you. The Women's Lib Movement has got dismantled. The Principal of your former college, Sekhar Bhowmick, who was the Secretary of the College, was charged with misappropriating the money allotted to it. Rumour has it that Sumit Mukhopadhyaya, Janardhan Kar and Arati Dastidar shared the money. Sumit Mukhopadhyaya had handled the fund.

Another interesting thing is that the students of your former college wanted you reinstated. It is quite likely that you'll get your post if you came back to Kolkata.

Arindam, think over the possibility of your being reunited with Susmita and Gautam. There are many gateways to heaven, as our scriptures say. You know heaven means happiness. Why not open one of Gautam at least?

Love and regards

Kumud

Kumud's letter and his good wishes for Arindam and his family show that he is a catalytic agent for the coming together of the separated couple. His letter testifies to Susmita's realization of the irrelevance of Women's Lib Movement to the Indian patriarchal society and of the importance of the institution of marriage involving the harmonious relationship among the members of the family. The slow realization has helped her to overcome her status-consciousness, hauteur and egotism. Kumud's letter shows further how Rebati Guha has lost his position as the President of the College Management due to his corrupt practices. Susmita seems to have realized belatedly that her loyalty is due to her husband and no longer to her status-conscious and high-handed father. Susmita's mental transformation is in conformity with Arindam Basu's attitude to life. Now that she has repented and shown the inclination to be reunited with her husband, Arindam Basu thinks seriously and positively about it. He feels that it is his duty to give a meaningful life to his son, Gautam and open the gateway to the heaven of happiness. He, therefore, decides to go back to Kolkata and rejoin his original post as a Professor of Bangla. His departure from the village would create a vacancy in the local college for Subrata Roy, who hated him for depriving him of the privilege. Similarly Arindam's reunion with his wife and son would satisfy and lend moral support for the young lovers like Arati and Abhik to get married. By opening the gateway to heaven Arindam Basu is able to solve many problems for himself as well as for others simultaneously. He has not started writing his novel about eh village life. People like Amulya Datta have discontinued their research into the supernatural mystery. Yet Arindam's separation from wife and child and his stay in the village away from Kolkata have given him wider knowledge of human life. That is the reason why he has acquired the ability to forgive the wife and forget the past and open the gateway to the heaven of domestic happiness. His reunion with his wife and son gives a sense of satisfaction to his readers like Arati and Abhik thereby hastening their marriage. Like in Kalidasa's *Sakuntala* and Shakespeare's Last Plays, exile and separation in this novel have a curative and ripening effect upon the protagonist and his wife and finally preparing them for the happy reunion. The hell of misunderstanding is followed by the heaven of happiness. The credit of bringing the separated couple together must go to Kumud who tries to his best to see them reunited and that without any axe to grind.

The novelist employs the third person narration to depict the experiences of the writer-protagonist. The style is terse and realistic although the title sounds quite romantic. Since memory plays a dominant role in the novel, it has a recapitulatory element in it. The past lurks again and again in the present through the protagonist's memories thereby giving a psychological dimension to the novel. *Gateway to Heaven* happens to be one of the very few meta-literary novels in the realm of Indian English fiction. The supernatural event in the novel easily brings Saratchandra's *Srikanta* to our mind. On the whole the novel testifies to the triumph of patriarchy over feminism and of Indian culture over the so-called westernization and modernization. It reinforces our faith in the time-tested Indian values of life and acts as an antidote to the modern abnormal and radical feminist, lesbian and gay literature foolishly imported from the West.

Works Cited

Barman, Bhaskar Roy. *Gateway to Heaven*, Guwahati: Spectrum Publications, 2004.

(28)

Trauma of Insurgency in Indira Goswami's *Pages Stained With Blood*

Ankush Chutia

Indira Goswami, (Mamoni Raisom Goswami and popularly Mamoni Baideo) has exhibited an inclination towards blending scholarliness with creativity. She prefers to absorb the environment of the topic she is writing on; and in order to achieve that end, she would travel extensively both within India and abroad to amass first-hand experience for her novel. Hiren Gohain, an eminent litterateur from Assam, writes the following words in his essay "Ineffable Mystery" applauding the creative flair of Goswami,

> It is the lack of love in the people and the world as she has known them, shocking the reader into an awareness of the horror and pity of it. Her writing is like a stifled cry of pain at man's inhumanity to man, which modulates sometimes in quiet bitterness and at times into poignant pathos. An obstinate feudal way of life has survived into our times, which crushes the soul with rigid dogma and inhuman ritual and squeezes into a husk the life-blood of healthy emotion. The results are a staggering inferno of broken lives, frustrated dreams, wasted promises and monstrous distortions of humanity. (Gohain 26).

Her novel *Tej Aru Dhulire Dhukhorito Pristha*, later translated into English as *Pages Stained With Blood* by Pradip Acharya, a lecturer in the Department of English at Cotton College, Guwahati, had initially appeared an innocent portrayal of the city of Delhi, where she appeared intending to paint Delhi "in broad swathes of color the days and lives of the Mughals and the British Raj" (Goswami 8). Soon this description of the city turns into pages stained with blood. Presented in the form of a diary, it is a depiction of the helpless and wretched conditions of the innocent victims of the riot that had engulfed Delhi, the capital city of India, during the later half of 1984 following the various acts of violence spread by the Punjab extremists, particularly in East Punjab and generally in the whole of Northern India, culminating in the assassination of Indira Gandhi, the then Prime Minister of India. It leads to the carnage of Sikhs and the writer is a witness to terrible scenes. Around that time the author was working in Delhi University as a lecturer in the Department of Modern Indian Languages and Literary Studies. The writer is seen roaming the city and recording in her diary what she witnessed and what she heard from the people she met during her wanderings. But slowly, she feels drawn to some queer character who are Sikhs living in slums and leading a wretched life. Her concern for them makes her actually aware of the unhappy situation. Sikhs in the city find themselves in because of the events in East Punjab. The Golden Temple had been ransacked and the Sikhs were in trouble. And in this novel, she has depicted the events that passed across her seeking eyes in a candid manner and has presented to the reader a brutal reality that had trampled on the very foundation upon which humanity and its values lie.

During the early eighties, the northern India saw the spurt of terrorism in the state of Punjab. Simultaneously, various acts of terrorism like bombings, hijacking, looting, killing, kidnapping,, intimidation, and similar activities began to show their ugly faces. The heat of such activities also reached the neighbouring states like Delhi, Haryana and even Jammu and Kashmir. Around the period, various acts of looting were also reported from the state of Punjab as well as the neighbouring places. The terrorists targeted the inadequately protected banks for such looting. The instances of bank robberies "which stood at 24 in 1980 and 40 in 1981" shot up to 70 in 1982. While in Delhi alone, many banks and jewellery shops were raided in 1983 and the total amount was recorded to be above 25 lakhs of rupees (Anand 134). Many businessmen and some well-to-do houses were also robbed during the same period.

They also targeted a few of the police personnel and many were killed. On April 23, 1983, the Director General of Police in Punjab, Attwal

> ...was shot dead by terrorists...on the steps of the Golden Temple. The body lay riddled with bullets, the Prasad halwa scattered. Blood spurted from his head and chest and flowed down the steps. The personal security guards...fled to safety. (Goswami 65).

When the lives of the chief of the security providers are insecure, what might happen to the common people? Bombs were placed in public places and even the places of worship were also used for such hideous activities. On March 1, 1984 a bomb was exploded "at a place of worship in Amritsar which resulted in the death of three persons and injuries to scores of others". (Anand 19)

Indeed, killing, exploding bombs, looting and hijacking became the order of the day. Such acts of violence—either demonstrated, threatened or implied, appeared to have achieved the desired objectives of the terrorists. After the killings, most of the family members of the police personnel became so fear-struck that they were believed to have "begged the militant leader Jarnail Singh Bhindranwale...to spare their lives." (ibidem).

In an effort to intimidate Jammu's senior political leader Tarlochan Dutt, some Punjab terrorists placed "a bottle on his lawn containing a live snake wrapped in a paper with the slogan 'Khalistan Zindabad' written on it." (ibidem 18). The Khalistani movement was not only restricted to the state of Punjab. The situation in the neighbouring states was also worsening as a result of the same. Satnam Singh alias Chinni, one of the chiefs of the Bhindranwale Tiger Force, had

> ...twenty nine people hung in the Terai region of Uttar Pradesh and had shot dead fifteen farmers at Ropar. He demolished the Special Police outpost at Athiyaan. Killing people was a sort of addiction for him—he's supposed to have killed five-hundred people. (Goswami 51).

It was amidst such tense situation that the author found some time to record the ups and downs, the joys and sorrows, the feelings and sentiments of a few common hard-working Sikhs, who had become a part of her life in Delhi. Her work is not directly concerned with the Sikh extremists; but it is, no doubt, a projection of real-life experiences and a depiction of the contemporary events and the miseries and sufferings that the people had to undergo as a result of the radical movements and activities. The imbroglio is presented, in the very beginning, by the image of the "half-clad or completely naked children" who look like "dead soldiers on a battlefield" (ibidem 7). The imagery of the bodies of the children being cut into "bits and pieces with a sword" foreshadows the sufferings of the innocent people accruing from the Sikh terrorism.

The Sikhs are the very sons and daughters of the conglomeration of the Indian society and they too had celebrated and suffered along with the others in their time of weal and woe respectively. The Partition of India in 1947 had also inflicted upon the people a lot of bitter suffering as well as unforgettable memories. The Sikhs, too, had to bear the brunt of the onslaught. In the book, one character, an old Sikh, found special mention. The author had noticed the old Sikh with his snowy hair and bear closely but she hardly ever saw him moving his lips at all. The old six-foot-three-inch tall Sikh baba with "a look of great sadness on his face" (ibidem) does not talk to anyone. As revealed later by Balbir, during the Partition when the old man, named Nanak Singh Bhalla, had left Pakistan for Delhi, his daughter Kuldip Kaur along with two other girls "vanished" at the Khankhana check post and her "dead body was found a week later in a wheat field", She had no clothes on. Her breasts had been cut off and hung on a peepal tree...Baba has not spoken since that day. (ibidem 25).

The writer knew a number of Sikhs varied in their professions and they, like other people too, share the peculiar common human feelings. They are "large-hearted and willing to give their lives for friendship." (ibidem 10-11). Santokh Singh was one such handsome enthusiastic Sikh youth, who took it upon himself to drive her to the university by his three-wheeler. He "wouldn't let others get into his vehicle" and would eagerly wait for her all day long at the main entrance of the campus like any lovelorn youth. He is also anxious to take her around Delhi as he would say to her, "You don't have to spend a paisa. I'll take you around delhi. Believe me, you don't have to spend anything." (ibidem 11)

Another common Sikh whom she was attached to is the "Kabadiwala". (ibidem 13). Balbir Singh who "pulls his old cycle up and down" (ibidem) the roads, lanes and bylanes of Delhi in search of kabadi. Almost everything about Balbir emphasizes the stamp of poverty and the daily struggle that he has to go through to make a living. The pair of chappals, which he put on, have worn off and a part of his heels scrape the road as he drags them along the road (ibidem). He has a son Gurdeep alias Sonnu, who, instead of attending the school, often wanders around with his father in order to help him. They form a part of the poverty-ridden people of Delhi who "...have to first feed the raging fire in the pit of your stomach and then worry about other things." (ibidem 14).

The lives of the people moved along through the mundane day-today activities with Balbir often stealing some of his precious time out of his routine job to have a cup of tea at the author's "cramped, claustrophobic flat" (ibidem 12) in Shakti Nagar and narrate some of the stories which the writer was eager to write down in her note book.

Although the writer and her acquaintances seemed to live a quiet and peaceful life, it was, in fact, the period when the terrorist activities in Punjab shot up to immeasurable heights. The country seemed to be in a state of turmoil. In Delhi itself it was not safe in those days to spend much time in the balcony. Therefore, Balbir warns the author,

> Bibiji, don't spend too much time in the balcony. Times are bad. At Tel Mandi and Kucha Ghasiram, many balconies that stood out like beehives have been blown up by bombs. (ibidem 50).

There was always a kind of "suppressed excitement in the air" (ibidem 124) and on the eve of such deteriorating situation and regular shoot outs, curfew was imposed in Punjab and the police checks were "becoming more intensive" in the neighbouring places with every passing day. In Delhi too, the vigil and the patrolling of the police has been intensified on its streets and lanes. All the Sikhs were suspected to be involved with the extremists and the Delhi Police since 1982 had spent "a great deal of time keeping the Sikhs under close surveillance and studying their behaviour" (ibidem 37). The Sikh had to live under a constrained state of mind. The excesses and harassment on the Sikh people were frequently reported. Sikhs were being pulled out from buses at Sarai Rohilla, Rani Jhansi Marg, Kingsway Camp and at many other places by the police and searched thoroughly. On the way to Fardkot, Balbir himself had to...get down from the bus three times and open his tin suitcase to be searched. (ibidem 36)

Once when he went forward to defend some Sikhs, being tortured and humiliated by the police, Balbir had to "take a beating" and got one of the glasses of his spectacles cracked.

With the government agencies turning against the whole race of Sikhs, the social security of the ordinary Sikh people gradually appeared to be slacking. It became very hard for the innocent ones to lead an unaffected life. The stance adopted by a few extremists had begun to take its toll on the Sikhs in general. They had to adjust themselves to a life where harassments and humiliations became a sort of day-to-day common affair for them. As a result, the dignity and status of the people on the social front had shown a slump.

Delhi has always been like a crossroad, bearing the marks of being a meeting place of many cultures. It has a long political history since the times old and under the constant mingling of different races and their respective cultures, it has achieved a renewed look with each and every part reverberating its past. The alluring and fascinating sights of Delhi have beckoned many artists and 'shaiirs' all the same. Khusro, Ghalib and others were enticed by the mysterious beauty of Delhi. It was in Majnu ka Tila that Guru Nanak spread his message of love and humanity (ibidem 68-69) Chandni Chowk, one such place within Delhi, bears the mark of the torture meted out to the Sikh religious leader Guru Tegh Bahadur and his followers. The Seeshganj Gurudwara stands there echoing the suffering of the leader. It also accounts for the blood of the people killed by ancient marauding invaders. It is also a testimony to the blood splattered from the wounds of the dying soldiers during the Sepoy Mutiny. Blood and dust has always been associated with the history of Chandni Chowk. (ibidem 93).

The capital city of Delhi has been from ages past a place where the people, despite their religious differences, could live peacefully. It is obvious in the following lines written by Mirza Abdul Rahim Khankhana,

> I am Rahim.
> This heart of mine is restless.
> All through the night it yearns
> For a glimpse of Lord Krishna. (ibidem 95).

But the times have changed for the worse and the differences have widened among he public. Almost anything pertaining to the Sikhs were looked at with a suspicious attitude. Even the Gurudwaras, the places of worship of the Sikhs, were suspected to be the hide-outs of the terrorists. The suspicion was firmly rooted in no time when in January 1984, in a daylight bid to rob a bank in New Delhi, one terrorist was apprehended by the police; and later he confessed of having been "trained in the use of arms and commando tactics within the premises of the Golden Temple complex at Amritsar." (Anand 135).

The search parties of the police kept strict vigil near the Sikh temples. While going to the gurudwara at Majnu ka Tila by the National Highway Number One, the author herself saw the police stopping the buses and searching for suspicious objects and people. Amidst such vulnerable conditions, it was not easy for the Sikhs living in Delhi to lead a secure life. Therefore, Balbir wanted to keep his earnings with the author. He felt that he could not safeguard his money at home since

> ...the police are on the prowl in Kabadi Bazaar...Their roving eyes seem to centre around the belongings of the Sikhs. (Goswami 36-37)
>
> The situation had deteriorated and the Sikhs looked concerned, The Sikh drivers at Najia Park look drawn and nervous. (ibidem 81)

The author too was concerned about the whereabouts of Santokh Singh and Balbir Raddiwala—two of the three Sikhs who have "somehow become a part of my family" (ibidem 113). Therefore, she felt distressed for showing her unwillingness to keep Balbir's money with her as "the police must be after them, like a pack of wild dogs (ibidem 86). Moreover, her hesitation to keep his money might be due to the reason that she suspected Balbir could not probably amass "so much money in such a short time" (ibidem) by the sweat of his brow. Balbir was deeply hurt by he could hardly blame her as the time itself was running through a bad phase. He rushed downstairs and there was no trace of him. It was really hard to trust another and it was already too late when the writer realized that

> In this atmosphere of fear and uncertainty, running from the police and from other men, he will be blundering about like one who has lost his way. (ibidem)

The chronicler of the events seemed to be full of anxiety regarding the well-being of the absconding Balbir and Santokh Singh. With an unknown desire to know the conditions of the latter, she even went down "the muddy path" (ibidem 77) across the extensive wasteland near the Majnu ka Tila Gurudwara and gulped down a few glasses of courtry-made liquor "in such a dirty place and among such dirty people" (ibidem 79) in the hope that "Santokh Singh will pass by" (ibidem). She also found out some time to 'have a look around' Kabadi Bazaar in search of Balbir, but her "hopes of meeting Balbir and Santokh Singh steadily wanted" (ibidem 96).

In Pubjab, the situation had worsened with 'loot, arson, rape and murder' becoming the order of the day and adversely affecting the lives of the common people. The anti-terrorism measures were intensified and the army had closed in on the Golden Temple. The huge buildings around the temple were evacuated and 'converted into fortresses'. There seemed to be hardly any doubt that the holy place of worship would be 'bombarded with bullets' in order to wipe out the Bhindranwale forces. Newspaper reports and radio news bulletins were crowded with information regarding the aggravating situation in Punjab. The author too could feel the intensity of the developments and express her concern at the thought that "every bullet fired at the temple will wound the Sikh heart" (ibidem 88-89). Murder and destruction ruled the day in Punjab and the ominous shadow of such activities "spreads over Delhi like the shadow cast by vultures on a corpse" (ibidem 89). Many Hindus and Nirankaris were either killed or injured; and

> Hindu refugees from Punjab have come and started living in certain areas. Similarly, many innocent Sikhs have left Delhi out of fear of the police." (ibidem 89-90)

The shadows of insecurity and terror still loomed large; and be it Punjab or Delhi, the common mass could no longer keep themselves aloof from the undesired swings of events, threatening to engulf and destroy the very existence of humanity. There was "anxiety on the faces of the Sikhs" (ibidem 93) on the verge of the impending attack on the Golden Temple. The Sikhs were "dissatisfied" (ibidem 101) and many students displayed their unhappiness by some bizarre writings on the walls which "draw a clear picture of these times". (ibidem).

Finally, the sanctity of the Golden Temple had been ravished by the Indian Army on 4 June, 1984, albeit "punctuated by the reiterated assurance of the commanding officer that the army would succeed in flushing out the extremists without causing any damage to the Harmandir Sahib" (ibidem 107). The attack had pierced through the heart of every Sikh. Some soldiers belonging to the Sikh Regiment "had rebelled and Brigadier Puri had been assassinated" (ibidem 108). There were heavy losses, of both man and material. The devastating and horrific scenario on the battle-front could be grasped when the author says,

> ...Killings and more killings!...heaps of used cartridges. Some images are etched in my mind, too deep to be wiped away. The bodies of a woman, her child and an old man, caught in the crossfire...riddled with bullets...a soldier... blown apart by the explosion, pieces of his flesh flying up could be seen from a distance. I could not help imagining the contorted look on the face of the soldier, the hazy image haunting me for a long time. (ibidem 109)

The attack continued for three consecutive days; and at last, it resulted in the death of Bhindranwale and the surrender of Sant Longowal and G.S. Tohra follwed by the arrest of hundreds of the extremists. The reports carried by the Newspapers

...reek of blood and gunfire. They are filled with snapshots of people killed by bullets and explosions, dismembered limbs, ugly pictures. The genteel ambience of Delhi seems to be disappearing into some dark cavern. (ibidem 47)

But the unrest continued with freshly brewed protests and incidents of mobbing in various parts of Delhi. Most Sikhs had closed their shops in Delhi and the neighbouring areas in protests. All throughout the Shakti Nagar area, the numerous Sikh traders "have downed their shutters". In anticipation of the growth of any hideous activity, Section 144 "had already been clamped" around many places in Delhi and in Punjab, too. (ibidem 110-112).

The Akal Takht had been "destroyed" (ibidem 112) during the exchange of bullets and with it the sentiments of the Sikhs were also hurt. Could any measure mitigate the lost pride of the Sikh heritage? History shall always be a testimony to the excesses done to the Sikhs. The humiliation meted out to them is clearly reflected through the words spoken by Santokh, who had unexpectedly reappeared towards the end of the month of June,

> No, no, I don't want tea or anything. No one offers a Sikh three-wheeler driver a chair or asks him for tea. When it rains, we stand drenched and in sweltering heat we do not even get water to drink, unless we ask for it with folded hands. (ibidem 114).

Moreover, they were suspected of surreptitious involvement and this feeling is also distinctly felt when he utters, These days, commuters avoid three-wheelers driven by Sikhs. They suspect us. (ibidem)

Violence always begets violence. This is an unending process. and there was no difference to the developments that followed the onslaught on the Sikhs. The repercussions of the same were realized when Indira Gandhi, the then Prime Minister of India, was murdered by her Sikh security personnel. There was "a kind of lull" (ibidem 130) everywhere and the author felt "the silence ominous and disturbing" (ibidem 131) as an indication the turmoil that was going follow. The situation was grave and a few Sikhs here and there were roughed up. The writer saw the marks of some scuffle on the road, "Turbans on the road…and stains of blood, like dried paan juice." (ibidem)

The heart-rending cries for help went unheard. Even there was hardly any "response from the police post". (ibidem) In such a state of affairs the heart of the author cried for the well-being of Santokh Singh, Balbir and the Sikh Baba. Innocent Sikhs were targeted and there was "crackling and bursting sounds of something going up in flames." (ibidem 133). There was occasional "heart-rending cries" followed by "cruel shout of triumph" giving an indication of unleashing of the beast within:

> Thud, thud, thud!
> Finish them, kill them all!
> accompanied by anguished cries,
> Wahe Guru! Wahe Guru! (ibidem 135)

Everybody looked worried about his own security. Madan Bhaisahab, the owner of the building, where Dr. Goswami was staying, took the necessary precautions in order to safeguard the family and the tenants since the police, the agents for restoring order, "can't be relied on. We have to look after ourselves". (ibidem 134). It was risky to move out of the household. Human beings were burnt alive and the "stench of burning tin, rexine, gunny bags, petrol and human flesh spreads all around". (ibidem). Civilization had drifted back to the primitive barbaric times. Outside the author could hear the perpetrators of violence—the monsters—shouting:

> "Khoon ka badla khoon se..."
> "...Indira Gandhi Zindabad."
> "Bring out the traitors..." (ibidem 138)

A few wounded Sikhs with their clothes "just clinging to their bodies" were saved and brought into the narrator's flat by the landlord. Soon the room was "wet with blood" and her clothes were "soaked in blood". (ibidem 160)

Everything belonging to the Sikhs was either 'looted' or 'razed to the ground'. Everything happened "in front of hundreds of people. Nobody protests or prevents it" (ibidem 142). The restraints of civilized existence had been abandoned. And the narrator stood as "a passive onlooker, an unwitting witness" (141) to the murder of humanity. Hospitals and places of worship were also not spared. Scenes of "burnt cars", long trails of "smoke from the gurudwara at Singh Sabha Road", "sounds of explosions" became an ordinary sight around Delhi, vanquishing its long-cherished claims towards modernity. The narrator used to go to the Singh Sabha Guradwara "to listen to the sweet Sukhmani Path and the Ashadiwar sung by the raagis. The gurudwara has been reduced to ashes. The granthi pierced with a trident and the half burnt copy of the Granth Sahib lies in a corner of the veranda". (141-42 & 145).

The "dance of death" (143) happened in the surrounding places all the same and the newspapers carrying the news, photographs, etc. of contemporary times were a proof to the stark reality of the situation. People seemed to have turned into 'automatons'—devoid of any feelings towards the fellow beings. Delhi had become a heaping ground of dead bodies which were "put into gunny bags and then loaded onto trucks like sacks of potatoes." (144) The "scenes of carnage" (ibidem) haunts the narrator continuously. The narrator witnesses harrowing scenes of this kind and turns back. The shock inside is expressed when she wrote:

> I come back home and scrub the bloodstains on my floor. In fact, there are no stains, but I keep seeing them all the time. And at times I feel I'm standing on a chunk of burnt flesh. (ibidem 146).

As time passed by, her anxiety grows stronger to get any kind of information about the duo—Santokh Singh and Blabir Raddiwala. Relief Camps were set up for the "riot-stricken people" who looked like "animals caught in the jungles" (ibidem 148) In trail of the two, the author narrator too visited many such camps were she saw compensation forms being distributed among the uprooted families. Can the lives, the attachment, the love and hate of the dear and near ones be compared with and replaced by a few sheets of crispy notes? But the government had other plans:

> The family members of those killed will get ten thousand rupees, the injured will get two thousand and for houses destroyed, ten thousand rupees. Loans on liberal terms will be allowed to rebuild the houses. People engaged in transport and other businesses can avail of government loans to enable them to start their businesses afresh. The Reserve Bank has issued details and specific instructions to the banks... (ibidem 149)

In such a camp, the narrator had witnessed a rare sight—of women—"widowed" on the same day at the same time, but there too she could not find Balbir or his family. She was determined to find them and hand over the wooden cigar boxes with some cash inside it. Her efforts ultimately paid back and she succeeded in spotting Balbir's wife in the Ludlow Castle Relief Camp alongwith his son, Sonnu. Balbir himself was "missing" and she had no idea whether he was dead or alive. In agony, her eyes "are sunken" and she had almost lost the other hope of living, too, since the eyes of her son "were pierced with a sword". She refused to accept the "boxes" and the author was thrown into a situation where she would be tormented by the stench of blood and stale sweat. (ibidem 150-152).

The small "family" belonging to the author could not escape the brutality of the situation. It is mainly through her attachment with the two Sikhs that the author has provided a realistic touch to the gravity of the situation. Caught in the heat of the cauldron, Santokh Singh too met with his lot. One Thursday morning, the author was awakened by a tremendous commotion only to find.

> "...a dead body. At the gol chakkar. It's horrible sight. It's been cut into pieces with a sword."
>
> ....
>
> ....
>
> "This the corpse of Santokh Singh." (155-56)

The earth "seems to slip" from under her feet as soon as she heard the name. Though she belonged to none of the parties involved, yet "the events of the past fifteen days eat into my heart, penetrating recesses I never knew existed. (156). For her, life in Delhi became very distressing. She could no longer open the door of the balcony facing the gol chakkar. It was there that the dismembered corpse of Santokh Singh had lain. (158)

Throughout the novel, the writer has woven the ruthless events in such a fashion that they appear as if someone is perusing the pages of a diary. But they indeed are the very depiction of life that the Delhi in 1984 witnessed. Indira Goswami in depicting this plight is genuine, without being sentimental. It seems that the author has shifted her attention from her troubletorn homeland in North East India to Delhi and Punjab and the condition and trauma of insurgency in North East has been translated intc the situations in Punjab and Delhi.

Works Cited

Anand, V.K. *Terrorism and Security.* New Delhi: Deep & Deep Publications, 1984.

Gohain, Hiren. "Ineffable Mystery": *Indira Goswami (Mamoni Raisom): A Critical Study of Her Writings.* ed. Malaya Khaund. Delhi: B.R. Publishing Corporation, 1994.

Goswami, Indira. *Pages Stained With Blood.* Tr. Pradip Acharya. New Delhi: Katha, 2002.

(29)

Postcolonial Writing from Tripura

Bhaskar Roy Barman

I shall not discuss the kind of literature from Tripura that obtained before the Independence of India but the kind of literature that flourished after the Independence for obvious reason. The achievement of Independence and its resultant partitioning and the merging of Tripura in Indian union have effected a drastic change in the political, geographical and economic setup of Tripura in general and its cultural status in particular. The partitioning of India brought on its heels about an exodus of Bengali refugees uprooted from their original home, Bangladesh (erstwhile East Pakistan) and many of them took shelter in Tripura. The inflow of the Bengali refugees shattered the age-old tranquility of Tripura and the folklife surrounded all around with hills and forests and eking out its existence on cultivation of jhum, felt the impact of the intrusion. The refugees carried along their agonies due to their being rendered uprooted and homeless as a curse of the partitioning of India and the agonies got reflected in their poetry and short stories. Achieving of independence by India exercised no effect on them and, thus, in their writing. Their poetry and short stories reminisce of how the authors used to live in their original land and what problems they faced in settling in a different land. They were not sure of a stability of life they came over to this different land to live.

As I have said earlier, writers must need be assured of a stability of life in order to write satires or humorous pieces, because satire or humour demands a deep-rooted attitude to life.

The conflict between two separate and distinct cultures that confronted each other monopolized the poetry and the stories written in the fifties and particularly in the poetry of the fifties are discernible the influences of Rabindranath Tagore and Jibanananda Das. Besides, the effect of partitioning of India dominated the poetry of that period, but petered out in the poetry written in the sixties. Many poets and short story writers felt themselves settled after a decade had elapsed since the mass-exodus and indulged in, or tried to indulge in, satire or sarcasm and their sarcasm characterized their poetry or short stories. But no novel worth mentioning was written in the fifties or sixties. In order to stand on their own feet, many writers in the sixties shook themselves free of the influences of Rabindranath Tagore and Jibanananda Das and created a commonwealth of writing through the establishment of a literary group called 'Sahitya Basar'. Many poets and writers assembled under the umbrella of Sahitya Basar. Salil Krishna Deb Barma stood out distinct and prominent among the poets who had got associated with Sahitya Basar and died a premature death. Though his poetry smelt of the water, the land and the sky of Tripura, it was infused with a satiric flavour. His first poetry collection, *Jaler Bhetar, Buker Bhetar* (*Inside the Water, inside the Heart*) established him as an important poet . This was only one poetry collection he had published before his death, but all the poems he had written since the fifties spread over different literary journals which helped him on with continuity of writing. Though Salil Krishna wrote original poetry, the influence of Jibanananda is distinctly visible in it and so his poetry is not spiced with satirical or humorous flavour. He tried to point in some of his poems at some social follies, but it sounds shallow. You can't write a satire or a humorous piece if you have not developed a personal and independent attitude to life by yourself experiencing the problems surrounding you and peculiar to the land you are living in and by interpreting the experience in your own way. Before he could shake himself free of the influence of Jibanananda Das he died.

Another poet who deserves a mention is Bijan Krishna Chaudhury who took to writing poetry after the Independence. A few poems written during the first phase of his writing career were imbued with a flavour of influence of Jibanananda Das. Fortunately in course of time when his poetry matured, he successfully unshackled himself from the extraneous influence and started producing poems impregnated with his own feelings vis-à-vis the problems surrounding him and established himself as a distinct poet. His later poems displayed a truthful portraiture of man and nature and the inherent characteristics of the culture and atmosphere of Tripura, and carry a toothsome flavour of sarcasm.

It is worth quoting a few lines—I have translated them—of a poem of his, entitled 'Atayeb' enriched with sarcasm. The reader might notice a tinge of humour in it.

> I don't enter the examination hall,
> for before my eyes the examinees open books to become learned.
> I don't go to the cinema
> lest I should buy tickets
> at the expense of my conscience
> I don't board a city bus,
> for both urchins and conductor
> delightedly violate strictures
> upon smoking.

The poet wrote the poem from the angle of his profession—he was a well-known professor teaching Bengali. In this poem he satirizes the go of the present-day life obtaining in Tripura, as in other parts of India. He projects himself as a prototype of all the professors and teachers. He does not dare enter the examination hall lest he should be humiliated by the examinees who take to copying from books in order to 'become learned'. Thus he satirizes the way the would-be scholars—they are aiming at becoming professors—aim to become learned. The poet does not let slip the opportunity to castigate the aura of separateness professors (and teachers also) tend to create around themselves, for 'professing' (and researching) is a noble profession, as in the fourth, fifth and sixth lines. Quite aware of the nobleness of his profession, he is entitled to see films free. No one gives him free tickets. So he does not go to cinema, because he is required to 'buy tickets/at the expense of conscience'. The last four lines tell us that the poet does not board a city bus, because both "urchins" and "conductor" violate the strictures upon smoking. The reader can't help laughing over the pseudo-prestige he and his like desperately adhere to.

Anil Sarkar, another important poet, reveals dexterity in sarcasm in his poetry. In his poetry as a poet and in his speeches as a minister he champions the downtrodden and so his poetry and speeches abound in sarcastic interludes. His satire or sarcasm is directed against the rich and the privileged who ride roughshod over the poor. His poetry and his speeches are couched in a simple language which appeals directly to the heart and helps manifest his sarcasm. I forbear translating a few lines of a poem of his, for just a few lines won't help bring home the pungency of his sarcasm. If I quote few lines, I shall have to quote two or three paragraphs of one of the speeches already published, for his poetry and his speech are, I think, interrelated and interlinked.There are other poets who have attempted at sarcasm, but their sarcasm is not as rich as that of Bijan Krishna Chaudhury and Anil Sarkar. But they are more or less good poets.

A distinct flavour of sarcasm reveals itself in a poem of Bhaskar Roy Barman's, entitled 'The Cascade of Rhythm' that appeared in an anthology, called *Paul Lawrence Dunbar: An Anthology in Memoriam* (1872-1906) edited by M. Myers and published by Bristol Banner Books, Bristol, USA. In the poem the poet who generally writes in English satirizes the establishment and the carving on the part of the poet for awards. I quote just a few lines. The poem tells of a poet awarded and felicitated by an institution and thus enslaved to the establishment.

> The institution institutionalized him
> by awarding and felicitating him,
> the recital couched in a florid language,
> and distanced him from the love
> that was once his poetic inspiration.
> Yonder was his dwelling house,
> a shady abode mothered and nourished by faineance.
> His childhood lay hidden and forgotten
> beyond the autumnal leafage.

No sound impinged on his ears;

> before his eyes was the world profaned and corrupted.
> A glow-worm wriggled out of the smidgin of idée fixe
> and burned itself in its own fire.
> The festivities round the felicitations just ended
> The frost shut in under the awning looked up
> through the chinks at the pale moon
> and understood it was time for it to be released
> from under the awning.

The lines quoted tell of how poets crave after awards at the expense of their love and familial happiness and how the establishment capitalizes upon their craving after awards to institutionalize them.

In the following poem by Bhaskar Roy Barman, entitled 'The Amaranth'—I quote it whole—the poet tells of the Utopia every poet is striving after. It appeared in another poetry anthology *in Memoriam,* edited by M. Myers and published by Bristol Banner Books, USA.

> The kaleidoscope stood befrilled with splendour;
> no messenger from on high did descend to hand
> it blessings, though.
> The rassling trees coruscated in an interplay of light and dark,
> the sun dipping down the western horizon
> Exuding a unisonant desire to search for the amaranth,
> a group of youths were changing their way along the path
> that led into forest.
> They had heard elders gossip about the amaranth
> they had never themselves seen,
> and tell themselves they had heard of the flower
> from the cowboys who herded cows into the forest.
> The youths wished the cowherds had sculpted the image of the amaranth
> on the bark of the trees.
> The amaranth was said to blossom when the light of the departing day
> intermingled with the darkness of the incoming night.
> Save for the interplay of light and dark
> the kaleidoscope has nothing else to boast.
> No messenger did descend from on high
> to hand it blessings from High.
> Someone might have deciphered the speech of the forest
> Ahead was a great ole caressed by darkness,
> where no light was allowed to intrude.
> The kaleidoscope uncrowned with blessings from High
> always changed colours to beguile you off the great hole.
> Did the amaranth bloom in or around the great hole?
> wondered the youths.

The amaranth is an imaginary flower that blooms at night and no one has ever seen it. In the poem it is the Utopia of poetic perfection. The youths in the poem are young poets who have joined together in search for the Amaranth they have just heard of. They have just started writing poetry and their pietism has not yet ripened. No poet, however great, has ever achieved poetic perfection; it always keeps eluding them. It is like the amaranth which is often heard of, but not seen. It is the common belief that only cowherds who herd the cows deep into the forest have seen the amaranth. They have nothing to crave after, for the moment they have seen the amaranth, they became satisfied with what they have had and with the way of life they have accustomed themselves to living. It is believed that once you have seen the amaranth you will become satisfied with what you have had ceased craving after anything else. No messenger descends from the sky to bless the kaleidoscope that lies on the way to the amaranth and it beguiles searchers for the Amaranth off the path.

The poem satirizes craving on the part of almost every poet after the impossible, after the Utopia never to be achieved.As I have said earlier, I shall discuss a few of the poems and short stories written after the Independence.In fact short stories in the true sense started being written after the Independence. It was Bimal Chaudhury who pioneered the short story writing in Tripura by writing his first short story, 'Jagaran' (Awakening) in 1947 just on the heels of the achievement of Independence. Under the influence of this short story awakened the trend of short story writing. The story tells of how Nagurai, the protagonist in the story, is awakened to need of asserting himself and others humiliated and oppressed and to the feeling that their superstition and ignorance bedevil their life, as they have killed his parents. His second story, *Hijla Khaler Kanna* (*The Cry of Hijla Canal*), Bimal Chaudhury gives expression to the agonies of the Bengali refugees who migrated to Tripura, uprooted from their homeland, East Pakistan (now Bangladesh) in the person of an eight-year or nine-year old boy. In this connexion it should be mentioned that Bimal Chaudhury had begun writing poetry before turning to writing short stories. Though the short stories I happen to have read do not smack of sarcasm, I have mentioned him and his two short stories, because he pioneered short story writing in Tripura, as I have said a bit earlier. In fact almost all the short story writers wrote short stories, centring on the effect of the refugee problems, and later in the eighties, on the impact of the communal riot that occurred in the first part of the eighties, which has shattered the stability of life. Even today the people, particularly the Bengali inhabitants, feel their life unstable.

A story by Subimal Roy, a short story writer contemporary with Bimal Chaudhury, has struck me as short story with a satirical tone. I have read a few other short stories of him. They are not as pungent as the short story, entitled *Yatri* (passenger), they are just representations of what their author has experienced. *Yatri* is the title of the short story collection published in 2003 and is a social satire. It, though representation of his personal experience, reveals a sarcasm on the mental set-up of all the passengers habituated to traveling like sardines on buses or jeeps. The story satirizes adjustment of passengers to their wonted feeling of inconveniences, winnowed of the courage to protest and they even coolstare into silence whoever dares protest. In the story we come across a variety of passengers traveling on a jeep. The jeep is packed full of passengers. Many passengers are standing on the iron deck attached to the jeep. A well-dressed and trimly bearded youth in his early thirties is standing near the jeep, looking for a vacant seat in the jeep to sit on. He is known to the driver chewing a paan. A personal interest of the driver lies with the well-dressed youth who has some influence with the government. Jeep-drivers have demanded of the government increase in jeep fare, as their conversation between them later reveals. He believes, like other jeep drivers, if he exercises his influence, the government will approve the increase in jeep fare. A rustic- and innocent-looking youth is sitting on a front seat. The driver forces him into vacating the front seat so that the well-dressed youth can sit on it. No other passengers protest at such humiliating behaviour; rather they insist on the rustic- and innocent-looking youth vacating the seat for the well-dressed youth. The rustic-and innocent-looking youth has no alternative but to vacate his front seat and go to the back of the jeep. The helper somehow manoeuvres him onto the iron desk.

A policeman stops the bus on the way for carrying passengers beyond its capacity. He examines all the papers of the driver. He then asks every passenger whether he or she will be a witness at the court. The well-dressed youth sitting beside the driver says he has come from Kolkata; an old passenger says he does not see well; a woman, a school teacher, implores the policeman not to put her to the trouble of going to the court; a smart boy, sitting at the backside, gives the policemen false information about himself and his address. But the rustic and innocent-looking youth gives the police his exact name and address, for he has not learnt the art of telling lies.

For the crime of giving the police his exact name and address, the driver forces him off the jeep before the very eyes of the passengers and drives the jeep away with other passengers packed in like sardines, leaving the youth helpless on the road. He has silently endured the humiliation, without any protest,

There are a few stories by Bhaskar Roy Barman which have a distinct flavour of satire. They are the "Jinxed House Balderdash", "Root", "The Learned Man", "Defeat and Champanula". They are contained in the short story collection, *Modern Short Stories: The Trap and Other Stories* published by Book Palace, New Delhi in 1995. I shall only discuss short stories, 'The Jinxed House' and 'The Learned Man', because the satires in them are distinct and pungent. 'The Jinxed House' satirizes the individual desire to be politically powerful. Though the story will sound like a ghost story at a first reading, when you read it a second time, the sarcasm will be revealed to you. The story narrated by the janitor of the house jinxed now living away from the house to a reporter who has come down from Kolkata to write on the house for his newspaper, tells of how the house has got jinxed. The house gets jinxed because of the lowering of the rents to the consternation of the tenants. The following passage reveals how the tenants react to the lowering of the rents:

> Next morning, as they learnt from Rebatibabu, the janitor, that the present proprietor had lowered their rents by one third, the tenants abandoned themselves to a fit of deliriousness. The tenants who had previously not so much as exchanged formal greetings when they bumped into one another found themselves drawn together, inasmuch as their interests homed in on the conundrum that presented itself to them. (p.25)

They are conjecturing on why the present proprietor has lowered the rents. They put forward different views, but they are not accepted. They are so consternated by the conundrum they start seeing something uncanny, as in the following passage:

> The next day the whole house was agog with commotion. The wife of Mr. Bose lodging on the third floor had stridden out on the terrace last night and walked along to the lavatory at the corner of the terrace. She had suddenly come across the phantom of Jagannath Mitra. He was holding a receipt book in a hand. Much scared, she had run back to her room and swooned off. (p.32)

Rebati Das, the janitor, goes over to the present proprietor to inform him that Mrs. Bose saw his late father, Jagannath Mitra sporting a receipt book, and requests him to rescind his decision to lower the rents by one-third. The present proprietor. Ashoke Mitra browbeats his appeal and sends him back.

By way of explaining to the reporter from Kolkata, Samir his name, why Ashoke Mitra has lowered the rents, Rebati Das says:

> An energetic young man possessing a generous bent of mind, Mr. Ashoke Mitra had been ashamed of his father's miserliness. Jagannath Mitra... had often made a fuss over his son's going astray, Ashoke had associated himself with a charity club that professed itself to be devoted to the uplift of the downtrodden. Since Ashoke was the scion of the richest family in the locality, the club hinged upon him in monetary matter and over it there would often ensue quarrels between the father and the son.(p.23).

He further says:

> The charitable activities that Ashoke had taken on as his pastime brought him into close contact with political-minded and influential people. Gradually he had insinuated himself into the favour of some influential leaders who were supposed to have assured him that they would see to him being given a party-ticket in the next election,(23)

The ghostly appearance almost every night scares the tenants off the house. The fact of the house being haunted spreads far and wide. No would-be tenant dares rent a room in the house. The terror grips the janitor and his wife. The janitor admits to himself being terrified.

> 'Even the terror gripped us', he said.. 'We heard every night howling and sinister murmurs. We couldn't sleep. Our house was in the vicinity of the haunted house. We were so gripped by the terror that I decided to renounce my duty as the janitor of the house. I saw the proprietor, resigned my post and handed him the key of the house and rented a house not far from the haunted house and opened a grocery.' (p.35)

When the janitor grieves that the house 'got jinxed as a result of the generosity of the proprietor', Samir, the reporter from Kolkata opines that the craving on the part of the proprietor, Ashoke Mitra after something he has 'no capacity to achieve' has jinxed the house.

The satire rests on capriciousness of the tenants that reveals itself when they have heard their proprietor has lowered their rents and on the desire on the part of the proprietor to stand for election and to win by duping people into believing that he is a generous person by experimenting his generosity on his tenants. His experiment has miserably failed because of the capriciousness of his tenants who negatively react to his lowering of the rents.

"The Learned Man" is an interesting story and satirizes learnedness. The leaned man has not married in his search for knowledge and prides himself on having learned everything. He doles out pieces of advice to his numerous disciples and other people who come over to seek his device. One day he hears that a Chinese, monk has come out and has lodged in a slum and propagates the doctrine that there does not exist anything called knowledge. Many of his disciples, attracted by this doctrine, flock round him. He feels his reputation challenged and decides to face him. His disciple, Subir who often goes down to the Chinese monk, takes him along to the slum to have him face the monk. When the learned man is walking with Subir through a maze of alleys, he is confronted with many vistas he has never before seen. He is particularly stuck by the uniqueness of the following vista:

> ...The Learned Man's eyes roamed hither and thither. It was still morning. In the alleyways awash with slime, beside a disease-ridden stream, some people, male and female, were subjecting themselves to a ritual of rigorous toilet. They banished, the Learned Man thought, the miasma of the previous night to which they had been

> exposed. The women, without revealing so much as a patch of their nudity, managed to wash themselves all over, fromt heir long hair to the soles of their feet...Mothers delused their children before soaping their little, naked bodies with vigour, undiminished even by the bitter cold of this winter morning. (139-140).

This vista moves the learned man. He can't help thinking that he has shut himself against this aspect of human life and that he has fled from people and insulated himself against love.

When he meets the Chinese monk, the Chinese monk enjoins him to write down those aspects of knowledge he is supposed to know in a separate room. When he sets to writing down the aspects he thinks he knows, he finds himself assailed with a feeling that he knows nothing at all. In this story, the satire rests on the Learned Man's feeling that he has learned all that is to be learned.

The postcolonial writers of Tripura reflect on ethnic diversity and problems in their creative writing both in English and Bangla.

List of Contributors

Bijay Kumar Danta is Professor of English and Dean of Humanities and Social Sciences at Tezpur University, Assam.

Jaydeep Chakravarty is an Assistant Professor of English at Assam University, Silchar, Assam.

Nigamananda Das is the editor of this anthology. He teaches in the Department of English, Nagaland University, Kohima, Nagaland.

A.J. Sebastian sdb is Associate Professor and former Head, Department of English, Nagaland University, Kohima, Nagaland.

Ms. Priyanka Sarmah teaches English at Pragjyotish College, Guwahati, Assam.

Ms. Dikshita Bhuyan teaches English at Madhabdev College, Narayanpur, Assam.

Buddhadeb Roychoudhury is Editor, Cambridge University Press, Hyderabad.

Bhaskar Jyoti Gohain teaches English at Dhemaji College, Assam.

Narendra Tiwary is the Principal of Mount Olive College, Kohima, Nagaland.

Nityananda Pattanayak teaches English at ADP College, Nagaon, Assam.

Basavaraj Naikar is Professor and Chairman, Department of English, Karnataka University, Dharwad, Karnataka.

Juri Dutta was teaching English at Rajiv Gandhi University, Arunachal Pradesh and now lives in Tezpur, Assam

Rupam Gogoi teaches English at North Lakhimpur College, Assam.

Binda Sah teaches English at North Lakhimpur College, Assam.

Satyendra Prasad Singh teaches English at H.R. College, Mairwa(Siwan), Bihar.

Ankush Chutia teaches English at Dhemaji College, Assam.

Bhaskar Roy Barman teaches English at a Higher Secondary School at Agartala, Tripura.

Index

●●●